THE POETRY OF THE
THIRTIES

A. T. Tolley

LONDON
VICTOR GOLLANCZ LTD
1975

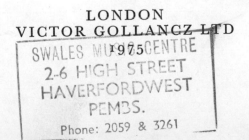

© A. T. Tolley 1975
ISBN 0 575 01976 x

Printed in Great Britain by
The Camelot Press Ltd, Southampton

Aut'

THE POETRY OF THE THIRTIES

To
Margaret
in memory
and to Mr W
because you said so

CONTENTS

PREFATORY NOTE

The Poetry of the Thirties is intended to offer a critical account of the work of British poets of the nineteen-thirties. In a sense, any book is a continued demonstration of the validity of its own conception of the boundaries of its subject; but there may be some value at the outset in giving an indication of what is included or omitted. The change that is associated with the new poets of the nineteen-thirties is the appearance of a dominating concern with political themes; but this will not do to define the subject, as it would lead to the exclusion of poets and poetry that clearly have a place in the book. However, the list of poets usually thought of when the thirties are mentioned —C. Day Lewis, W. H. Auden, Stephen Spender, Louis MacNeice, John Lehmann, Geoffrey Grigson, William Empson, Dylan Thomas, George Barker, David Gascoyne— attests to the way in which certain young writers who were at Oxford and Cambridge in the late twenties brought about a change in English poetry in the succeeding decade; and it is with the work of those writers that the book begins. The oldest of them, C. Day Lewis, was born in 1904. Three writers, a year or two older, became associated with these poets with the publication of the anthology *New Signatures*—Michael Roberts (born 1902), A. S. J. Tessimond (born 1902), and William Plomer (born 1903). Roy Campbell, slightly older still (born 1901), seems to stand apart as a poet, and the discussion is not extended to include his work. Similarly, the work of writers like Laura Riding, who began publishing books in the twenties, is not discussed, even though it was an important part of the literary output of the decade. The same applies to older writers, such as T. S. Eliot, who continued publishing work of the first significance during the thirties.

The historical approach has been chosen out of a sense of its appropriateness to a subject so intimately involved with the events of its time, and out of a desire to show the development of poetry over the period. In addition, it is felt that the literary historical approach can often give a better insight into the idiom of a body of poetry than does the analytic approach, which, in the hands of some of its more highly developed practitioners, has often become a means of unloading their own philosophical preoccupations on to the poetry.

It is a pleasure to be able to recommend to readers a book that is more than a worthy companion to the reading of this one—Robin Skelton's anthology *The Poetry of the Thirties* (Penguin Books); it should be invaluable in providing access to material otherwise hard to obtain.

Finally, it is perhaps appropriate, writing on a British subject from a Canadian University, to say, for the benefit of any reviewers of the book, that the author was born and educated in England.

A. T. T.

Carleton University
Ottawa

ACKNOWLEDGEMENTS

MY ADMIRATIONS AND indebtedness will, I hope, be clear from the book itself and from the bibliography and references. What follows is a record of specific indebtedness or service, together with acknowledgement of those works from which quotation has been made. I have tried to be as accurate as possible in the latter, and apologise for any errors or omissions in what is a rather long listing from a wide variety of sources.

The book was written during a period of normal duties as a professor in the English Department at Carleton University, and later as Dean of the Faculty of Arts (Division I). It was done without benefit of sabbatical leave, leave of absence, fellowships, travel grants, or other grants in aid. Carleton University, through its Research and Publications Fund, paid for the preparation of the typescript and provided a grant in support of publication. I should like to express my gratitude to the University for this and other types of assistance.

My initial thinking about the subject owed a great deal to my late wife, Margaret, who had considerable experience of the Left-wing in the nineteen-thirties. George Johnston read the whole of the typescript and made many suggestions that I have incorporated. George Steiner read part of the typescript and gave valuable help at a time when help and encouragement were needed. Frank Wilson gave a great deal of time and support to the project of publishing the book; and Eva Kushner gave similar assistance. Part of the book was written in the house of Peter and Kirsten Lamb.

Jean Rogers of the National Library of Canada helped me in tracing books in my original bibliography. Very considerable assistance in obtaining texts was given over the years by the Inter-library Loan Departments at Monash University and at Carleton University. Material was also brought to my attention by the G. J. Wood Memorial Clipping Service. Barbara Sudall, my secretary for many years, helped put the typescript into good shape and corrected the spelling. Pamela Going and Jean Smith did a great deal of typing for me. My wife, Glenda, helped revise the Introduction.

Chapter 2 originally appeared, in more extended form, as an article in the *University of Toronto Quarterly*, to whom I am grateful for the re-use of this material.

I should like to say that it is a pleasure to appear under an imprint that saw the publication of so much work that was a vital part of the life of the thirties.

Acknowledgement is made for quotation from the following:

Kenneth Allott	*Poems* (Hogarth Press) *The Ventriloquist's Doll* (Cresset Press) *The Penguin Book of Contemporary Verse* (Penguin)
W. H. Auden (with Faber & Faber)	*Poems, The Orators, Look Stranger!, Spain, Letters from Iceland, Journey to a War, The Dance of Death, The Dog Beneath the Skin, The Ascent of F6, On the Frontier, Another Time* *The Poet's Tongue* (Bell) *The Oxford Book of Light Verse* (Oxford University Press) *Poems* (1928) (University of Cincinnati)
George Barker (with Faber & Faber) (with Parton Press)	*Poems, Calamiterror, Lament and Triumph, Janus* *Thirty Preliminary Poems, Alanna Autumnal* *The True Confessions of George Barker* (Fore Publications) *Essays* (MacGibbon & Kee)
Julian Bell	*Winter Movement* (Chatto & Windus) *Work for Winter* (Hogarth Press)

	Essays, Poems and Letters (Hogarth Press)
John Betjeman	*Collected Poems* (John Murray)
	First and Last Loves (John Murray)
Ronald Bottrall	*The Loosening and Other Poems* (Heffer)
	Festivals of Fire (Faber & Faber)
J. Bronowski	*The Poet's Defence* (Cambridge University Press)
	William Blake (Secker)
Norman Cameron	*Collected Poems* (Hogarth Press)
Christopher Caudwell	*Poems* (Lawrence and Wishart)
	Studies in a Dying Culture (John Lane)
John Cornford	*John Cornford: a memoir* (Jonathan Cape)
Idris Davies	*Gwalia Deserta* (J. M. Dent)
C. Day Lewis	
(with Hogarth Press and Jonathan Cape)	*Transitional Poem, From Feathers to Iron, The Magnetic Mountain, A Time to Dance, Overtures to Death, Noah and the Waters, The Aeneid of Virgil*
	A Beechen Vigil (Fortune Press)
	Country Comets (Hopkinson)
	A Hope for Poetry (Basil Blackwell)
	The Buried Day (Chatto & Windus)
William Empson	*Collected Poems* (Chatto & Windus)
C. P. Fitzgibbon	*The Life of Dylan Thomas* (J. M. Dent)
Roy Fuller	*Poems* (Fortune Press)
David Gascoyne	*Roman Balcony* (Temple Bar Press)
	Man's Life is this Meat (Parton Press)
	Poems 1937–42 (Poetry London)
	A Short Survey of Surrealism (Cobden-Sanderson)
Robert Graves (and Alan Hodge)	*The Long Week-end* (Faber & Faber)

Geoffrey Grigson	*Several Observations* (Cresset Press)
	The Crest on the Silver (Cresset Press)
	New Verse (anthology) (Faber & Faber)
Frederick Grubb	*A Vision of Reality* (Chatto and Windus)
Christopher Isherwood	*Lions and Shadows* (Hogarth Press)
	Exhumations (Methuen)
Humphrey Jennings	*Poems* (Weekend Press)
F. R. Leavis	*New Bearings in English Poetry* (Chatto & Windus)
Laurie Lee	*The Sun my Monument* (Hogarth Press)
Julius Lipton	*Poems of Strife* (Lawrence & Wishart)
John Lehmann	*A Garden Revisited* (Hogarth Press)
	The Noise of History (Hogarth Press)
	Collected Poems (Eyre & Spottiswood)
	The Whispering Gallery (Longmans)
Louis MacNeice	
(with Faber & Faber)	*Poems, The Earth Compels, Letters from Iceland, Plant and Phantom, The Strings are False, Autumn Journal*
(with Oxford University Press)	*Modern Poetry, W. B. Yeats*
	Blind Fireworks (Victor Gollancz)
	I Crossed the Minch (Longmans)
	Poems, 1925–1940 (Random House)
Charles Madge	
(with Faber & Faber)	*The Disappearing Castle, The Father Found*
Ralph Maud	*Entrances to Dylan Thomas's Poetry* (University of Pittsburg Press)
Philip O'Connor	*Selected Poems* (Jonathan Cape)
	Memoirs of a Public Baby (Faber & Faber)

Elder Olson — *The Poetry of Dylan Thomas* (University of Chicago Press)

William Plomer
(with Jonathan Cape) — *Visiting the Caves, At Home*
Selected Poems (Hogarth Press)

F. T. Prince — *Poems* (Faber & Faber)
Henry Reed — *A Map of Verona* (Jonathan Cape)
John Pudney — *Home and Away* (Michael Joseph)
James Reeves — *The Natural Need* (Seizin Press)
W. R. Rodgers — *Awake: and other poems* (Secker)
D. S. Savage — *The Autumn World* (Fortune Press)
Francis Scarfe — *Inscapes* (Fortune Press)
Auden and After (Routledge)

Bernard Spencer — *Collected Poems* (Alan Ross)
Stephen Spender
(with Faber & Faber) — *Poems, The Still Centre, Trial of a Judge*

(with Hamish Hamilton) — *World Within World, The Creative Element*
Nine Experiments (University of Cincinnati Press)
Twenty Poems (Basil Blackwell)
The Destructive Element (Jonathan Cape)
Forward from Liberalism (Victor Gollancz)

Julian Symons — *Confusions About "X"* (Fortune Press)
The Thirties (Cresset Press)

Dylan Thomas
(with J. M. Dent) — *Collected Poems, The Notebooks of Dylan Thomas, Adventures in the Skin Trade, Selected Letters, Letters to Vernon Watkins*

Henry Treece — *How I See Apocalypse* (Lindsay Drummond)

P. Waldberg — *Surrealism* (Thames & Hudson)
Rex Warner — *Poems* (Boriswood)
Vernon Watkins
(with Faber & Faber) — *The Ballad of the Mari Lwyd*

| | *The Lamp and the Veil* |
| W. B. Yeats | *Essays and Introductions* (Macmillan) |

Acknowledgement is made for quotation from the following collections of material by the authors indicated:

The Arts Today ed. G. Grigson (John Lane)   W. H. Auden
The God that Failed ed. R. H. S. Crossman (Hamish Hamilton)
   R. H. S. Crossman
In Letters of Red ed. E. A. Osborne (Michael Joseph)   Rex
   Warner
Modern British Poetry ed. L. Untermeyer (Harcourt)   Stephen
   Spender
New Country ed. M. Roberts (Hogarth Press)   W. H. Auden,
   Richard Goodman, C. Day Lewis, Charles Madge,
   Michael Roberts, Stephen Spender
New Signatures ed. M. Roberts (Hogarth Press)   Julian Bell,
   William Plomer, Michael Roberts, A. S. J. Tessimond
Oxford Poetry (Basil Blackwell)   W. H. Auden (1927), Norman
   Cameron (1928), Stephen Spender (1930), Bernard
   Spencer (1932)
Poems for Spain ed. S. Spender and J. Lehmann (Hogarth
   Press)   Charles Donnelly, T. A. R. Hyndman, John
   Lepper, Tom Wintringham, anonymous poem
Public School Verse (1924) (Heinemann)   W. H. Auden
The Poet Speaks ed. P. Orr (Routledge)   Ronald Bottrall,
   John Lehmann, Stephen Spender, Rex Warner
The White Horseman ed. J. F. Hendry and H. Treece (Routledge)   J. F. Hendry, Nicholas Moore, Henry Treece
T. S. Eliot: a Symposium ed. R. March and Tambimuttu
   (Poetry London)   Nevill Coghill, Kathleen Raine, James
   Reeves
Vernon Watkins, 1906–1967 ed. L. Norris (Faber & Faber)
   Vernon Watkins

Acknowledgement is made for quotation from the following periodicals of material by the authors indicated and of editorial material:

The Atlantic Monthly	Stephen Spender
Contemporary Poetry and Prose	Kenneth Allott, Edgar Foxall, Humphrey Jennings, Roger Roughton, Francis Scarfe, editorial material
Encounter	W. H. Auden, Stephen Spender
Granta	William Empson
Kenyon Review	W. H. Auden, William Empson
Left Review	George Barker, Maurice Carpenter, C. Day Lewis, Jack Lindsay, Charles Madge, Randall Swingler, editorial material
Life and Letters Today	Randall Swingler
London Magazine	Dylan Thomas
New Verse	W. H. Auden, Edgar Foxall, David Gascoyne, Kathleen Raine, Allen Tate, Geoffrey Taylor, Dylan Thomas, editorial material, the Oxford Collective Poem
New Writing	Ewart Milne, Stephen Spender, Randall Swingler, editorial material
Poetry	W. H. Auden, Michael Roberts
Poetry and the People	J. R. Walker, anonymous poem
The Review	Ian Hamilton, James Reeves, Edgell Rickword, Julian Symons
Scrutiny	F. R. Leavis, Geoffrey Walton
Southern Review	W. H. Auden
The Spectator	Stephen Spender
Times Literary Supplement	Review of *Poems* by W. H. Auden
Twentieth Century	J. Bronowski
Twentieth Century Verse	Julian Symons, Ruthven Todd, editorial material
Wales	Editorial material

THE POETRY OF THE THIRTIES

Peace Pledge Movement; and Winston Churchill, the outcast of the Conservative Party, demanding attention to British air power.

These attitudes must be borne in mind in reviewing the familiar pattern of the main international events of the decade that seem so decidedly to presage war. In January, 1933, Hitler became Chancellor of Germany. In March the Nazis assumed dictatorial powers, and Germany left the League of Nations in October. Italy attacked Abyssinia in October, 1935, completing the conquest in May, 1936. In the meantime, Germany had remilitarised the Rhineland in March; and in July right-wing elements of the army in Spain revolted to begin the Spanish Civil War. The Sino-Japanese conflict was renewed in July, 1937, with the taking of Peking, Nanking and Shanghai. Germany occupied Austria in March, 1938; and followed this with the annexation of the Sudetan areas of Czechoslovakia under an agreement reached with Britain, France and Italy at Munich in September. The remainder of Czechoslovakia was taken over in March, 1939, the month in which the fascists achieved victory in the Spanish Civil War. Germany and the Soviet Union signed a pact of non-aggression in August; and in September Germany invaded Poland and the Second World War began.

In retrospect these events seem to lead inexorably towards war; yet various things contributed to the pattern not being generally recognised. Hitler's anti-Bolshevism appealed to many Conservatives. The Labour Party was by tradition— and by the action of many of its leading members in the Great War—pacifist. The public overwhelmingly desired to believe that peace was possible. After 1935, however, a change in attitude becomes noticeable. The Hoare–Laval agreement between the British and the French, whereby Mussolini was to be offered a partition of Abyssinia, although disowned publicly by the British, nevertheless marked the abandonment of the League of Nations as an organ for the settlement of international disputes. The same year, 1935, saw rearmament planned in the White Paper, *Statement Relating to Defence*, and the open acknowledgement by Hitler that Germany was building up a military air force. The Left, however, did not become militant until the outbreak of the Spanish Civil War

Chapter 1

INTRODUCTORY

THE NINETEEN-THIRTIES belong to the mythology of our time as well as to its history. In retrospect they seem startlingly encapsulated: they begin with the Wall Street crash in 1929 and end with the invasion of Poland in 1939. They are the "hungry" thirties; the era of appeasement: before, there was unthinking prosperity; afterwards, war. In fact the thirties were not so dramatic in their inception or conclusion. The economic difficulties of parts of Great Britain had their origins in the twenties and were manifest in the General Strike of 1926; while, at the end of the period, there is a gradual change after the Munich agreement in 1938, though the event that truly closes the era is the fall of France in 1940.

The thirties were not as homogeneous as they appear in popular memory. What images does the period evoke? The hunger marches; the Nuremberg rallies; frontiers disappearing; unemployed miners scrambling for coal on dirt tips? Or Baldwin, with his pipe, cannily moralising to the public during the abdication crisis of 1936, or making Mary Webb's fortune by publicly mentioning her novels? George V was concerned most, when a Labour government came into power, about whether proper protocol would continue to be observed in dress for visits to the palace. Both outwardly and inwardly, the thirties had an element of the Victorian as well as an element of the progressive.

No event in the period itself had as great an influence on the course of events as did the memory of the Great War. War was to be avoided at all costs; so war must never be resorted to to settle international differences. These attitudes were associated with policies of pacificism and disarmament. On the other hand, Germany had started the Great War, and German rearmament under Hitler threatened renewed war. It could only be stopped by firm action; and firm action demanded strength, which in turn demanded rearmament. The poles of policy were represented by Canon Dick Shepherd and The in 1936. No series of events in the twentieth century has had so stirring an ideological effect on British intellectuals as did this war. The result was a change of rôles: the Left demanded that the struggle against fascism be opened at once; the government adopted a policy of non-intervention, and, later, of appeasement. Nevertheless, it must be remembered that, even after the Munich agreement with Hitler, appeasement was still popular. This was partly due to the belief that air bombardment would result in wholesale destruction on both sides. It was only after the annexation of the whole of Czechoslovakia that war was at all widely accepted as fairly inevitable.

Hoping for the best was very much a policy in foreign affairs. The War had been fought to end all wars, and the League of Nations had been set up to see that there was no doubt about this. The question of what was to be done if all men did not prove to be men of goodwill and obey the League (or even stay in it) was left vaguely open. When Italy invaded Abysinnia, it was felt that economic sanctions would bring the aggressor into line without recourse to arms; though the half-hearted pursuit of this policy in the light of dividing economic interests made it ineffective and let go by a major opportunity to halt the series of aggressions that eventually led to war. The pressure exerted by the remembered horrors of war is seen in the way that the disarmament conference of 1933, set up, in part, to conciliate Germany, was allowed to drag on, even though it had opened with Germany's departure from the League. A similar hopeful farce was kept up over the matter of non-intervention in Spain. Committees met to discuss and oversee the policy, even though every member of such committees knew that the German and Italian members were using the policy to limit intervention to their own side. So long as discussion went on, it was hoped, there was something to hope for.

War and the inevitability of war was not the main preoccupation of most people in Great Britain throughout the decade. Unemployment and economic difficulties were of much more continued concern. Regarding unemployment and financial crises, few people in public life could discover any solution. The Labour Chancellor, Snowden, was an unshakeable believer—a moral believer—in the balanced budget. For this was a period, both on the Right and on the Left, when politics and economics were still seen very much in moral terms. The image of the thirties as an era of economic devastation is the one projected by books like George Orwell's *The Road to Wigan Pier* (1937). Orwell's book takes much of its material from the traditionally industrial North, a part of the country containing "depressed areas". These areas were ones dependent on industries in which Britain had been predominant in export before the Great War, and depression in these areas in the thirties was a continuation of a pattern of the twenties. These were the areas from which the hunger marches began, and where older men were to remain unemployed throughout the decade.

Yet there was another Britain, apart from the Britain of industrial depression and the traditional Britain of rural areas and country towns. In 1934 in Jarrow, unemployment stood at 67·8 per cent; in High Wycombe it was 3·3 per cent. There were areas of the South of England in the thirties that, in absolute terms, might be regarded as prosperous. These were the "other" Britain—the new Britain of light industries, semi-detached houses and ribbon development. This new Britain had features that represented a break with tradition, disconcerting to many. Improved bus services and the low price of small cars made new out-lying housing estates possible. Leisure was transformed, even for the unemployed. With the coming of talking pictures, the cinema swept aside every competitor. Alongside the cinema grew up the *palais de danse*, catering for the new lower middle-class craze for ballroom dancing. At home, the invention of the loudspeaker radio, replacing the crystal set with its earphones, made listening a source of entertainment rather than an eccentric hobby.

Reading through a popular but responsible journal like *The Listener* in the thirties, one is struck by the extent to which discussion is concerned not only with the achievements, but, more vociferously, with the shortcomings and cultural dangers of the new Britain. Throughout the thirties, people of every persuasion—apart, it would seem, from the builders and buyers of new houses—were concerned with the disappearance of traditional aspects of English life. On this matter Right and Left agreed that the country was going to the dogs—literally and metaphorically, as dog racing was one of the new and despised sports.

There is, however, no escape from the fact that the thirties was a period of great social shortcomings and injustice, and of destitution and economic strain for many people. Over eight and a half million families had an income of £4 a week or less in 1934, while nearly twenty thousand people had incomes exceeding £5000 a year. In such a situation, with its surrounding pattern of international bumbling towards disaster, the poets of the thirties made their protest. Yet it would be wrong to imagine that the combined voice of the left-wing poets was a powerful one. In the early years, when they warned of disaster ahead, the number of people who read their work were in the hundreds. When they spoke with the popular left-wing movements of the later thirties, their readers might have been counted in the thousands. It was only in the forties that they reached a reasonably large poetry reading public—a public created by the cultural consciousness produced by the war. In the thirties, the main middle-class reading public stayed with their Francis Brett Young, Mary Webb, and *Gone with the Wind*.

II

Sympathy with the Left was widespread in intellectual circles in the thirties: none of the poets discussed in this book was Right in sympathy; and very few could be described as a-political. In this period it is hard to assess the extent of an individual writer's involvement with Marxist ideology, partly because the amount of left-wing journalism in the late thirties was so overwhelming that someone of left-wing sympathy might well have been described as living in a culture as pervasively Left as the culture as a whole was pervasively Christian. Many Marxist notions were commonplaces of the time. On the other hand, the extent of a writer's affiliation with the Communist Party is not necessarily a measure of his commitment to left-wing ideas. Discussions of the influence of Marxism in the thirties may easily fail because they ignore the pervasiveness as well as the cogency of Marxist ideas.

The relationship between the Communists and other left-wing movements changed radically in the course of the thirties. Up to 1928, the Communist International had adopted a policy of a united front from above—that is, by short-term agreement with democratic socialist parties. In 1928, this was replaced by a policy of a united front from below—that is, by bringing the proletariat under the Communist Party alone, and by rejecting co-operation with democratic socialist parties. This policy, which involved taking every opportunity to destroy other parties of the Left, proved disastrous, particularly in Germany, where the triumph of the Nazis, to an extent assisted initially by the Communist Party, resulted in the annihilation of Communism in Germany. It became clear to the Comintern that the most notable political trend of the thirties, the replacement of liberal democratic governments by right-wing totalitarian régimes, was a menace to the continuation of Communism in the one country in which it had established itself, the Soviet Union.

From 1928 to 1934, the Comintern had emphasised economic factors in speaking of the capitalist world; from 1935 to 1939, political factors were emphasised. "In face of the towering menace of fascism to the working class . . . at the present historic stage it is the main and immediate task of the international labour movement to establish the united fighting front of the working class . . ."[1] (*The Resolution of the Seventh Comintern Congress on Fascism, Working Class Unity, and the Tasks of the Comintern*: 20th August, 1935). The guiding notion of the later thirties was a "popular" or "people's front", uniting all left-wing movements: this involved a return to the idea of the united front from above. The united and popular front policies continued until they no longer appeared to give any hope of successfully halting fascism: they were then superseded by the Hitler–Stalin pact of August, 1939.

The attempts to set up a united front with the Labour Party met with no success in England. The idea of a united front was first brought forward by the Communists in 1933, but was denounced by the Labour Party and the Trade Union Congress (T.U.C.). The Communist Party of Great Britain (C.P.G.B.) continued, however, to attempt to pursue the Comintern policy of reconciliation; and, to the embarrassment

of the Labour Party, later attempts were made from the
Labour side to establish a popular front. During 1938 and
early 1939, such a movement got under way. Little was
achieved, though these widespread "popular" left-wing movements had the effect of increasing very greatly the small
audience of the left-wing writers of the period.

Despite the strength of the Labour Party and the T.U.C.,
it is surprising that the C.P.G.B. had so little success among
the working class. It has been in this field that its main efforts
have been made and its main interest shown. The real life
of the C.P.G.B. is not seen in the autobiographies of intellectual
affiliates, nor even in a book like *I Believed* (1950) by Douglas
Hyde of the *Daily Worker*, but in Bob Darke's *The Communist
Technique in Great Britain* (1952). Here we see the world of the
C.P.G.B.'s attempts to infiltrate the trade unions by a body
of dedicated Communists getting control of elective offices.
It is to this activity that the Party has shown its most steady
dedication.

Indeed, it may be argued that the C.P.G.B. acquired much
of its intellectual support in the thirties by accident; and
that those intellectuals who gained the greatest prominence as
writers were the most loosely attached. Well before the formation of the "popular front" policy, Stalin evidently saw the
value of influencing the intellectuals. There existed an International Bureau of Revolutionary Literature, with which
American writers had contact, and which held its Second
World Plenum in Kharkov in 1930. Yet the British Section
of the Writers' International was not formed until 1934.
There seems to have been, in the case of people like Philby,
Burgess and MacLean, deliberate recruitment of a small
number of secret Communists among intellectuals; but this
appears to have been international rather than British in
origin. The intellectuals in Britain do not seem to have had as
decided a place in the Party as they did in the United States;
nor were they as exposed to the realities of politics and oppression as were European intellectuals.

In the late twenties there was little political concern among
British university students. If any sentiment was strong politically among undergraduates of 1930, it was pacifism; and a
pacifist leaning was to mark the attitude of British left-wing

intellectuals throughout the period. The collapse of the Labour government in 1931, and the separation of its leaders from their party, seems to have been a decisive event in the spread of Communism among British intellectuals. With MacDonald and members of his Labour cabinet designated "National Labour" and in coalition with the Liberals and Conservatives in a National government, the hope of any action from the democratic Left in Britain seemed gone.

The case of John Strachey throws an unusual light on the development of the British Left in the thirties. Strachey became a Communist and wrote one of the few classics of the British Left, *The Coming Struggle for Power* (1932). However, he did not become a Communist immediately: he first joined Oswald Mosley in the formation of the New Party. In 1930 Mosley was a Labour M.P. and one of the few politicians to come forward with any intelligent plans to deal with the economic and financial crisis. Mosley resigned from the party, and in February, 1931, formed the New Party. Strachey resigned from the New Party in July, 1931, when he became aware of its totalitarian and thuggist tendencies; but the party had a considerable attraction for intellectuals at the time of its formation, and many contributed to its periodical, *Action*. Among these contributors was Christopher Isherwood.

The appeal of Mosley was similar, in fact, to the appeal of Communism. If the Communists offered the "struggle for power", the New Party presented itself as the party of action and change. Action, above all, was what many younger intellectuals were looking for after the collapse of the Labour government. The rightist potentiality for following a strong leader was present in some of the young people who later turned Left. W. H. Auden, in his Foreword to the third edition of *The Orators* (1932), remarks: "My own name on the title-page seems a pseudonym for someone else, someone talented but near the border of sanity, who might well, in a year or two, become a Nazi."[2] Both parties offered action in the face of the supposed bankruptcy of liberal democracy. Both parties sought to replace liberalism by totalitarianism.

Auden and Spender were also contributors to a periodical, *The Twentieth Century*, which ran from 1931 to 1934, and which was edited by David Archer, who kept the famous left-wing bookshop in Parton Street. *The Twentieth Century* was styled the journal of the Promethean Society. The name is suggestive of the notion of rejuvenation of society behind the early work of Auden and Spender. Their notion of rejuvenation owes a good deal to Lawrence, who saw this rejuvenation of society as taking place through the physical and spiritual rejuvenation of the individual. The differences in political orientation in the earliest work of Auden and Spender suggest how much more important to them may have been the idea of change or transformation than was the ideal of social equality.

However, it was an early awareness of the dangers of the Fascist movement in Germany that helped to turn Spender, Auden and Isherwood towards Communism. Auden had gone to Germany after leaving Oxford in 1928. Isherwood joined him in March of 1929. Spender was in Germany in the summer of 1929, and returned after leaving Oxford in 1930. William Plomer was in Berlin in 1930; and Edward Upward was also in Germany around this time. It was initially the moral emancipation of Germany of the Weimar Republic that attracted some of these young writers to it. The Germany they knew was the Germany of Isherwood's *Goodbye to Berlin* (1937). It was in Germany that Spender first came face to face with the effects of unemployment. Yet important as was the horror at the effects of economic depression, anti-fascism seems to have been the strongest formative element in the left-wing sympathies of these British literary intellectuals.

The appeal of Communism to intellectuals at the beginning of the thirties is not entirely explained by the circumstances so far outlined. Just as the western world entered a startling depression, people began to hear of the success of the Soviet Union's first five-year plan. This impression of Soviet society being alive while western European civilisation was moribund was reinforced by the arrival of great Soviet films like *Mother* and *Potemkin*. Communism also had a fundamental intellectual and emotional appeal. R. H. S. Crossman, in introducing *The God that Failed* (1950), said: "The intellectual attraction of Marxism was that it exploded liberal fallacies—which really were fallacies. It taught the bitter truth that progress is not automatic, that boom and slump are inherent in capitalism, that social injustice and racial discrimination are not cured merely by the passage of time, and that power politics cannot be 'abolished', but only used for good or bad ends."[3] C. Day Lewis saw his Communism as having had a "religious quality", and attributed the attraction left-wing beliefs had for him and, for friends such as W. H. Auden, Rex Warner, Stephen Spender, to the fact that they had grown up in a Christian, liberal tradition, and had ceased to believe in Christianity and despaired of liberalism.[4] The "religious" aspect of the Party's appeal extended to the sense of community in rightness that it gave to the individual, a feeling that all his actions contributed to a movement of history whose aim was good and which transcended his own being. And, as has so often been pointed out, these "religious" satisfactions were what enabled some Communists to ignore inhuman features of the Party's activities: for the true believer, it had to be right.

III

The largest groups of poets dealt with in this book are those who were at Oxford or Cambridge around 1930. Almost without exception, these writers had come from public schools. Public school and Oxford: C. Day Lewis, W. H. Auden, Louis MacNeice, John Betjeman, Stephen Spender, Rex Warner, Norman Cameron, Bernard Spencer, Geoffrey Grigson. Public school and Cambridge: William Empson, Julian Bell, John Lehmann, Charles Madge—plus the novelists Christopher Isherwood and Edward Upward. William Plomer was a public school boy, but did not go on to university. Vernon Watkins was also a public school boy: he went up to Cambridge, but left in disgust. Kathleen Raine was at Cambridge around 1930, as was James Reeves. It is safe to say that no generation of writers has been so preoccupied with school as was this generation. *The Old School* (1934), edited by Graham Greene, and devoted to reminiscences of school from various young writers—including several of those listed above—is only the most obvious evidence of this preoccupation.

This was the generation of schoolboys who just missed fighting in the war, but who were at school in a wartime atmosphere and, for all anyone knew, were being prepared for the war. The grotesque simplicities of propaganda in the

Great War are too well known to need illustration. The attitudes symbolised by the figure of Colonel Blimp were merely an extension of the attitudes inculcated by the public school and their nurseries, the preparatory schools. It must have been impossible for a sensitive boy to go through the Great War unaffected by the slaughter he heard reported and the bogus patriotism that attended it.

The generation to which these writers belonged came to maturity in the years of disillusionment following the war. It is not surprising that, when they came to criticise their society, these writers saw it in the image of Blimpism and the public schools. These stood for the past and all that had gone wrong. According to William Plomer, Christopher Isherwood related how Kipling's works "were read aloud on Sunday afternoon at his preparatory school, almost as if part of the curriculum, and how the things Kipling approved of seemed to him aspects of an Enemy he knew he would have to fight for the rest of his life".[5]

This generation constitutes a moral watershed. Spender described himself as growing up in the "Puritan decadence". This decadence of puritanism involved its breakdown, and there was a great contrast between the world in which this generation of writers grew up and the world into which they emerged at maturity. They had gone to schools which imposed, in their most rigid and humbug-ridden forms, the puritanical values of the Victorian age (particularly regarding sex); and they had emerged into an age that no longer held these values or the religious beliefs that gave them sanction. It was at last possible to name openly what had been unmentionable. It is not surprising that this generation turned on those whom they felt had poisoned their youth.

The image of the middle class as a doomed class was a constant one in the poetry of the thirties. It was connected with what was perhaps the most original mode of the period: satirical fantasy. The doomed world was projected as the "mad" world it was. This was the mode of Isherwood and Upward's Mortemere elaborations and of Auden's *The Orators* (1932). Yet though these writers often wrote of the class from which they came as doomed, they were of that class and wrote with a feeling and authority concerning what

B

they ostensibly condemned. For all their apparent certainty concerning the future, the upper middle-class radicals of the thirties betrayed a sadness for the era that was passing:

> You dowagers with Roman noses
> Sailing along between banks of roses
> > well dressed,
> You Lords who sit at committee tables
> And crack with grooms in riding stables
> > your father's jests;
>
> Solicitors with poker faces,
> And doctors with black bags to cases
> > hurried,
> Reporters coming home at dawn
> And heavy bishops on the lawn
> > by sermons worried; . . .

In these opening lines of "The Witnesses", Auden not only shows an insider's feeling for his subject; a certain affection goes along with the satire. There is a sense in which these radical poets of the thirties were also the valedictorians of the class from which they came. Auden, MacNeice, Day Lewis—as well as the non-radical Betjeman—have such a strong feeling for the England in which they had grown up. This is one of the things for which we value them most.

IV

Although politics were a dominant concern of many writers of the thirties, the most important literary fact of the period was that, for the first time, there existed a generation of writers who had grown up under the influence of the great makers of twentieth-century literature and thought—under the influence of Proust, Eliot, Joyce, Lawrence and Freud. Freud, almost as much as Marx, was a patron saint of the period, and the attempt to combine his social analysis with that of Marx is seen in, for instance, the work of Auden. Freud and D. H. Lawrence expounded the danger to the individual and to civilisation of repression of natural tendencies —particularly the sexual instinct. The appeal of their teaching to the writers growing up in the post-war period is obvious.

Lawrence saw the rejuvenation of society as coming with the sexual rejuvenation of the life of the individual; and this association of social change with the death of puritanism and an acceptance of the body clearly had a considerable influence, especially on Auden, Spender and Rex Warner. The influence of Freud was to extend beyond providing a rationale for instinctual freedom. His writings—and those of Lawrence—brought the unconscious into great respect and became the basis for anti-rational theories of art, such as surrealism. In addition, Freud saw the artist as a type of neurotic who used his art as a substitute satisfaction for what he could not attain in reality; and it became something of a minor doctrine that the artist must be neurotic and even nourish his neuroses.

Iconoclasm is a natural prelude to freedom; and two of the most influential books of the period were ones that attacked and disdained the older values: Lytton Strachey's *Eminent Victorians* and Aldous Huxley's *Crome Yellow*. The twenties was an era of "debunking". The word "debunk" seems to have come into British English during that decade from the United States. Strachey and Huxley were great "debunkers"; and, as such, were hailed by the upper middle-class intellectuals of the late twenties. "Debunking" got further impetus from the large number of war books that appeared at the end of the twenties: Erich Maria Remarque's *All Quiet on the Western Front*; Richard Aldington's *Death of a Hero*; Edmund Blunden's *Undertones of War*; Robert Graves's *Goodbye to All That*. These books stressed the horrors of war, and undoubtedly had a great impact on a generation that had just missed fighting in the Great War.

Of the writers admired by the poets and novelists of the thirties, some were influential because they showed new possibilities for literature, but others were more important in the rôle of "culture hero". Christopher Isherwood has said of T. E. Lawrence: "He was the myth-hero of the 'thirties. Auden and I consciously tried to recreate him in our character of Michael Ransom in F.6."[6] He was at once the man of action—Lawrence of Arabia—and the tortured intellectual at war with himself—Aircraftsman Shaw. In the case of Katherine Mansfield, the *Journal* and her struggles against disease seem to have meant most to the thirties writers: "To be rooted in

life, That's what I want" Auden quotes in Poem XVII of
Look Stranger! E. M. Forster was something half-way between
a literary influence and a hero. His tolerant liberalism and his
distrust of high sentiments made him an exemplar of attitudes
admired in the thirties; but the naturalness and simplicity
of his manner of writing had a considerable stylistic influence.

Another writer who was both hero and influence was Wilfred
Owen. In their poetry, Auden and Spender owe something
to Owen's technical innovations, and his unusual combination
of the lyrical and the satirical. However, it was as one who had
faced war and attained through it a more humane vision that
Owen meant so much to the poets of the thirties. It was this
that made C. Day Lewis name him, along with Hopkins
and Eliot, as one of their "immediate ancestors".[7]

Undoubtedly the work that had the greatest literary influence on the poetry of the thirties was T. S. Eliot's *The Waste
Land*. It seemed to offer a vision of what civilisation had been
brought to by the errors of former generations. Eliot contended
that an ugly world was as valuable to a poet as a beautiful one,
and he demonstrated this in *The Waste Land*. The idea that
the subject matter of poetry could be ugly, or merely ordinary,
was still a shocking and exciting one in 1930. Eliot's methods—
his discontinuities, his images that faded into one another,
his reliance on images and his use of quotation: all these
were startlingly new and set the poetic fashion for poetry
that was compressed, strongly visual and, ultimately, obscure.
The influence of the Imagist doctrine of the hard, clear,
definite image was particularly pervasive in the thirties, and
became one of the dogmas of Geoffrey Grigson's *New Verse*.
In addition, as Stephen Spender has remarked: "What
attracted the young poets to *The Waste Land* was that rhythmically the language was so exciting."[8]

A writer whose influence joined with that of Eliot was
Gerard Manley Hopkins. Although the first edition of his
poems had appeared in 1918, long after his death, it was
only with the second edition in 1930 that he became widely
known among readers of modern poetry. With his sprung
rhythm, his distortions of syntax, his startling verbal combinations and his vivid and sometimes overloaded imagery, he
was seen as a modern poet before his time. He seems to have

been a liberating example for Auden, Day Lewis and Rex
Warner, though it would be easy to over-estimate his influence,
as the style of many of the poets discussed in this book had
been formed by the time the influential second edition of
Hopkins appeared.

The writers whose influence has so far been discussed might
be described as constituting the "official list" of approved
modern influences. Most of them are mentioned in, for instance,
the first chapter of John Lehmann's *New Writing in Europe*,
which he wrote in 1940. When, however, he came to write
his autobiography in the 1950s, Lehmann named the Georgian
poets as important examples to him as a beginning poet.
William Plomer has said the same of them. However, they
were under a cloud in the 1930s, because they had been
attacked by Eliot and Pound, and because they were associated
with beery Chestertonianism.

In fact, many of the older and less "modern" poets were
equally important with Eliot as models to the poets of the
thirties. While Hardy, Edward Thomas and the Georgians
did not give a precedent for the new doctrine that any subject
was fit subject for poetry, their directness of expression and
simplicity of diction—as contrasted with the decidedly
"oblique" manner of Eliot and Pound—were an important
formative influence. Equally important was their preoccupation
with the actual, the local, the everyday, for its own sake.
Both Auden and Bernard Spencer attested to the influence
of Hardy's poetry on their work. Yeats, too, was not, in the
twenties, on the list of great moderns: he was still regarded
suspiciously, because of his nineties beginnings. During the
thirties, there is a growing awareness of his greatness, as
seen in the attention given to him in Spender's *The Destructive
Element* (1935), and, at the end of the decade, in Louis Mac-
Neice's *The Poetry of W. B. Yeats* (1941), one of the first books
on Yeats, and still a very good one.

Of the poets who emerged in the twenties, the Sitwells
had little influence on the poetry of the thirties. However,
the work of Robert Graves was emulated by some of the
new poets, including Auden; though except in the cases of
Norman Cameron and James Reeves, this influence has been
discounted. This is understandable, as Graves has himself

consistently disparaged the work of Auden and his friends. In the thirties, the Gravesians were a group apart, and have largely remained so. Considerably more important, though more pervasive, was the influence of Laura Riding. The impact of the sophistication of her language and rhythm is felt in Auden's early poetry, where her poems are directly imitated. Her work was clearly well known to Louis MacNeice and many others and was an important model.

It is interesting to see that, apart from the expatriates, Eliot and Pound, and the well-known Robert Frost, the American poets who so largely made the revolution in twentieth-century poetry had scarcely any influence on English poetry in the 1930s. Indeed, until the publication of *The Faber Book of Modern Verse* in 1936, poets like Wallace Stevens and John Crowe Ransom were scarcely known in Britain, and William Carlos Williams, for instance, remained unread by English readers until much later. Similarly, the only European poet to make a noticeable mark on British poetry in the thirties was Rilke; and his influence was nowhere near as widespread as it was in the forties, when Leishman's translations had made their impact. The most interesting aspect of European/ British literary relations throughout the inter-war period is how little influence the poetry of Apollinaire and his literary descendants had on British poetry. For a short time surrealism had a vogue and an influence among the younger poets in the late thirties. Otherwise, British insularity continued to have its day, despite the international flavour of periodicals like *New Writing*, and isolated efforts like the special American number of Julian Symons's *Twentieth Century Verse*.

Chapter 2

OXFORD

Oxford Poetry, 1925–32 – C. Day Lewis – W. H. Auden – Louis MacNeice – Stephen Spender – Influence of Eliot

MANY OF THE poets who were to shape English poetry during the nineteen-thirties were at Oxford between 1925 and 1930. These five years saw the presence of Rex Warner, Norman Cameron, the "big four"—Cecil Day Lewis, W. H. Auden, Louis MacNeice and Stephen Spender—and John Betjeman, who was already producing poems like "Death in Leamington" as an undergraduate. Among those present at Oxford during these years was Geoffrey Grigson, later editor of *New Verse*. He seems to have known few of the poets whom he was later to publish, and to have published very little himself as an undergraduate. A little after came Richard Goodman, and Bernard Spencer, later to be assistant editor of *New Verse*. While the undergraduate writings of some of these poets do not seem very remarkable, the concentration of talent was.

II

Between the wars, Blackwell's in Oxford published annually a series of volumes called *Oxford Poetry*, devoted to undergraduate poetry and edited by undergraduates. The great question of the day—as aired in the prefaces of the late twenties —was whether the modern or the traditional in poetry was most representative of Oxford. The first poem to stand out as decidedly modern—and it stands out, despite the obvious talent, rather like a sore thumb—is Auden's "Thomas Epilogises", in 1926. The influence of Eliot, whom Auden had recently discovered, is ill absorbed; though in spite of the immense vogue enjoyed by *The Waste Land* among undergraduates at the time, this is the only poem to appear in *Oxford Poetry* in any year with obvious imitation of Eliot's celebrated poem. The influence of the Sitwells was the modern influence most noticeable in *Oxford Poetry* at the end of the twenties: Louis MacNeice and his friends, Graham Shepherd and John Hilton (all of whom appear in the volume for 1929), had been Sitwell admirers since their days together at school; and Geoffrey Grigson recalls a meeting of the English Club at which Edith Sitwell declared that Tom Driberg, one of her admirers and soon to be a well-known gossip columnist, was "the hope for English poetry". Driberg evidently dominated the undergraduate literary scene at the time.

Over the years, one can see an increasing modernity in the contributions; but this manifests itself, not in a deliberate choice of "non-poetic" subjects, or in social awareness, but merely in a freedom (or looseness) of verse form, a contemporaneity of diction, and a general modishness of attitude. The only poets who seem to have been imitative in a conscious and deliberate (and creative) way are Norman Cameron and Clare Parsons. Cameron's Gravesian poems are perhaps the most satisfying poems in *Oxford Poetry* during this period. Parsons, whom MacNeice described as being (with Auden) the most important poet in Oxford at the time, was an admirer of Cummings, whom he imitated with considerable facility. He was then already ill with diabetes, and considered unlikely to live. He died in 1931.

Louis MacNeice also recalled that Parsons was one of the first poets at Oxford to be interested in politics. There is no sign of this in his undergraduate poetry, nor in the early poems of Rex Warner, a strong left-winger in the thirties. The first poem on a political theme in *Oxford Poetry* in this period is in the 1930 volume: Stephen Spender's "Now you've no work, like a rich man . . ."—an early version of "Moving through the silent crowd. . . ."

III

Cecil Day Lewis was the first of the "big four" to arrive in Oxford, coming up to Wadham College in October, 1923. His tutor was Maurice Bowra, whom Day Lewis was later to succeed as professor of poetry at Oxford. Bowra encouraged Day Lewis's taste for the middle Yeats, introduced him to *The Waste Land*, and later took him to Garsington. Day Lewis's principal friend throughout his Oxford years was Rex Warner.

Though each was a member of the Communist Party in the thirties, politics were not a theme of their acquaintance. Both studied classics, and poetry and philosophy seem to have been their chief interests.

Day Lewis had written poetry before coming to Oxford, but he did not become an immediate celebrity there. In fact, he did not appear in *Oxford Poetry* until 1925—the end of his second year. In that year he also published, at his own expense, his first volume of poetry, *Beechen Vigil*. This was not a book to produce a poetic revolution. It contained twenty-four poems in a rather literary and ethereal manner, somewhat reminiscent of de la Mare and the early Yeats. Only occasionally does anything like the authentic Day Lewis voice appear. What strikes one about the volume as a whole is the competence of the writing—the general impression of smoothness and facility.

An added facility is the impression given by Day Lewis's second volume, *Country Comets*, which he finally got published in 1928, and in which he collected most of his undergraduate poems. During the years since the publication of *Beechen Vigil*, he had got to know the work of Eliot, and had become a friend of W. H. Auden—two years his junior at Oxford—with whom he edited *Oxford Poetry*, 1927. Day Lewis has said that he became Auden's disciple in poetry,[1] but there is no sign of this, or of the influence of Eliot, in *Country Comets*. Among those who helped Day Lewis as a young poet was Humbert Wolfe, a civil servant and an amateur of poetry, then highly regarded. Day Lewis was a great admirer of his poems.[2] Wolfe's influence is behind a number of poems in *Country Comets*; we have the author's word for it in one case—"Naked Woman with Kotyle":

> She moved to the slow
> Dance of supplication
> Her body's flow
> Was a moon in motion . . .

The verse pattern is stylishly handled, and is one that Day Lewis was to use in the thirties in lyrics like "Can the mole take/A census of the stars? . . ."

One of the earliest poems in *Country Comets* (it appeared in

Oxford Poetry, 1925) exemplifies Day Lewis's obvious talent at that time, but also shortcomings that were his then and which were to remain with him:

> On the heart's hidden verge
> To mark where love is buried
>   Mourner lilies spring
> Out of the stunted spurge.
> And a small wind sings dirge
>   Under the last leaves fluttering.
>   ("Autumn of the Mood")

The poem is still an enjoyable one, yet it cannot aspire to being more than pleasant. What is attractive about it is the particularity with which the visual elements are developed, coupled with the lightness of rhythm; but the imagery has a decorative function, and seems developed for its own sake. The stanza quoted is merely a pretty way of saying that the poet feels only slightly sad at the death of love. The poem's felicities and its defects were to remain characteristic of Day Lewis throughout his career. The authentic Day Lewis voice, relaxed and reflective, is certainly present, intermittently, even from the start:

> Now you have gone, I remember only your smile,
> Flame-like and vivid as first green in March hedgerows,
> Telling the wayfarers that every mile
> Is bringing them nearer to sunshine and dog-rose.
>   (*Beechen Vigil:* "An April Mood")

But also present from the start are the facile rhetorical features, such as the love of musical imagery, evocative merely of stock responses:

> See how the wind's bleak trumpet stuns each hill
>   To colder immobility!
>   (*Beechen Vigil:* "Song of the Sirens")

The voice that is heard in the early poems might be described as "Georgian"; but it is not a voice of Georgian firmness. There is a "literary" quality about the writing that points forward to the facile pastiche of some of the later poetry (in volumes like *Poems*, 1943–47).

Before he ceased to be an undergraduate, Day Lewis had begun, at Auden's suggestion, a sequence of poems to be called *Transitional Poem* (1929). The subject was love, not politics; the most noticeable model was Yeats, not Eliot; the source of ideas and imagery was most frequently the philosophers Day Lewis had studied at Oxford, not Marx and the industrial world. An early part of it appeared in *Oxford Poetry* for 1927:

> Now I have come to reason
> And cast my school-boy clout,
> Disorder I see is without,
> And the mind must sweat a poison
> Keener than Thessaly's brew
> A pus that, discharged not thence,
> Gangrenes the vital sense
> And makes disorder true.
> It is certain we shall attain
> No life till we stamp on all
> Life the tetragonal
> Pure symmetry of brain.

It is an impressive and lively beginning. But the writing seems a little over-pitched—a conventional talent straining to be up to date. A good deal of Day Lewis's writing in the thirties was to give this feeling.

IV

When W. H. Auden arrived in Oxford in 1925, he might have claimed to be a "published poet" already. *Public School Verse* for 1923–4 had contained the following poem—"Woods in Rain" by W. H. Arden [*sic*]:

> It is a lovely sight and good
> To see rain falling in a wood.
> The birds are silent, drunk with sound
> Of raindrops kissing the green ground,
> They sit with head tucked under wing
> Too full of joy to dare to sing.
> Flowers open mouths as wide I say
> As baby blackbirds do in May:

> While trees shake hands as grave and slow
> As two old men I used to know,
> And hold out smiling boughs to find
> Whence comes this sweetest breath of wind.
> But now the sun has come again
> And he has chased away the rain.
> The rain has gone beyond the hill,
> But leaves are talking of it still.

This was Auden's first published poem. Auden, in 1940, summarised his development during this period: ". . . it was Hardy in the summer of 1923; for more than a year I read no one else . . . In the autumn of 1924 there was a palace revolution after which he shared his kingdom with Edward Thomas, until they were both defeated by Eliot at the battle of Oxford in 1926."[3] In fact, this first poem seems to echo one of Auden's earliest admirations: W. H. Davies.

When Christopher Isherwood, who had been at the same preparatory school as Auden, met him again in the autumn of 1925, Auden sent him an envelope of manuscripts of his poems. Isherwood later published some of them.[4] While, as he points out, Hardy and Edward Thomas are the models, Auden's originality shows itself in adapting their medium to deal with the industrial landscape that had fascinated him since the days when he had dreamed of being a mining engineer.

> It was quiet in there after the crushing
> Mill; the only sounds were the clacking belt
> And the steady throb of waters rushing
> That told of the wild joy these waters felt
> In falling. The quiet gave us room to talk:
> "How many horse-power is the large turbine?"
> "Seventy. The beck is dammed at Greenearth Fork; . . ."
>> [The Edward Thomas manner]

> The smelting-mill stack is crumbling, no smoke is alive there,
> Down in the valley the furnace no lead ore of worth burns;
> Now tombs of decaying industries, not to strive there
> Many more earth turns.
>> [The Hardy manner]

Isherwood remarked that, if he had read him, he might also have recognised the influence of Frost.

Auden's dictum in those days—as throughout his Oxford

period—was that poetry should be "classic, clinical and austere".[5] Auden was to say later that Hardy taught him a lot about colloquial diction, "all the more because his directness was in phrasing and syntax, not in imagery. . . ."[6] Another poet whose example for a time (in 1926) contributed to his development in this direction was Edwin Arlington Robinson, whom Auden considered "very austere indeed".[7] Auden wrote about half a dozen poems in Robinson's manner, among them "Portrait", which appeared in *Best Poems of 1926*.

It is a good thing that Isherwood preserved some of Auden's early poems, as "the battle of Oxford" was evidently a massacre. Neville Coghill recalled that Auden turned up one morning for his tutorial hour and announced that he had torn up all his poems.[8] The reason was the discovery of Eliot. According to Isherwood, "The discovery of *The Waste Land* marked a turning-point in his work—for the better certainly; though the earliest symptoms of Eliot-influence were most alarming. Like a patient who has received an over-powerful inoculation, Auden developed a severe attack of allusions, jargonitis and private jokes. He began to write lines like: 'Inexorable Rembrandt rays, which stab . . .'."[9] This line is from "Thomas Epilogises", a poem that displays all the symptoms, well developed, as well as the celebrated "clinical" manner:

> Inexorable Rembrandt rays, which stab
> Through clouds as through a rotting factory floor,
> Make chiaroscuro in a day now over,
> And cart-ruts bloody as if Grendel lately
> Had shambled dripping back into her marshes.
> The train runs on, while in the sagging West
> Gasometers heave Brobdignagion flanks
> Like dragons with their bat-wings furled for sleep.
> (No rock nor twisted thorn was there to fill
> Uneasy silences, save once a poplar
> Wrung its bewildered leaves, and once a mill
> Raised heavy hands and dropped them to its side.)
> I, Thomas, the disappointed lover
> My reins protected by one flaccid hand,
> Trace thumb-nail sketches on the sweaty pane,
> Sole audience of the coach-wheels clattering
> (οἴκαδε, οἴκαδε, οἴκαδε, Home!)

> For thoughts of you and of the growth of love,
> A sigmoid curve, that dwindled suddenly
> As love grew hungry, but the diet stale.
> Love mutual has reached its first eutectic,
> And we must separate . . .
>
>   (*Oxford Poetry*, 1926)

The jerky discontinuities, the unevenness of tone, the way some lines seem to stick out of the poem (quite apart from the ill-absorbed Eliotian display of culture): all these things bring to mind what Isherwood said about the way some of Auden's poems were composed in those days:

> If I wanted an adjective altered, it was altered then and there. . . . If, on the other hand, I had praised a line in a poem otherwise condemned, then that line would reappear in a new poem. And if I didn't like this poem, either, but admired a second line, then both lines would appear in a third poem, and so on—until a poem had been evolved which was a little anthology of my favourite lines, strung together without even an attempt to make connected sense.[10]

Isherwood was slightly older than Auden; their friendship was the most important one to Auden at the time, so far as his literary development was concerned. To others—even to Day Lewis, who was three years older—Auden was dogmatic and dictatorial; but to Isherwood (who was from Cambridge) he deferred, as to a more experienced writer. For those at Oxford, who, like Stephen Spender, were privileged to be introduced by Auden to Isherwood, Isherwood was preceded by his "legend".

On Auden's recommendation Isherwood read some Norse sagas: they were the background of Auden's family history, and Auden disliked French literature. Isherwood found the people and the atmosphere of the sagas familiar: ". . . they were the boys at our preparatory school. Weston [Auden] was pleased with the idea. . . ." In time the two developed a saga fantasy world based on their preparatory school days, though the world of Auden's ruined industrial landscape, the Northern moorlands, the ominous saga tone, do not appear in a developed form in any of Auden's poems that may definitely be traced to his undergraduate period. "About a year later,"

Isherwood goes on, "I actually tried the experiment of writing a school story in what was a kind of hybrid language composed of saga phraseology and schoolboy slang. And soon after this, Weston produced a short verse play in which the two worlds are so confused that it is almost impossible to say whether the characters are epic heroes or members of a school O.T.C." This was "Paid on both Sides", written in Germany in the months after Auden left Oxford in 1928. The story was "Gems of Belgian Architecture", included in Isherwood's *Exhumations* (1966).[11]

An interesting sidelight on his collaboration is given by an anonymous poem in *Oxford Poetry* for 1927, "Souvenir des Vacances":

> That day the steak was bad, he came. We found
> The cormorant shot last year as a spy
> My friend the author in the Lisbon hat
> Was ordered from the pub for quoting Tourneur;
> Read us, after lunch, Professor Stinkbomb
> On the Greek Games. Wilde would have been appalled.

There are two more stanzas of the same kind. The poem is by Isherwood, and seems to refer to Auden's visiting him at the seaside in July, 1926. This might suggest that the abrupt, article-free, pseudo-Norse style of some of Auden's early poetry was one developed by the two of them in evolving their fantasy world, though Isherwood now rejects the poem as ". . . a feeble attempt to parody the current *avant-garde* poetic manner. . . ."[12]

Auden's work at this time seems less all of a piece than that of, say, Louis MacNeice. This might partly be put down to Auden's having further to go, more to explore. But one might also recall the way in which Auden was to retain the habit of exploiting the manners of other poets: some of his best poems have involved an element of ventriloquism. The more obvious features of Auden's undergraduate poetry—the more flashy ones—are not a measure of his real originality. They belong with the Auden of the anecdotes—the walks in his clerical coat by the gas-works with Day Lewis, the dictatorial "interviews" with Stephen Spender in his rooms at Christchurch, where the light was shut out with sackcloth: there may have been some spontaneity in these eccentricities, but not much originality. Again, Louis MacNeice spoke of the Auden of those days as "someone to whom ideas were friendly";[13] yet there was a certain glibness in Auden's ideas then—a glibness connected with a detachment that Spender noted; a glibness that was in part to remain with Auden. What was truly original was the direction of his interests—his feeling for the industrial landscape, which was unpoetic to most people then, but of which Auden was to realise the essential poetry in his writing.

Most original of all was what one might call his poetic conservatism. Speaking of Hardy's world, Auden described it as "... above all a world that had nothing to do with London, the stage, or French literature". Although Auden learned a great deal from Eliot about the poetic possibilities of the contemporary world and of contemporary diction, he did not imitate the more superficial features of modern poetry. Speaking of free verse, Auden said: "Hardy saved me from this. . . . Here was a 'modern' rhetoric which was more fertile and adaptable to different themes than any of Eliot's gas works and rat's feet which one could steal but never make one's own."[14] The ability to learn from Hardy, Edward Thomas, and Frost when Eliot and the Sitwells were the rage was remarkable; from it derives the firmness and resilience of diction and phrase that was Auden's, and which enabled him to develop an idiom that could deal poetically with the England of his day and provide a model for others to do the same.

v

Louis MacNeice, in 1926, was the next of the four to arrive in Oxford. Although he knew Auden and Spender, his friends seem principally to have been those with whom he had been at school at Marlborough. Auden recalled him as "a tall dark languid undergraduate from Merton, rather foppishly dressed"[15]—but had no clear recollection of when he met MacNeice. Good, in his own words, as "an intellectual window dresser",[16] he surprised his tutor by getting a first in Greats (the final examination in classics) and went on to teach at Birmingham and London universities. He was the only one

of the four poets to gain any distinction academically: Day
Lewis got a fourth-class degree in classics; Auden, a third in
English; Spender left without getting a degree at all. Neverthe-
less, for MacNeice, "The only serious activity was poetry".[17]

The relative ease with which MacNeice distinguished himself
academically was merely an extension of the considerable
precocious ability he had shown from early childhood. His
description in *Modern Poetry* (1938) of a paper he read to a
school society in his seventeenth or eighteenth year gives a
good idea of his particular kind of brilliance. His contention
was that "the business of the poet was to produce rabbits
out of apparent vacancy. . . . They supply the missing pieces
to our jigsaws. They delve into our brains and fish up the
king of the salmon from beneath the weeds of convention."
And finally: "I end the paper by quoting Yeats's 'Happy
Townland', the 'Pervigilium Veneris' and Theocritus refrain:
Ἴυγξ ἕλκε τὺ τῆνον ἐμὸν ποτὶ δῶμα τὸν ἄνδρα with the typical
romantic comment—'She may chant on, she may mix her
philtres, he will never come.'"[18]

His precocity had included poetry. From the age of seven
he wrote poems, and continued to do so throughout his
school years. During his seventeenth year someone told him
that his poetry was like that of the Sitwells, so he read them.
A little later he was introduced to Eliot's poetry, which he at
first found repellent, but later, attractive because of the
contemporary content.[19] No doubt this reading influenced
his writing; but there is every indication that he developed
early what was to be, basically, his characteristic manner,
and that he did so without much recourse to literary example.
The poem, "Genesis" (originally "The Universe: an excerpt"),
which opens *Collected Poems, 1925–1948*, was written in 1925,
when he was still in school. Another poem, written during his
last year at school, in 1926, is, with its rococco manner and
echoing sounds, recognisably his ("The Sea"):

> The sea, now hoary with desire,
> Yet follows feet that walk the beach;
> The sensual plumes of brine aspire
> But cannot reach beyond their reach—
> Will amour'd Neptune never tire?

Both poems appeared in MacNeice's first volume of poetry, *Blind Fireworks* (1929), which evidently contains other poetry from his school days. These early poems show what MacNeice was to term "an excessive preoccupation . . . with things dazzling, high-coloured, quick-moving, hedonistic or up-to-date".[20]

He went up to Oxford believing in something close to automatic writing as the means of producing poetry. No doubt this accounts for the diffuseness of some of the poems in *Blind Fireworks*, and of his early contributions to *Oxford Poetry*. However, in these poems certain aspects of the authentic MacNeice manner are already established: the ringing of changes on particular words, combined with a subdued rhythm that never becomes cantabile; the concentration on surface, with metaphor relatively unimportant in function.

> The glass is going down. The sun
> Is going down. The forecasts say
> It will be warm with frequent showers.
> We ramble down the showery hours
> And amble up and down the day.
> Mary will wear her black goloshes
> And splash the puddles on the town;
> And soon on fleets of macintoshes
> The rain is coming down, the frown
> Is coming down of heaven showing
> A wet night coming, the glass is going
> Down, the sun is going down.
> [*Oxford Poetry*, 1928: "Glass Falling"]

His first book of poems, *Blind Fireworks*, was published by Gollancz in March, 1929. Of it, MacNeice later said: ". . . it is . . . full of mythological tags, half-digested new ideas and conceits put in for the hell of it . . . The images are rarely structural; they are too often not merely decoration . . . but *random* decoration."[21] At about that time he became engaged to be married. Neither family approved of the engagement. MacNeice found that he had less and less time and energy for writing. He got married on Midsummer Day 1930—the day after the last of his final examinations. He went to Birmingham as a lecturer in the university there, and almost gave up reading or writing modern poetry for three years. But, by the time he left Oxford, he was already an accomplished poet, with his own distinctive manner. One of the few surviving poems written between the publication of *Blind Fireworks* and his marriage was "Spring Sunshine", still one of his best and most characteristic pieces. It was dated "April, 1929":

> In a between world, a world of amber
> The old cat on the sand-warm windowsill
> Sleeps on the verge of nullity.
>
> Spring sunshine has a quality
> Transcending rooks and hammering
> Of those who hang new pictures,
> Asking if it is worth it
> To clamour and caw, to add stick to stick for ever.
>
> If it is worth while really
> To colonize any more the already populous
> Tree of knowledge, to portion and reportion
> Bits of broken knowledge brittle and dead,
> Whether it would not be better
> To hide one's head in the warm sand of sleep
> To be embalmed without hustle or bother.
>
> The rooks bicker heckle bargain always
> And market carts lumber
> But I in the calm of the all-humouring sun
> Will too indulge my humour
> And bury myself beyond creaks and cawings
> In a below world, a bottom world of amber.
>
> *(Oxford Poetry, 1929)*

Like a great deal of MacNeice's poetry, it is a poem of directness and of the surface. It gets a lot of its life and evocativeness from the use of two figures of which MacNeice remained very fond: the revived *cliché*—"To hide one's head in the warm sand of sleep"; and the juxtaposition of words and phrases of disparate quality—"Sleeps on the verge of nullity", "Transcending rooks". Both figures enliven the surface, rather than give added depth, as does metaphor. This concern with the disparate aspects of reality was to remain a feature of Mac-Neice's poetry.

VI

Christopher Isherwood was introduced to Stephen Spender by Auden in the summer of 1928, at the end of Spender's first year in Oxford: "He burst in upon us, blushing, sniggering loudly, contriving to trip over the edge of the carpet—an immensely tall, shambling boy of nineteen, with a great scarlet poppy-face, wild frizzy hair, and eyes the violet colour of bluebells."[22]

Spender became, in the year they were at Oxford together, Auden's protégé. He found himself "in the position of a pupil learning from a schoolmaster".[23] When Spender first called on Auden, the meeting had the character of an interview, in which Auden tersely quizzed Spender on his tastes in poetry. He then told Spender who was good: Owen, Hopkins, Edward Thomas, Housman, Eliot. When Spender told him that he wrote four poems a day, Auden replied: "What energy! . . . I write about one in three weeks." Spender cut his output at once. He continued to see Auden, and showed him his poetry. Auden told him to "drop the 'Shelley stunt'. The poet is far more like Mr Everyman than Kelley and Sheets. He cuts his hair short, wears spats, a bowler hat, and a pin-stripe city suit. He goes to the job in the bank by the suburban train." Spender described his talks with Auden as ". . . the witches' brew from which a literary movement is made".[24]

If Auden changed Spender's view of poetry, there is little evidence of this in Spender's first book, *Nine Experiments* (1928), which he printed during his first year as an undergraduate on his own hand press. The poems are rather characterless and conventionally poetic. There is only one line that has the real Spender note:

> The snow has explored the very heart of innocence.
> [*Nine Experiments: "From* 'The Enshrinement of the Ideal',
> Part iv"]

The book was shown to Louis Untermeyer by Anna Wickham, and this led to Untermeyer's including some of Spender's poems in his *Modern British Poetry* (1930).

The rather conventional character of *Nine Experiments* is not what one might expect from Spender's account of his relationship with Auden. A line of Spender's that had impressed Auden was: "In a new country shooting is necessary."[25] There is nothing like this in his first book. Among the poems published only by Untermeyer, however, there is a very uncharacteristic poem, "Statistics", that clearly stems from Auden's teaching:

> Lady, you think too much of speeds,
>   Pulleys and cranes swing in your mind;
>   The Woolworth Tower has made you blind
> To Egypt and the pyramids . . .

The big step forward poetically came for Spender after Auden had left Oxford in 1928, and as a result of something that had nothing to do with Oxford literary circles. Spender had become emotionally involved with another undergraduate, who attracted Spender because of the apparent "purity of his ordinariness". Spender's feelings were not returned; and after a walking tour along the River Wye, Spender saw the impossibility of the relationship. "Immediately after the walking tour I began to write poems different from any others I had done."[26] In his autobiography, *World Within World*, Spender refers to the young man as "Marston". Spender's second book of poems, *Twenty Poems* (privately printed in 1930), has a first section called "The Marston Poems". These eleven poems, written in the latter part of 1928 or early in 1929, include well-known pieces like "Acts passed beyond the boundary of mere wishing", and "He will watch the hawk with an indifferent eye". This last poem, written when he was nineteen, remains one of his best.

> He will watch the hawk with an indifferent eye
>   Or pitifully;
> Nor on those eagles that so feared him, now
>   Will strain his brow;
> Weapons men use, stone, sling, and strong-thewed bow
>   He will not know.
>
> This aristocrat, superb of all instinct,
>   With death close linked

> Had paced the enormous cloud, almost had won
>   War on the sun;
> Till now like Icarus mid-ocean-drowned,
>   Hands, wings, are found . . .

His changed awareness of his own experience may have been connected with the reading of D. H. Lawrence, by whom he was greatly affected at that time. His best poetry has a suffused and burning intensity reminiscent of Lawrence's poems of the natural world. *Twenty Poems* was perhaps the most impressive of the volumes produced by these poets in their undergraduate years. Other first-rate poems in it were "The Port", "Beethoven's Death Mask" and "Written Whilst Walking Down the Rhine".

> Now I suppose that the once-envious dead
> Have learnt a strict philosophy of clay
> After these centuries, to haunt us no longer
> In the churchyard, or at the end of the lane
> Or howling at the edge of the city
> Beyond the last bean-rows, near the new factory.
>   ("Written Whilst Walking Down the Rhine")

The nature of the self-discovery that had so opened up poetry for Spender is indicated by the way in which he contrasts himself with Auden in *World Within World*: "When Auden said at one of our earliest meetings, 'The subject of a poem is a peg to hang the poetry on', he had indicated what I gradually realised to be another basic difference between our attitudes. For I could not accept the idea that the poetic experience in reality which led into a poem was then, as it were, left behind, while the poem developed according to verbal needs of its own which had no relation to the experience. My poems were all attempts to record, as truthfully as I could, experiences which, within reality, seemed to be poetry."[27] In the truthful recording of his personal experiences in *Twenty Poems*, Spender's introspection begins to get into his poetry—an anticipation of poems, like "The Double Shame", that were to be among the best of his later work.

> His figure passes, and I confess
> No suddenness of pain, but an old pain
> More constant in the heart that heart lives by

Again revived: as though from happiness,
Freshness of wind and the cloud-breathing sky,
All happiness rolled away—again revealed
That sore and flaming wheel I must live by.

[*Twenty Poems*, IV]

"Written Whilst Walking Down the Rhine" ("In 1929")
was the only poem of anything like political theme in *Twenty
Poems*. The first truly political poem by Spender appeared a
few months later in *Oxford Poetry*, 1930: "Now you've no
work, like a rich man . . .", later rewritten as "Moving through
the silent crowd. . . ."

> Now you've no work, like a rich man
> You'll sleep long hours and rise at ten;
> And stand at corners of the street
> Smoking continual cigarettes.
>
> Your pockets gape with wry dismay,
> Turned inside-out we find them funny:
> Strange, now I cannot laugh again
> For fear my tears should fall like rain.
>
> I'm jealous of your empty hours
> Spent staring with such hungry eyes,
> Or greeting friends with a shrugged shoulder,
> The cynical gesture of the poor.

Indeed, Spender seems to have been the only one of the "four"
concerned with politics in his undergraduate years. "I was
always interested in politics, but . . . [Auden's] interests were
poetry, psychoanalysis and medicine. I think he disapproved
of my politics. . . ."[28]

VII

What was the nature of Eliot's influence on these young
writers? There is no doubt that Eliot was widely read and
admired in undergraduate literary circles at the time. The
Oxford gas-works—not really so far from Auden's Christchurch, but in an area where nobody would normally go—
seems to have become an emblem of modernity under the
influence of *The Waste Land*. Auden used to take Day Lewis

for walks along the canal by the gas-works, and Louis MacNeice recalled canoeing past the place.

In "Eliot and the Adolescent", MacNeice describes the impact Eliot's poetry had on him and on his friends at school in 1926. One thing that it is easy to forget today is that Eliot was appreciated before he was understood. This was certainly the case with MacNeice and his friends. *The Waste Land* had the greatest impact, opening up for them a new conception of poetry. Poems like "Prufrock" they unconsciously adapted to their own emotional experience. But, above all, Eliot served an emblematic or exemplary function. They knew Picasso and Matisse, but had not yet found any English poet who was modern in the way that they were. Eliot, they sensed, was the poet they were looking for.[29]

That Eliot was an example rather than a model is the key to his influence on the Oxford poets. He showed the possibility the "unpoetic" had as poetry—the ugly, the ordinary—both in subject matter, and in rhythm and diction. But the landscape and furniture of Eliot's poetry they could not, as Auden remarked, make their own. The transformation of Auden's North of England industrial landscape into the ruined world of *Poems*, 1930, no doubt owed something to *The Waste Land*. But Eliot was a poet concerned with the past, with culture, with his own particular spiritual vision. Beyond showing these poets the possibilities that contemporary material and contemporary diction had in freeing poetry from the conventionally poetic, he could not help them.

VIII

In the thirties, of course, these poets were identified as a group by their common involvement in left-wing politics, but, at Oxford, there is scarcely any sign of this in their poetry. It was Auden's genius to learn from Eliot, and yet to retain what he had inherited from Hardy and Edward Thomas. On this basis, he evolved a medium that could capture the essential poetry of the physical and social features of modern English life; and the ability to do this, he passed on to his Oxford friends. At a poetry reading, just after the war, Louis MacNeice introduced Auden as the poet who had made

the work of his generation possible. It must be remembered
that these poets were known, after one of Spender's more
popular poems, as the "Pylon poets"—the poets who had
introduced the imagery and the landscape of industrialism
into English poetry. The preparation of the idiom in which
they could do this went back to their days together at Oxford
with Auden. From him they took their orientation. Thus
whether the four may be spoken of as a movement in the
thirties—or in their undergraduate days—is a question
involving something more complex and truly literary than
an alignment of ideologies. Their designation as a group came
early, and was not merely the product of ill-informed journalism. *Oxford Poetry* for 1932, edited by Richard Goodman and
Bernard Spencer, contains the following dedication:

Dedicated to
WYSTAN AUDEN, CECIL DAY
LEWIS, and STEPHEN SPENDER

Chapter 3

CAMBRIDGE

Cambridge, c. 1930 – Ronald Bottrall – Julian Bell –
John Lehmann – William Empson – James Reeves

CAMBRIDGE OF THE late twenties is remembered as a place
of great intellectual excitement and undergraduate achievement. It inherited the philosophical tradition begun there in
the first two decades of the century by Moore, Russell and
Whitehead. Wittgenstein, who was to lecture there, had
submitted his *Tractatus* as a doctoral thesis at Cambridge;
the young Frank Ramsay was still alive; and, most importantly for literature, Ogden and Richards had carried the
tradition into the fields of linguistics and literary criticism.
Cambridge in the twenties was also the Cambridge of Ruther-
ford and of J. M. Keynes; and it was the chief centre of propaganda for the importance of T. S. Eliot as a poet and a
critic. Richards had written admiringly of *The Waste Land*
in an appendix to *The Principles of Literary Criticism*; in the last
years of the twenties, F. R. Leavis was giving the lectures
that were to become, in 1932, *New Bearings in English Poetry*;
and, in 1926, Eliot delivered his Clark Lectures on Donne.

The importance of Eliot is emphasised by all those who were
at Cambridge at the time. As James Reeves put it:

> The stranger who enters an Anglican church at service time is
> handed two books, *Hymns Ancient and Modern* and *The Book of
> Common Prayer*. When I went up to Cambridge twenty years ago,
> I was handed as it were, in much the same spirit, two little
> books, the one in prose, the other in verse. They were *The Sacred
> Wood* and *Poems 1909–1925*. Those who played the part of the
> sidesmen were not, it should perhaps be said, my tutors but my
> fellow undergraduates. Eliot was not at this time 'officially'
> recognised.[1]

Kathleen Raine has said that ". . . T. S. Eliot's early poetry . . .

enabled us to know our world imaginatively".[2] William Empson met Eliot while he was giving his Clark Lectures.

It was not merely that Cambridge provided the setting and stimulation for undergraduate brilliance: the brilliance was also strikingly apparent. James Reeves again epitomises the scene:

> Two magazines were started in Cambridge about this time. [Autumn, 1928] 'This time', by the way, was the beginning of what I think was the last generation of undergraduates to remain more or less indifferent to politics. Few read a daily newspaper; on the rare occasions when one wanted to consult *The Times*, the copy in the Union reading-room was sufficient, and one was sure to find it unclaimed. *Cambridge Left* and undergraduate Communism, began, I think, after the national crisis of 1931. *The Venture* run mainly by Michael Redgrave, and *Experiment*, under J. Bronowski, William Empson and Hugh Sykes Davies—these two contemporaries were pure of all politics; there was scarcely a reference to the world outside, over which lingered the last golden rays of Locarno sunshine. *The Venture*, tastefully produced, adorned with woodcuts and filled with neo-Georgian poems and stories, was in reality an undergraduate heir to Sir John Squire's *London Mercury*; but *Experiment*, claiming to be youthful, rebellious, provocative, and to be concerned with 'all the intellectual interests of undergraduates', contained articles on science as well as literature, stills from modernist films, photographs of surrealistic paintings, much obscure poetry and experimental prose, of which latter our proudest example was a hitherto unpublished extract from Joyce's *Work in Progress*. We published articles on Hemingway, Hopkins, Joyce, Eliot; an attack on Wyndham Lewis; poems influenced by Hopkins, the Metaphysicals, the Imagists, Laura Riding and of course Eliot. Regular contributors, apart from the three editors named above, included Elsie Phare, John Davenport, T. H. White, George Reavey, Humphrey Jennings, Basil Wright, Richard Eberhart, Kathleen Raine, Edward Wilson and myself.[3]

Experiment went through seven numbers, the last appearing in May, 1931; *The Venture* had six numbers, closing in June, 1930. Other contributors to *Experiment*, not mentioned by Reeves, included Malcolm Lowry and Martin Turnell. *The Venture* published the poems of Julian Bell, along with those of his friend, John Lehmann, who also provided some of the woodcuts.

Something of the brilliance of the Cambridge of those days can be felt from the two volumes of *Cambridge Poetry*, 1929 and 1930, published by the Woolfs' Hogarth Press, evidently as a counterpart to Blackwell's annual *Oxford Poetry*. The first volume is particularly impressive, with poems by Richard Eberhart, William Empson, Ronald Bottrall, Julian Bell, John Lehmann, and James Reeves. What is notable is how much of the poetry is still pleasing and rewarding to read, and not, as one feels in reading *Oxford Poetry* of the same period, merely the interesting work of writers who later became famous.

> I could hear silence now,
>
> or snow, falling,
> that the ear echoes
> and forgets.
>
> If the silence pricked this restlessness,
> this drone, suddenly,
> a star to the heat—
>
> silence under the ice
> and in the long arches of snowdrifts—
>
> breaking
> the exigence, to and fro,
> swelter, and street-mouthed echo,
>
> I could hear it
> tighten
> like a tree to the rime,
> or a bird's wing
> that splinters the frost.
>
> ("City Summer": *Cambridge Poetry*, 1929)

This poem is far from being the best in a volume that contains Empson's "To an Old Lady" and "Legal Fiction". However, it illuminates another facet of literary Cambridge in 1929. Its author, J. Bronowski, was to become well known as a scientist, and also won distinguished literary prizes. Bronowski was one of the editors of *Experiment*. Just as in *Oxford Poetry* of the late twenties we find contributors like

R. H. S. Crossman who were to become famous in humane fields other than literature; so in *Cambridge Poetry* we find poets like Michael Redgrave (an editor of *The Venture*) who was to make his name as an actor; but we also find writers like Bronowski, whose studies lay outside the arts in the sciences for which Cambridge was famous. William Empson began—and excelled—as a mathematician. Kathleen Raine studied biology.

In reviewing *Cambridge Poetry* for 1929, F. R. Leavis, quite rightly, picked Eberhart and Empson as the star contributors. Both were precocious in their poetic achievements. Eberhart arrived in Cambridge with the poems already published in *Poetry*. The firm individuality of his early poetry is illustrated by a poem (not included in *Cambridge Poetry*) which, he tells us, ". . . was written after seeing a dead lamb among daisies in a field near Cambridge, England in 1928". In theme and manner it anticipates his celebrated "The Groundhog" of 1933.

> I saw on a slant hill a putrid lamb,
> Propped with daisies. The sleep looked deep,
> The face nudged in the green pillow
> But the guts were out for crows to eat.
>
> Where's the lamb? whose tender plaint
> Said all for the mute breezes.
> Say he's in the wind somewhere,
> Say, there's a lamb in the daisies.[4]

Eberhart went on to be one of America's more distinguished poets. In his *New Bearings in English Poetry*, in 1932, F. R. Leavis saw Empson and Ronald Bottrall as the "hope for poetry" in England—not Auden, Spender and Day Lewis, whom he did not mention. In his "Notes on English Poets" in *Poetry* for February, 1932, Michael Roberts spoke of ". . . Julian Bell, whose volume *Winter Movement* . . . was, with Mr Auden's *Poems* . . . the outstanding achievement of the younger men in 1930".[5] Bottrall never established himself as an important poet; Empson wrote more really good poems as an undergraduate than he was ever to write later, and he published little poetry after 1940; Julian Bell was, in fact, never to hit form again after *Winter Movement,* and seems to have stopped writing poetry in the two years preceding his death in the Spanish Civil War in 1937. Ironically, no poet who came out of the brilliant Cambridge of *Experiment* and *The Venture* showed the fecundity or staying power of the contemporary Oxford poets, Auden, Day Lewis, Spender and MacNeice.

II

Ronald Bottrall was introduced by F. R. Leavis in *New Bearings in English Poetry* as a "young poet whose achieved work leaves no room for doubt about his future".[6] A contemporary of Bell and Empson at Cambridge, he made little mark on the literary scene there. As he disclosed, he wrote poetry at school that he considered bad, and only wrote one poem while at Cambridge.[7] The poem was published in *Cambridge Poetry 1929* and was "E Il Modo Ancor M'Offende":

> How if the past be past? Sublimed in me
> That moment's residue now emanates
> A cosmic sense, still crescent through entry
> To the universal; firmly adumbrates
> A knowledge that those few words on the stair
> Figure the world in little; not poorly
> Spoke by one for one, a lover to his fair,
> But proudly claiming perpetuity.

Sophisticated, and with a certain elegance, it is characteristically contorted and over-written. It serves to show that his reconditely pompous diction was an early habit, not one later developed in imitation of Pound. By 1931 he had produced his first book, *The Loosening*—the book on which Leavis based his claim for Bottrall.

It seems to have been a word from Leavis that opened up the world of poetry for him.

> The two writers of poetry who particularly influenced me (and I can say that without hesitation, I can use the word *influence*) were Ezra Pound and T. S. Eliot. I read Eliot first, but I didn't see a great deal of possibility in Eliot as a model, but

when I read Ezra Pound, and in particular 'Hugh Selwyn Mauberley', I thought I saw how you did it: how I thought contemporary poetry ought to be written, how it could be written. And I owe a great debt to 'Hugh Selwyn Mauberley' and to Dr. Leavis who, when I was in Finland, suggested to me that I should read and study that poem.[8]

In praising Bottrall, Leavis made clear how invaluable the tip was:

> Nightingales, Anangke, a sunset or the meanest flower
> Were formerly the potentialities of poetry,
> But now what have they to do with one another
> With Dionysus or with me? . . .

Obviously the study of *Hugh Selwyn Mauberley* was decisive for Mr. Bottrall. But his debt to Mr. Pound serves to bring out his own strong originality: it takes unusual independence to learn in this way.[9]

It is certainly unusual for such "strong originality" to be able to accommodate itself, not only to the manner of another poet, but also to his choice of classical references. "Anangke" and "Dionysus" are both to be found in *Mauberley*—as are the "epitaphs" of the last line of Bottrall's five stanza poem.

The other poems from *The Loosening* that Leavis chose to praise seem only to illustrate Bottrall's weaknesses. Leavis remarks of the following passage: "Must we despair of attaining a new naturalness at the far side of the experience of disharmony?"

> Poised herself like a falcon at check
> Amid the unfooted ploughland,
> Laughter splashing from her mouth and
> Rippling down her brown neck;
> Not passion-rent she
> But sensing in the bound
> Of her breasts vigours to come, free
> As air and powered to make her one
> With the stream of earth-life around.[10]

One would be inclined to despair of anything new from a poet who got three clichés and a semi-archaism into nine would-be impressive lines: "amid"; "laughter . . . rippling"; "free / As air"; "stream of . . . life". There is some evidence in *The Loosening* that Botrall was able to write with precision and economy when some incident moved him and he could forget about the need to be culturally significant. The great failing of his poetry in the thirties was an over-preoccupation with literature. Most often he offers sentiment dressed up in poetry, spun out into pretentiousness.

Bottrall produced two other books of poetry in the thirties: *Festivals of Fire* in 1934; and *The Turning Path* in 1939. The title poem of the first marks an advance of pretentiousness, as its preparatory "Note" might make one expect:

> For the idea of the ground-plan of the poem, 'Festivals of Fire', and for certain details of the first three sections, I owe much to *Balder the Beautiful*, Part VII of Sir J. G. Frazer's *The Golden Bough*.
>
> The poem might have been provided with a full apparatus of notes, but I believe that the labour-saving value of the annotations would be outweighed by the distraction and misconception which they would cause in many readers.[11]

The poem, written in 1932, is in four sections, with the titles: "Allegro Moderato E Rubato"; "Mässig, Doch Immer Noch Etwas Feierlich"; "Larghetto—Con Fuoco—Ruhig Und Bemerkt"; "Andante—Allegro Energico". The plan is obviously copied from *The Waste Land*, and the manner suggests an attempt to vie with that model:

> Came as hostess, extending a drooping
> Hand, the Queen of Sheba, her
> Robe brocade of gold, quartered
> By falbalas of pearls, jaspers and
> Sardonyx. "Come in dearie, come in
> And have a glance over my scarlet
> Garters." She came sidlin' up
> Half canned, makin' as if
> To say to mad Hieronimo
> "Fitchew yourself!" *What are whores?*
> *Cold Russian winters.* Came the Bolibochki
> With Romanoff faces. Came a stag

With gilded antlers, came Wall Street
Bears, politicians with dromedary
Humps, came goats and monkeys,
Sun-worshipping baboons. A bully-rook, coat-armoured
As herald of France, cried, "Montjoye! Make way
For an alligaitered Bishop, advancing from Q3!"
The Bishop took a chair and said, "Alice,
My dear, I have heard that young ladies
Frequently do smoke nowadays."
Then, bowing carelessly to Tertullian,
He passed a mild Laurens Khédive.

(Part III)

The Turning Path is again conceived on the grand scale. All the poems are said to be arranged to form a unit. The book is dedicated to Laura Riding, and contains a commendatory letter from Robert Graves. There is less tendency for the imagery to obscure the thought than there was in *Festivals of Fire*, but the imagery seldom has the inevitability one associates with the best poetry. Behind some of the poems of *The Turning Path* there is a concern for the political problems of the day. Oddly enough, Bottrall's most likeable poem from the thirties is something of a sport—a poem of social concern, "Epitaph for a Riveter" from *Festivals of Fire*.

There need be no haste, slowly bear
Him along by the tenements;
He will never give heed to the Metro
Crisply accelerating below the fence.

Womb's entourage gave him small respite
From the forensic bark of punctual steel:
Expend no curses on the pathogen
That stars him in his last newsreel.

III

Julian Bell would hardly be known today if Peter Stansky and William Abrahams, in their *Journey to the Frontier*, had not made him—somewhat inappropriately—an image of what drew English intellectuals to the Spanish Civil War. He was the son of Clive and Vanessa Bell; the nephew of Leonard and Virginia Woolf: the friends of the family included most of

C

the great Bloomsbury figures. A second-generation Blooms-buryite, with all the opportunity that that implied, he seemed at first to live up to his opportunities. At Cambridge he was elected to the Apostles—an intellectual society of limited membership to which, three-quarters of a century before, Arthur Henry Hallam had introduced an embarrassed Alfred Tennyson. An admirer of Georgian poetry, Bell had contributed poetry and prose to the middle-of-the-road *The Venture*. The poetry he had written up to the end of 1929 (and of his second year in Cambridge) was collected to form his first book, *Winter Movement*, in 1930. Though it sold only forty-four copies in its first six months, it impressed those who read it, and was the reason why Michael Roberts asked him to contribute to his symposium of new poets, *New Signatures*, in 1932.

Nobody today would be likely to class *Winter Movement*, as did Michael Roberts, with Auden's *Poems* (1930), either as poetry or as a publishing event. Yet the book remains fresh today, and was a considerable achievement for so young a writer. In one respect, at least, it is superior to *Poems* (1930): it has a certainty and individuality of style that is not broken in upon by pastiche and literary echoes. Dedicated to Richard Jefferies, it is made up principally of poems of the countryside; but it is not the nostalgic townsman's countryside of most Georgian poems. In their firmness of diction and exactness of observation, Bell's poems remind one of the early work of Edmund Blunden.

> Bleached stubble on a hillside, winter late,
> Trodden, rain-beaten, no longer bristling and straight.
>   Among the blades chaffinches seek
>   With conical, tusk-curving beak
>   The scattered seed
>   Of grain and weed . . .
>
> ("Chaffinches")

John Lehmann has described very well the essential quality of his friend's poetry:

> . . . the poetry he was writing at that time was remarkable because it was an attempt to let the countryside, the moods of wind and weather and life outside the cultivated human pale, speak for themselves without any interference of the poet's own moralising thoughts.[12]

The careful observation and the chastity of diction and impulse that allowed these things to "speak for themselves" was undoubtedly the strength of these poems, though perhaps a dubious one. Did such finished and controlled performances imply the possibility of development? Sometimes the poems have the air of being jottings from a painter's notebook—as though the gift for observation had taken control of the poetic process. Only one poem suggests the direction in which Bell's talent might have been expected to expand. It is not the long poem in varying stanzas, "Winter Movement", which is evidently intended to be the *tour de force* of the volume; but the somewhat shorter "Marsh Birds Pass over London". The poem opens with a poignant and eerie evocation of the migration of the marsh birds, high over the night-life of London. The birds, unheeded by those below, pass on, having "shrieked a prophecy of fear". Their passage is followed by a vision of the dissolution of the city:

> Fallen, fallen and fallen,
>   The city fallen and gone.
> The marsh birds' desolate calling
>   Comes menacing from the sky,
> The city is falling, falling,
>   The passing Whimbrel cry.
> And the down shepherds with their sheep
> See the advancing grasses creep,
>   Walls crumble stone from stone,
>   Bone fall from bone.
> The city now gleams white and fair
>   For no smoke clouds the air
>   Or blackens any wall
>   At all.
> So white, so quiet, it seems to be
> A seaside hamlet's cemet'ry,
>   Covered in ground mist chill
> On some September morning calm and still
>
>   Grey clouds from the north-east,
> Where the river mouth is wide;
> The waters piled in a tattered hill
>   Sweep in on the spring tide.
> The waters tower above the shore,

> Grow higher and higher yet,
> Steep curling waves that leap before
> The heaved swell of the tidal bore
> That hurries up the town.
> Each ruined bridge comes tumbling down,
> The waves pour through each gap
> That bombs have torn in great stone dykes,
> Steadily rise and lap
> Against what doors and window-panes
> Men had the time to close,
> Cascades down every flight of steps,
> And still the flooding grows: . . .

Coming so surprisingly in this volume, the poem shows the extent to which the British, between the wars, were haunted by the possibility of a second world war. "Marsh Birds Pass over London" sees Bell giving his earlier themes a deeper resonance; but it did not show the direction he was to take later. At the end of *Winter Movement* are "Characters in the manner of Pope: Nimrod, Sporus, Pyrrha". The "manner of Pope" was to be the manner that Bell, unfortunately, would cultivate for the next year or two.

In the February, 1930, issue of *The Venture*, there appeared an eight page poem in heroic couplets: "An Epistle on the Subject of the Ethical and Aesthetic Beliefs of Herr Ludwig Wittgenstein (Doctor of Philosophy) to Richard Braithwaite, Esq., M.A." This was the first of Bell's poem's in "the manner of Pope". He could get Pope's tricks of style well enough, as he shows in the highly imitative "Characters":

> Nimrod between two joys his life divides,
> By night he dances, and by day he rides;
> Now toys with spaniels, now with Pyrrha's locks,
> And now a nymph pursues, and now a fox . . .
>   ("Nimrod")

Yet it is an empty triumph—superior pastiche; and, in a world where "good sense" could not be felt to be an adequate criterion by which to judge the ills of the period, the style of Pope could hardly be a fruitful starting point. The new manner was to be a dead end for Bell.

The notion that poetry should be classical, austere, clear,

with the virtues of good prose and with the freedom of subject matter of prose, was a common one in the thirties. It arose from the teaching (if not the example) of Eliot and Pound, and also in reaction to the often noted obscurity and esotericism of early twentieth-century poetry. Though Bell had read Eliot, and "Tom" was a friend of the family, he seems never to have come under the spell of his poetry. Indeed, he felt his own conception of poetry to be challenged by the followers of Eliot who dominated undergraduate literary Cambridge; and it is understandable that he should see Empson and the *Experiment* group as making poetry narrower and even more limited in its audience than was Eliot's poetry in the late twenties. (*Poems, 1909–1925,* the "*Hymns Ancient and Modern*" of the Cambridge admirers of Eliot in those days, was printed in an English edition of 1,460 copies.) In the June, 1930, issue of *The Venture*, there appeared "A Brief View of Poetic Obscurity", in which Bell attacked ". . . poetry that the well educated 'common reader' . . . is unable to understand".[13]

Bell's career after this can be sketched briefly. He appeared with Lehmann, Auden, Spender, Day Lewis, Empson and Eberhart in *New Signatures*. He was represented by two rather ordinary poems in something like his early manner, and by a long poem—by far the longest in the collection—"Arms and the Man". This was a satire on the folly of armament—a familiar Bloomsbury position, explored with somewhat obvious common sense. Yet, despite moments when it has a contemporary life—

> . . . We conquered half the world, so now it's best
> We should go on, and conquer all the rest,
> Till all the lesser breeds have owned our rule,
> Till all the world's become a public school
> (Where once again the senior prefect brags
> Of all the beatings that he gave the fags) . . .

—it remains a treatment of a contemporary subject in an eighteenth-century manner, pounding out its sentiments with an eighteenth-century certainty and generality that is incongruous.

He was sceptical of appearing in a collection with Auden,

Spender and Day Lewis, whom he considered "romantic", both in their poetry and in their attitudes to politics. Feeling himself opposed to the growingly dominant movement in poetry that they represented, he seems to have given up the notion of poetry as a central vocation. Then, in 1933, he experienced another productive spurt, no longer as a militant classicist, but as an occasional or personal poet.

These new poems were collected in *Work for the Winter* (1936) which contains no poems in his Popean manner, and which was to mark the virtual close of his career as a poet. The first section of *Work for Winter* is headed "Political Poems". In "Bypass to Utopia", Bell criticises the revolutionary Left, both for the simplistic nature of their hopes and for their glib acceptance of violence. He sees violence as destroying all that the revolutionaries hope for; and, as a pacifist, contends that violence only leads to violence. Yet with the revolutionary poets of the thirties he shows the upper middle-class disquieted nostalgia for the world of his childhood before the Great War—disquieted, because he knows that it was based on economic injustice:

> For here was good, built though it was, no doubt,
> On poverty I could not live without,
> Yet none the less, good certain and secure,
> And even though I see it not endure,
> And though it sinks within the rising tide,
> What can for me replace it good or sure?

Work for the Winter contains occasional passages that remind one of Bell's earlier works; while some of the personal poems have a winning poise. However, the book has none of the intense vividness of *Winter Movement*. What virtues its poems have are largely conventional. All the poems were written before he left England to be Professor of English at Wuhan in China in 1935. He had only two years to live until his death in the Spanish Civil War in 1937. During these last two years he ceased writing poetry.

No doubt there were features of Bell's personality and upbringing that led to his decline as a poet. A restless character —a pacifist drawn temperamentally to war, he seems to have been unable to find any vocation sufficiently acceptable to devote enough energy to it to excel. He was surprised and hurt when, in the last years of his life, the Woolfs were not interested in publishing the rather desultory essay he had written on Roger Fry. With no decided vocation, he stayed on at Cambridge. Yet the thesis he produced, even though one of the readers was a friend of the family, could not be accepted—and not surprisingly. Whatever its merits, its form clearly indicated the writer's disdain of thesis writing.

Poetry might have provided him with a vocation, despite the absence of feeling that excellence must be striven for that seemed to be the result of his belonging at the centre of the Bloomsbury group of promise. But both politically and in literary terms he could not accept the main poetic movement of the thirties. Bell had become a socialist in 1922, at the age of fourteen. During the early thirties, until he left England to be Professor of English at Wuhan in China, he worked for the Labour Party. He could not make the essentially "romantic" leap that Spender and Day Lewis and Lehmann made, to see the salvation of Europe in Communism, even though he sympathised with their anti-fascist tendencies and with their desire to widen the audience for poetry. There was a sense in which he may be said to have seen through them.

> Certainly it would be a mistake to . . . neglect the very large element of rather neurotic personal salvationism in our brand of Communism . . . Our generation seems to be repeating the experience of Rupert Brooke's, the appearance of a need for "the moral equivalent of war" among a large number of the members of the leisured and educated classes. And Communism provides the activity, the sense of common effort, and something of the hysteria of war.[14]

However one looks at it, he was of the Left and of the upper middle class, yet unable to identify himself with the dominant upper middle-class left-wing movement in the poetry of his day. Spoiled, perhaps, initially by his Bloomsbury upbringing, he could not feel at home in the movement that Bloomsbury approval had done so much to launch. In this respect he contrasts with his friend John Lehmann, who was able to step out of Julian's world to play an important rôle in the literary Left of the thirties.

IV

Like his great friend Julian Bell, John Lehmann was associated with *The Venture*: though he admired Empson's poems
and critical writings in *Experiment*, he felt that *The Venture*
was his spiritual home. *Experiment* regarded *The Venture* as
Georgian, and Lehmann's early poems have a Georgian
flavour:

> The sycamore, the lime, the poplar now
> Their rich design,
> Their Autumn harmonies of leaf and bough
> Compose, combine; . . .
> ("October": *Cambridge Poetry*, 1929)

Lehmann later recalled that he had deliberately gone to
school with the Georgians, and he felt that it had a beneficial
effect on his poetry. This is no doubt the origin of the subdued
directness of Lehmann's diction compared with that of Spender
or even Auden.

> I read all Eddie Marsh's volumes of Georgian Poetry through,
> and Squire's fat volumes of Selections from the Georgian poets
> again and again in order, not merely to find the real and nourish-
> ing food I wanted, but to purge myself, by surfeit, of all con-
> temporary clichés of attitude and metaphor and phrase-making.[15]

His first book, *A Garden Revisited* (1931), is Georgian in tone,
though there is none of the brilliant observation and evocation
of nature to be found in Bell's *Winter Movement*. The presentation of a scene or incident, as often in his maturer poetry, was
likely to be the occasion for psychological exploration:

> How strange it was so quietly to meet,
> In sleep returning where we walked before,
> To hear the equal pacing of our feet
> Sound down the long, straight, dream-built corridor.
>
> All the September day we roamed alone;
> Low clouds were kindling, as we climbed the stair,
> Leaving the labyrinth of naked stone
> To breathe the evening fragrance of the air.

From the wide roof we heard the pheasants call,
We saw the chestnut leaves in yellow waste,
With glossy nuts, and dahlias by the wall,
The ladders in late apple branches placed;

We had no need of words: our thoughts were phrased
By flowers, and trees, and evening sky behind,
Summer with Autumn blending: and we gazed
As down the distance of each other's mind.

("Return to the Chateau")

When Lehmann was at Cambridge the "atmosphere . . . was strongly pacifist . . . the memory of horror and the sense of futility and waste were uppermost . . .":

I suddenly saw, or seemed to see, that war might come about, not because one nation deliberately planned it, but because of the anarchy that was inherent in the idea of sovereignty and the unchecked competition of great industrial interests, national in scope and repercussion but controlled by private individuals or groups.[16]

A Garden Revisited contains one rather suprising poem: "Talk on the River" evokes, in its opening and closing, an evening on the Thames near Lehmann's family home. The nostalgic tranquillity of the poem is broken by the middle section, in which the two lovers speak of the possibility of another war. Similarly, in a poem called "Ruin" that presents a psychological landscape, the imagery is that of revolution and seems to portend the Europe Lehmann was to know.

. . . As one who, waking in the startled night,
Hears firing in the street below,
Rises in horror at the sudden fight,
And prays that it may quickly go, . . .

Lehmann's time at Cambridge was a period of constant discussion and correspondence with Julian Bell; but, as his period at Cambridge drew to an end, Bell was developing his notions of a neo-classicism, which became increasingly alien to Lehmann. Lehmann, on the other hand, through his meeting with Stephen Spender in 1930, was on the threshold of his collaboration with the Oxford poets—a grouping that was to be the most prominent one in the literary Left of the thirties.

v

A man who had done nothing else with his life but write "To an Old Lady", "Camping Out", "Arachne", "Legal Fiction", "This Last Pain", "Homage to the British Museum", "Note on Local Flora", "Aubade", and "Missing Dates" would not need to feel ashamed; though he might feel disheartened to reflect that seven of the nine were written while he was an undergraduate. It seems fairly clear now that nearly all the poems in William Empson's *Poems* (1935) were written before the end of 1930, and a large number before the end of 1928, when Empson was still studying mathematics.

Both as poet and as critic, Empson belongs strongly to the traditions of the Cambridge of his youth: the tradition that includes Moore's *Philosophical Studies*; Russell and Whitehead's *Principia Mathematica*; Wittgenstein's *Tractatus*; Ogden and Richards' *The Meaning of Meaning*; and, of course, the Cambridge Mathematical tripos, the examinations that Empson wrote before switching to English. Randall Jarrell once called the later poetry of Wallace Stevens "G. E. Moore at the spinnet"; and one might be tempted to apply the phrase to Empson as a poet, if it were not that his own critical writings provide the parallel to his poetry. In his criticism—taking his example from Graves and Riding's *A Survey of Modernist Poetry*—Empson applied to poetry the Cambridge habit of turning every word round and round to contemplate its meaning; a method that was given an extended scope by the Freudian thesis (from *The Psychopathology of Everyday Life*) that even our mistakes are meaningful. "Whereof one cannot speak, thereof one must be silent" (*Tractatus*, 7): everything in a poem can be and is to be made explicit. This is Empson's system as a critic—and also his vice. When every implication of a word has been hunted down and dragged into full light, every element in the poem seems to exist on the same level, and the poem becomes a tissue of conflicting intellectual viewpoints to be reconciled intellectually. A good deal of

Empson's critical discussion of poetry suffers because of this; but one comes to feel that this is the right way to read *his* poetry, and the one he consciously or unconsciously expects us to adopt, even though his own statements about what his poems mean can be startlingly simple.

The piece of criticism that gives the best insight into Empson's own poetry is "Donne the Spaceman"—an article of his that appeared in *The Kenyon Review* in 1957. Donne is seen as an up-to-date young intellectual, whose theological and scientific tropes are not merely a vehicle of expression, but are there because the poem is concerned with a particular intellectual position with regard to the material of these tropes. Donne is seen as steadily preoccupied in his youth with the problem of other worlds and with the theological implications of their existence. Empson describes this notion of Donne as "part of the atmosphere in which I grew up as an undergraduate at Cambridge", and says ". . . I was imitating it in my own poems . . ."[17] Presumably the imitation lay both in his conception of human beings as isolated worlds and in the use he made of the then novel notion from the Theory of Relativity that the universe was finite but unbounded: you lived in a closed universe, but there was no "great beyond" to which you were prevented from travelling.

Empson's Donne is the Donne of Eliot's "The Metaphysical Poets": a poet with his intellect at the tips of his senses; the poet, the imitation of whom was compatible with the imitation of Eliot himself. Donne purged the "Muses garden [of] Pedantique weedes" and took his tropes from theology and astronomy; Empson, the poet and Cambridge mathematician, takes his from philosophy and modern cosmology. However, Empson's Donne is not just interested in other worlds: when he mentions them, he is concerned with all the ramifications of such a notion, and his reader is supposed to spot just what Donne's position is. Of "The Good Morrow" Empson writes:

Instead of simply backing Copernicus, Donne gets a kind of lock-grip on his reader by arguing from both Ptolemy and Copernicus at once. According to Ptolemy, the planets are more or less in heaven, and matter is much better-class than matter here. Copernicus merely showed that it was convenient for calculation to treat the earth as one of the planets . . . , but the obvious deduction was that life on other planets is simply like it is here. Matter is very refined on Donne's secret planet, as in Ptolemy, and this allowed him to treat his refined lovers as still material; but without Copernicus their position in the universe would not have seemed plausible. It is a charming argument, but it gives us no reason to suppose that he meant by his love something purely spiritual.[18]

Discussing the line from "Love's Growth", "Stars by the sun are not enlarged, but shown", he makes a strangely down to earth and practical point: ". . . a man like Donne, who wanted them to be like the earth, and to colonise them with a pair of lovers, would want them not to be balls of fire".[19] It is as though the figurative use of statements did not control and limit the aspects of the statements to which we give attention.

"Camping Out" seems to ask of the reader the sort of close and ingenious spelling out of implications that Empson practices on Donne's poetry.

> And now she cleans her teeth into the lake:
> Gives it (God's grace) for her own bounty's sake
> What morning's pale and the crisp mist debars:
> Its glass of the divine (that Will could break)
> Restores, beyond Nature: or lets Heaven take
> (Itself being dimmed) her pattern, who half awake
> Milks between rocks a straddled sky of stars.
>
> Soap tension the star pattern magnifies.
> Smoothly Madonna through-assumes the skies
> Whose vaults are opened to achieve the Lord.
> No, it is we soaring explore galaxies,
> Our bullet boat light's speed by thousands flies.
> Who moves so among stars their frame unties;
> See where they blur, and die, and are outsoared.

Like many of Empson's poems, "Camping Out" is accompanied by a note as long or longer than the poem:

The intention behind the oddness of the theme, however much it may fail, was not satirical but to show indifference to satire from outside. She gives the lake its pattern of reflected stars, now made of toothpaste, as God's grace allows man virtues that nature wouldn't; the mist and pale (pale light or boundary) of morning have made it unable to reflect real stars any longer. *Soap tension* is meant to stand for the action of surface tension between more and less concentrated soap solutions which makes the specks fly apart. *Their frame unties*: if any particle of matter got a speed greater than that of light it would have infinite mass and might be supposed to crumple up round itself the whole of space-time—"A great enough ecstasy makes the common world unreal."

The way this last notion fits into the poem is clear enough. The girl's face is reflected in the water, like that of a Madonna among stars (the patches of soap); but it is not the prelude to the coming of a god whose presence will transcend, shape and give meaning to the material universe. It is we who do this. If our ecstasy were great enough, it could transform the whole universe for us, just as an object that attained to sufficient velocity to exceed the speed of light would have an infinite mass, and hence be associated with an infinite gravitational field which would crumple up or obliterate the contours of space time. Yet this power only derives from the motion of the body relative to the rest of the universe. Presumably, to an observer on the particle (or heavenly body) things *there* would be normal: the relation to the rest of the universe would be transformed. Was the reader intended to think along these lines, and how far? This way of thinking parallels the way Empson thinks about Donne and the way he writes in the notes to some of his poems. Yet, oddly, when one has poked around in the intellectual corners of "Camping Out", so that one finally has the hang of it, one can stand back and see it as a rather simple poem in its poignant nostalgia for certainty and for a transfiguration of the ordinary—a nostalgia that is plangently evoked by the movement of the second stanza, and that is a frequent theme of Empson's poetry.

The reader is frequently left with the problem of how far he is intended to follow the logical ramifications of the imagery: Empson's poems, unlike most poems, don't establish the boundaries for us clearly, and sometimes they unload implications that are clearly at odds with the tone of the poem, but cannot be avoided. "Camping Out", for all its success, may not be successful in its "indifference to satire". The connotations of used toothpaste are not suppressed by the poem; and the word "milks", not merely suggestive of the dairy, but also, applied to a woman who is to be associated with the Madonna, suggestive of giving milk, gives one a distasteful and, one supposes, an unintended jolt.

It is not merely a question of how far we go, but also of where we go. "Note on Local Flora" begins

> There is a tree native in Turkestan,
> Or further east towards the Tree of Heaven, . . .

Kathleen Raine has suggested that the poem is perfectly clear when one remembers that the tree is in Kew Gardens. The second line refers to its position there. In the introduction to the notes in *Poems*, Empson said: "It is impertinent to expect hard work from the reader merely because you have failed to show what you were comparing to what, and though to write notes on such a point is a confession of failure it seems an inoffensive one." He goes on to say: "Also there is no longer a reasonably small field which may be taken as general knowledge." This last remark used to be a common enough apology for the obscurity of *The Waste Land*. Empson's poetry shows how far, as a result of the success of Eliot's poem and of poems like it, obscurity had come to be thought of as natural and inevitable. Empson seems nonchalantly to accept the cultural privacy of his poems as unavoidable.

It is Empson's own best poems that show up the weakness of the rest of his writing. In a poem like "Arachne", his ingenuity is completely and clearly under the control of the central feeling of the poem as described in his note: "Man lives between the contradictory absolutes of philosophy, the one and the many, etc. As king spider man walks delicately between two elements, avoiding the enemies which live in both. Man must dance, etc. Human society is placed in this matter like individual men, the atoms who make up this bubble." The poem proceeds by controlled analogy, as often in Donne's poetry:

> Twixt devil and deep sea, man hacks his caves;
> Birth, death; one, many; what is true, and seems;
> Earth's vast hot iron, cold space's empty waves:

King spider, walks the velvet roof of streams:
Must bird and fish, must god and beast avoid:
Dance, like nine angels, on pin-point extremes.

His gleaming bubble between void and void,
Tribe-membrane, that by mutual tension stands,
Earth's surface film, is at a breath destroyed.

Bubbles gleam brightest with least depth of lands
But two is least can with full tension strain,
Two molecules; one, and the film disbands.

We two suffice. But oh beware, whose vain
Hydroptic soap my meagre water saves.
Male spiders must not be too early slain.

Even where the poem depends on technical references to the
sciences, it establishes the significance of these references
sufficiently for the reader not to need to turn to the notes.
The poignant fragility of human achievement and security is
beautifully established by both the argument of the poem and
its imagery.

There are only a few poems where Empson follows Donne
so well: "Legal Fiction"; "To an Old Lady". In "Legal
Fiction" he begins with a display of his celebrated Donnean
wit with ambiguities: "Law makes long spokes of the short
stakes of men." In fact, Empson's wit seldom has the power
to resonate throughout a poem, or clinch its argument emotionally as in Donne's poems. This is partly because Empson
is too interested in the arguments of his poems: unlike Donne,
he does not use false argument (with an undercurrent of emotional truth) as an important rhetorical device. In his poems
there is usually a clear strain of argument, which carries
the main import of the poem: the wit merely consists in sharp
or obscure ways of saying what is said. It is a kind of "extra",
thrown in to make the poem more attractive. It may seem far
fetched to compare Empson to his friend Dylan Thomas,
yet they can sound alike, oddly enough:

. . . Groyned the white stallion arches of the main
(And miner deeps that in the dome of the brain
Take Iris' arches' pupillage and Word)

> Walked on the bucking water like a bird
> And, guard, went round its rampart and its ball . . .
>
> ("Bacchus")

Thomas loved a play on words almost as much as did Empson, and he frequently went over his poems to make them denser by introducing puns. Yet, while Empson's word play often seems incidental to the poetry and sometimes a red herring, it contributes a great deal of life to Empson's early poetry, even though it is a superficial life.

One of the early poems in which one might have seen an indication of a maturing talent was "To an Old Lady"—not merely because in it the wit was controlled by the central impulse, but because the life of *things* entered in for once. Things appear in Empson's poetry, but as an illustration of ideas, or to be overlaid with ideas, as in "Camping Out". The critic of "Donne the Spaceman", like the young Empson, the poet, seems to find the incidental ideas of the poem as containing its *raison d'être*. Empson's own early poems seem too concerned with peripheral ideas—lacking any centre or any root in the actual. Reading them, one feels as if one were playing musical chairs in a room overcrowded with superb but incongruous furniture. One of his earliest poems, "Value is in Activity", involves a juggler with an apple who is also the worm at the heart of the apple. The "things" of the poem are there as illustrations of these opposing positions, the intricacies of which concern Empson. There is no evocation of an experienced example of the duality, but rather a contrived handling of contradictions that are disquieting to Empson, but which were intellectualised before the poem was written.

Empson's poems are ironical and paradoxical, concerned with the disparities of the world: the satisfactions of this world are finite, but imagination is infinite; with knowledge and experience come pain and disillusion; each person is a separate world, and we must choose between the boons of privacy and communication. In *Seven Types of Ambiguity*, Empson showed himself adept at spotting unconscious strategies in poets. In "This Last Pain" Empson speaks of learning "a style from a despair", and his despair does not seem to arise merely from those disparities that he is conscious of in his poems. The imagery of "Arachne" is appropriate, yet the killing of the male spider, together with the fragile vulnerability of the spider and his bubble, with which the human condition is compared, suggest there are pressures too disquieting to the poet for direct confrontation, and that these pressures are the real reasons for the choice of imagery. Ian Hamilton remarks that, in "Plenum and Vacuum" (where, as Empson explains in his note, ". . . scorpions kill themselves when put under glass and frightened with fire . . .") the incident with the scorpion is ostensibly there "for the sake of argument", and is distanced by so being. However, it can be seen as another manifestation of fears too disquieting to be brought out into the open.[20] The existence of such unconscious pressures would go a long way towards explaining the character of Empson's early poetry. The bizarre incongruity of the images would then go along with the intense intellectualisation as a means of masking or distancing these pressures, while at the same time allowing them to get a veiled expression through some of the imagery.

After leaving Cambridge, Empson spent the early part of the thirties teaching in Japan. During this period—and possibly before he left Cambridge—he seems to have stopped writing poetry at all regularly. The only piece that can with any certainty be said to have been written during his years in Japan was the first section of "Bacchus", a long and intellectually impenetrable poem that he seems to have laboured over throughout the decade.

On his return to England in 1934, Empson brought together his early poems, which were published, along with the first section of "Bacchus", in 1935 as *Poems*. Collecting them together may have stimulated him to start writing again: he published a number of poems in the villanelle form, or forms close to it, in the middle thirties, and the most famous of them, "Missing Dates", is strongly reminiscent of "Villanelle", one of his undergraduate poems collected in *Poems*. Once started again, Empson produced poems slowly but steadily up to the outbreak of war. These poems were brought together in *The Gathering Storm* in September, 1940.

In most respects these poems are totally different from his

earlier ones. The subject is frequently, if rather generally, political. "Courage means Running" is in praise of the wisdom of avoiding what you rightly fear (the element of good sense in policies of non-intervention). "Reflection from Rochester" has a similar theme. Empson dissociates himself from most of the political poetry of the period, guying Auden in "Just a Smack at Auden", while he writes with his own sense of the political situation in the short poem "Manchouli":

> I find it normal, passing these great frontiers,
> That you scan the crowds in rags eagerly each side
> With awe; that the nations seem real; that their ambitions
> Having such achieved variety within one type, seem sane;
> I find it normal;
> So too to extract false comfort from that word.

The poem exemplifies the virtues of the poetry of *The Gathering Storm*. It has the power of clear direct statement, coupled with a very sane wit in the choice of phrase. There is none of the dazzling ambiguity of the early poems. Something of that earlier brilliance of word play is present in "Aubade", a poem about an incident in a love affair in Japan; and the much admired "The Teasers" appears to have this earlier wit:

> Not but they die, the teasers and the dreams,
> Not but they die,
> and tell the careful flood
> To give them what they clamour for and why.

The verse form is beautiful and highly original, but Empson has confessed: ". . . I cut it down to rags so that it doesn't make sense, you can't find out what it's about".[21] "Ignorance of Death" perhaps best typifies Empson's later poetry; though it must be admitted that the poems of *The Gathering Storm* show the kind of variety of style that suggests a poet groping for a manner. "Ignorance of Death" concludes:

> Otherwise I feel very blank upon this topic,
> And think that though important, and proper for anyone to
>   bring up,

It is one that most people should be prepared to be blank
upon.

The whole poem is written in this manner. It is a sequence of
connected general remarks, all well put. There is a tension
between the various remarks, but little of the interplay between
words found in the early poems. This manner has its one real
success in the moving "Missing Dates", in which Empson
shows his gift for the sententious phrase, a gift that goes along
with a decided wisdom: the wit of "The Canonization" has
been replaced by the wit of "The Vanity of Human Wishes".

> Slowly the poison the whole blood stream fills.
> It is not the effort nor the failure tires.
> The waste remains, the waste remains and kills.

It is only when one stands back from Empson's *Collected
Poems* as a whole that the important link between *The Gathering
Storm*, with its awareness of the political pressures that are
growing, and the scientific wit of *Poems* becomes clear:

> It is the two
> Most exquisite surfaces of knowledge can
>
> Get clap (the other is the eye). Steadily you
> Should clean your teeth, for your own weapon's near
> Your own throat always. . . .
> ("Courage Means Running")

This passage shrieks as it illustrates its sensible point. Once
again, as in *Poems* (but more obviously), fear is the really
pressing theme.

VI

Not all the poets associated with *Experiment* were to remain
so recognisably rooted in the Cambridge of their undergraduate years as did Empson. Two of the editors of *Experiment*,
Humphrey Jennings and Jakob Bronowski, were to meet
again in the early forties to discover that both of them had
come to the conclusion that William Blake was a better
social critic than Marx. Jennings, who became well known
as a film producer, collaborated in the late thirties with

Charles Madge, also from Cambridge, in the movement known as "Mass Observation". Madge was married to Kathleen Raine, who found poetry impossible in Cambridge, and who was later to become a leading interpreter of Blake, as well as a poet. She also had contributed to *Experiment*. Another Cambridge man who found Cambridge of the period impossible was Vernon Watkins, who left in disgust after a short time there.

A poet associated with *Experiment*, but largely unexperimental in manner, was James Reeves. Reeves was among the poets included by Michael Roberts in the *Faber Book of Modern Verse* in 1936, after his first book of poems, *The Natural Need*, had been published in 1935 by Graves and Riding at the Seizin Press.

Although Reeves was a friend and admirer of Graves and Riding, his work does not show their influence in the way that Norman Cameron's does. Indeed, Reeves's work, excellent in its own minor way, gives little suggestion that the author had, as a young man, been associated with one of the most go-ahead experimental undergraduate periodicals. He is decidedly a traditional poet; and his later resuscitatory editing of an anthology of Georgian poetry is not surprising. Of the poems by Reeves included by Roberts in the *Faber Book*, the longer ones seem diffuse and somewhat shapeless. His quality is given best by the one short poem chosen by Roberts:

> Then more-than-morning quiet
> The pretty lawn extended;
> And rooted trees stood tall
> On westward shadows pointing.
>
> Answering no will my hand
> Dropped from the window catch,
> My throat to know faltered
> Whether sob or sing.
>
> Why trees were not, nor morning,
> No flash of mind revealed;
> Maybe throat found and hands met
> A memory more clear than sight.
>   ("At the Window")

Chapter 4

FORWARD FROM MORTMERE

"Mortmere" – Homer Lane – *Poems*, 1928 – "Paid on
Both Sides" – *Poems*, 1930 – Graves and Riding –
Impact of *Poems*, 1930 – *The Orators* – Poems in *New
Country* – *The Dance of Death* – *The Dog Beneath the Skin*

"ARRIVAL AT THE country of the dead," said Edward
Upward, when he and Christopher Isherwood first saw
Cambridge. "They"—the "Enemy" of schooldays, would be
lying in wait for them. They came to see Cambridge in terms
of two sides, the other side being "the Combine", the official
Cambridge, the Cambridge that was a continuation of the
values that they had rebelled against at school. The college
waiter who murmured: "Most *certainly*, sir", was undoubtedly
"an important spy". They developed a whole hidden side
of fantasy as a reverse to the apparent Cambridge of ordinary
experience. This led on to the notion of "The Other Town"—
a town not Cambridge, but hidden within it: a town at
first escape, but then recognised as a criticism of the actual
Cambridge. This "Other Town" became peopled with fictional
characters for whom they evolved a series of adventures.
Finally, the fantasies became detached from Cambridge
altogether. They decided that the "Other Town" had nothing
to do with the actual town. They looked round for a name:
Mortmere—to them a remote village in the downs which now
became the setting for a whole world of fantasy, with characters
like Gunball, Hearn and the Reverend Welken.[1]

It was in the most flourishing days of Mortmere that Isherwood made Auden's acquaintance again. The way in which
they developed a world of schoolboy saga fantasy has already
been described. "In time, the school-saga world became for
us a kind of Mortmere—a Mortmere founded upon our
preparatory-school lives, just as the original Mortmere had
been founded upon my life with Chalmers [Upward] at
Cambridge."[2] This saga world was to flower eventually in

Auden's charade of 1928, "Paid on Both Sides", and in the landscape of Auden's early poems and *The Orators* (1932). Traces linger in the first dramatic collaboration of Auden and Isherwood in 1935, *The Dog Beneath the Skin*.

Auden, Isherwood, Spender, Day Lewis, Rex Warner and Edward Upward were, as has already been pointed out, closely acquainted in their early years as writers, and were often with one another. They may be thought of as constituting a not necessarily self-conscious group. Upward went on from Mortmere to develop a Marxist fantasy in his novel *Journey to the Border* (1939). Rex Warner's first novel, *The Wild Goose Chase* (1937), involves a quest for salvation in a journey into a fantasy world beyond the border. The border, the ruined landscape, the doomed bands of endurers, the feuds—these features of Auden's poetry enter into the imagery of Day Lewis's work in the early thirties. These fantasies were sometimes given a Marxist extension; and it is possible to explore the psychological reasons for the way they preoccupied this group of writers. However, it would be wrong to regard them as pure fantasies or as convenient metaphors for archetypal concerns. The writers were, above all, concerned with the material of their fantasies: Auden's ruined landscape, his sick, doomed society is the Blimp-ridden England with its sickness truly revealed. The double vision of Upward's hero is a manifestation of the Marxist situation in a bourgeois society.

In addition to the Mortmere fantasies, Isherwood developed another imaginative concern while at Cambridge. This he called "The Test". Mortmere as such was abandoned by Isherwood shortly after he left Cambridge, and exists only in his account of it in his autobiography, *Lions and Shadows* (1938), and in Edward Upward's story, "The Railway Accident".[3] However, "The Test" seems to have been a more lasting concern, and the idea was evidently passed on to Auden, and perhaps developed during their time together in Berlin in 1929. Isherwood remarked:

> Like most of my generation, I was obsessed by a complex of terrors and longings connected with the idea "War". "War", in this purely neurotic sense, meant The Test. The test of your courage, of your maturity, of your sexual prowess: "Are you

really a Man?" Subconsciously, I believe, I longed to be sub-
jected to this test; but I also dreaded failure. I dreaded failure
so much—indeed, I was so certain that I *should* fail—that,
consciously, I denied my longing to be tested, altogether. I
denied my all-consuming morbid interest in the idea of "War".[4]

"The Test" was associated with the conceptions of "The
Truly Strong Man" and "The Truly Weak Man". "The
Truly Weak Man" is "the neurotic hero": ". . . the Test exists
only for the Truly Weak Man: no matter whether he passes
it or whether he fails, he cannot alter his essential nature."[5]
These preoccupations were to emerge frequently in the work
of Auden and Isherwood: in the cult of T. E. Lawrence; in
the hero as neurotic; in the Oedipal concern for the approval
of a dominating mother in "Paid on Both Sides" and *The
Ascent of F.6* (1936); and in the central figure of the airman in
The Orators. They are decidedly fascist preoccupations. They
also reflect the public school ideals that centred around the
playing of games: "Truly Strong"/"Truly Weak" parallels
the division of "hearties" and "aesthetes".

II

Auden's interest in people and society, psychological rather
than political in his undergraduate days, took a new turn
when, in Berlin, he met an anthropologist, John Layard,
who was a disciple of the psychologist, Homer Lane. Isherwood
sums up Lane's teaching, as he heard it from Auden:

Every disease, Lane had taught, is in itself a cure—if we know
how to take it. There is only one sin: disobedience to the inner
law of our own nature. The results of this disobedience show
themselves in crime or in disease: . . . the disobedience . . . is
the fault of those who teach us, as children, to control God (our
desires) instead of giving Him room to grow . . . God appears
unreasonable because He has been put in prison and driven
wild. The Devil is conscious control, and is, therefore, reasonable
and sane. Conventional education . . . inverts the whole natural
system in childhood, turning the child into a spurious adult . . .
Diseases are . . . warning symptoms of a sickness of the soul;
they are manifestations of God—and those who try to "cure"

them without first curing the soul are only serving the Devil. The disease of the soul is the belief in moral control: the Tree of the Knowledge of Good and Evil, as against the Tree of Life.

. . . One of the greatest evils of our civilisation is the invention of the idea of pity. Pity consciously induced, loveless and sterile, is never a healer, always a destroyer. Pity frustrates every attempted cure.[6]

In this summary can be found many of the key ideas and attitudes of Auden's early years as a poet: the forces that make for health in the individual are, when perverted, those that manifest themselves as disease. This ambivalence is a very important aspect of the world of the early poetry. Neurosis appears as destructive, but also as an important force for change. This fits in with the significant position given to the neurotic hero. The notion of the diseased and doomed society is there; as also is the disdain for pity that is connected with the unpleasantness of poems like "Miss Gee".

The system, which places the blame for all shortcomings on upbringing and education, would naturally appeal to Auden and his friends. It is a system that puts its converts in a very smug and knowing position, and a smug knowingness is one of the disturbing features of Auden's early work. Finally, as is apparent in the terms Isherwood used, this system is just a version of the Protestant conception of salvation—an heretical one, in that, like Romanticism, it gets rid of original sin.

Auden has described the teachings of Blake, Lawrence, Freud and Marx—all early masters of his—as "Christian heresies".[7] "Lawrence, Blake and Homer Lane" are grouped together as healers in poem XXII of *Poems*. In Christian terms, their "heresies" include a belief in the possibility of human perfection and of heaven on earth. There is little value, of course, in emphasising the similarity of Auden's early views to Christianity, except by way of cultural explanation. He was not then a Christian; and all views of the world are the same if we simplify them sufficiently to eliminate the differences. However, Lawrence and the psychoanalysts had in common with Protestantism that they offer extreme versions of the view that putting the inner man right will put the world right. In this they contrast with Marx, who saw things the other way round. The contrast illuminates the difference between Auden's outlook up to 1933, and his attitudes during the remainder of the thirties.

Lawrence's ideas, though not his poetry, had a considerable influence on Auden as a young man. Lawrence, like Freud, identified the erotic instincts as the life-giving instincts. Freud opposed to them the "death wish"—the instincts that tend to make the living being return to inanimate matter. The closest analogue to the "death wish" in Lawrence's thought was the state of "funk". Auden, who makes great play with the "death wish", particularly in *The Dance of Death* (1933), seems at times to equate it with a state of "funk" endemic in a society. Lawrence, like Lane, believed that repressed natural instincts would return to tear the individual and his society; and he saw the malaise of modern society as arising from the failure to face up to the demands of the god within, the dark natural instincts. For Lawrence, this was a failure of courage. Again we find a similar analysis behind the doom-ridden society of Auden's early poetry.

Lane considered that all diseases were psychosomatic. In this he was in agreement with the German psychoanalyst Georg Groddeck, author of *The Book of the It* (1923), a thinker who also influenced Auden. Auden told Isherwood: "When people are ill, they're wicked . . . You must be pure in heart." Isherwood's sore tonsils were due to his having told lies—"the liar's quinzy" of poem XXX of *Poems*.[8] These views are to be associated with a good deal of the silliness in Auden's early work. Nevertheless, he only occasionally attains to the extremes of sweeping silliness to be found in psychoanalysis in its hey-day, and in that frequently reprinted classic of the subject, *The Book of the It*.

III

In order to see the way in which these ideas became absorbed into the vision of Auden's early poetry, it is necessary to form some idea of the order in which the poems were written. The ruined landscape of a sick, doomed, feuding society does not appear in any of the poems included in undergraduate publications. The first of the twenty poems in his *Poems*, 1928, is in eight sections, one of which is a poem that first appeared in *Oxford Poetry*, 1927 ("Consider if you will . . ."), while another section is a poem that was among those that Auden showed to Isherwood when they renewed their acquaintance in 1926 ("This peace can last no longer . . ."). In his autobiography, *World Within World* (1951), Stephen Spender recounts what was evidently an early editorial session on Auden's book,[9] at which Isherwood objected to an image ("The frozen buzzard / Flipped down the weir . . .") that appears in fragment (c) of poem I. Auden and Isherwood, to whom *Poems*, 1928, is dedicated, may have been going through Auden's earliest poems, selecting passages for inclusion; and this would suggest that *Poems*, 1928, opens with a series of fragments that Auden felt worth preserving from his work up to the end of 1927. The remainder of the poems in the volume would then have been written in the latter part of 1927, or in 1928. It would seem that the poems at the end of the book were written in Germany at the end of 1928, it is not impossible that the poems are arranged roughly in the order of composition.[10] If this is taken to be the case, we can see in *Poems*, 1928, the slow coming together of images and attitudes that finally form the landscape and society of "Paid on Both Sides" and most of the other poems in *Poems*, 1930.

The austere landscape of poem II—"I choose this lean country / For seven days content, . . .", reminiscent of Graves's earlier poetry, becomes the ruined industrial landscape with the impassable frontier of "Who stands, the crux left of the watershed . . ." (poem VI). It merges, too, with the remote valley of the lover who "decent with seasons, move[s] / Different or with a different love, . . ." (poem XI). Poem II also contains a rather lurid nightmare in "[a] buried engine-room". A nightmare situation occurs in poem IV about two lovers who "slept apart, though doors were never locked".

> The womb began its crucial expulsion.
> The fishermen, aching, drenched to the skin
> The ledge cleared, dragged their boat upon the beach.
> The survivor dropped, the bayonets closing in.

A preoccupation with puritan constraints lies behind poem
X, "The mind to body spoke the whole night through . . .":

> Never to the Dark Tower we rode,
> But, turning on the hill crest, heard,
> Catching the breath for the applause,
> A tolling disillusioned bell . . .

The association of erotic love and religious redemption is
found in poem VII:

> ["] . . . Wonderful, was that cross, and I full of sin."
> "Approaching, utterly generous, came one,
> For years expected, born only for me."
>
> Returned from that dishonest country, we
> Awake, yet tasting the delicious lie;
> And boys and girls, equal to be, are different still.

Four men in a "bare room" each give reminiscences of love,
in poem XII, as they sit "waiting the enemy . . . / Beyond the
reef high-breaking surf".

These images and concerns come together in poems XIII to
XX, six of which were included in "Paid on Both Sides",
to give us the first glimpses of the world of Auden's early
poetry in fully developed form. Poem XV is the famous
sonnet of the captured spy, "Control of the Passes was, he
saw, the key / To this new district . . ." We have here, for
the first time, a figure frequently met in Auden's early poetry:
the spy or secret agent as the emissary of health in the doomed
society. Sometimes this figure is the outcast survivor of some
group; on other occasions he is the frustrated questor, impelled
against his will on a quest he knows will end tragically. In
all cases, success or rest or ease is denied. The concluding
picture of the man alone, waiting for death, evokes marvel-
lously this atmosphere of doom and denial that haunts these
early poems, setting death beside the longed-for fulfilment:

> The street music seemed gracious now to one
> For weeks up in the desert; woken by water
> Running away in the dark, he often had
> Reproached the night for a companion
> Dreamed of already. They would shoot of course,
> Parting easily who were never joined.

Poem XVI, "Taller today, we remember . . .", brings together the various elements of Auden's early poetic world in an austere and beautifully achieved unity: "in the windless orchard" the "glacier" at the source of "the brook" is remembered; in the room, they turn to the landscape "hearing our last / Of Captain Ferguson". The world of feud is here: "excellent hands have turned to commonness. . . . / One sold all his manors to fight, broke through, and faltered." ". . . the dead howl / Under the headlands . . . Because the Adversary put too easy questions / On lonely roads." They were deceived concerning Death and the demands of life. The "we" of the poem are "happy", "though no nearer each other": communion—perhaps sexual—is not attained, even in this domesticated valley, where men leave work and "go home".

> Noises at dawn will bring
> Freedom to some, but not this peace
> No bird can contradict, passing but is sufficient now
> For something fulfilled this hour, loved or endured.

The peace associated with love is, even in the valley, transient and threatened—threatened by the harsh, glaciated world of the feud and the Adversary. The threat is associated with a failure of those—us—who inhabit that world. "One, staring too long, went blind in a tower": the power that should dominate the world has been turned inward. The Adversary—death—triumphs.

It is fairly clear how the erotic forces, seen as those of purity and peace, but capable of perversion into something destructive, together with the notion of the death wish, have been transformed into elements of Auden's saga landscape, in which is enacted the sickness of society. Particularly significant in this connection is the opening of poem XIX, later included in "Paid on Both Sides":

> Some say that handsome raider still at large,
> A terror to the Marches, in truth is love . . .

The raider is "handsome" and a "terror" and "in truth is love": love accepted is handsome; rejected, a terror, as in the thought of Lane and Layard. This possible ambivalence of what is malignant in the world of Auden's early poetry is an important key to a good deal of its apparent obscurity.

Reading through *Poems*, 1928, one is aware of an increasing suppleness and muscularity of rhythm, a growing firmness of diction, a greater density and suggestiveness. Details are more starkly evoked, more memorable, as in "Taller today . . .". At the same time, the relationship between the details becomes harder to grasp, and the overall situations of the poems is more elusive. This is to be a notable feature of *Poems*, 1930, as a whole.

IV

By Christmas 1928 six of the poems in the 1928 volume had grown into the dramatic poem, "Paid on Both Sides", which was published in *The Criterion* for January, 1930. It is the opening poem of *Poems*, 1930. The setting and action of the poem recall the Icelandic sagas. The action is a part of a feud between two families, the Nowers and the Shaws. John Nower is tired of the feud and sickened at the killing. He decides to marry Anne Shaw and put an end to the feud. Seth Shaw's brother is captured by the Nowers in the course of the action, and executed as a spy. At the behest of his mother, Seth Shaw kills John Nower and many of his family at the wedding feast, thus reopening the feud. He acts as he does in order to gain the approval of his mother, as does Ransom in *The Ascent of F.6*. The relationship of both of them with their mothers is clearly meant to be seen as an example of the Oedipus complex. In performing a dubious act of courage merely to prove that he has the courage, Seth is evidently the Truly Weak Man facing "The Test". The poem concludes with a chorus: "Though he believe it, no man is strong."

The plot clearly portrays a clash between the forces of love (the erotic instincts) and those that make for death. Auden said, in *Letters from Iceland* (1937): "I love the sagas, but what a rotten society they describe, a society with only the gangster virtues."[11] The gangster virtues triumph in the end; and the piece as a whole gives one, not merely through the action, but also through the sombreness of the writing, the feeling of a society doomed to its feud.

It goes back to the collaborative fantasies with Isherwood, and the style recalls his phrase "a kind of hybrid language composed of saga phraseology and schoolboy slang".[12] The language is more powerful than this would suggest, and the deliberate avoidance of the definite article gives the feeling of Old English poetry.

> Can speak of trouble, pressure on men
> Born all the time, brought forward into light
> For warm dark moan.
> Though heart fears all heart cries for, rebuffs with
>   mortal beat
> Skyfall, the legs sucked under, adder's bite.

It was this feature that was most noticed among the stylistic innovations of *Poems*, 1930; and it was the subject of a celebrated essay, "The Tell-tale Article" by G. Rostrevor Hamilton.[13]

"Paid on Both Sides" is marred by satire that, as so frequently with Auden, degenerates into schoolboy ragging of the subject. Yet it is powerful and impressive, in spite of its obscurity and the sense it gives of being tangled, clotted and overloaded. The overall impression is hard to characterise: an analysis of what appears to have been the intended meaning makes the piece seem hopeful; after all, Seth is "The Truly Weak Man". Not all need be like him. Yet the laconic tenseness of the verse, the sombreness of the writing leave one with the impression that hope is a very tenuous thing in this world. The plot exists, presumably, as an embodiment of certain tensions that Auden felt in himself and society. These we feel are powerfully there; but what they are and in what their conflict consists, is just beyond the power of the author to bring into focus and to resolve. The radical uncertainty of tone is symptomatic of this, and is characteristic of many other pieces in *Poems*, 1930.

v

In the poems that are new in *Poems*, 1930, and not carried over from the 1928 volume, the world of saga and feud is replaced by the image of modern society as a sick society. An example is the hortatory poem XXII:

> Get there if you can and see the land you were once
>   proud to own
> Though the roads have almost vanished and the expresses
>   never run:
>
> Smokeless chimneys, damaged bridges, rotting wharves and
>   choked canals,
> Tramlines buckled, smashed trucks lying on their side
>   across the rails; . . .

The landscape is the ruined industrial landscape found in "Who stands, the crux left of the watershed, . . ." in the 1928 volume. "Get there if you can . . .": there is still a mysterious danger overhanging everything; yet the landscape of XXII is also the landscape of England of the depression, and exists in the historical framework of the depression. However, the poem is not Marxist. The healers who are mourned are "Lawrence, Blake and Homer Lane". Even though one may "listen for the crash / Meaning that the mob has realised that something's up, and start to smash; . . .", the solution is to "Drop those priggish ways for ever, stop behaving like a stone: / Throw the bath-chairs right away, and learn to leave ourselves alone." Society is in a bad way because society is sick; and the sickness is due to mis-direction of the sexual impulse. The message is that of Lane and Lawrence.

Some of the new poems in the 1930 volume may be seen as being close in style to the 1928 poems. They include II, "Which of you waking early and watching daybreak . . ."— a rather diffuse poem, which appears only in this first edition; III, "Since you are going to begin today . . .", written in couplets that are linked by assonances in the manner of Owen (as opposed to the "bad" rhymes of Yeats and Graves); XXX, "Sir, no man's enemy . . .", a fourteen line poem in the same manner; "Consider this and in our time . . ."; and the four part XVI, later called "1929", which features Auden's early article-free style almost to the point of parody.

"Consider this . . ." is one of the most impressive poems in the volume, and interesting too in that it relates the distorted sickness of modern society to the public school ethos:

Financier, leaving your little room
Where the money is made but not spent,
You'll need your typist and your boy no more;
The game is up for you and for the others,
Who, thinking, pace in slippers on the lawns
Of College Quad or Cathedral Close,
Who are born nurses, who live in shorts
Sleeping with people and playing fives.
Seekers after happiness, all who follow
The convolutions of your simple wish,
It is later than you think; nearer that day
Far other than that distant afternoon
Amid rustle of frocks and stamping feet
They gave the prizes to the ruined boys.

The idea of a society near the point where the upper classes
meet their doom seems Marxist, though in fact the feeling
that things had reached the point of disaster was common
to both Left and Right. Clearly here the "ruined boys"
(ruined by the public school values instilled in them) and
those who "are born nurses" are those who are sick—protec-
tively sick—in modern society. The "supreme Antagonist"
of the second section of the poem is reminiscent of "the Adversary" in "Taller today . . .": he starts his "rumour" that will
eventually scatter the people, "Seized with immeasurable
neurotic dread." The rather portentous writing at the conclusion contrasts very unfavourably with the aplomb of
". . . In strangled orchards and the silent comb / Where dogs
have worried or a bird was shot". As in "Paid on Both Sides"
the uncertainty of touch indicates how poorly focused some
elements of the poem were for the author.

It was not the poems from the 1928 volume and those close
to them in style, however, that contributed most to the impression of linguistic and musical vitality that the 1930 volume
gave—an impression given more strongly by the second
edition of 1933. The newness and vitality of Auden's rhythms
was one of the things that excited contemporary readers
most, and is found in poems like "Watch any day . . ." (IV),
"Upon this line . . ." (VII), "Again in conversation . . ."
(VIII), "Love by ambition . . ." (X)—poems that recall the
work of Laura Riding or Robert Graves.

The debt to Laura Riding's *Love as Love, Death as Death*
(1928) is an obvious and easily demonstrated one. There
are clear examples of imitation:

> The standing-stillness
> The from foot-to-foot
> Is no real illness . . .
>   (Riding)

> This gracious greeting
> "Good day. Good luck."
> Is no real meeting . . .
>   (Auden)

The debt is, however, more than a superficial one; and,
coming at this early stage in the career, is much more considerable than it has been acknowledged to be. Apart from
the greater sophistication of language, it shows itself in a
tremendous compression; but it is not the compression of
"Paid on Both Sides" and "Consider this . . .", which get
their power in part from the terse collocation of vividly realised
details, or from the omission of parts of speech. The poems
in the manner that recalls Riding have a sparseness of sensuous
detail, as has much of Riding's poetry. They get their compression from a directness of expression, from their economy
of syntax. Their life is very much in the voice and in the
suggestiveness of statements on the surface very plain. It was
these poems of short lines, with their powerful rhythms, that,
quite as much as the celebrated ruined landscape or the
article-free diction, gave Auden's first volume such an impact.

Auden himself said that he was a regular reader of Graves
from before 1929; and Graves's poetry seems to have made a
fairly lasting impression upon him. "O love, be fed . . .",
in Graves's *Poems* (1929), evidently impressed Auden considerably: it is imitated in "Watch any day . . ." (*Poems*, IV),
and there is a second poem in the 1930 volume that echoes it,
"Upon this line between adventure . . ." (VII). It concludes:

> On neither side let foot step over
> Invading Always, exploring Never,
> For this is hate and this is fear.

D

> On narrowness stand, for sunlight is
> Brightest only on surfaces;
> No anger, no traitor, but peace.

As in "Watch any day . . .", Auden copies Graves's device of rhyming stressed and unstressed syllables to obtain a muted rhyming effect; and once again the language has a notable spareness and muscularity. In this poem, as in Graves's poem, the advice of the speaker is to live in the present, because love is so vulnerable.

This feeling of the vulnerability of human feelings and attainments, already noted in "Paid on Both Sides", is a particularly strong one in Auden's 1930 volume, and gets very vital expression in the poems that echo Laura Riding. In these poems, such as "Before this loved one . . ." (XVIII), we encounter features of Auden's doomed landscape: ". . . Frontiers to cross / As clothes grew worse . . ."; ". . . This gratitude for gifts is less / Than the old loss; / Touching is shaking hands / On mortgaged lands . . ." The very urgency of expression seems to be associated with a fear that cannot be located. Nothing can assuage the menace and the frustration that go together and hang like a curse.

> Again in conversations
> Speaking of fear
> And throwing off reserve
> The voice is nearer
> But no clearer
> Than first love
> Than peace-time occupations.
>   [Than boy's imaginations (1933)].
>
> For every news
> Means pairing off in twos and twos
> Another I, another You
> Each knowing what to do
> But of no use.
>
> Never stronger
> But younger and younger
> Saying goodbye but coming back, for fear
> Is over there
> And the centre of anger
> Is out of danger.
>   [VIII]

Poems was not widely reviewed in its first edition of 1930. *The Times Literary Supplement*, under the heading, "Poetry and Disintegration", found it "baffling, if not unintelligible".[14] It was only as Auden got to be better known that his work was more fully and respectfully reviewed. The edition of *Poems* by which Auden became best known to readers was the second edition of 1933, which was kept steadily in print from then on. The substitution of seven poems written before the beginning of 1931 for some earlier ones merely increased the impression of linguistic vitality given by the volume as a whole. Before this edition appeared, however, Auden had produced (in 1932) a new and highly idiosyncratic book, *The Orators*, which, in style and in outlook, can be grouped with *Poems*.

VI

The Orators is subtitled "An English Study"; and it embodies the psychological analysis of the ills of society derived from Lane, Lawrence, Freud and Groddeck found in *Poems*. Auden has called it a "fair notion fatally injured".[15] His remarks on its fascist tendencies were quoted in Chapter 1. It is extremely obscure, and its composition in the form of juxtaposed set pieces, together with an uncertainty of tone in many parts, make any surety of comprehension impossible. The obscurity of the book is in part wilful, and in part comes from the fact that the author is not wholly consistent in his attitude to his subject.

The sick modern society, with its sickness projected as feuds within it, is the setting for the book. The relationship of this society to the earlier Mortmere evinces itself in the mention of some of the Mortmere characters in one of the included poems. Indeed, *The Orators* marks the decadence of the fantasies that began with Mortmere. The work is in three parts: "The Initiates", consisting of four "speeches"; "Journal of an Airman"; and "Six Odes". There are also two poems as Prologue and Epilogue. Book one consists of: "Address for Prize-day"; "Argument"; "Statement"; and "Letter to a Wound".

The heart of the book is "Journal of an Airman". The form of this part was suggested by Baudelaire's *Intimate Journals*, which Christopher Isherwood had translated in 1930. Viewed

historically, Baudelaire's *Journals* might be said to offer the
first instance of the neurotic as culture hero, or the neurotic as
saviour. The neurotic is sick, but he has, as a result of his
neurosis, an impulse to change things. He also has a greater
awareness of things than the undisturbed person. This ambivalence regarding the neurotic is reflected in the presentation
of the Airman: he is a tortured figure, but he is also "The
Agent of this Central Awareness", which is the awareness of
likeness (sympathy) and of difference (love). The Airman is
homosexual. His neurosis involves a lack of control over his
hands. He is, it would seem, a kleptomaniac; though the tone
of his concern about his hands and their secret would much
better fit masturbation, as Joseph Warren Beach suggests.[16]
This would also fit in with the schoolboy concerns that keep
cropping up in the book, and with the book's concern with
perverted sexuality or love as social ill.

The enemy is the old "Enemy", traditional English society
in love with the death-wish, afraid of change. Like the Devil
in Isherwood's description of Lane's ideas, he is the friend
of Reason and Organisation. There exist, however, those
whom the Enemy fears, the Truly Strong—the Hollies whom
the Airman visits on the final day before "The Test", with
which his journal evidently culminates. The enemy thinks
and pretends that he stands for the normal and desired state
of affairs: there is no sickness in society; to become aware of
the sickness is to join the forces against the Enemy.

The Airman's mother, whose dominance is connected in an
Oedipal manner with the disease of self-regard, hated the
boy's uncle, who was evidently homosexual, and who killed
himself in an incident connected with evidence faked by a
boy. The Airman sees his uncle as his true ancestor. This
notion is very important in the Journal; and the Airman's
salvation comes after a realisation of what the words "I have
crossed it" ("words in my dream under Uncle's picture")
(p. 74) mean. The final understanding of the nature of the
struggle only comes, via this dream, when the Airman is close
to "The Test". "Conquest can only proceed by absorption
of, i.e., infection by, the conquered. The true significance
of my hands . . . They stole to force a hearing . . . / To my
Uncle, perpetual gratitude and love for this crowning mercy.

For myself, absolute humility" (p. 75). Those who have seen this, as did Randall Jarrell, as a submission to authority, can hardly be blamed. The book is deeply authoritarian in its Lawrentian hero-worship of "the Truly Strong". However, it seems more likely that the Airman finally faces the fact that it is he who is to be tested, and finds the right attitude in which to face "The Test": not the grandiose battle with outside forces but the change within. The Journal concludes: "Pulses and reflexes, normal . . . / Some cumulus cloud at 10,000 feet . . . / Hands in perfect order" (p. 77).

In the six odes that conclude *The Orators*, there is considerable virtuosity, but it is a vulgar, theatrical virtuosity. The famous fifth ode ("Which side am I supposed to be on?") contains the passage: "The agent clutching his side collapsed at our feet, 'Sorry! They got me!'" (p. 104). Perhaps the final phrase was new in 1931, after only a few years of talking pictures. Today it makes the poem quite unreadable aloud. Indeed, reading through this poem aloud, one becomes aware of just how many places there are where one is embarrassed to know what tone of voice to adopt, while at other times the writing has the superb aplomb of the best of *Poems*: ". . . the bitter psalm is caught by the gale from the rocks: / 'How long shall they flourish?'" (p. 106).

Of all Auden's work, it is to the poems in *The Orators* that one might point and justly accuse him of in-group self-satisfaction. Equally depressing is the strongly fascist tone that pervades the whole work. It is a fascism latent in all systems of thought that see the difficulties of life as arising from human lack of courage to accept the message of the true prophet. It is also a fascism of 1931—the year in which Mosley had his greatest appeal for intellectuals.

One has to admit that *The Orators* does not owe all its tone of immaturity to its author: it partly reflects a ridiculousness to be found in some of the sexual prophets of the age; and particularly in psychoanalysis. Nevertheless, although Auden is using similar ideas to those used in *Poems* and "Paid on Both Sides"—and using them in the same setting—he is no longer involved in the attendant emotions, as he was in the earlier work. He stands back, knowingly laughing: he catches the headmaster with his trousers down.

VII

Shortly after the publication of *The Orators*, Auden seems to have abandoned many of his earlier beliefs and fantasies. The nature of this change is seen in two crucial poems: "A Happy New Year", published in Michael Roberts's symposium, *New Country*, in 1933; and "The Witnesses", published in *The Listener* of 12th July of the same year. "A Happy New Year" is in two parts, the second of which became poem X of *Look Stranger!* The first part is a peculiar and unsatisfactory performance. It is written in rhyme royal and portrays a vision of the people of England. In this it is reminiscent of Skelton's "Garland of Laurel". In its "blurring images / Of the dingy difficult life of our generation" (*New Country*, p. 205) there is a good deal of horse-play and fantasy reminiscent of *The Orators*. However, in spite of the elements of fantasy in the poem, this is one of the first of Auden's poems where the public world appears without being acclimatised to a special world of the poet's creation. This is particularly true of the second part of the poem, where Auden portrays the Helensburgh of the school in which he is teaching:

> Now from my window-sill I watch the night
> The church clock's yellow face, the green pier light
> Burn for a new imprudent year;
> The silence buzzes in my ear;
> The jets in both the dormitories are out.
>
> (p. 205)

It is the actual world of a clear night, serene and unhaunted, in contrast with the setting of his earlier poems. The poet stands outside of the world on which he comments, instead of projecting his own preoccupations into it in the form of fantasy.

At the beginning of the first part of the poem he writes:

> Motion reversed, blood to the day had turned,
> For justice rather than for love was burned,
> Withdrawn from loins into a quickened mind
> In spiritual use to find.

> The old old arguments were still as dangerous
> As I walked by myself in the sun; . . .
>
> (p. 195)

The "old arguments" are evidently being rejected: "justice rather than love" is to be the key concern. In the second part of the poem, "we are sick, / Using, the mole's device, the carriage / Of peacock or rat's desperate courage . . ." (p. 206); but it is not an acceptance of our erotic impulses that will right things.

> But deaf to prophecy or China's drum
> The blood moves strangely in its moving home,
> Diverges, loops to travel further
> Than the long still shadow of the father
> Through [Though?] to the valley of regret it come.
>
> (p. 205)

The distinction is made between the private and public worlds; and the indifference of one to the other is pointed out. This was to be a basic theme in Auden's poetry in the middle and later thirties. Erotic love is no longer the panacea; it is in fact distrusted, because of its lack of public concern. Instead, Auden invokes the "Lords of limit, training dark and light / And setting a tabu 'twixt left and right . . ." (p. 205). Discipline and limitation are the way to the good life. The actual is accepted and praised, not fantasied into an image of sickness. Traditional forms are being used; the voice is relaxed, taking time over its effects.

Auden has undergone some sort of conversion. His orientation is reversed, and his relation to the actual has completely changed. The Pure in Heart are no longer perfect and immune. They must respect the "Lords of limit". These figures appear in "The Witnesses", another poem of traditional form, and one of Auden's first pieces of satirical light verse.

In a system of thought like that of the early Auden, where a broken arm would be the manifestation of a guilty wish, the Reality Principle has little place. Only when the outside world is seen as "other", as something to which we have to accommodate our inner life, does such a principle have validity. It is this recognition of the outer world as something exerting pressure on us, something to be respected and dealt with, that differentiates so startlingly the world of *Poems* from that of *Look Stranger!* (1936), in which Auden collects together his poetry of the middle thirties, where the psychology becomes more orthodoxly Freudian, and is accommodated to another creed, Marxism.

VIII

The first work in which the new analysis appears is the dramatic sketch, *The Dance of Death*, published in 1933. It opens with the announcement: "We present to you this evening a picture of the decline of a class, of how its members dream of a new life, but secretly desire the old, for there is death inside them. We show that death as a dancer." This is about the best thing in the piece, which is written in lyrics that recall intimate review, are not particularly effective, and leave one at times wondering whether they are intended as parody or not. The characters belong to the "smart set", and are pictured in a Grand Hotel setting. The notion that these people might be effete is hardly new, so that the satire goes off a bit damply. They are all pictured as deluded victims of the death wish, not realising that they are a doomed class. Death, the dancer who enchants these people, eventually dies, and the figure of Karl Marx appears:

> O Mr. Marx, you've gathered
> All the material facts
> You know the economic
> Reasons for our acts.
>
> (p. 38)

After which Marx pronounces on the dead dancer: "The instruments of production have been too much for him. He is liquidated" (p. 38). This Marxist conclusion, while consistent with the play, is very much an appendage. The whole work is rather crude and superficial, and altogether too clever as an analysis of what, after all, was an aspect of a very sombre reality at the time.

The same may be said of the first dramatic collaboration of Auden and Isherwood, *The Dog Beneath the Skin* (1935). The genesis of the play is not clear. Isherwood has recently written: "In the *Notes* ["Some notes on Auden's Early Poetry" (1937)] I write that we revised the best parts of our earlier, unpublished play, *The Enemies of the Bishop*, and used them again in *The Dog Beneath the Skin*. This statement is oddly misleading. *The Dog Beneath the Skin* was based almost entirely on a later play, *The Chase*, which Auden wrote independently in 1934."[17] The impression of its being a doctored piece of work is most strongly given in its last line: "To each his need: from each his power." It is hard to see what this had to do with the adventures of Alan Norman who goes in search of the lost heir of his village of Pressan Ambo, who is in fact disguised all the time as a dog—a theme that recalls Mortmere, though, in fact, there seems to be no significance to the disguise: it is merely a device. The same may be said of the action of the play. A series of not too funny sketches, with visits to places like the red light district, it is again intimate review, and its social commentary is, in most scenes, about as significant as one might expect of that medium. The play is given a Marxist conclusion by having the hero return to his village to find that it has been transformed into a parody of the old enemy, Blimpism. The hero finds himself at a celebration for The Lads of Pressan, a reactionary, quasi-military, quasi-religious organisation. He leaves to join the forces of light.

The triviality of the play is revealed in contrast by the marvellous poetry of some of the choruses, where Auden displays the feeling for contemporary England that was a mark of his best work of the middle thirties:

> Paddington. King's Cross. Euston. Liverpool Street:
> Each hiding behind a gothic hotel its gigantic green house
> And the long trains groomed before dawn departing at ten,
> Picking their way through slums between the washing and the
>   privies
> To a clear run through open country,
> Ignoring alike the cathedral towns in their wide feminine
>   valleys, and the lonely junctions.
>
> (p. 80)

The Dog Beneath the Skin is the last gasp of the early fantasies. Unlike them, it is vapid and the authors seem uninvolved.

Fantasy is no longer an impelling mode in Auden's hands. By the middle thirties he is the detached moral commentator, and his work is very different in character from that of *Poems* and *The Orators*.

IX

The unassuageable terror, the amities broken for no apparent reason, "the gradual ruin spreading like a stain" haunt Auden's early poetry. All are guilty in some never to be specified way. The secret agents of the forces of life can never hope for happiness or real success in the face of the Enemy. Sex is associated with guilt and nightmare—ostensibly, one might say, in the doctrinaire psychoanalytic manner, but in fact more compulsively than at first appears. There is an ambivalent feeling about strength and weakness: a power of analysis that explains the sickness, coupled with a despising of the sick. The laconic writing and the admired virtues remind one strongly of the early Hemingway: the terseness of statement; the concentration on "things", which are often rendered with a hyper-aesthesia; a hopeless courage as the greatest virtue. In Hemingway's work, these qualities appear as the natural outcome of a loss of confidence in traditional beliefs. They are associated with a similar feeling in Auden's portrayal of a sick society. Yet, in Hemingway, it becomes increasingly clear, they were associated with a tendency towards depression that had to be kept at a distance at all costs. Similarly, Auden's attitudes and the landscape of his ruined society can be felt to be projections of a clash of feeling that he was unable to deal with directly. The clear evocation of the actual goes along with confusion and contradiction concerning the total situation. The call for renewal, made in terms of psychological theories of the world's ills that make them childishly simple to right, is accompanied by attitudes of romantic despair, a pervading nostalgia and hopelessness. The lapsed puritan did not find it all that easy to be clinical.

Auden's peculiar relationship to his material manifested itself in fantasy and reality becoming confused in his early poetry, frequently when the tone became satirical. How seriously and how literally to take him becomes a problem;

and one has the feeling that it was a problem the author would not have been happy to face. There is a certain amount of unconscious sleight of hand. The mysteriousness that arises from this may have been part of the initial appeal of his poetry; and the air of mystery was added to by the absence of titles. *Poems* seemed to younger writers to show them new possibilities for poetry. The new imagery was highly exciting; and, if Auden had done no more for English poetry than acclimatise the industrial landscape of modern England to poetry, he would have done a great deal. *Poems* also provided, sometimes for the worse, a great deal of the rhetoric and furniture of thirties poetry: frontiers, spies, the madness of rulers, the general tendency to present social comment in the form of fantasy or satirical fantasy. There is no doubt that, in terms of developing an idiom, Auden's early poetry made possible much of the poetry of the decade; so that it is important in approaching the poetry of the period to see just what is nonsense and immature in the early Auden, and what not. Related to this problem is that of seeing just what is being said. Because Auden became the leading poet of the Left, *Poems* and *The Orators* were seen as Marxist works. They clearly are not. It is ironical that the very personal early poetry provided the stylistic basis for much left-wing poetry in the thirties.

Chapter 5

NEW SIGNATURES: NEW COUNTRY

New Signatures – New Country (A. S. J. Tessimond,
Michael Roberts) – *The Listener*

AFTER THE PUBLICATION of his first book of poems, John
Lehmann received a letter from someone he had never heard
of, Michael Roberts. Roberts had read Lehmann's poetry
and that of his contemporaries and felt "that they belonged
together . . . in spite of wide apparent differences".[1] This
was to lead to the publication (by Leonard and Virginia
Woolf, for whose Hogarth Press Lehmann was working) of
the anthology, *New Signatures*, edited by Roberts. Included
were poems by three poets from Oxford—Auden, Day Lewis
and Spender; four poets from Cambridge—Lehmann, Bell,
Empson and Eberhart; and two poets whom Lehmann had
got to know in London, A. S. J. Tessimond and William Plomer.
Lehmann, through his sister Rosamund, had met Spender;
while Day Lewis was already being published by the Woolfs.
Auden was recruited by Christopher Isherwood.

Born in 1902, Michael Roberts was a little older than any
of the poets whose work he was to introduce. He had studied
chemistry at King's College, London, and mathematics at
Trinity College, Cambridge. In the twenties he had joined
the C.P.G.B., but had been expelled after a year or two as a
Trotskyite. A poet and a reviewer, he had contributed to
The Criterion, The Listener and many other periodicals. At the
time at which he met Lehmann, he was a mathematics teacher
in a London school. He was later to marry Janet Adam Smith,
who did so much for the new poetry as assistant editor of
The Listener.

As a scientist, Roberts was, not surprisingly, attracted by the
critical writings of I. A. Richards, whose early work is so
influenced by psychology, and, who, in his book *Science and
Poetry* (1926), discusses the ways in which scientific theories of
knowledge tend to undermine the status of poetry. He was

also concerned with the extent to which a poet, in writing a poem, committed himself to any system of belief—a problem that concerned Eliot, particularly around 1930. Roberts, in *New Signatures* and in later collections, tends to discuss the poetry of his day in the framework of these preoccupations. They were certainly not the most pressing concerns for the poets included in *New Signatures*.

In his introduction, Roberts indicated what he felt was new in the poems he had edited:

> The poems in this book represent a clear reaction against esoteric poetry in which it is necessary for the reader to catch each recondite allusion. Even Mr. Empson, whose poetry may still be difficult, is definitely trying to say something to an audience. (p. 12)

> Mr. Auden's *Poems* and Mr. Day Lewis's *From Feathers to Iron* were, I think, the first books in which imagery taken from contemporary life consistently appeared as the natural and spontaneous expression of the poet's thought and feeling. (p. 15)

> It is natural that the recognition of the importance of others should sometimes lead to what appears to be the essence of the communist attitude ... (pp. 18–19)

He notes the reacclimatisation of traditional forms being made by these poets after the dominance of *vers libre* in the twenties. He sums up the character of his authors in terms that recall what he has learned from Richards and Eliot:

> The writers in this book have learned to accept the fact that progress is illusory, and yet believe that the game is worth playing; to believe that the alleviation of suffering is good even though it merely makes possible new sensitiveness and therefore new suffering; to believe that their own standards are no more absolute than those of other people, and yet to be prepared to defend and to suffer for their own standards; to think of the world, for scientific purposes, in terms which make it appear deterministic, and yet to know that a human action may be unpredictable from scientific laws, a new creation. (pp. 12–13)

A candid reading of the poems in *New Signatures* would not lead one to make such a characterisation, except in the case of William Empson, who, oddly enough, had, in 1928, summarised his own outlook in words very like those of Roberts.[2] Although Roberts became a spokesman for the new poetry in the early thirties, his outlook was that of Cambridge of the twenties, and he tended to project his attitudes on to the younger writers.

Julian Bell's contributions to the anthology have already been described. Empson's—because he was in Japan, and writing very little—were in fact all taken from Cambridge undergraduate publications, with the exception of the celebrated "This Last Pain", which seems, however, to date from his Cambridge days. "Camping Out", "Invitation to Juno" and "Note on Local Flora" were reprinted. The poems by the American poet, Richard Eberhart, who was presumably back in America when *New Signatures* was prepared, seem likely to have been taken from undergraduate periodicals. Auden contributed three poems. They included what was to be the fifth ode ("Though aware of our rank . . .") in *The Orators*, and "Chorus from a Play"—the famous "Doom is dark and deeper" that became poem II in the second edition of *Poems*.

None of the poems so far mentioned, with the exception of Bell's long "Arms and the Man", has any political flavour. The same appears largely true of the poems by William Plomer and John Lehmann—and entirely true of the poems by A. S. J. Tessimond. The nearest thing to a unifying feature is the one named by Roberts, the absorption of the modern world—and particularly its technology—into poetry. Empson's use of scientific imagery and Auden's ruined industrial landscape have been remarked upon already, though the latter obtrudes very little into Auden's contributions. In the poems by Day Lewis, Spender and Tessimond, the industrial imagery is a striking feature.

What Roberts had to say about the use of this imagery by Day Lewis and Auden has already been quoted. In speaking of Tessimond, he makes a comparison with the Imagists—a comparison whose validity is illustrated by the following poem:

La Marche des Machines

This piston's infinite recurrence is
night morning night and morning night and
death and birth and death and birth and this
crank climbs (blind Sisyphus) and see

steel teeth greet
bow deliberate
delicately lace
in lethal kiss

God's teeth bite whitely tight
slowly the gigantic oh slowly the steel spine dislocates
wheels grazing (accurately missing) waltz

two cranes do a hundred-ton tango against the sky

In its purely aesthetic approach to the objects described, this poem has much in common with Imagist poetry (even if the immediate model is e. e. cummings). There is not an imaginative absorption of machinery: the machine is merely written about in the terms one might have used in describing the movements of something conventionally beautiful that impressed one by its power. In contrast, though Day Lewis does not make industrial imagery a part of his poetry as fully and successfully as does Auden, whom he too frequently seems to be imitating, the following stanza illustrates what Roberts had to say about the new imagery:

> Somewhere beyond the railheads
> Of reason, south or north,
> Lies a magnetic mountain
> Riveting sky to earth.
> [Poem 3, p. 50]

Instead of features of modern industry being given the traditional poetic treatment of the beautiful, traditional matters of poetry—reason and emotion—are presented in terms of modern industrial metaphors.

One of the most celebrated poems of the thirties on an industrial subject is included in *New Signatures*—Spender's "The Express". It is not so "poetic" in a limiting sense as is a poem often linked with it, and written at about the same time—Spender's "Landscape near an Aerodrome"—with its "burring furred antennae", "soft as any moth". Nevertheless, its approach to its subject is of the same type as that of Tessimond:

> . . . It is now she begins to sing—at first quite low
> Then loud, and at last with a jazzy madness—
> The song of her whistle screaming at corners,
> Of deafening tunnels, brakes, innumerable bolts.
> And always light, aerial underneath
> Goes the elate metre of her wheels.

It is as though the poet were trying to convince us that trains are as beautiful as songs and poems—*not* in their own ways but in the way that songs and poems are beautiful. Perhaps this is to belittle an impressive and original poem. However, it does not have the power and originality that we find in Baudelaire or Auden—the power to draw out the essential poetry of the modern city or modern industry, with indifference to conventional notions of what is aesthetically pleasing.

The two obviously politically conscious poets in *New Signatures* are Day Lewis and Spender. Day Lewis contributes seven poems from *The Magnetic Mountain*, his third book, and the first to be overtly left-wing. Readers might be excused for not noticing that these were political poems at all, as Day Lewis's call for change tends to expend itself in the type of generalised aspiration hinted at in the stanza quoted above. His contributions also contain a good deal of Audenesque posturing concerning "frontiers". However, Spender's poems are among the most successful political poems of the period. They include "Oh Young Men", "The Prisoners", "I Think Continually" and "The Funeral".

New Signatures was an unexpected success: it ran to a second impression in a few weeks. It brought the new poets to the attention of the poetry-reading public. Not all of them had published volumes of poetry; and the early books by Bell, Day Lewis, Lehmann, Plomer and Spender had received little attention. One result of the success was that the poets became lumped together by that public as the "*New Signatures*" poets. In fairness to the public, it should be pointed out that these writers rather reinforced the impression that they were a group by reappearing the next year, 1933, in a new anthology, *New Country*, under the same editor, Michael Roberts.

New Country was more of an Oxford product than had been *New Signatures*. Empson, Bell and Eberhart were not among the contributors. Of the contributors to *New Signatures*, Auden, Day Lewis, Spender, Lehmann and Tessimond all contributed poems. William Plomer was represented by a short story. New contributors included Richard Goodman and Rex Warner, both of whom had appeared earlier in editions of *Oxford Poetry*. *New Country* included prose as well as verse, and one of the prose contributions was a short story by Christopher Isherwood, "At the Bay". There were also short stories by T. O. Beachcroft and Edward Upward.

New Country was avowedly political. Roberts presented his contributors as the truly post-war generation, moving towards a new faith in Communism. The writing he had collected, he claimed, showed "how some of us are finding a way out of the individualist predicament". However, Communism was not to mean "any diminution . . . of personal identity": it was to bring "that extension of personality and consciousness which comes sometimes to a group of men when they are working together for some common purpose". The book did not represent "proletarian art" (pp. 20–1). However, the Left orientation of the writers would have an artistic consequence—an extension of the revolt against esoteric art remarked on in the introduction to *New Signatures*. As the writer ". . . sees more and more clearly that his interests are bound up with those of the working class, so will his writing clear itself from the complexity and introspection, the doubt and cynicism of recent years, and become more and more intelligible to that class . . ." (p. 18).

In illustrating what he meant by ". . . that extension of personality . . . which comes . . . when . . . working together for some common purpose . . .", Roberts gives an illustration that shows the tone of many of the contributions: "a fortnight of wind and heavy snowstorm in the Jura. . . . I remember only, at the end of each day's work, standing at nightfall on the last spur of the ridge, counting the tiny figures moving down the slope in sight of food and warmth again: nine, ten, eleven, black dots against the snow, and knowing that again the party was complete, uninjured, tired and content" (p. 21) Y.M.C.A.: Young Men's Communist Association. This sort of thing makes one give three cheers for Cyril Connolly. Roberts was not a liberal beginning to lean towards Communism; he had been a member of the C.P.G.B. Yet he can choose as his example of dedication to a purpose what is merely an upper middle-class leisure occupation. The extent to which he is imbued with the attitudes of that class is seen in the fact that he shows that class's tendency to treat games as one of the most serious things in life, certainly not to be slighted by being regarded as mere pleasure. He writes like the Duke of Edinburgh recommending the Outward Bound schools.

A similar alarming unawareness of class tone is seen in Day Lewis's "Letter to a Young Revolutionary". He had either become or was to become a member of the C.P.G.B. His letter begins: "Dear Jonathan, So you are thinking of joining the Communist Party" (p. 25). Comment seems unnecessary. Like so many of his fellow upper middle-class left-wing intellectuals, Day Lewis could not see that, as class consciousness was so central to British life, everything that he said or did had class implications, and thus might clash with his Communist doctrines. It was not the liberalism of his class that was their stumbling block in truly entering into Communism, but the innate snobbery and politeness in everything that made up their way of life.

Stephen Spender's article, "Poetry and Revolution", is a good deal more sensible. He is concerned with the problem of the bourgeois artist who has become a Communist, and with the problem of the individuality of the artist who accepts a dogmatic system of belief:

> Of human activities, writing poetry is one of the least revolutionary . . . Separate poems are separate and complete and ideal worlds. If a poem is not complete in itself and if its content spills over into our world of confused emotions, then it is a bad poem . . . This is what people mean when they say that it is impossible to write propagandist poetry. A work of art cannot reach out into everyday life and tell us whom to vote for and what kind of factories to build, because injunctions how to act in a world that has nothing to do with the poem destroy the poem's unity. (p. 62)

Spender characterises fairly well the situation of intellectuals like himself. What must surprise anyone unfamiliar with the writing of the thirties is the ease with which the word revolution—which implies death, anarchy, disruption—is used by Spender and other contributors to the anthology; with no sense that their calm in the face of this word is a measure of the order and subdued tenor of British life.

Not all of the contributions in *New Country* had a left-wing flavour. This is particularly true of the short stories. Edward Upward's two pieces, which were later incorporated in his novel, *Journey to the Border* (1939), were clearly political in intent. However, the best of the stories—and perhaps the best contribution to the anthology—William Plomer's "Child of Queen Victoria", had nothing to do with politics. Oddly enough, Plomer's story, with its strong portrayal of situations that involve feelings basic to life, shows up the other contributions, some of which, however much the writers fulminate, seem the product of a limitingly sheltered experience. This seems true of Upward's stories, which were picked out at the time as being among the more distinguished pieces.

The poetry is more decidedly left-wing than the short stories. Oddly enough, none of Spender's poems is political in any way. All four are concerned with personal themes, and are also decidedly less impressive than his poems in *New Signatures*. Day Lewis contributes four more poems from *The Magnetic Mountain*. One of them, "Fireman, and farmer, father and flapper . . .", an imitation of a rather regrettable poem in the same form in *The Orators*, hits a low in vulgar, superficial tub thumping:

> Scavenger barons and your jackal vassals,
> Your pimping press-gang, your unclean vessels,
> We'll make you swallow your words at a gulp
> And turn you back to your element, pulp . . .

The most directly political of Auden's poems, "A Communist to Others", is also an unfortunate performance. The voice is evidently that of a Communist other than the poet, as the poet is appealed to at the end; though there is little sense of any created "persona". The second stanza adds to the confusion:

We know the terrifying brink
From which in dreams you nightly shrink
"I shall be sacked without," you think,
    "A testimonial."

The intention is evidently sympathetic; though the handling of the verse, with the hold-off before "testimonial" is dropped into the comically deflating short line, suggests that the person addressed is being satirised. However, the real damage comes from the fact that it is clear that Auden did not know that only the lower middle classes—never the "saved" of Marxism—got "testimonials". Working-class people were just laid off without ceremony. This causes the passage to have the reverse tone of the one intended.

Rex Warner contributes some rather prolix poems, the style of which is a mixture of Hopkins, Warner's friend Day Lewis, and Auden. Auden is saluted with a ludicrous imitation of his mannered private references: "What has happened to Colonel Humphries? Will he come?" (Presumably he is off "seeing [his] last of Captain Ferguson".) A poem entitled "Hymn", concludes: ". . . All Power / to lovers of life, to workers, to the hammer, the sickle, the blood." This is not only a sample of its rhetoric, but also an expression of its key position. The main interest in the poem arises from the fact that it opens with: "The splendid body is private, and calls for more." The Marxist revolution is seen as inaugurating a sexual revolution of guiltless, healthy fulfilment.

Roberts introduced two younger poets in *New Country*, both of whom contributed much more doctrinaire poems than the older poets. By this time left-wing clubs had begun to dominate intellectual life at the universities. Charles Madge, a South African from Cambridge, had joined the C.P.G.B. in 1932. His poem, "Letter to the Intelligentsia", is a description of his progress to Communism. First he is rescued from lassitude and despondency: "But there waited for me in the summer morning, / Auden, fiercely. I read, shuddered and knew . . ." His conversion is completed by seeing a "hunger march": ". . . since more than in name / The day has been a communist one . . .". (For those who missed the Wordsworthian echo, there is an easier one shortly: "Lenin, would you were living at this hour: / England has need of you . . .") In this poem, we see the way in which the Auden/Day Lewis apparatus of urgency—maps and telegrams and rushed journeys—is catching on as the normal furniture of political poetry: ". . . telegrams come in / From China, and the world is mapped on our brains . . ." The poem is an excellent sample of how damaging sure intellectual positions unbacked by experience can be to poetry.

The other younger poet is Richard Goodman, who had been an editor of *Oxford Poetry* in 1932. Goodman was also a Communist. His father had kept the sweet shop at Eton; and Goodman had been the butt of former Etonians while at New College, Oxford. He was a friend of Spender, and his most finished poem in *New Country*, "It is too late for pity now or striving with love . . .", is an imitation of Spender's "I think continually . . ." Like Spender, because he is caught up in an apocalyptic response to the Communist vision, he comes close to bringing off poems rooted in extremely simplified attitudes:

Over the face and the brilliant features of love—
those fields below the snow-line he thought safe from
    death—
where for a space beneath the promising sky
hope, like the erect brave flowers, burnt massive with joy,
standing alone once more, the young Communist sees
sorrow, the glacier, raiding, barrage of ice

Those towns he had planned and had built already in dreams . . .

Goodman's poems, unfortunately, do not have sufficient maturity of style for a distinctive voice to emerge.

Not all the poems of social and political theme in *New Country* are marred. The book includes Auden's marvellous "Prologue"—the poem that opens *Look Stranger!*. The poems by John Lehmann stem from his experiences in Europe, and are more poised and unassuming than most of the poems in the book.

The only unpolitical poet in *New Country* was A. S. J. Tessimond. His retrospective *Selection* of 1957 is impressive enough in an unassuming way; and a reader of that volume, which is marked by plainness and directness, would hardly recognise Tessimond in his work in *New Signatures* and *New Country*. "Marche des Machines", quoted earlier, is typical of his contributions to the anthologies. "Epitaph on a Disturber of His Times" begins:

> We expected the violin's finger on the upturned nerve;
>   its importunate cry, too laxly curved:
> and you drew us an oboe-outline, clean and acute;
>   unadorned statement, accurately carved.

"Unadorned statement" is, unfortunately, what Tessimond does not give us. His poetry reads like something simpler dressed up in a rhetoric that is straining to heighten the effect of what is being said. The preciousness of the musical imagery in the above extract seems to indicate a talent fundamentally more literary and conventional than the surface of the poetry might make us expect. Tessimond seems excessively concerned with subtleties of sense experience, as in the poem "Discovery", in *New Country*, which evokes the way things appear when one is drunk.

His poetry was to become plainer and less pretentious, but it remained concerned with an obvious and often sensuous treatment of its material. However, his "England", included in the last issue of John Lehmann's *New Writing*, is one of the poems that captures most firmly the flavour of the end of the decade.

It might be more accurate to say that there are two poets in *New Country* who are unpolitical. Michael Roberts, in spite of his introduction, does not touch on politics in his poems in this book. His themes are two most dear to him, mountaineering and stars. It is a little hard to take seriously his cult of mountaineering as a self-sacrificing and heroic activity, epitomising the best in man. However, "Kangchengjunga" is movingly evocative in parts. It is not in terms of subject matter or attitude that Roberts falls down, but in the quality of the writing. "Sirius B" is asked to "be mine / Own thought." Roberts continues "And march imponderable stars / In mind's dimension . . ." The language is made up of poetic clichés, which evidently had for the author the emotions associated with their original literary settings. This tendency to lapse into cliché goes along with a similar proclivity for pastiche:

> ... Whose thought racks cloud-confusion, sheer
> Black vitreous wall, blank precipice
> Grown final. No analysis
> Can find familiar footing. Here
>
> All reason ends; ends summer; ...

These cliffs of the mind are the cliffs of Hopkins ("No worst, there is none"), not of Kangchengjunga. There is no definiteness of style in the five poems of his own that Roberts prints. In *New Country* he lacks that certainty of voice that is the mark of an individual poetic vision.

Robert's outlook was predominantly religious rather than political. The radical politics were only an extension of his religious attitudes. In his second book, *Orion Marches* (1939), he writes, under the influence of a religious view of man's rôle, archetypal poems redolent of the work of Edwin Muir— though without Muir's sure and subtle handling of tone. They remind one that he was a friend of Kathleen Raine, who wrote well about him after his death in 1948.[3] In his later poems Roberts often wrote with a simplicity that avoids both cliché and literary posturing and produced more satisfying poetry than that included in *New Country*.

New Signatures and *New Country* brought together before the public a group of poets not yet established who were, from that time on, to dominate the new poetry of the decade. *New Country* made clear their political inclination; but to the poetry-reading public of the time they became known as the "Pylon" poets, after Stephen Spender's poem on that subject, and in recognition of the scientific and industrial imagery that was the striking feature of their poetry. In these anthologies it is associated with hopefulness and renewal; but, as the decade advanced, machinery was to become increasingly associated by these writers with the oppressive industrial society and with the vulgar materialism of the new suburbia.

II

In 1935, Michael Roberts married Janet Adam Smith, assistant editor of the British Broadcasting Corporation's new periodical, *The Listener*, in its beginning years. From very early on, *The Listener* regularly included poems. The issue for 12th July, 1933, included a supplement of "Nine Poems", with poems by C. Day Lewis, Bernard Spencer, John Hewitt, Herbert Read, W. H. Auden, John Lehmann, Charles Madge, T. H. White, and Arthur Ball. In the issue for 14th June that year there had been a full page review by Bonamy Dobrée of *New Country*, Auden's *Poems*, Spender's *Poems* and C. Day Lewis's *The Magnetic Mountain*. The choice of poems published in *The Listener* had caused a certain amount of complaint, both within and outside the B.B.C., and Janet Adam Smith recalls how she was sent for by Sir John Reith, the director general, to justify her policy. She suggested sending a portfolio of contributions to T. S. Eliot for an opinion. This was done, and an encouraging opinion returned. The portfolio included poems by Conrad Aiken, George Barker, Julian Bell, J. N. Cameron, Gavin Ewart, David Gascoyne, Louis MacNeice, Edwin Muir, William Plomer, Kathleen Raine, Michael Roberts, Stephen Spender, A. S. J. Tessimond, and R. E. Warner. Some of the poems included in *New Signatures* and *New Country* had already appeared in *The Listener*. Janet Adam Smith in 1935 collected together the best poems she had published in an anthology, *Poems of Tomorrow* (1935).

The mere listing retrospectively of the poets published is no measure of what she had done. One has to remember that she had published all these poets by the middle of 1933, when very few of them had had books out. In 1931 *The Listener* included poems by Julian Bell, Richard Goodman and Stephen Spender; in 1932, it included poems by Goodman, Spender, Tessimond, Day Lewis, and John Lehmann. All this was before these poets had had much publicity, and before *New Verse* had appeared. What was most important was that it brought them before the main body of the intelligent reading public, which the little magazines, with their circulation in the hundreds, did not reach. This must have been especially important in the earlier years.

The Listener continued to publish new poets throughout the thirties, though less actively in the second half of the decade. In addition to the poets already mentioned, early work by the following poets appeared in *The Listener*: Edgar Foxall, George Barker, Randall Swingler, Rayner Heppenstall, Dylan Thomas, Roger Roughton, Richard Eberhart, D. S. Savage, William Empson, Ruthven Todd, H. B. Mallalieu, Henry Reed, Kenneth Allott, John Betjeman, Keidrych Rhys, F. T. Prince, Julian Symons and Nicholas Moore. In terms of the volume of poems published—nearly two hundred by the poets named—*The Listener* did more for the new poetry of the thirties than did *New Writing* or *Left Review*; but the contribution is perhaps best measured in terms of the number of poets brought before a wide audience.

Chapter 6

POETRY AND POLITICS

Stephen Spender – John Lehmann – C. Day Lewis –
Rex Warner – The Problems of Political Poetry –
The First Phase of Political Poetry

OF THE POETS in *New Signatures* and *New Country* whose early
work has not yet been dealt with extensively, the most interesting were Stephen Spender, John Lehmann and Cecil Day
Lewis—all poets with decidedly left-wing orientation. Their
emergence as political poets between 1931 and 1933 marks
the first phase of left-wing poetry in the thirties.

Of 1931 Christopher Isherwood records:

> I was living mostly in Berlin at the time, which seemed especially
> romantic to Spender; for Germany was then pre-eminently
> the country of the wandervogel movement, of nudism, hiking-
> trips, leather shorts, accordions and free love. So Spender came
> to Germany, and wrote in his diary: "Now I shall begin to
> live."
>   What he actually did there was to write some of his best
> early poems; and to expose the utter absurdity of the sex-freedom
> myth by living up to it with his ruthless *naïveté*.[1]

The incongruous aspects—moral libertarianism and incipient
Fascist reaction—that Germany of the day presented have
already been mentioned; while it was in Berlin that Spender
first became aware of the effects of unemployment at first
hand.

The two years after he left Oxford were, for Spender, his
great period. In 1931 in Germany he developed the intensely
lyrical poem of political concern that was his peculiar invention. From the evidence of periodical publication, and from
the order of poems in the manuscript book in which he made
his drafts,[2] it is clear that the first of these poems, "The Prisoners", was written about the middle of 1931; and that in
the next twelve months or so he wrote a dozen of his best

poems which include "I think continually . . .", "After they have tired . . .", "The Funeral", "The Express", "The Landscape near an Aerodrome", "In railway halls, on pavements . . .", "The Pylons" and "Not palaces, an era's crown . . ." (in that order). This group of poems includes most of the poems by which Spender is represented in anthologies. He was 23 when he completed the last of them.

Although these poems are perhaps the first poems that come to mind when one thinks of the political poetry of the thirties, many of them are very lacking in any direct political reference. "Oh young men, young comrades" disturbed Virginia Woolf when it appeared in *New Signatures*. It is certainly a political poem, but it is also a very Lawrentian poem. It says that it is "too late" for "those financiers like fossils of bones in coal"; but it speaks of renewal in terms of exultance in the body:

> Count rather those fabulous possessions
> which begin with your body and your fiery soul
> the hairs on your head the muscles extending
> in ranges with their lakes across your limbs . . .
> *(New Signatures)*

As has been seen, Lawrence was an important example in the early development of Spender's poetry; and the conjunction of sexual freedom with social and political renewal was a frequent one in the thirties. The importance of Lawrence to the thirties poets arose from the fact that they were revolting against the puritanism of the society in which they were born as much as against its economic system. Spender diagnosed his position:

> I shall have to admit that puritanism may indirectly have started me on a path which has lead to communism; but communism so far from being a revived puritanism resolves . . . the problems arising from puritanism in a synthesis which is far from being puritanical . . . it is an alternative to the extremes of puritanism and a life devoted to the equally purist crusade of eliminating every trace of puritanism from one's being.[3]

The puritan ideal and the ideal of freedom come together in the tone which dominates the group of poems being discussed.

The poems are full of light and wind and unsullied bodily activity; and it is to an attitude of idealistic aspiration that Spender responds most. This was to be found in *Twenty Poems*, particularly in "Beethoven's Death Mask". It is expressed most forcibly in "I think continually of those who were truly great. . . .":

> Near the snow, near the sun, in the highest fields,
> See how these names are feted by the waving grass
> And by the streamers of white cloud
> And whispers of wind in the listening sky.
> The names of those who in their lives fought for life,
> —Who wore at their hearts the flame's centre:
> Born of the sun, they travelled a short while towards the sun
> And left the vivid air signed with their honour.
>
> *(New Signatures)*

Those who are praised are those true to their vision. In the context of poems like "After they have tired of the brilliance of cities . . ." (the next poem written by Spender), "I think continually . . ." might seem to be political. Both poems have similarly intense imagery of light and purification; yet the only "message" spelled out in "I think continually . . ." is:

> What is precious is never to forget
> The essential delight of the blood, drawn from ageless springs
> Breaking through rocks in worlds before our earth.
>
> *(New Signatures)*

The imagery of this poem and of many of Spender's poems is not "modern": indeed, it is traditional to a point that might seem mawkish: ". . . corridors of light where the hours are suns / Endless and singing"; ". . . the Spirit clothed from head to foot in song". The comparison has been made with Shelley; and the comparison suggests a limitation in Spender's world. It is frequently forgotten, however, that Shelley was not only the poet of "Adonais" and "Epipsychidion"; he was also a radical poet, who, throughout the nineteenth century, was the admired poet of English radicalism. In *Forward from Liberalism* (1937), Spender tried to show that Shelley had inadequacies that were related to his not having the true

Marxist social vision; yet, what Spender says of him epitomises very well the mode of his own political poems of the early thirties: "He turns the future communal and just society into a myth and then insists that is is realizable. . . ."[4]

Shelley was, along with Keats, one of the major influences on the poetry of Wilfred Owen. Owen's particular originality was to see in the intense idiom of these writers a means of communicating his own horror and pity concerning war. He evolved a form of poem that combines intense lyricism with intense realism, as in "Strange Meeting", with its echoes of both Shelley and Keats. Spender said of Owen's subject: ". . . if it had not been the War, it might have been the industrial towns, and the distressed areas".[5] The early poem by Spender most reminiscent of Owen is "The Prisoners":

> . . . My pity moves among them like a breeze
> On walls of stone
> Fretting for summer leaves, or like a tune
> On ears of stone. . . .
>
> If I could follow them from room to womb
> To plant some hope
> Through the black silk of the big-bellied gown,
> There would I win.
>
> No, no, no,
> It is too late for anger.
> Nothing prevails
> But pity for the grief they cannot feel.

While the strength of the poem lies in its simplicity and directness, and in the way in which the poet projects his bafflement in rhythms that are constantly being drawn up or made halting, the poem is very far from being a poem of simple realism—or even lyrical realism. At points the poem is phantasmagoric rather than realistic: "The silted flow / Of years on years / Is marked by dawns / As faint as cracks on mud-flats of despair." He speaks of his own generation not resting in pity, but moving to action; yet he is in fact a much more subjective poet than Owen, as he seems to admit when he says: ". . . what I write are fragments of autobiography . . ."[6]

It is the intense subjectivity of these early political poems that is the source of their success. Experience, doctrine, response are all suffused with an intense inner light that gives a unity to the poem. The intensity of the impulse, and the way it is maintained in an unbroken surge through the poem is what carries "Not palaces, an Era's Crown". The poem ends: ". . . Death to the killers, bringing light to life." It is utterly bald and uncompromising in the statement of its sentiments. There is a monolithic certainty, with no suggestion that there might be an alternative view. Standing by itself, the last line is almost hysterical. Yet the reader is carried over and into the final lines, without the feeling that he is being asked to accept something he would prefer to reject or qualify. The sweep of the poem is such that the reader is carried to an emotional pitch where he can understand someone speaking with such certainty and simplicity.

The music of the poems does not depend on the tension between the pattern of the poem and some implied norm of form. These poems succeed by building an overall pattern of rhythm and sound that is sustained at every point: any flagging in intensity (as opposed to modulation of intensity) would deflate them. In this they resemble Lawrence's poems: in a poem like "Snake", we do not feel that tensions are resolved, but that a single impulse has been followed through with complete integrity.

Spender is seldom attracted to set forms. He said that he "wasted time by paying heed to criticism that I had no skill in employing rhyme".[7] It is interesting to consider this in the light of what he says in "The Making of a Poem" about his methods of composition, and in the light, too, of the original drafts of the 1931-2 poems in his manuscript book, "Sketch Book III", where the drafts may be seen evolving into the finished poem. Spender evidently worked by compression. He does not begin, like Eliot and Valéry, with a rhythm that slowly builds into a phrase and then a poem: he is more like Yeats, who began with images. Spender's poems are generally much longer in first draft than in their final version. Furthermore, he does not work merely by cutting out whole sections. Phrases are often combined, and any diffuseness is eliminated. If this can be achieved throughout the poem, then we have one of Spender's successes. His failures are generally marked by a laxness of music and an overdevelopment of individual images.

Spender, like Yeats, had a leaning towards painting rather than music: ". . . the thing I wanted to be almost more than to be a poet was to be a painter when I was young, and painting is a tremendous interest to me. I think I'm really too visual as a writer because I always tend to think of things in terms of painting."[8] In "After they have tired of the brilliance of cities", this visual gift is what makes it one of Spender's finest poems, and one of the most successful political poems of the period. Not only does it have the sweep and intensity of some of its companion poems, but it gets both life and unity from the use that is made of images of whiteness:

> . . . death stalks through life
> Grinning white through all faces
> Clean and equal like the shine from snow.

> . . . the hard light of pain gleams at every street corner, . . .
> . . . our strength is now the strength of our bones
> Clean and equal like the shine from snow . . .

> . . . We have come at last to a country
> Where light equal, like the shine from snow, strikes all faces, . . .

> . . . through torn-down portions of old fabric let their eyes
> Watch the admiring dawn explode like a shell
> Around us, dazing us with light like snow.

The recurrent phrases and imagery not only give unity to the poem, but also give the feeling of transformation, as Spender moves through the various suggestions that white can carry—death; simplicity and nakedness; purification and illumination; exultance, a new dawn.

During this period Spender was reading the poetry of Rilke, and, in 1933, published translations of two of his poems, "Orpheus Eurydice Hermes" (included in *Collected Poems*, 1955), and "Autumn Day" (never republished since its first appearance in *The Spectator* for 28th July, 1933):

> Lord, it is time. The summer was so huge.
> Now lay your shadows on the sundials
> And across the floor let the winds loose.

Command the last fruits to be fine;
Give to them yet two southerly days more;
Drive all their ripeness in and pour
The last sweet drop into the heavy wine.

Who now no home has, builds himself none more.
Who now alone is, he will stay so, long,
He will watch, read, write letters that are long
And through the avenues here and there
When the leaves run, restlessly wander.

Writing later about Rilke, Spender remarked: "Everything comes from an interior life where even the most outside things . . . are given this interior quality."[9] Something like this might be said of Spender's early political poetry; and the influence of Rilke is directly felt in "I Think Continually . . .".

In his writings of this period, Spender felt a conflict between his private and his political feelings. The former were the centre of his emotional life; yet he felt a duty to make his anti-fascism the subject matter of his poetry. The four-part poem *Vienna*, which Spender wrote in 1934, is intended to project the tension that the poet feels between his personal feelings in a love affair, and his feelings concerning the putting down of the Viennese socialists by Dollfus. The tension he is dealing with is one felt by many of the poets of the period, including Auden. The sense of guilt concerning one's private feelings, the feeling that they are irrelevant, are emotions that must have been experienced by most people. Unfortunately, they are neither effectively evoked nor resolved in *Vienna*. The poem is a collection of stylistic mannerisms attempting to grapple with a subject. There is little that can be found good about the writing, with its sloppy rhythms, its over-realised images that clash with one another, and its wandering syntax. Indeed, Spender's poetry in 1934 seems to lack the intensity of the best poems of the previous year or so. The contributions to *New Country* were disappointing; so were nearly all the poems added to *Poems* for the second edition of 1934, the only exception being "Shapes of Death . . .". He was seldom to regain the form he showed before 1933.

Spender's *The Still Centre*, his next collection of poems after the second edition of *Poems* in 1934, was not to appear until three months before the beginning of the war, in May, 1939. Its foreword is subdued and retrospective in tone:

> I think that there is a certain pressure of external events on poets today, making them tend to write about what is outside their own limited experience. The violence of the times we are living in, the necessity of sweeping and general and immediate action, tend to dwarf the experience of the individual, and to make his immediate environment and occupations perhaps something that he is even ashamed of. For this reason, in my most recent poems, I have deliberately turned back to a kind of writing which is more personal, and I have included within my subjects weakness and fantasy and illusion.[10]

There are only ten poems in *The Still Centre* written between 1936 and 1939 that are not about the Spanish Civil War, and only two could be called political. Apart from his poems about the Spanish Civil War, Spender's association with politics was not very fruitful poetically in the late thirties.

In the concluding section of the book, Spender returns to the vein of introspection present in *Twenty Poems* (and intermittently from then on). The first poem in this section is "Darkness and Light", which he prefixed to his autobiography, *World Within World*, in 1951.

> To break out of the chaos of my darkness
> Into a lucid day is all my will.
> My words like eyes in night, stare to reach
> A centre for their light: and my acts thrown
> To distant places by impatient violence
> Yet lock together to mould a path of stone
> Out of my darkness into a lucid day.
>
> Yet, equally, to avoid that lucid day
> And to preserve my darkness, is all my will.
> My words like eyes that flinch from light, refuse
> And shut upon obscurity; my acts
> Cast to their opposites by impatient violence
> Break up the sequent path; they fly
> On a circumference to avoid the centre . . .

Towards the end of *World Within World*, looking back on his

E

childhood, Spender makes some remarks that illuminate this poem and its companions in *The Still Centre*:

> My difficulty was to connect my interior world with any outward activity. At what point did my inner drama enter into relation with the life which surrounded me?

The way out he glimpsed through an acquaintance with the Romantic poets and

> . . . the quality . . . whereby they broke all the rules, diving as it were into the depths of their own isolated being, and fetching up pearls of the creative imagination which had no apparent relation to existing knowledge.[11]

The reconciliation of the private and public self is one that Spender saw as central to the composition of his autobiography, and it is an important theme of these poems of the late thirties. The peculiar intimacy with self, the preoccupation and the sense of being locked in, may have been something Spender shared with his father, who had the habit of addressing himself as "H. S." However, there is a strong feeling of guilt in these poems of introspection—the sort of guilt one might expect in someone who, like Spender, had broken with a highly moralistic tradition in which he had been brought up. This same feeling is more explicit in "Variations on my Life".

> To knock and enter
> Knock and enter
> The room white as paper
> With light falling on a white space
> Through high windows of power
> On hands resting on the controlling table,
> Hands severed from the wrists
> Moving only with the thoughts in fingers . . .

The poem is impressive in a rather ostentatious way: "Hands severed from the wrists / Moving only with the thoughts in fingers" is a powerful image of dissociation, though it does not have the effect of focusing the emotion of the poem. The verse pattern is reminiscent of that of Eliot's "Ash Wednesday", and its sonorities are relished for their own sake to the extent that one feels that the poet is drawing things out. Indeed, diffuseness is a fault of this as of other poems in the last section of *The Still Centre*.

No poem illustrates this better than "The Little Coat". When Spender rewrote this poem for his *Collected Poems* in 1955, he used only the first lines nearly as they were. In re-writing, he considerably compressed and altered the remainder. The first section is excellent in the way in which the feeling is brought out by the imagery. In the third section the imagery, though logically handled, and though intended to evoke a feeling which in essence is not one of clarity, teeters on the edge of the bathetic because the images are close to clashing in their over-realisation. This use of clashing and over-realised images was one of the faults of Spender's poetry of the later thirties.

Along with the general diffuseness and rhythmic slackness of some of these poems, the clash of imagery may have been part of a failure to bring feeling into poetic focus. In addition, Spender, during the late thirties, was tempted to try to combine the career of poet with that of painter. He studied with the Euston Road Group—William Coldstream, Victor Pasmore, Claud Rogers and Graham Bell. (At the same time he was being psychoanalysed.) Perhaps this explains the quality of the poems at the end of *The Still Centre*—both their subject matter and their faults. A painter's preoccupation with the visual for its own sake could lead to a poet's realising his images with a clarity and assertiveness at odds with the need of the subject. It could also lead to the development of individual images at the expense of the orchestration of a poem as a whole. Spender's poetry of the late thirties has both these faults.

II

John Lehmann's second book of poems, *The Noise of History* (1934), was produced in circumstances similar to those in which Spender wrote the important poems in *Poems*. In his introduction, Lehmann wrote:

The poems in this book were written during the latter part of 1931, and 1932, with the exception of the last, which belongs to the beginning of this year. The prose begins in 1933, at the time of the Nazi conquest of power in Germany, and ends soon after the suppression of the February Insurrection in Austria. Much of it was written in Berlin and Vienna.[12]

Both he and Spender developed their political awareness in the presence of the unemployment and the violence in Germany and Austria, symptoms of the convulsions of the society that had never recovered from the Great War. The comparison of Lehmann and Spender is an instructive one. Lehmann's "Like the Wind" is similar to Spender's "In Railway Halls":

> The singers wandering before the door
> Come empty-handed from shut factories;
> Suffering is in their faces, but no greed;
> Their voices are not strong, but like the wind
> Straying in gusts about the littered road.
> Yesterday came three boys from an Alpine village,
> Fair, with brown skins, and one had a violin;
> They moved like twigs that fall in a sluggish river,
> They held out caps for coins and passed by,
> And the violin grew faint, as the voices now;
> To-morrow these too will be gone, but more will come.

Spender's poem begins: "In railway halls, on pavements near the traffic, / They beg, their eyes made big by empty staring . . ."; but it moves quickly off into a typical Spender atmosphere:

> No, I shall weave no tracery of pen-ornament
> To make them birds upon my singing tree:
> Time merely drives these lives which do not live
> As tides push rotten stuff along the shore.

Spender's poem is much more subjective, developing a rhetoric of imagery which evokes the poet's response to the situation, but which has the effect of submerging the situation itself. Lehmann's poem dwells in the actual, recreating the poet's response by the evocation of the situation itself. His poem is more direct, more subdued in diction, less rhetorical, in that it does not work through a figurative use of language in which the figures call attention to themselves. In Spender's poem,

the imagery and language is to be experienced: it gives rise
to the mood. In Lehmann's poem, the language carries us
through to the subject. Here one may recall the influence that
Lehmann said the Georgian poets had on his Cambridge
poetry.

Reference to the Georgians might suggest that the virtues of
Lehmann's poems were largely negative—a firm and unassuming diction, subdued and natural rhythms. In fact, his
poems are a good deal subtler than this would suggest. He
was trying to move beyond the restricted manner of his
undergraduate poetry towards a style that involved "a mingling
of outer and inner, of the beleaguered past and the dissolving
present, of the conscious mind with . . . the deeper intuitive
mind . . ."[13]—trying to become the poet that he felt Rilke
had pictured in *The Notebook of Malte Laurids Brigge*.

Below them, in the street, the linden shook
Raindrops, in sudden pelting, to the ground,
Splashing the hollows in the stones, reflecting
The broken moonglow of the lamp.
But the rain had finished, the cloud birds took
A northward course, warm winds directing.
Across their open window came
The smell of leaves, fresh, damp.

One said: tell me your name.
Why were you standing there alone?
Tomorrow, even, I had planned my train,
But on the bridge I turned, I saw
The slow derisive offer of your mouth.
I had friends waiting, a light heart again,
I was impatient for the lakes, the south;
Now all that's dropped and gone.

Now, as I lean towards your face,
A diver watching the wave smile, so soon
To leap to him, engulf, caress,
I think, still poised—this place
I fix with a falling gesture, I press,
Pressing your lips, a signet of my life,
Imprint deep, deep, this moon, this lamp,
And from the linden, after storm in June,
The smell of leaves, fresh, damp.

The attempt to get the same qualities into political poetry is not so successful. In fact, Lehmann gets little political event into his poems in verse; much more directly political are the "prose poems" he wrote at this time.

Lehmann has given this account of what he was trying to do in these prose poems:

> . . . they came about from a deliberate attempt to write prose poems, a kind of poetry which I think has been very much neglected in this country. It's surprising how very few poets have tried prose poetry in our tradition compared with continental tradition, the tradition of French, Italian and German poetry. *They* are constantly trying. It is very difficult, of course. 'Poetic prose' has a very bad name in our country and rightly, but prose poems are by no means necessarily in 'poetic prose'.[14]

These prose poems were usually vignettes of the life of the time. "Quickened by Horror", from *The Noise of History*, shows how prose pieces of this type might attain a poetic quality and yet be written in a subdued style. It is the unity of atmosphere and the transition of images that make this passage a prose *poem* with an insinuatingly evocative quality:

> In the days before Easter, the haze vanishes early before the sun, and innumerable tips of branches are set glowing with a soft green flame. But when we look out of our windows, we see the trees as if they were dripping blood.
>
> Down there, below the lilac-bushes, rank ivy creeps and sucks among the bulbs of the crocuses. Over the first folded heads of daffodils a shadow seems to hang, that will not turn with the turning light.
>
> A body lies on the cobbles of an industrial city's suburb, covered with a stained green coat, and casts its shadow over these fields. The mind, quickened by horror, darkens here and now with shadows of the images of other time and place.
>
> There is a horror to be fought, to be wrenched away as the ivy is wrenched from the crocus-bulbs by the gardener.
>
> The smooth-running river is foul with the twisting bodies of the massacred beneath its smile of glass. It is poison-gas, the mist that still floats and curls there after the night.
>
> Looking out of our windows, in the days before Easter, we cannot see the soft green flame of Spring, we are obsessed by the red that drips from the ends of the branches.

Lehmann clearly knows the scene from personal experience. In the thirties, Lehmann in fact lived in the Europe of closing frontiers and secret police, and even acted as a secret courier. Nevertheless, he sometimes creates an Eric Ambler atmosphere in his treatment of these themes.

Lehmann may appear a rather pale poet beside some of his friends, because his work is unpretentious and subdued in rhythm and diction; yet it is these unostentatious qualities that give certain of his poems immediacy and lasting power. In the later thirties, when he was editor of *New Writing*, Lehmann wrote very little poetry. It was not until the middle of the Second World War that he began to write freely again.

III

Transitional Poem (1929) was the first of three sequences of poems that constituted Day Lewis's poetic output between 1928 and 1933. The others were *From Feathers to Iron* (1931) and *The Magnetic Mountain* (1933). *Transitional Poem*, in homage to *The Waste Land*, was accompanied by a set of notes as pretentious as those on which they were modelled. The head note gives an idea of the tone of the notes as a whole, and also explains the theme and pattern of the poem:

> The central theme of this poem is the single mind. The poem is divided into four parts, which essentially represent four phases of personal experience in the pursuit of single-mindedness: it will be seen that a transition is intended from one part to the next such as implies a certain spiritual progress and a consequent shifting of aspect. As far as any definitions can be attached to these aspects, they may be termed (1) metaphysical, (2) ethical, (3) psychological; while (4) is an attempt to relate the poetic impulse with the experience as a whole. Normally, the parts fall with fair accuracy into the divisions of the theorem in geometry, *i.e.* general enunciation, particular enunciation, proof, corollaries. The following notes may be of assistance to the diligent; they are intended simply for the elucidation of the text, and do not necessarily imply assent to any proposition that may be advanced in them.[15]

Without the note, it would be hard to recognise the patterns. The poem vacillates between thought dressed up in imagery and imagery that is the means of argument by analogy.

I thought, since love can harness
Pole with contrary pole,
It must be earthed in darkness
Deeper than mine or mole.
Now that I have loved
A while and not gone blind,
I think love's terminals
Are fixed in fire and wind.

(Poem 19)

It is hard to find any steady development in the poem, even though one was apparently intended. The chief poetic models are Yeats and Donne, and their influence is obtrusive. Only the scientific imagery and an occasional touch ("Seventeen months ago / We came to the mine on the moor . . ." [Poem 33]) suggest that Auden had had any influence on his friend. One or two of the lyrics, with their stylish handling of rhythm, still seem lively and individual today:

Come up, Methuselah,
You doddering superman!
Give me an instant realized
And I'll outdo your span.

(Poem 4)

The second of the sequences, *From Feathers to Iron* (1931), is very similar in manner. It deals with Day Lewis's experiences during the nine months before the birth of his first child, and traces his own growing feeling of responsibility and maturity. Looking back on this poem, Day Lewis wrote:

When . . . I was writing *From Feathers to Iron*, . . . I found that my own excitements and apprehensions linked up quite spontaneously with a larger issue—the struggle and joy in which our new world should be born—and derived strength from it, so that I could use naturally for metaphors or metaphysical conceits the apparatus of the modern world, the machinery which, made over for the benefit of all, could help this world to rebirth.[16]

The influence of Auden, to whom the epilogue is addressed, is now more noticeable; but, in this poem, even more than in *Transitional Poem*, the subject is swamped by the imagery.

Now the young challenger, too tired to sidestep,
Hunches to give or take decisive blow.
The climbers from the highest camp set out
Saying goodbye to comrades on the glacier,
A day of rock between them and the summit
That will require their record or their bones.
Now is a charge laid that will split the hill-face,
Tested the wires, the plunger ready to hand.
For time ticks nearer to a rebel hour,
Charging of barricades, bloodshed in city:
The watcher in the window looking out
At the eleventh hour on sun and shadow,
On fixed abodes and the bright air between,
Knows for the first time what he stands to lose.

(Poem 27)

Who would imagine that this was from a poem about the last few days of waiting for the birth of a child? The lack of connection between subject and imagery goes hand in hand with the prevalence of pastiche and the general unsureness of tone. The sequence contains what is perhaps the most gauchely snobbish expression of political-cultural renewal to be found in the whole period: ". . . Petty-officer be rapt in the Seventh Symphony . . ." (Poem 29). Once again, it is one or two lyrics that redeem the sequence.

The Magnetic Mountain (1933) is a political poem, and the influence of Auden predominates, so that any authentic voice Day Lewis had is stifled. Day Lewis has said that he was writing "revolutionary poems" before he joined the Communist Party;[17] and it seems unlikely that he was a member when *The Magnetic Mountain* appeared. The poem is an amalgam of Marxism, Christianity and D. H. Lawrence. He adopts the mythology of Auden's early poetry: the frontier as dividing the degenerate society from a renewed world; the notions of the Adversary and of the feud; the landscape of industrial ruin; and the symbol of the kestrel, a bird to be met with in Auden's *Poems*, which seems to be associated by Day Lewis with the airman of *The Orators* and with Auden himself. The sequence takes its title from the image of the magnetic mountain in the world of truth and renewal beyond the frontier:

> Somewhere beyond the railheads
> Of reason, south or north,
> Lies a magnetic mountain
> Riveting sky to earth.
>
> No line is laid so far.
> Ties rusting in a stack
> And sleepers—dead men's bones—
> Mark a defeated track.
>
> Kestrel who yearly changes
> His tenement of space
> At the last hovering
> May signify that place. . . .
>
> Oh there's a mine of metal,
> Enough to make me rich
> And build right over chaos
> A cantilever bridge.
>
> (Poem 3)

It is clear that the imagery of Auden's early poetry, which was not connected primarily with political ideas, has here been given a political interpretation.

A Time to Dance, Day Lewis's next volume, was completed in November, 1934, though it was published in 1935. By this time Day Lewis was a member of the C.P.G.B. It is perhaps his least congenial book, and one of the least attractive collections produced by a poet of any talent in the thirties. This is partly due to the naïve crudity of outlook behind the poetry, which manifests itself in poetic effects of a vulgarity that one feels only a blinkered sensibility could allow to go to print.

The volume takes its title from a long poem that occupies most of the book. The poem is subtitled "a symphonic poem", and is in several sections, into some of which short poems have been built. The whole is intended as a memorial to Lionel Hedges, a fellow master at Cheltenham, where Day Lewis was teaching—a man a little older than Day Lewis, and a county cricketer, a fact that was the source of a good deal of the admiration for him. The dead man is remembered by ". . . not a dirge, not a funeral anthem, / But words to match his mirth, a theme with a happy end . . ." This notion of remembering his friend by a celebration of the spirit that he exemplified is the most congenial thing about the book.

A Time to Dance is an intermediate volume between *Transitional Poem*, *From Feathers to Iron* and *Magnetic Mountain*, in which a unifying theme is treated obliquely and metaphorically through a sequence of poems; and Day Lewis's work since the end of the thirties, in which personal experience is dealt with more directly in unconnected short poems. The "symphonic poem", with its narrative section telling the story of the famous flight of Parer and MacIntosh from England to Australia in a D.H.9 after the Great War, marks an abandonment of the "philosophic" ambition behind the long poetic sequences of the earlier volumes. It looks forward to "Nabara", the narrative of the Spanish Civil War; to the translation of the *Aeneid*; and, regrettably, to the ghastly "Flight to Italy" (1953).

The narrative is presented in regular rhyming stanzas containing some short lines, but with a basic line that might be described in the terms Day Lewis uses to describe the metre of his translation of the *Aeneid*: ". . . a six-stress one, which enables me to protract a line to at least 17 syllables or contract it to 12 . . ."[18] The model for the versification seems to be Hopkins's sprung rhythm. The choice of verse form and the pacing of the material are good: the story of the flight is exciting, and Day Lewis gets that excitement. One wants to know what happens next, even if the adventures are a bit *"Boys' Own Paper"*.

It is in matters of detail that the poem seems least successful. In introducing his translation of the *Aeneid*, Day Lewis speaks of ". . . introducing here and there a sharp bold colloquialism, or a deliberate cliché which might stimulate by appearing in an unfamiliar context".[19] As in the translation of Virgil, the effect is of a deliberate jazzing up of the poetry. In "A Time to Dance", while magnetos are called magnetos, and compasses, compasses, the subject is poeticised with the conventional rhetoric of aspiration usual in Day Lewis's poetry, this time with a Hopkinsesque flavour. Indeed, the rather blatant pastiche of Hopkins is one of the off-putting features of the poem, which might, for its style, be called "The Flight of the Deutschland".

> Sing we the two lieutenants, Parer and M'Intosh,
> After the War wishing to hie them home to Australia,
> Planned they would take a high way, a hazardous crazy
>   air-way: . . .

In Day Lewis's handling of contemporary imagery there is not the naturalness that would make one feel that he had achieved fully the imaginative absorption of the industrial landscape that was felt to be a mark of his work. The "new" imagery is handled like conventional poetic imagery, as though to be "modern" the poetry merely had to undergo a change of interior decoration. This produces some staggering unintentional lapses of taste in the elegiac section of the poem; and there are some remarkable metaphors that are "mixed", not merely in the sense of being ancient and modern:

> . . . Let the masked batteries of spring flash out
> From ridge and copse, and flowers like shrapnel burst
> Along the lanes, and all her land-mines spout
> Quick and hanging green.

The insensitivity of the clashing connotations of the imagery and the overall vulgarity of the writing cannot here be connected with ideological simplification. They reflect a conventional and limiting conception of poetry—a feeling that a subject does not become "poetic" until it is dressed out in gratuitous metaphors and similes. Day Lewis of the "shrapnel" and "land-mines" is merely the conventional poet turned upside down—the "unpoetic" put in the place of the conventionally poetic. The quality of the sensibility from which his poetry proceeds is caught in a poem where he feels that modern imagery is not called for, "The Ecstatic":

> . . . Buoyed, embayed in heaven's noon-wide reaches—
> For soon light's tide will turn—Oh stay!
> Cease not till day streams to the west, then down
> That estuary drop down to peace.

It is this conventional sensibility that vitiates the political poems in the volume, just as much as does the crude simplicity of outlook. There is plenty of evidence of the latter in the third section of "A Time to Dance":

As the tape-worm they relent not, as the hook-worm
   they pity not; more vile than blowflies, insidious
   as the ichneumon and like the trypansome in
   their multiplying—these, the deadly exploiters.

．　．　．

The director placing explosives under the infant's
   cradle, the editor keeping a nursery for snakes: . . .

Day Lewis himself became quite aware of how bad the type
of poetry in this section is, and for that reason rejected it.
In his autobiography he wrote, presumably alluding principally
to *A Time to Dance*:

> . . . it is significant that the only two political poems of any
> value which I wrote—"The Conflict" and "In me Two Worlds"
> —though they end with a confident statement of the choice
> made, are poems of the divided mind, while the shrill, school-
> boyish derisiveness which served for satire in other political
> verse of mine demonstrates the unnatural effort I had to make
> in order to avoid seeing both sides.[20]

It is hard, however, to feel that there is much to be said even
for the poems that Day Lewis names. They are too full of
the rhetoric of "effort and expectation and desire" that informs
so much of his political poetry:

> . . . These have the spirit's range,
> The measure of the mind:
> Out of the dawn their fire comes fast
> To conquer and to change.
>
> So heir and ancestor
> Pursue the inveterate feud,
> Making my senses' darkened fields
> A theatre of war.

Quite apart from the monotonous, exhorting rhythm and the
clichés passed off as poetry, the poems hardly mirror the
divided mind that they speak of. Although they are spiced
with unconventional "modern" images, such as "blood's
. . . semaphore", they are all of a piece with the inveterate

politeness that characterises Day Lewis's poetry. In his "Letter to a Young Revolutionary" in *New Country* he had written:

> It is easy enough to despise the trappings and trimmings of one's own class; and a sight more difficult, I imagine, to discard them in the eyes of another class. You are a very charming person, you know, and your manners are terribly good.[21]

This applied rather pointedly to himself.

The conventional nature of the sensibility is borne out by another group of poems in *A Time to Dance*, the "light" poems. In all the shorter poems in the volume there is evidently an attempt to attain to the simpler more popular style that the Left ideology of the day seemed to call for. An example is "Johnny Head-in-Air", written in ballad form in a style that from time to time recalls "The Rime of the Ancient Mariner". In the third section of "A Time to Dance" there are a number of attempts at light verse, some of which recall Auden's *The Dance of Death*. These poems are ham-fisted and unsuccessful. However, among this group of poems are three parodies, one of them of Jane Elliot's "Lament for Flodden", more commonly known as "The Flowers of the Forest":

> I've heard them lilting at loom and belting,
> Lasses lilting before dawn of day:
> But now they are silent, not gamesome and gallant—
> The flowers of the town are rotting away.

Here Day Lewis's touch seems more sensitive. He is more at home, because, in parody, a main element is the imitation of the original style, and Day Lewis evidently finds this light romantic style congenial. There is less sense of strain than in the straight poems.

Day Lewis left the C.P.G.B. in 1938. Addressing a large political meeting, he suddenly felt a revulsion for the self that engaged in political activities, and resentment at the way in which it depleted the energies that were available to what he felt to be his true self, the poet.

> It was not that I was disillusioned in Communism, or even that my initial enthusiasm had, like so many of my enthusiasms in

the past, too rapidly burnt itself out, but that I was giving far more time and energy than I could afford to political work. . . . If my poetry had gained by the enlargement of my interests, it was now losing because of the many distractions this broader life had brought with it.[22]

His development away from the party can be traced in *Overtures to Death* (1938), his next collection of poems. Aside from "Nabara", "Bombers" and "Volunteer", poems on the Spanish Civil War, there are only two distinctly political poems from this period of Day Lewis's most intense political activity: "Newsreel", which had appeared in *Left Review*; and "Sonnet for a Political Worker", which shows by contrast how unpolitical the rest of the book is. The poems that give the book its name are a set of seven, originally published in *New Writing* for spring, 1938, as "Addresses to Death". They form a somewhat long-winded, diffuse sequence, reminiscent of Day Lewis's sequences of the early thirties, but they capture the sombre mood of the time. Political blame is apportioned in the usual way; but there is little doctrine in the poem, just as there is little feeling that anything can be done to put off disaster.

The first really striking poem in the book is "In the Heart of Contemplation", which appeared in *The Listener* for 1st September, 1937.

> In the heart of contemplation—
> Admiring, say, the frost-flowers of the white lilac,
> Or lark's song busily sifting like sand-crystals
> Through the pleased hourglass an afternoon of summer,
> Or your beauty, dearer to me than these—
> Discreetly a whisper in the ear,
> The glance of one passing my window recall me
> From lark, lilac, you, grown suddenly strangers.

This poem seems to have been a turning point for Day Lewis. Though it has a political meaning in the context in which it was written, and appears to advocate the doctrinaire choice, "action", it is really a poem about one of Day Lewis's perennial themes, the divided self. The rhythms and imagery are very different from the strident rhythms and "up-to-date" images

of his poetry of the early thirties. Both rhythm and rhyme
are muted to give the effect of intimate self-address rather
than of public exhortation. There is a delicacy and a finish
that had not been a feature of his poetry before.

From this time Day Lewis's themes become increasingly
personal, with a concomitant improvement of his poetry.
One of the last poems in *Overtures to Death* is "Passage from
Childhood", a poem that in form and mood looks forward
to the poems in which Day Lewis explores his early recollections
in *Word Over All* (1943), the book in which he seems most
fully himself.

> His earliest memory, the mood
> Fingered and frail as maidenhair,
> Was this—a china cup somewhere
> In a green, deep wood.
> He lives to find again somewhere
> That wood, that homely cup; to taste all
> Its chill, imagined dews; to dare
> The dangerous crystal.

IV

A poet whose political poems exemplify even more than do
those of Day Lewis the split between ideas and sensibility
is Rex Warner, whose *Poems* appeared in 1937. Warner had
been a close friend of Day Lewis at Oxford, and has, later in
life, become known as a classical scholar. In the thirties he
was a Communist and a contributor to *New Country*, *Left
Review* and *New Writing*. He was better known for his novels,
which appeared in the late thirties and early forties. In the
first of them, *The Wild Goose Chase*, the theme of the quest is
given an effective political adaptation, with an atmosphere
between Kafka and Bunyan.

Warner has recalled that he was one of the first people at
Oxford to read Hopkins.[23] There is not a great deal that shows
Hopkins's influence in Warner's contributions to *Oxford
Poetry*, but, in *Poems*, he is clearly an admirer of Hopkins, to
the point, at times, of pastiche.

There are two important groups of poems in Warner's
book: the political poems, and the poems about birds.

"Chough", one of the simplest and best of the poems about birds, is a valid and touching poem, with that particularity that is the sign of something actually experienced. To say that it is a poem of conventional sensibility—a poem showing that detailed knowledge of flora and fauna characteristic of Englishmen of good class—is no denigration of it.

> Desolate that cry as though world were unworthy.
> See now, rounding the headland, a forlorn hopeless bird,
> trembling black wings fingering the blowy air,
> dainty and ghostly, careless of the scattering salt.

> This is the cave-dweller that flies like a butterfly,
> buffeted by daws, almost extinct, who has chosen,
> so gentle a bird, to live on furious coasts.

> Here where sea whistles in funnels, and slaps the back
> of burly granite slabs, and hisses over holes,
> in bellowing hollows that shelter the female seal
> the Cornish chough wavers over the waves.

> By lion rocks, rocks like the heads of queens,
> sailing with ragged plumes upturned, into the wind
> goes delicate indifferent the doomed bird.

The extent to which this sensibility is not engaged by politics is shown by a comparison with the next poem. What success it has comes from the directness and bareness with which the simplistic attitudes are stated. Even if one did not object to the simplification of life implied by these sentiments—and it is easy to sympathise with them in the light of the events of the period—one still has the feeling that they are "dragged into prominence" (to adapt a phrase of Marianne Moore).

> So that men might remain slaves, and that the little good
> they hoped for might be turned all bad and the iron lie
> stamped and clamped on growing tender and vigorous truth
> these machine guns were despatched from Italy.

> So that the drunken General and the Christian millionaire
> might continue blindly to rule in complete darkness,
> that on rape and ruin order might be founded firm,
> these guns were sent to save civilisation.

Lest the hand should be held at last more valuable than paper,
lest man's body and mind should be counted more than gold,
lest love should blossom, not shells, and break in the land
these machine guns came from Christian Italy.

And to root out reason, lest hope be held in it,
to turn love inward into corroding hate,
lest men should be men, for the bank-notes and the mystery
these guns, these tanks, these gentlemanly words.

("Arms in Spain")

The rhetoric is one of submerged cliché: "iron . . . stamped
and clamped"; "love . . . blossom".

One of his few successful political poems underlines his
difficulties as a political poet:

How sweet only to delight in lambs and laugh by streams,
innocent in love wakening to the early thrush,
to be awed by mountains, and feel the stars friendly,
to be a farmer's boy, to be far from battle.

But me my blood binds to remember men
more than the birds, not to be delicate with squirrels,
or gloat among the poppies in a mass of corn,
or follow in a maze endless unwinding of water.

Nor will my mind permit me to linger in the love,
the motherkindness of country among ascending trees,
knowing that love must be liberated by bleeding,
fearing for my fellows, for the murder of man.

How should I live then but as a kind of fungus,
or else as one in strict training for desperate war?

The phrase "the motherkindness of country among ascending
trees" might have been written by Rupert Brooke. The poem
is successful because Warner is able to write about the things
he genuinely responds to; and the tension in it arises from
his sincere feeling that he should reject them. All the same,
the "lambs" seem to dominate the impression the poem leaves
when one has put the book down.

v

One of the most recurrently discussed topics of left-wing
poetic criticism in the thirties was the relationship of the
poet and poetry to politics. It can be argued, of course, as

it was then, that politics are unavoidable and that every poem is hence a political act, even if it ignores politics. More unexceptionably it can be suggested that, in a decade where political concerns were obvious in every area of life, no poem could be free of political implication. There are many poems discussed in this book that would seem to contradict this position; though it would have to be admitted that a great deal of the poetry of the period that is not overtly political draws strength and sustenance from the political concerns of its authors. Some of the most moving poetry of the decade was written, in fact, by poets who were weighing and questioning the demands of their political beliefs and their capacity to respond to them: Auden's "Summer Night" and Bernard Spencer's "A Cold Night" are two striking instances. The contending demands of the personal and public concerns of the poet—sometimes associated with the conflict between the middle-class liberal cultural heritage in which the poet has been educated and the political beliefs he has embraced—are a frequent theme, as in Bell's "Bypass to Utopia", Allott's "Men Walk Upright", Day Lewis's "In the Heart of Contemplation", and Swingler's "Sussex in Winter". Such weighing and questioning was not acceptable to the orthodox Marxist. If the Marxist view of history was correct, then the poet who accepted Communism and wrote out of that acceptance was writing out of what was most vital in the present. The vexed question was the extent to which the poet was to be committed to Marxism in the actual writing of his poetry. Stephen Spender, in the essay he contributed to *New Country* in 1933, stood out for the independence of the poet and for the autonomy of the poem. The young Communist poet, John Cornford, writing about that essay in *Cambridge Left* for Winter, 1933–4, held that ". . . Spender adheres to the doctrine that has become fundamental to the bourgeois writers of our epoch—the contradiction between art and life, between the life of the artist and the life of society". His premise was that "the traditional artist's 'impartiality' is unmasked as a denial of the class struggle . . .". The poet could only write truly revolutionary poetry "by direct participation in the revolutionary struggles". In a similar vein, Montagu Slater attacked Day Lewis in *Left Review* (July, 1935) in an article entitled "The

Fog Beneath the Skin". This division of opinion, while a very real one, was by its nature fruitless, and seems to have had no obvious poetic manifestations, except in so far as poets of little talent, but strong persuasion, found themselves more and more committed to emotionally crass attitudes.

More interesting are the implications of another of Cornford's remarks. He speaks of ". . . a very dangerous attempt to deck out the old class literature in new revolutionary-utopian trappings, . . . to make a literary fashion of 'revolution' among bourgeois intellectuals while denying the possibility of growth of a genuinely revolutionary literature with a new class-basis."[24] This last phrase, "a genuinely revolutionary literature", was one of the cant phrases of the period. What it would be like nobody seemed to know; though, as Day Lewis remarked in "Revolutionaries and Poetry", "The tradition of poetry for the last hundred years has been developed by a dominating class, the bourgeois. . . . The worker poet at present has to write in a tradition not built for the material he wishes to put into it."[25] The remedy, "direct participation in revolutionary activity", was always clear; though it was by no means so clear that all "participants" produced poetry that was revolutionary in anything other than sentiment. However, there was more truth to these ideas than those who voiced them perhaps imagined.

The poetry of revolution frequently betrayed the conventionality of its idiom in its imagery, as it did in the work of Day Lewis. Randall Swingler, an editor of *Left Review* and a much more died-in-the wool Communist than Day Lewis, frequently turns to images of dawn and fertility—the conventional poetic images of hope and new life—in writing about revolutionary themes:

> Acres of power within me lie,
> Charted fields of wheat and rye
> And behind them, charted too,
> Brooding woods of beech and yew.
> Beyond them stretch, uncharted yet,
> Marsh and mountain, dark and wet,
> Whence sometimes in my dream and ease
> Strange birds appear among the trees.
> (*New Writing* V (Spring, 1938) 197)

The poem from which this is taken, "Acres of Power", is, within its limitations, quite an acceptable poem. Poetry of this type was, at the time of its writing, often preferred by ordinary readers to poetry more genuinely modern and adventurous. Politics, not very "poetic", is made "poetic" by the poet's imagery. However, this is not the objection to this type of poetry. Given that "mountains" suggest aspiration; "glaciers", elemental energy; "spring", joy; "wheat", fertility; etc.; there is no reason why one should not write in this way about the Salvation Army, vegetarianism, fascism, the euphoria of drug-taking, sex . . . the list can go on for ever. The imagery has no root in the attitudes and emotions that particularise the poem. It is a version of the conventional imagery of hope, joy, energy and aspiration. Some of the superiority of Auden's "Spain", or of poems like his "Here on the cropped grass . . .", derives from the fact that they take an actual situation for their starting point, and that both the attitudes and the sensory elements of the poems have their roots in that situation. The same may be said in some measure of the early poems of Spender and Lehmann.

Allen Tate summed up the poetic problems of writing political poetry very well in reviewing Spender's *Poems* for *New Verse* in May, 1933:

> It is one of the defects of revolutionary thought, in this age, so far as poetry is concerned, that it is not assimilable to any great body of sensuous forms. It was possible for Shelley to imagine, at least, that he was rewriting the classical mythology. Our own contemporaries have the gospel according to Father Marx, certain passages of which are almost as moving as Dickens; most of it is merely engaging dialectically, leaving the young humanitarian to flounder in an opaque mass of abstraction that is not easily translated into the mere physical objects that the distressed Platonist, in all times, is compelled to see. The raw initiate into the Society of Friends would suffer, as poet, a similar disability. (*NV* 3, p. 21)

VI

The presentation of *New Signatures* and *New Country* in an earlier chapter brought out the distinction between them as it appeared to contemporaries in retrospect. However, though *New Signatures* as a volume may not appear overtly political, it contained in the contributions of Spender, Lehmann and Day Lewis poems that were decidedly political when presented in other contexts. *New Country* is seen as the volume that marks the emergence of left-wing poetry in England in the thirties. Certainly, it marks the beginning of public awareness of this poetry. However, there is a sense in which it is the culmination of the first phase of the political poetry of the decade. Spender and Lehmann had written their best political poetry by the end of 1932; Auden and Day Lewis, as well as Spender and Lehmann, wrote little political poetry after the end of 1934, until the period of the Popular Front and the Spanish Civil War in the later thirties.

The political poetry of the early thirties might be called apocalyptic. It was a poetry of change and renewal. Though Communist in sympathy, it was only vaguely doctrinaire before the end of 1932. Social renewal was frequently associated with sexual freedom, just as the old, moribund society was associated for these writers with puritanism. For Spender and Warner, social renewal had a Lawrentian tone. Day Lewis took the setting and the imagery of Auden's early poetry—the frontier, the feud, the glaciers, the moribund society—and, clothing it in the conventional rhetoric of change and renewal, gave it a political meaning; though, once again, the demand for political renewal is embedded in a longing for a vague, general revitalisation. Auden himself abandoned the setting and imagery of his early poetry, though he retained the notion of a moribund society that fears change, giving it a Marxist and a Freudian interpretation. Lehmann also wrote of renewal, but he did not develop a Romantic quasi-mythology to embody his vision. His frontiers are the actual frontiers of the Europe he knew.

This poetry had its origins in the desire for change that was felt by young intellectuals after the collapse of the Labour government in 1931. The imagery of this early apocalyptic poetry is that of the new technology, which the poets evidently associated with the transformation of life that they longed for. As they became more doctrinairely Left, the new technology became suspect as a tool for the exploitation or deception of

the working class. The desire for change was, in the beginning,
potentially right-wing as well as left-wing, as the admiration
of D. H. Lawrence and the hero-worship of *The Orators* shows.
In this respect, these intellectuals had much in common
with the intellectuals of the Weimar Republic, which several
of them visited and admired. In the Germany of the time there
was an attractive abandonment of puritanical standards; a
great cultural flowering in the work of artists like Brecht,
Hesse, Kokoschka, Kandinsky, Klee and Gropius; and an
insistent longing for change and renewal. There, very soon,
"the Old Gang" were to rally under the leadership of the
puritanical, artistically conservative Hitler. Premonitions of
what this might mean had something to do with the English
poets turning strongly to the Left.

   This turn to the Left on the part of the younger British
intellectuals—especially the literary ones—took place during
the period when the official Communist policy was one of
"united front from below", and when there was no overt
attempt to come to terms with the educated middle classes.
Ironically, this first phase of left-wing political poetry, during
which Auden, Spender, Day Lewis and Lehmann wrote the
larger part of their political poetry, came to an end on the
eve of the adoption by the Comintern of a policy of a "united"
(later "popular") front. By the time the movement for a
popular front had got going in the late thirties, these poets
were writing less enthusiastically and less frequently on
overtly political themes. It was only the Spanish Civil War
that seemed to stir the old fire.

Chapter 7

MARX, FREUD AND CHRIST

W. H. Auden and Communism – *Look Stranger!* – W. H. Auden in the late thirties

AT A TIME when frontiers were about to become an important symbol in connection with the growing barbarism, oppression and restriction of personal freedom, Auden, as was clear from his contributions to *New Country*, abandoned his mythology of feuds and frontiers (which had, in fact, had little or nothing to do with politics). At the same time, Auden's poetry became overtly political; and from late 1932 to the end of 1934 seems to have been the period of his greatest sympathy with Communism.

New Country contained a poem, "Prologue", which was to appear again in 1936 as the prologue to *Look Stranger!* It is the poem most directly expressive of Auden's new outlook:

> O love, the interest itself in thoughtless Heaven
> Make simpler daily the beating of man's heart; within
> There in the ring where name and image meet
>
> Inspire them with such a longing as will make his thought
> Alive like patterns a murmuration of starlings
> Rising in joy over wolds unwittingly weave;
>
> Here too on our little reef display your power, . . .
>
> .   .   .
>
> For now that dream which so long has contented our will,
> I mean, of uniting the dead into a splendid empire,
> Under whose fertilising flood the Lancashire moss
>
> Sprouted up chimneys and Glamorgan hid a life
> Grim as a tidal rock-pool's in its glove-shaped valleys,
> Is already retreating into her maternal shadow;
>
> Leaving the furnaces gasping in the impossible air
> The flotsam at which Dumbarton gapes and hungers,
> While upon wind-loved Rowley no hammer shakes

The cluster of mounds like a midget golf course, graves
Of some who created these intelligible dangerous marvels;
Affectionate people, but crude their sense of glory.

. . .

Yet, O, at this very moment of their hopeless sigh

. . .

Some dream, say yes, long coiled in the ammonite's slumber
Is uncurling, prepared to lay on our talk and kindness
Its military silence, its surgeon's idea of pain.

Those who created the "intelligible dangerous marvels" are
clearly the capitalists, who, in Communist theory and in
the poem, are seen as a declining class. The descendants of
the early capitalists are in fact a decadent class who

          . . . inertly wait
     In bar, in netted chicken-farm, in lighthouse,
     Standing on these impoverished constricting acres,
     The ladies and gentlemen apart, too much alone.

The description is reminiscent of Auden's presentation, in
Poems and *The Orators*, of the middle classes as doomed. However, after 1932, the psychological perversion associated with
social disintegration and decadence is not explained in terms
of theories derived from Lawrence and Lane, but in Freudian
terms. The conjunction of Marx and Freud, while not an
obvious one, is a natural one. Both thinkers contend that the
unhappiness of civilised life is caused by human institutions:
for Marx, these are economic institutions; for Freud, the
perverting institutions are human mores. Both believe that
adjustment (of social institutions or of the human psyche)
will bring the desired condition: for Marx, the classless society;
for Freud, normality.

However, it is "Love" that is invoked in "Prologue";
and here it is clearly not primarily erotic love. "Love" was
to be one of Auden's favourite words in the thirties, but it
was to be one of his vaguest. At times it stood for erotic love;
at other times for loving one's neighbour; and at other times
still it had the best of these impulses by confusing them. In

"Prologue", human solidarity of a Communist type is identified with the Christian love of one's neighbour.

Auden's new scheme of ideas is made explicit in an essay, "The Good Life", that he contributed to a symposium, *Christianity and the Social Revolution*, in 1935.

> The two commandments of loving God and thy neighbour imply that the good life is a product, and only a product, of an attitude of complete love and faith toward both. . . . The development of self-consciousness in man marked a break with the rest of the organic world. Henceforward the conscious image or idea could interfere and govern the unconscious impulse which had hitherto governed it. What we call evil is a consequence of this. . . . Psychology and Communism have certain points in common:
> (1) They are both concerned with unmasking hidden conflicts.
> (2) Both regard these conflicts as inevitable stages which must be made to negate themselves.
> (3) Both regard thought and knowledge not as something spontaneous and self-sufficient; but as purposive and determined by the conflict between instinctive needs and a limited environment. . . .
> (4) Both desire and believe in the possibility of freedom of action and choice, which can only be obtained by unmasking and making conscious the hidden conflict. . . .
> Communism is the only political theory that really holds the Christian position of the absolute equality in value of every individual, and the evil of all State restraint.[1]

The poem in which Auden's political attitudes at the time are most fully developed is "The Malverns" ("Here on the cropped grass of the narrow ridge I stand . . ."), originally published in November, 1933, and included as Poem XVII in *Look Stranger!* The conjunction of Marxism and "Love" is made in the last four lines:

> These moods give no permission to be idle,
> For men are changed by what they do;
> And through loss and anger the hands of the unlucky
>   Love one another.

"For men are changed by what they do . . ." echoes the words of Engels. The middle-class English of Auden's day are seen as the inheritors of a bankrupt tradition. They have the same longing for death as had the society of *The Orators*, though this now seems to be associated with the Freudian "death wish". The vision of the poem is presented explicitly by "the bones of war" that speak "out of the turf":

> But pompous, we assumed their power to be our own,
> Believed machines to be our hearts' spontaneous fruit,
> Taking our premises as shoppers take a tram.
>
> While the disciplined love which alone could have
>   employed these engines
> Seemed far too difficult and dull, and when hatred
>   promised
> An immediate dividend, all of us hated.

The cultivation of the private life was seen by Auden, as by many left-wing intellectuals in the thirties, as an evasion of public responsibility. This is presented by Auden in terms of a clash between the two meanings of the word "love": erotic love and love of one's neighbour; "eros" and "agape". This clash is at the heart of some of his few political poems of the period: "Me, March, you do with your movements master and rock . . ." in *New Country* (later Poem XV in *Look Stranger!*); "Easily, my dear, you move, easily your head . . ." (Poem XXI); and, most notably, "Summer Night" (Poem II), which first appeared in *The Listener* for 7th March, 1934.

This poem is the most celebrated expression of the dilemma of the middle-class intellectual in the thirties:

> For what by nature and by training
> We loved, has little strength remaining:
>   Though we would gladly give
> The Oxford colleges, Big Ben,
> And all the birds in Wicken Fen,
>   It has no wish to live.

The traditions with which they had grown up, and which embody all they have learned to value, they must reject because they are moribund. Similarly, it is these traditions and their material surroundings which make possible the cultivated personal life, which must also be viewed suspectly because it may constitute a temptation to ignore the historical necessities of the public life of politics:

> The creepered wall stands up to hide
> The gathering multitudes outside
>   Whose glances hunger worsens;
> Concealing from their wretchedness
> Our metaphysical distress,
>   Our kindness to ten persons.

What makes the poem so compelling is the warm and vivid evocation in its opening of the English scene: for this Auden has an intimate and particularised feeling. In contrast, the conclusion of the poem is vague, and little more than a pious hope that things will be better:

> May this for which we dread to lose
> Our privacy, need no excuse
>   But to that strength belong;
> As through a child's rash happy cries
> The drowned voice of his parents rise
>   In unlamenting song.
>
> After discharges of alarm,
> All unpredicted may it calm
>   The pulse of nervous nations;
> Forgive the murderer in his glass,
> Tough in its patience to surpass
>   The tigress her swift motions.

What "this" is is not altogether clear; and how it might "to that strength belong" is the crux of the poem's dilemma. The stanza form (that of Smart's "A Song to David", which is echoed in the last stanza) is not well suited to a poem of continuous meditation. It is interesting that, in the stanza where Auden tries to bring the poem to a resolution in his rather vague hope, the stanza form trips him into a grammatical clash. Auden seems to be pushing himself here.

There are other points in the poem where the language makes one suspicious of the inspiration. The first stanza ends ". . . my feet / Point to the rising moon." The form is again obtrusive, as "feet" is given an unduly emphatic position. In addition, read in the most unsympathetically critical manner, the information about where Auden's feet are pointing might seem inanely gratuitous. Yet the lines just come off, because their relaxed manner is a part of the general relaxedness that gives the poem such charm. However, a little later, we come on some very mixed writing of this sort:

> Moreover, eyes in which I learn
> That I am glad to look, return
>   My glances every day;
> And when the birds and rising sun
> Waken me, I shall speak with one
>   Who has not gone away.
>
> Now North and South and East and West
> Those I love lie down to rest;
>   The moon looks on them all:
> The healers and the brilliant talkers,
> The eccentrics and the silent walkers,
>   The dumpy and the tall.

The first of these stanzas is guilefully simple, yet highly effective. The last three lines quoted show Auden's customary gift for evoking the particular with a tremendous suggestion of generality. "The dumpy and the tall" is just the right variation on "short/tall" to make it come alive, to give a fruitful interplay between the words. The enumeration of the four points of the compass, however, is mock-naïve padding. This manner presses towards a simplification and sentimentalisation of the situation, without openly recognising that it does so. Similarly, in a later stanza there is a mock-Shakespearean synecdoche in the lines: "And, gentle, do not care to know, / Where Poland draws her Eastern bow, / What violence is done; . . ." Does it not, in fact, cunningly "distance" the dilemma the poet purports to be facing?

There is something altogether devious about the poem. Its very virtuosity betrays it, because those aspects of the situation that are most evocatively rendered are the ones Auden suggests he is rejecting. The dominant response evoked by the poem is one of nostalgia for the upper middle-class life that is found insufficient. This no doubt accounts for its popularity; and it is also what makes it a classical expression of the mood of the times. The tone is a frequent one in Auden's poetry in the middle thirties; but the devious poetic strategies, the softness behind the marvellous aplomb, are also characteristic. Auden's aplomb often got the better of him: the temptation "to ruin a fine tenor voice / For effects that bring down the house" was one Auden no doubt understood well.

Look Stranger! constitutes the high-water mark of Auden's political poetry, and the vision of experience that it projects is one that was enriched by the political ideas, even when they were not directly expressed. However, the overtly political poems were nearly all written well before the appearance of the book in 1936. Except for "Spain" (1937) and the poems in *A Journey to a War* (1939) and the small amount of verse in the pot-boiling *On the Frontier* (1938), Auden wrote little political poetry after the end of 1934. "Letter to Lord Byron" (in *Letters from Iceland* (1937)) is brilliant and wide ranging in its social commentary; yet its very congeniality and wit suggest a lessening of political engagement, and leave one disinclined to speak of it as "political poetry". The very generalised philosophical response of the sonnets in *Journey to a War*, in the face of the opportunity to write out of first-hand experience of an anti-fascist war, attests to Auden's growing estrangement from the political struggles. It was evidently difficult for Auden to love the working-class comrades:

> . . . A digit of the crowd, would like to know
> Them better whom the shops and trams are full of,
> The little men and their mothers, not plain but
>   Dreadfully ugly.
>   (Poem XVII, *Look Stranger!*)

II

If one could have only one book of poetry from the thirties, *Look Stranger!* (1936) would be a natural choice. Certainly, if one were allowed only one of Auden's books, this would be the one to go for—at once the most felicitous and the most representative of his variety. Auden had intended to call the book *On this Island* (the title used in America); and the choice seems to indicate an awareness of how English the book was. To a contemporary reader it must have been a revelation to see traditional forms like the sonnet, the sestina, the song, revived and given all the new life of modernity. There are only a few

poems in the book that are not written in regular stanza
forms. Auden had never been an exponent of free verse; and
the metrical revivals, turning their back on the Franco-
American practices of Eliot and Pound, were one aspect of the
Englishness of *Look Stranger!*

Auden uses the traditional forms with a feel for their historical
associations, just as his friend, Benjamin Britten, used the
forms of Purcell with an historical feeling. There are poems
in lyric form (some written for Britten), ballads, a sestina
and, most notably, sonnets. One reason why Eliot and his
generation had turned their back on traditional forms was
that these forms were so closely associated with traditional
attitudes; and of no form was this more true than of the sonnet.
Yet Auden makes the sonnet a vehicle of expression quite
unencumbered by literary echoes (except when he imitates
Rilke).

A poem almost perfect in its sensitivity to the English
landscape is the poem from which the British title is taken:

> Look, stranger, at this island now
> The leaping light for your delight discovers,
> Stand stable here
> And silent be,
> That through the channels of the ear
> May wander like a river
> The swaying sound of the sea.
>
> Here at the small field's ending pause
> Where the chalk wall falls to the foam, and its tall ledges
> Oppose the pluck
> And knock of the tide,
> And the shingle scrambles after the suck-
> ing surf, and the gull lodges
> A moment on its sheer side.
>
> Far off like floating seeds the ships
> Diverge on urgent voluntary errands;
> And the full view
> Indeed may enter
> And move in memory as now these clouds do,
> That pass the harbour mirror
> And all the summer through the water saunter.
>
> (Poem V)

The gift for the telling detail or the right comparison that indicate a particularity of experience are there: "the small field's ending"; "like floating seeds the ships". The musical evocation of sensation in the second stanza is dazzling: the placing together of three stressed syllables of the same sound—"chalk wall falls"—with the repeated falling intonation, evokes the sensation of coming on a precipitous drop; while "the shingle scrambles after the suck- / ing surf, . . ." imitates, in its consonants, and in the drag over the line end created by splitting "sucking", the motion of the water that is described.

However, it is impossible to notice the felicities just remarked upon without recalling that they both turn on tricks to be found in Hopkins's "The Windhover" and "No worst, there is none". This reflection leaves one feeling uneasy about "The swaying sound of the sea", which might easily have been derived from a memory of Hopkins's phrase "out of the swing of the sea". Place these lines beside the marvellous and truly individual "And all the summer through the water saunter", and one begins to feel that there is an element of pastiche in the poem that comes close to vitiating it. This feeling is much stronger in other places in the volume, and often when the virtuosity is most marked: "To settle in this village of the heart, . . ." (Poem XXIII) is an imitation of Rilke, and recalls the poem, "Ausgesetzt auf den Bergen des Herzens" (translated variously as "Exposed on the alps of the heart" or "Lost on the mountains of the heart").

Apart from any question of literary indebtedness, there is one line in Poem V that pulls one up: "Diverge on urgent voluntary errands; . . ." Why "voluntary"? It is not that the errands of the ships are not in a sense "voluntary"; but they are so in a sense that is gratuitous, as far as the poem is concerned. "Compulsory" would have made just as good sense, suggesting the urgency and necessity of the voyages. The word "voluntary" seems to be there because Auden likes it and associates it with desirable conditions. It floats loosely in the atmosphere of afternoon ease; yet it is ultimately forced on the experience, not derived from it.

This habit of bringing in favourite words loosely and gratuitously is another recurrent blemish in the book. "Lucky" is a great favourite:

    ... Lucky to Love the new pansy railway,
    The sterile farms where his looks are fed,
    And in the policed unlucky city
        Lucky his bed.

(Poem XXI)

There is some tricky semantic footwork here: the first use of
the word seems to imply either "favourable" or "lucky to
get away with it"; the second seems to be trying to imply at
once "unluckier than other places (perhaps than other cities)"
and "a place where unlucky things are bound to happen
(perhaps because it's a bad place)", whereas a choice between
the meanings affects the meaning of the poem in an important
way; the third usage is more normal, suggesting a place of
fortunate happiness for those who are favoured by fortune in
a doomed world. The second usage is the most disturbing.
The ambiguity is not a fruitful and deliberate one; it is more
like a cloudy attempt to dodge the issue. This may be said of
many of Auden's favourite words of the period: they come
loaded with desired implications that find no correspondence
in the experience behind the poem. Words like "necessary",
"deliberate", "dare", or "voluntary", often come loaded
with Freudian implications concerning unconscious motives
that involve nasty and deliberate attempts to dodge the
reality we dare not face; and finally there is "Love", the
great panacea of Auden's middle period—a word very soft
at the centre.

Consideration of Auden's use of these words leads inevitably
to an examination of the main ideas with which he works in
the poems in *Look Stranger!*, some of which have already been
mentioned. The change to traditional forms had begun in
1932, and had accompanied a change in outlook for Auden.
During 1933 and 1934, politics were strongly emphasised in
Auden's poetry. However, after 1934, and especially in 1935
and 1936, Freud seems to have been the most important
thinker for Auden. Auden's contribution to Geoffrey Grigson's
symposium, *The Arts To-day*, in 1935, is called "Psychology
and Art To-Day". Auden accepts Freud's view that art has
its origins in neurosis, and is, in etiology, a form of fantasy
satisfaction, though he sees the limitation of this view. Auden

F

gives a description of man's fallen nature that is Christian in terminology, but substitutes self-consciousness (with attendant neuroses) for the Fall. He still believes that all illness is purposive, and that all change, for good or bad, is caused by frustration or tension. He finds that the whole of Freud's teaching is implied in Blake's *The Marriage of Heaven and Hell*; but he is critical of Lawrence, in whom he now sees the fascist tendencies. These ideas of awareness and attendant neuroses as marks of the Fallen State, and of the animals existing in an unfallen condition where there is no gap between thought and action, were to be dominant in Auden's work in the later thirties, and recur throughout his career. The embarrassment concerning the conflict between action and awareness is paralleled by a concern with the dichotomy between fantasy and reality, which, with its strong but sneaking respect for what is loosely called "real", appears in Auden's startlingly simplistic definition of the two types of Art:

> There must always be two kinds of art, escape-art, for man needs escape as he needs food and deep sleep, and parable-art, that art which shall teach him to unlearn hatred and learn love . . .[2]

The characterisation of the fantasy element in Art as "escape" is very surprising in a poet for whom fantasy was as important as it was for Auden. The simple, dual classification gives a gross over-simplification. Yet Auden seems to have been very troubled by such simplistic dichotomies that appear to work out at the expense of the imagination and of the contemplative. His embarrassment concerning Art and Life is presented rather frighteningly in a review in *New Verse* in 1938:

> Does Life only offer two alternatives: "You shall be happy, healthy, attractive, a good mixer, a good lover and parent, but on condition that you are not overcurious about life. On the other hand you shall be attentive and sensitive, conscious of what is happening round you, but in that case you must not expect to be happy, or successful in love, or at home in any company. There are two worlds and you cannot belong to them both. If you belong to the second of these worlds you will be

unhappy because you will always be in love with the first, while at the same time you will despise it."[3]

In *Look Stranger!* the fantasy element merges most strongly with the reality principle in Auden's use of the *paysage moralisé*. The most striking example is the brilliant sestina, poem VII, "Hearing of harvests rotting in the valleys . . .", written in 1933. The poem works by exploring and defining certain associations of the six key words of the sestina, and concludes with the call for social reconstruction:

> It is the sorrow; shall it melt? Ah, water
> Would gush, flush, green these mountains and these valleys,
> And we rebuild our cities, not dream of islands.

Clearly "islands", for instance, stand for a state of mind as much as for a geographical location. In this interfusion of the·actual and the mental Auden is often considered to have been influenced by Rilke. However, the landscape of his early poetry, at once modern England and the world of fantasy, indicates such a proclivity for a merging of the actual and the mental that the continuation of this tendency in Auden would hardly seem to call for explanation. On the other hand, poems like "The Malverns" (which, in setting, recalls one of Auden's favourite poems, *Piers Plowman*), or poem X, "Now from my window-sill I watch the night . . ." keep their settings and the ideas that flow from them separate, and proceed from one to the other. They belong to a long tradition of English poetry, that of the meditative topographical poem, of which Denham's "Cooper's Hill", Dyer's "Grongar Hill" or Wordsworth's "Tintern Abbey" are examples. In these poems the setting provides the starting point for meditation, but the meditation is not conducted solely in terms of the images the scene provides.

In this respect Auden differs from another poet under whose influence he seems to have come in the middle thirties: Yeats. Yeats always thought in images, and setting, image and idea were inseparable in his poetry. Auden himself summed up what he felt to be Yeat's legacies, and his remarks apply particularly to his own poetry in the thirties:

His main legacies to us are two. First, he transformed . . . the occasional poem, from being either an official performance of impersonal virtuosity or a trivial *vers de societé* into a serious reflective poem of at once personal and public interest.

A poem such as *In Memory of Major Robert Gregory* is something new and important in the history of English poetry. It never loses the personal note of a man speaking about his personal friends in a particular setting . . . and at the same time the occasion and characters acquire a symbolic public significance.

Secondly, Yeats released regular stanzaic poetry, whether reflective or lyrical, from iambic monotony; . . .[4]

The poem that comes to mind when one reads these remarks is poem XXX of *Look Stranger!*, which is addressed to Christopher Isherwood:

> Our hopes were set still on the spies' career,
> Prizing the glasses and the old felt hat,
> And all the secrets we discovered were
> Extraordinary and false; for this one coughed
> And it was gasworks coke, and that one laughed
> And it was snow in bedrooms; many wore wigs,
> The coastguard signalled messages of love,
> The enemy were sighted from the norman tower.

Auden does not succeed in transforming his personal life and his friends into legend, as Yeats does. The best feature of the poem is what is usually best in *Look Stranger!*, the evocation of the particular scene, often by the telling selection of detail: "May climb the old road twisting to the moors / Play leap frog, enter cafés . . ." The influence of Yeats is also seen in poem IX, which is written in *ottava rima*, the form Yeats used so vitally and originally in his meditative poems; and again in one of the several remarkable lyrics contained in *Look Stranger!*, "Fish in the unruffled lakes . . ." (Poem XXVII), though here Auden spoils his poem by importing Yeats's poetic furniture in the line "Lion, fish and swan".

Auden's lyrics of this period are at once brilliant and touching, but we experience them as "performances". Stephen Spender commented on the impersonality of the famous lyric, "Lay your sleeping head, my love . . .", which appeared slightly after *Look Stranger!* in *New Writing* for Spring, 1937:

Lay your sleeping head, my love,
Human on my faithless arm;
Time and fevers burn away
Individual beauty from
Thoughtful children, and the grave
Proves the child ephemeral:
But in my arms till break of day
Let the living creature lie,
Mortal guilty, but to me
The entirely beautiful.

Spender writes:

> . . . his poetry is often depersonalised in the same way that a
> philosophic argument or an article in the newspapers exists
> simply as an argument or as information, so that the reader
> cannot identify himself with the situation out of which the writer
> is writing, even if he feels that his own situation is stated in it,
> and even if the writer writes in the first person singular.[5]

The feeling of impersonality and non-involvement in the
poetry of this period goes along with Auden's glibness in the
disingenuous or loose handling of certain words ("lucky",
"real", "Love") and with his taste for exercising his virtuosity
for its own sake, as at the end of "Prologue", where the subject
of the poem is virtually forgotten in the long Miltonic simile.
The facility and virtuosity seem to be intimately associated. In
part, the teachings of Freud and Marx are an invitation to
glibness: both explain that the reasons we may think we have
for doing things are not the real reasons; the adept of either
body of thought is put in a "knowing" position. Auden's
stance would also seem to be associated with his dilemma
regarding fantasy and reality. In Auden's earlier poetry,
fantasy had been a means of handling what were clearly very
urgent pressures. In 1932, he abandons the fantasies of his
early poetry, and his poetic stance becomes anti-romantic. In
view of Auden's critical embarrassment concerning fantasy in
the mid-thirties, could not both this and the glibness be a
means of distancing pressures that were ultimately to drive
him to adopt Christianity at the end of the decade? This
would go some way towards explaining Auden's "impersonality".

III

During 1938, Auden and Isherwood travelled to China and worked together on their book, *Journey to a War* (1939). The bulk of it is taken up by a prose account of the travels in China, mainly written by Isherwood. There are a few poems on the journey at the beginning of the book, but Auden's principal contribution is a sequence of twenty-seven sonnets, with a commentary in verse, called "In Time of War".

These sonnets are, at first reading, impressive, and have been highly praised since their appearance, when Geoffrey Grigson reviewed the book in *New Verse*. The sequence begins with a potted account of the evolution of civilisation, and the writing has that combination of breadth and brilliance that one often finds in Auden's work at its best. The sequence also has pace—something of the pace of the sequence that seems to have suggested it—Rilke's *Sonnets to Orpheus*. In some of the earlier sonnets, Auden shows Rilke's gift for revitalising a myth to embody an ideal condition against which the modern or normal human state is measured. Auden's Freudian conception of self-consciousness as the Fallen condition, which contrasts with the innocence and directness of the animals, is sufficiently close to Rilke's attitude to the animal world to make some of the echoes of Rilke's manner startlingly effective:

> We envy streams and houses that are sure:
> But we are articled to error; we
> Were never nude and calm like a great door,
> And never will be perfect like the fountains . . .
>
> (XXVII)

However, the poem from which these lines are taken begins "Wandering lost upon the mountains of our choice . . ." (another imitation of the opening of Rilke's poem "Ausgesetzt auf den Bergen des Herzens"); while the previous sonnet (XXVI) begins "Always far from the centre of our names, / The little workshop of love . . ."—a clear echo of "Immer wieder, ob wir der Liebe Landschaft auch kennen . . .". Rilke's mannerisms are adopted, as in "For who when healthy can become a foot? / Even a scratch we can't recall when cured . . ." (XVII), where the rhetorical question is answered by a statement. However, what is disturbing is that this echoing of Rilke's manner is accompanied by an echoing of Rilke's attitudes, not always appropriately. About the Japanese raiding China, Auden writes:

> . . . [they] will never see how flying
> Is the creation of ideas they hate,
> Nor how their own machines are always trying
> To push through into life.
>
> (XV)

This seems to echo Sonnet X of *Sonnets to Orpheus* (2nd part). In Rilke's poem the notion of machines pushing, having a mind of their own, is a part of his mythologising of the environment; in Auden's poem it is false, and a piece of rhetorical whimsy.

The Rilkean echoes are only one manifestation of a glibness that mars the sonnets. There are a number of striking but superficial similes, such as "They carry terror with them like a purse . . ." (XX) In what sense is "purse" appropriate, except that it surprises us in conjunction with "terror" and that it is something carried? The thirteenth sonnet epitomises so much that is wrong with "In Time of War" and with Auden's poetry of the period generally. After the Rilkean flourish with which the poem opens, it is conducted in terms of a series of rather deadening and over-simplifying abstractions: "the Unjust"; "the Good Place"; "all princes must / Employ the Fairly-Noble unifying Lie". What is the justification for the capitalisation in the last phrase, with its suggesting that a well established idea is being referred to? Why "must"? The poem moves from one sweeping generalisation to another, hardly one of which is true in the unexceptional sense that the poem suggests. The complexity of experience is at once distanced and ignored by this type of writing.

At the end of 1938 Auden went on a holiday to Brussels, and in spring, 1939, *New Writing* included eight poems by him that were evidently the product of this trip: "Palais [Musée] des Beaux Arts"; "The Capital"; "Gare du Midi"; "Brussels in Winter"; "The Novelist"; "The Composer"; "Rimbaud"; and "A. E. Housman". "Gare du Midi" is an effective thirties vignette. In "The Capital" Auden responds to his subject with his customary brilliance of phrase, at once witty and evocative:

> Quarter of pleasures where the rich are always waiting,
> Waiting expensively for miracles to happen,
> O little restaurant where the lovers eat each other,
> Café where exiles have established a malicious village ...

However, the last five poems listed, all sonnets, are of very different quality. "The Novelist" and "The Composer" might have been left-overs from *Journey to a War*. They have the same facile rapidity as the sonnets in that book, and flourish facile (and false) generalisations like "Encased in talent like a uniform, / The rank of every poet is well known . . ." The two sonnets on Rimbaud and Housman and "Brussels in Winter" are equally meretricious.

IV

In June, 1940, after a year in the United States, Auden produced his first collection of short poems since *Look Stranger!*. *Another Time* is considerably longer than its predecessor, but not nearly so impressive. It is divided into three sections: "People and Places"; "Lighter Poems"; and "Occasional Poems". The last section contains the only political poem in the book, "Spain".

In *Another Time* Auden collected nearly all the shorter poems he had written since 1936, with the exception of those contained in his two travel books, *Letters from Iceland* (1937) and *Journey to a War*. The immediately striking thing about the book is that the poems have titles, in contrast with Auden's previous books of short poems. This in fact is indicative of a fairly radical change in the poetry. The poem "Casino", included in *Look Stranger!* exceptionally with a title, contrasted with the other poems in that volume in being about a particular thing in the outside world: the subject was not a kicking off point for more general meditation. In addition, "Casino" was possibly Auden's first attempt at a poem in syllabic verse (perhaps under the influence of Marianne Moore's *Selected Poems*, which appeared, with an introduction by T. S. Eliot, in

1935). Many of the poems in the section "People and Places" in *Another Time* share these characteristics of "Casino". They are decidedly *about* the subjects stated in their titles: "School-children"; "Oxford"; "Dover"; "A. E. Housman". They give the impression, with their flat rhythms and lack of linguistic excitement, of a poet who is looking round for something to write about. Some of them seem to be just a sequence of bright remarks about their subject:

> Nature is so near: the rooks in the college garden
> Like agile babies still speak the language of feeling;
> By the tower the river still runs to the sea and will run,
>   And the stones in that tower are utterly
>   Satisfied still with their weight.
>
> ("Oxford")

This kind of wit, by the end of the thirties, has become Auden's substitute for the richly evocative verbal felicity that one finds earlier in *Look Stranger!* (and, later, in "The Sea and the Mirror"). There are a number of good lyrics in *Another Time*, among them the justly celebrated "Lay your sleeping head . . ." and "Madrigal"; but there are also some that are extremely dull and lifeless, both rhythmically and linguistically:

> The friendless and unhated stone
> Lies everywhere about him,
> The Brothered-One, the Not-Alone,
> The brothered and the hated
> Whose family have taught him
> To set against the large and dumb,
> The timeless and the rooted,
> His money and his time.
> ("Wrapped in a yielding air . . .")

Another noticeable feature of *Another Time* is the number of poems about literary figures: "A. E. Housman"; "Edward Lear"; "Rimbaud"; "Herman Melville"; "Pascal"; "Voltaire at Ferney"; "Matthew Arnold". The poems on Housman, Lear and Rimbaud are sonnets, and that on Arnold is sixteen lines long. They give a quick run down of the lives of the authors, incorporating the facts that everybody knows into a glib psychological explanation. They read in places like jazzed-up literary criticism. This is well illustrated by a section of "Herman Melville":

> Evil is unspectacular and always human,
> And shares our bed and eats at our own table,
> And we are introduced to Goodness every day,
> Even in drawing-rooms among a crowd of faults;
> He has a name like Billy and is almost perfect
> But wears a stammer like a decoration:
> And every time they meet the same thing has to happen;
> It is the Evil that is helpless like a lover
> And has to pick a quarrel and succeeds,
> And both are openly destroyed before our eyes.

Quite apart from the over-simplification, it is disturbing to find a poet of Auden's distinction having to turn to paraphrases of his reading for material.

The best known poem in *Another Time* is probably "In Memory of W. B. Yeats". This too is factitiously rhetorical, this time in a pseudo-Rilkean manner. The remarks in the first section about the instruments agreeing and the river being untempted by the fashionable quays seem gratuitous grandiosity. Perhaps it is because the poem is so rhetorical that it is so popular: it satisfies the taste for grand sounds on grand occasions. One part of the poem was cut by Auden in reprinting it after 1940:

> Time that is intolerant
> Of the brave and innocent,
> And indifferent in a week
> To a beautiful physique,
>
> Worships language and forgives
> Everyone by whom it lives;
> Pardons cowardice, conceit,
> Lays its honours at their feet.
>
> Time that with this strange excuse
> Pardoned Kipling and his views,
> And will pardon Paul Claudel,
> Pardons him for writing well.

The last four lines seem the best in the poem, because they say something perceptive, directly and with a wit that is a natural aspect of what is being said.

Another Time contains good poems: "Law"; "Musée des Beaux Arts"; "Lay your sleeping head . . ."; "Spain"; and the marvellous sonnet "The hour glass whispers . . .", which unconsciously echoes Graves's "A Cool Web", but which is nonetheless a truly individual poem. On the whole, however, a lack of engagement is a feature of a great deal of the poetry in *Another Time*. Auden goes through his old tricks, apparently either unable to respond to experience or else unable to handle those experiences that touch him most nearly. At first sight, the famous "Musée des Beaux Arts" is an exception:

> About suffering they were never wrong,
> The Old Masters: how well they understood
> Its human position; how it takes place
> While someone else is eating or opening a window or just
>   walking dully along;
> How, when the aged are reverently, passionately waiting
> For the miraculous birth, there always must be
> Children who did not specially want it to happen, skating
> On a pond at the edge of the wood:
> They never forgot
> That even the dreadful martyrdom must run its course
> Anyhow in a corner, some untidy spot
> Where the dogs go on with their doggy life and the tor-
>   turer's horse
> Scratches its innocent behind on a tree.

Here the rhythm is relaxed and perfectly modulated to direct our response to the subject. Auden's feeling for telling detail is well displayed. Yet the subject is at once both intimate and distant: the poem is about suffering, but it is also about another work of art. It is as though Auden could afford to let himself be involved only when the ostensible subject is distanced from experience.

This poem comes from the time when Auden was turning to Christianity, as a poem contemporary with "Musée des Beaux Arts" shows:

Perhaps I always knew what they were saying:
Even the early messengers who walked
Into my life from books where they were staying,
Those beautiful machines that never talked
But let the small boy worship them and learn
All their long names whose hardness made him proud;
Love was the word they never said aloud
As something that a picture can't return.

.   .   .

It was true.
For now I have the answer from the face
That never will go back into a book
But asks for all my life, and is the Place
Where all I touch is moved to an embrace,
And there is no such thing as a vain look.

(IX)

The poem is serene: but few conversions are serene. Frederick Grubb has suggested:

> Just before and after his removal . . . to America in 1939 . . . I believe that Auden underwent a cataclysm of feeling and that his insatiably developing intellect was unable to tolerate it. For long the poems seem stunned. Contrasts of abstractions is the method; out of the blue flights are the thought; the rhythm is that of the metronome. . . .[6]

The flat, distant quality of so much of Auden's work at the end of the decade supports this opinion.

On the outbreak of war Auden said goodbye to the thirties in "September 1st, 1939". The poem was evidently intended to contain an important exploration of one of Auden's recurrent themes: the conflict between the demands of the public and the private lives. When he writes about Thucydides and about the ideas with which he feels at home, he shows his usual gift for the apt phrase and the apt tone; while, when he writes about ordinary people, he shows his customary ineptness and distaste. For a conclusion, he first seizes on a highly exceptionable generalisation (which he himself has rejected)—
—"We must love one another or die", and then he goes on to the much quoted ending, which, nevertheless, sounds like whistling in the dark:

Defenceless under the night
Our world in stupor lies;
Yet, dotted everywhere,
Ironic points of light
Flash out wherever the Just
Exchange their messages:
May I, composed like them
Of Eros and of dust,
Beleaguered by the same
Negation and despair,
Show an affirming flame.

This affirmation of Justice was evidently the intended burden of
the poem; but other pressures emerge. There is one stanza in
the poem with real intellectual and emotional bite:

The windiest militant trash
Important persons shout
Is not so crude as our wish:
What mad Nijinsky wrote
About Diaghilev
Is true of the normal heart;
For the error bred in the bone
Of each woman and each man
Craves what it cannot have,
Not universal love
But to be loved alone.

This frightening vision of human beings as inveterately
selfish also suggests that being loved is seen by Auden as a
form of power. One recalls how, throughout his early work,
sensitivity is associated with weakness. To have power, and
to have it quite unreflectingly, was for Auden an enviable
condition (and in this, arguably, he followed Freud). This
led him to sympathise with Freud's underselling of art as a
form of wish-fulfillment, and, in particular, to associate
fantasy with escapism. *The Orators*, with its hero-worship, is
less of a fluke than it might seem. Even Auden's immature
and "naughty" iconoclasm may have been a manifestation
of his more than sneaking admiration of power—in this case,
as it showed itself in figures of authority. Faced, at the end of
the decade, with the full horror of power, even in what he

felt to be a just cause, like the Republican cause in Spain, the only road for Auden away from his ambivalent attitude towards power was the acceptance of humility and self-effacement as higher virtues, and the way to this was through Christianity.

Turning to Christianity was also a turning away from panaceas that always seem associated in his work with an ineradicable shortcoming: the notion of the perfection of the Pure in Heart went along with a tone of doom in the early poems; the Freudian analysis of psychological ills—as a tool, a thing of hope—was associated by Auden with the image of Fallen Man as the ill-adjusted; his poetic reaction to Marxism included an embarrassment with the demands of the personal life, clearly so natural and pressing for him, when they were set over against the urgent demands for action for the public good. To make the step from these paradoxical positions to Christianity may not have been a logical one (but rather one made in the teeth of logic); but it was a natural one, in that the paradoxes are contained and resolved in the Christian faith.

One way of viewing Auden's development during the thirties would be as a series of strategies for containing emotional pressures too deep or too severe for direct confrontation. Those pressures, associated with Auden's feelings about power, love and puritanism, find their most satisfying (if highly ambiguous) embodiment in *Poems*. After the change of heart in 1932, Auden begins to write with brilliant clarity and immense relaxation, but this degenerates into a glibness that is clearly associated with an inability to approach anything truly disturbing in poetic terms. This culminates in the conversion.

These changing attitudes of Auden must, of course, be seen in the general framework of the disillusionment of the literary intellectuals in Britain at the time. Auden told Stephen Spender, after the war, that he had gone along with the Left because he saw in it a hope of defeating fascism: when that hope was gone, he abandoned the Left; and this is true enough, despite the fact that something more profound and more disturbing seems to have been happening to Auden at the same time.

Chapter 8

THE OLD ORDER AND THE NEW

Louis MacNeice – John Betjeman

AFTER LEAVING OXFORD and marrying, Louis MacNeice wrote little poetry for about three years. (His second book of poetry, *Poems*, did not appear until 1935.) However, 1933 saw him writing fairly fertilely again, and, at the end of the year, surprising himself with the degree of social engagement of "Eclogue for Christmas": "Was I really as concerned as all that with the Decline of the West? Did I really feel so desperate? Apparently I did. Part of me must have been feeling like that for years."[1] "Eclogue for Christmas" in fact contains very little (if anything) that is unquestionably left-wing, though the feeling expressed in it that society is doomed might easily be mistaken for a leftist sentiment. In fact, "the Decline of the West" is seen in terms of the decay of traditional patterns of life and their replacement by new-fangled and standardised patterns and products:

> And over-elaboration will nothing now avail,
> The street is up again, gas, electricity or drains,
> Ever-changing conveniences, nothing comfortable remains
> Unimproved, as flagging Rome improved villa and sewer
> (A sound-proof library and a stable temperature).
> Our street is up, red lights sullenly mark
> The long trench of pipes, iron guts in the dark,
> And not till the Goths again come swarming down the hill
> Will cease the clangour of the pneumatic drill.

MacNeice was more truly the critic of the new England of the suburban villa, the motor car, the wireless and ribbon development than he was a critic of the economic rottenness of society. Left-wing criticism of society frequently merged with criticism of the new vulgarity, but MacNeice could never feel whole-heartedly devoted to left-wing principles; and, with characteristic honesty, he wrote (in 1938):

I would vote Left any day, sign manifestos, answer question-
naires. Ditto my soul. My soul is all for moving towards a classless
society.

With my heart and my guts I lament the passing of class. Of
class, property and snobbery. A man for me is still largely characterised by what he buys—his suits, his books . . .[2]

The centre of MacNeice's social criticism is concern with
the decay of traditional patterns of life, and, with this decay,
what he felt to be the destruction of individualism in a world of
mass-produced uniformity and slickness:

> Among these turf-stacks graze no iron horses
> Such as stalk, such as champ in towns and the soul of crowds,
> Here is no mass-production of neat thoughts
> No canvas shrouds for the mind nor any black hearses:
> The peasant shambles on his boots like hooves
> Without thinking at all or wanting to run in grooves.
>
> (*Poems:* "Turf-Stacks")

It is typical of MacNeice that the theme of individualism and
tradition should take him back to the Northern Ireland of his
childhood. It is not merely that that country contrasts strongly
with southern England—the new England—of the day.
MacNeice is a highly personal poet, and his Northern Irish
childhood is something to which he frequently recurs in
other connections.

In part, the memories of his childhood are important
because they are his only memories of the pre-1914 "Victorian"
peace. It is also clear, however, that through his memories of
childhood he was able to approach pressingly personal themes
that recur in his poetry:

> . . . in a poem called 'Perseus', presenting an experience and a
> mood from which I have often suffered, I write:
>
>> Or look in the looking-glass in the end room—
>> You will find it full of eyes,
>> The ancient smiles of men cut out with scissors and
>>   kept in mirrors.

> . . . I am describing a mood of terror when everything seems
> to be unreal, petrified. . . . In such a mood, both when a child
> and when grown-up, I remember looking in mirrors and . . .
> thinking that my own face looked like a strange face . . .[3]

The same preoccupation with fascination and petrification is
to be found in "Circe" (*Poems*), which concludes with the
image of a mirror, and which also deals with the inner life
by relating it to the mythological.

Alongside this preoccupation with the petrified and unchanging goes a delight in change and in the evanescent in
poems like "Morning Sun", "Train to Dublin" and "Contact"
(all in *Poems*). (These are all concerned with the movement of
trains, which MacNeice recalled first hearing lying in bed as a
child before he had ever seen them.) The tension between the
two concerns is made explicit in "Nature Morte":

> . . . Yet even so, no matter how solid and staid we contrive
> Our reconstructions, even a still life is alive
> And in your Chardin the appalling unrest of the soul
> Exudes from the dried fish and the brown jug and the bowl.
>
> (*Poems*)

Change and the elusiveness of experience touched MacNeice
closely: ". . . every year since [1929] I have been terrified
by the movement of the year. The bouyant months are May
and June. Once they are over, I feel defeated."[4] This feeling
is echoed in "August":

> The shutter of time darkening ceaselessly
> Has whisked away the foam of may and elder
> And I realise how now, as every year before
> Once again the gay months have eluded me.
>
> (*Poems*)

These feelings seem to be related to a quite natural, though
perceptively honest feeling about the self: "If you know
what my whole self and my only self is, you know a lot more
than I do. As far as I can make out, I not only have different
selves but I am often, as they say, not myself at all."[5] The
self is, of course, a construction, as is also the outside world,

and MacNeice seems to have been peculiarly and pressingly aware of this.

This leads back to what has been called MacNeice's "evasive honesty". In refusing to take definite and absolute positions, MacNeice attained to an honesty and clarity of perception that other writers of his period seldom have (though, looking at the same aspect of his work and personality from a less favourable point of view, he might be accused of confusion and uncertainty). In consequence of this outlook, MacNeice was suspicious of the intellect. He frequently turns from the "nostrums" of his day to celebrate ordinary things: "I do not want to be reflective any more" is the opening line of "Wolves" (*Poems*). His conception of the poet and of poetry is in keeping with these emphases:

> I consider that the poet is a blend of the entertainer and the critic or informer; he is not a legislator, however unacknow-ledged, nor yet, essentially, a prophet . . . I would have a poet able-bodied, fond of talking, a reader of newspapers, capable of pity and laughter, informed in economics, appreciative of women, involved in personal relationships, actively interested in politics, susceptible to physical impressions.[6]

He called his book, *Modern Poetry* (1938), from which the above quotation is taken, ". . . a plea for *impure* poetry, that is, poetry conditioned by the poet's life and the world around him . . ." This did not, however, mean that the poet must adopt a political creed and make his work its mouthpiece. "In a world intransigent and over specialised, falsified by practical necessities, the poet must maintain his elasticity and refuse to tell lies to order."[7]

The most celebrated poem in *Poems* is perhaps "Snow", and it epitomises MacNeice's orientation towards the world and the stylistic consequences of that orientation.

> The room was suddenly rich and the great bay-window was
> Spawning snow and pink roses against it
> Soundlessly collateral and incompatible:
> World is suddener than we fancy it.

World is crazier and more of it than we think,
Incorrigibly plural. I peel and portion
A tangerine and spit the pips and feel
The drunkenness of things being various.

And the fire flames with a bubbling sound for world
Is more spiteful and gay than one supposes—
On the tongue on the eyes on the ears in the palms of your hands—
There is more than glass between the snow and the huge roses.

It is a poem in which "things" exist in their own right, a
poem that is reflective, yet derives its strength from the tact
and integrity with which the poet refuses to extend that reflection beyond the limits that the experience allows. The experience itself is a personal one and is highly individuated in terms
of the outside world. Some years after the poem was written,
MacNeice remarked: ". . . it means exactly what it says; the
images here are not voices off, they are bang centre stage,
for this is the direct record of a direct experience, the realisation
of a very obvious fact, that one thing is different from another—
a fact which everyone knows but few people perhaps have
had it brought home to them in this particular way, i.e. through
the sudden violent perception of snow and roses juxtaposed".[8]
In spite of this directness, there is nevertheless a subtlety of
detail in the construction of the poem that is closely attuned
to the purpose of the poem as a whole. The diction may seem
in places flashily intellectual: "Soundlessly collateral and
incompatible . . ."; and this may seem to clash with the
simplicity of other phrases. Similarly, the poem may seem to
lurch rather suddenly from the abstract to the sensuous, or
from the conversational to the conceptual. All this is true,
but it does not constitute a criticism of the poem. The shifts
of tone and diction and imagery mirror "The drunkenness of
things being various", which is the subject of the poem.

However, as MacNeice himself puts it: "It is almost impossible either to explain in what sense a poem is 'about' something
or even to define, at all exactly, what any one poem is about."[9]
The diction and the images are, like good furniture, functional;
but, again like good furniture, they are also expressive of the
person who has selected them. A reading of *Poems*, or of
MacNeice's poetry as a whole, will leave the reader not merely

with the feeling that the poet has a very definite and personal style, but that a great deal of what the poems say resides in the style. This comes close, of course, to being a critical commonplace. However, in the case of MacNeice, we can go so far as to say that some of the poems—particularly in his early volumes—give the impression that they exist largely for the purpose of creating that style. Style for MacNeice, as for Yeats, is an attainment—at once an attainment and a projection of the qualities of being that the author values.

The style chosen by MacNeice has been criticised: Julian Symons, reviewing MacNeice's work of the later thirties, drew a distinction between MacNeice as an ordinary man and the "MacNeice character". The social implications of "the MacNeice character with its Hampstead flat and its big borzoi"—do represent a radical failure in MacNeice's writing as a whole, which manifests itself at times in a rather snobbish and superficial conception of the good life.[10] However, most frequently the "MacNeice character" is felt in the strawberry candy-floss aspect of his poetry—the overdeveloped surface of sensuous bric-a-brac of some of the lesser poems.

Writing about the aspects of his style exemplified by "Snow", MacNeice said:

> . . . my basic conception of life being dialectical (in the philosophic, not the political sense), I have tended to swing to and fro between descriptive and physical images (which are 'correct' so far as they go) and *faute de mieux* metaphysical, mythical or mystical images (which can never go far enough).

He adds, in a footnote: "Hence my fairly frequent use of oxymoron, the phrase which concentrates a paradox."[11] These effects are not confined to paradoxical phrases like "Spawning snow": the sensuous clash in language and in imagery is an ever-present feature of MacNeice's poetry, as the poems already quoted show: "fire flames with a bubbling sound"; ". . . the appalling unrest of the soul / Exudes from the dried fish . . ."; "smiles of men cut out with scissors"; "graze no iron horses". Metaphor is not an important figure in his poetry; nor is the device of the central metaphorical object or situation from which the other "figures" of a poem grow. Though he insisted that what distinguished his generation of poets from that of Eliot was their concern with subject and with things, he does not utilise "things" by drawing out their metaphorical implications, but rather (in *Poems*, especially) overlays them with his interacting images. His poems tend to say something *about* their subjects. The life of his poetry tends to be in its images.

Equally important with MacNeice's use of images and figurative language is his individual handling of rhythm, which suggests the subdued and mature poise of attitude behind his poetry. He described his own practice in terms of using "syncopation" to throw proper stress on the important words.[12] The frequent effect is the muting of what is always on the verge of becoming a definite and pronounced rhythm. Particularly effective in this respect is his handling of the couplet. Many of the poems in *Poems* are written in couplets, an example being "Sunday Morning":

> Down the road some one is practising scales,
> The notes like little fishes vanish with a wink of tails,
> Man's heart expands to tinker with his car
> For this is Sunday morning, Fate's great bazaar; . . .

The clinching effect of the couplet is there to be taken when needed. The basic pattern is of a hexameter rhyming with a fourteener—the dire Poulter's measure of Elizabethan poetry. Yet, so skilfully are the rhythms shifted, the long lines do not break up, and the artificial clippedness of the heroic couplet is avoided. MacNeice's breaking up of rhythm inside conventional forms is a device he shares with Robert Graves and John Crowe Ransom. Another "muting" device found in both these poets, and also used by MacNeice, is the rhyming of a stressed with an unstressed syllable.

MacNeice's liking for the revitalised cliché was remarked upon in an earlier chapter. One of his longer poems of the thirties is called "Homage to Clichés". MacNeice explained that by clichés he meant "the ordinary more pleasant sense-data of the sensual man".[13] He is the constant celebrator of the importance of ordinary things, and it is appropriate that he should suggest this ordinariness by the hint of cliché in his phrases:

> I cannot draw up any code
>   There are too many qualifications
> Too many asterisk asides
>   Too many crosses in the margin
> But as others, forgetting the others,
>   Run after nostrums
> Of science art and religion
>   So would I mystic and maudlin
> Dream of both real and ideal
>   Breakers of ocean.
> I must put away this drug.

These lines are from "Ode", a long poem included in *Poems*. They provide a fair summary of MacNeice's *credo*, which it is the aim of the poem to present.

It is in this type of longer "philosophical" poem that Mac-Neice most often uses his "cliché" style.

> I would pray for that island; mob mania in the air,
> I cannot assume their easy bravery
> Drugged with a slogan, chewing the old lie
> That parallel lines will meet at infinity;
> As I walk on the shore of the regular and rounded sea
> I would pray off from my son the love of that infinite
> Which is too greedy and too obvious; let his Absolute
> Like any four-walled house be put up decently.

The way in which the cliché about "parallel lines"—a cliché when used figuratively—deflates the pretensions of the poem both philosophically and poetically is excellent. The poem as a whole is effective, which is not generally the case with this type of poem as written by MacNeice. The denial of philo-sophic pretence is quite regular with him, yet he was drawn throughout his life to philosophise in verse. He was, in the first place, a muddled Idealist. Furthermore, the notion that one can write philosophical poetry by being chatty and explicit is false, and involves the besetting vice of his poetry. Writing that has neither the precision of prose nor the life of poetry can be illustrated even from "Ode".

> If God is boundless as the sea or sky
> The eye bounds both of them and Him,
> We always have the horizon
> Not to swim to but to see:

God is seen with shape and limit
More purple towards the rim,
This segment of His infinite extension
Is all the God of Him for me.

There was one form of long poem which MacNeice made his own in the thirties: the Eclogue, of which he wrote four—"Eclogue for Christmas", "Eclogue by a Five-Barred Gate", "Eclogue from Iceland" and "Eclogue Between the Motherless". The circumstances in which the first of the eclogues was written have already been mentioned. The model for the poems was the classical pastoral of Theocritus and Virgil (variously imitated in England in the Renaissance, but most notably in Spenser's *The Shepheardes Calendar*). MacNeice takes from his originals very little except the notion of a static dialogue poem; though, in "Eclogue by a Five-Barred Gate", where two shepherds converse with Death about his sheep, and each sing him a song which is a parody of a style of contemporary poetry, there is a closer connection with the originals, which dealt with philosophical themes by means of dialogues between shepherds, and with matters of poetry in terms of shepherds playing on pipes.

"Eclogue for Christmas", with its impressive opening, is easily the best:

A. I meet you in an evil time.
B.   The evil bells
   Put out of our heads, I think, the thought of
   everything else.
A. The jaded calendar revolves,
   The nuts need oil, carbon chokes the valves,
   The excess sugar of a diabetic culture
   Rotting the nerve of life and literature;
   Therefore when we bring out the old tinsel and frills
   To announce that Christ is born among the barbarous hills
   I turn to you whom a morose routine
   Saves from the mad vertigo of being what has been.

Once again the rhythms of the couplet are handled in such a way as to combine the impression of the natural speaking voice with the sense that there is a deliberate order and measure. The theme of the poem is the new England of suburbia; and the feeling that the present is shabby and effete compared with the more traditional past is behind all four poems, though the fourth of them, "Eclogue for the Motherless", deals with marriage, no doubt a pressing concern to MacNeice when it was written in 1937, his own marriage having broken up. "Eclogue from Iceland" in which two trippers meet the ghost of Grettir Asmundson is especially concerned with the shabbiness of the present. Grettir Asmundson reveals that indeed the past had enough of treachery and deceit. Those to be praised are the individualists, the men of sufficient courage and integrity to go against the crowd:

> Let us thank God for valour in abstraction
> For those who go their own way, will not kiss
> The arse of law and order nor compound
> For physical comfort at the price of pride: . . .

The reason why MacNeice was so successful with the eclogue and not generally with the longer poem is that MacNeice's self-deprecating, loose formulations seem natural in the dialogue form, and are protected from any demand for exactness by the fact that their looseness is dramatically appropriate. In addition, the dialogue form permits the poet to play off contrary points of view, while remaining in uncertainty himself. It is the ideal form for MacNeice's deliberately inconclusive honesty.

Much the same may be said of *Autumn Journal*, a long poem he wrote as a journal between the end of August, 1938, and the close of that year. The poem is written in a loose rhyming form, the length of line being free. Within this flexible form MacNeice can vary from the chatty to the lyrical. The chattiness of the poem has led many to dismiss it, yet that is its chief virtue. It once again protects MacNeice from his tendency to philosophise in a self-deprecating way, because the deliberate casualness of the poem creates an ambience in which nothing that is said has the manner of a considered formulation, and in which we feel that abstract precision would be out of place. Thus we can accept passages like the following which, if the poem were a "full dress" long poem, we might reject as superficial or sloppy. In *Autumn Journal* they have a dramatic rightness.

If you can equate Being in its purest form
  With denial of all appearance,
Then let me disappear—the scent grows warm
  For pure Not-Being, Nirvana.
Only the spider spinning out his reams
  Of colourless thread says Only there are always
Interlopers, dreams,
  Who let no dead dog lie nor death be final;
Suggesting, while he spins, that to-morrow will outweigh
  To-night, that Becoming is a match for Being,
That to-morrow is also a day,
  That I must leave my bed and face the music.
As all the others do who with a grin
  Shake off sleep like a dog and hurry to desk or engine
And the fear of life goes out as they clock in
  And history is reasserted.

                                                    (ii)

Throughout the poem cliché is used in a masterly way to
create the tone, an effect which reminds one of Clough's
Amours de Voyage (though the Satires of Horace are more likely
to have been an immediate model for the poem as a whole):

> *Dulce* it is, and *decorum*, no doubt, for the country to fall,—to
> Offer one's blood an oblation to Freedom, and die for the
>   Cause; yet
> Still, individual culture is also something, and no man
> Finds quite distinct the assurance that he of all others is
>   called on,
> Or would be justified even, in taking away from the world
>   that Precious creature, himself.
>
>   (*Amours de Voyage*, II, ii)

If one cannot see Clough's poem as having individuality,
perceptiveness and seriousness, one is unlikely to find these
qualities in *Autumn Journal*. In fact, MacNeice's attitudes are
more precise, less sentimental and more honest than those of
his contemporary poets.

    Like so much of MacNeice's poetry, *Autumn Journal* displays
his feeling for ordinary things and his gift for evoking happiness.
Nothing in it, in this respect, quite comes up to the magnificent
opening, which captures so well the mood of the months
preceding World War II:

Close and slow, summer is ending in Hampshire,
   Ebbing away down ramps of shaven lawn where close-clipped
      yew
Insulates the lives of retired generals and admirals
   And the spyglasses hung in the hall and the prayer-books ready
      in the pew
And August going out to the tin trumpets of nasturtiums
   And the sunflowers' Salvation Army blare of brass
And the spinster sitting in a deck-chair picking up stitches
   Not raising her eyes to the noise of the planes that pass
Northward from Lee-on-Solent. . . .
And I am in the train too now and summer is going
   South as I go north
Bound for the dead leaves falling, the burning bonfire,
   The dying that brings forth
The harder life, revealing the trees' girders,
   The frost that kills the germs of *laissez faire*;
West Meon, Tisted, Farnham, Woking, Weybridge,
   Then London's packed and stale and pregnant air.

(i)

A sadness for a way of life that is passing permeates the poem.
He recaptures brilliantly the ease of his early days of marriage
in Birmingham at the beginning of the thirties; and no passage
is more evocative, more nostalgic, or more poignant than that
where he remembers his former wife—a passage that becomes
a superb compliment. It is a considerable achievement to
have written, in the twentieth century, a continuous poem
of over two thousand lines that is not boring or self-defeatingly
literary. It is also a triumph to have developed an individual
form with such success. In addition, *Autumn Journal* is one
occasion when the thirties' conception of the poet as reporter
or journalist paid off.

Poems marked MacNeice's effective emergence as a poet.
Blind Fireworks, his undergraduate volume, got very little
attention. Wherever *Poems* was reviewed, it was highly thought
of: even *Scrutiny*, so critical generally of the new poets, could
not, at times, help giving MacNeice his due. His reputation
was sustained by his next collection of shorter poems, *The
Earth Compels*, in 1938.

The most striking difference stylistically between *Poems* and
The Earth Compels is the quality and use of the visual elements

in the poetry. In *Poems*, the "subjects" of the poems are sometimes overlaid with a web of visual images; in *The Earth Compels*, there is a greater and more direct concern with "subject", and what is notable is the visual clarity with which the world of things is realised. A poem very striking in this respect is the translation of Horace's Ode "Solvitur Acris Hiems" (Odes, I, 4):

> Winter to Spring: the west wind melts the frozen rancour,
>   The windlass drags to sea the thirsty hull;
> Byre is no longer welcome to beast or fire to ploughman,
>   The field removes the frost-cap from his skull.

Another characteristic of several poems in *The Earth Compels* is the delicate and precise handling of unusual verse movements, as for instance in "Iceland", where the clipped lines, suggesting an excess of restraint, nevertheless form parts of the steady flow of natural speech that the stanzas as a whole offer. The effect is intensified by the skilfully controlled near rhymes:

> Men have forgotten
>   Anger and ambush,
> To make ends meet
>   Their only business:
> The lover riding
>   In the lonely dale
> Hears the plover's
>   Single pipe
>
> And feels perhaps
>   But undefined
> The drift of death
>   In the sombre wind
> Deflating the trim
>   Balloon of lust
> In the grey storm
>   Of dust and grit.

MacNeice's gift for writing in long loose lines that do not break in two, but seem thought of as a unit, is also displayed. Perhaps this came from his familiarity with Latin metres, where the metrical forms are thought of as units rather than sets of repeated feet. One of the most famous poems in the volume, "June Thunder", is written in modified Sapphics, though the metrical pattern of the Sapphic stanzas is only loosely followed in MacNeice's stanza of three unrhyming lines of five beats with a short coda:

> The Junes were free and full, driving through tiny
> Roads, the mudguards brushing the cowparsley,
> Through fields of mustard and under boldly embattled
>   Mays and chestnuts
>
> Or between beeches verdurous and voluptuous
> Or where broom and gorse beflagged the chalkland—
> All the flare and gusto of the unenduring
>   Joys of a season
>
> Now returned but I note as more appropriate
> To the maturer moods impending thunder
> With an indigo sky and the garden hushed except for
>   The treetops moving.

However, in the coda the Sapphic pattern, $-\ \cup\ \cup\ -\ -$, is closely imitated: "Down like a dropscene"; "Joys of a season"; "Flashed from the scabbard"; "Now if now only".

"June Thunder" is the poem that perhaps best epitomises MacNeice's work of the late thirties, with its combination of nostalgia and honesty, of restlessness and poise. It was an aspect of MacNeice's originality that, in an era so suspicious of emotional self-indulgence (though not an era at all free of it), he readily admitted to nostalgia. Nostalgia admitted and seen for what it is can no more be rejected as a theme of poetry than can any other. It is only nostalgia that masquerades as something else that is objectionable.

> If only now you would come and dare the crystal
> Rampart of rain and the bottomless moat of thunder,
> If only now you would come I should be happy
>   Now if now only.
>
>   ("June Thunder")

A poem that combines MacNeice's poised felicity of movement (in a complex stanza) with his characteristic nostalgia is "The Sunlight on the Garden":

The sunlight on the garden
Hardens and grows cold,
We cannot cage the minute
Within its nets of gold;
When all is told
We cannot beg for pardon.

It is a poem that embodies a feeling widespread in the last years of the thirties—not merely a nostalgia for the things MacNeice mentions in the poem, but for the freedom and exultance and excitement that the struggle against fascism and the hope of a better society gave. From 1937 on, war became more and more imminent. It might be the final confrontation with fascism; but it offered little hope, and it would be the destruction of a way of life.

Except for the writing of *Autumn Journal* in its latter months, 1938 was an empty year poetically for Louis MacNeice: there are only three shorter poems dating from that year. It is possible, indeed, that one reason for writing *Autumn Journal* was to get his hand back in. However, in the spring of 1939 (presumably after the completion of *Autumn Journal*) he began to find form again, and between then and autumn 1940 produced nearly sixty short poems, most of which were collected in *Plant and Phantom* (1941), and some of which were earlier collected in a small volume published in Dublin in 1940, *The Last Ditch*. Nearly all of these poems were written in three comparatively short creative bursts in the summer of 1939, in February and March, 1940, and from August to October, 1940.

These poems are of a high standard, and some are of considerable felicity, though there are few that are as memorable as the best pieces in *Poems* or *The Earth Compels*. A case in point is the famous "Meeting Point":

Time was away and somewhere else,
There were two glasses and two chairs
And two people with the one pulse
(Somebody stopped the moving stairs):
Time was away and somewhere else, . . .

Only MacNeice could have written this; but it runs off a bit easily compared with "June Thunder" or "The Sunlight on the Garden", and the nostalgia of the poem as a whole is rather drawn out and decidedly self-indulgent.

During this same period he wrote the first four of a sequence of poems, "Novelettes", the best known of which is perhaps "Les Sylphides". For all their felicities, the poems are a little slick, so that one feels tempted to rename them "Potted Lives". The element of fantasy in the imagery marks the beginning of a new tendency in MacNeice's poetry. So too does the whole conception of the sequence. Once again, there is an increased emphasis on "subject". In the past, a subject had been the occasion for meditation; but throughout the forties his subjects seem much more deliberately chosen and to constitute in themselves the *raison d'être* of the poems. There is, however, a noticeable lack of pressure behind such poems when they are compared with his earlier work. Nevertheless, there are a few poems from this period that can be set beside MacNeice's best. One of them is "Cradle Song", one of the last to be written (in October, 1940).

> Sleep, my darling, sleep:
>   The pity of it all
> Is all we compass if
>   We watch disaster fall;
> Put off your twenty-odd
>   Encumbered years and creep
> Into the only heaven,
>   The robbers' cave of sleep.

Marked "for Eleanor" it reminds one of one of his most delightful early poems, "Cradle Song for Miriam", written in 1928.

The two bursts of creativity in 1940 may have been occasioned by MacNeice's visit at that time to America. He brought together all the poems he wanted to collect in *Poems 1925–1940*, published in the United States and Canada, but not in Great Britain. This book is his true monument. It contained the best poems from *Blind Fireworks*, along with *Poems*, *The Earth Compels*, *Autumn Journal*, pieces from his travel books, *Letters from Iceland* and *I Crossed the Minch*, and the poems written in 1939 and 1940—altogether over 350 pages of poetry. There are, perhaps, no great poems, but many have an individuality that makes comparison with other poets irrelevant. Few are trivial, and hardly any—above all—are dull.

II

> There are few songs for domesticity
> For routine work, money-making or scholarship
> Though these are apt for eulogy or for tragedy.
> ("Hidden Ice")

These lines are from MacNeice's book of 1938, *The Earth Compels*. In many respects they might be applied to another book that appeared in the previous year: John Betjeman's *Continual Dew*. Betjeman is not usually thought of as a poet of the thirties; and *Continual Dew*, with its drawings of churches, its *art nouveau* decorations and its deliberately dated cover, is not, at first sight, the book to make one connect Betjeman with the decade. Yet he produced his first book, *Mount Zion*, in 1932, and two other books of poetry in the period: *Continual Dew* (1937); and *Old Lights in New Chancels* (1940). He was a friend of Auden and of Bernard Spencer, and his preoccupations were not so different from theirs as they might appear to be.

It is not at all fanciful to group Betjeman with MacNeice. MacNeice's connection with Auden and the *New Writing* group was a very loose one. In Oxford his principal friends seem to have been Graham Shephard and John Hilton, who, along with Betjeman, had been with him at Marlborough. Betjeman's background was Highgate, Chelsea, Marlborough and being sent down from Oxford. His circle as an undergraduate included Harold Acton, Evelyn Waugh and C. M. Bowra. He married the daughter of a Field-Marshal; and his *Collected Poems* is introduced by the Earl of Birkenhead. However, his poetry shares with that of Auden and MacNeice a concern with capturing the quality of middle-class life, and shares with their poetry an ambivalent attitude to that life, at once affectionate and critical.

Betjeman, like MacNeice, was appalled at the new England of the growing suburbia: not the Edwardian and late Victorian suburbia of London and the Home Counties; but the suburbia of ribbon development and speculative building that spread out during the thirties. Betjeman's feelings are summarised in the following passage (written in 1952, but applicable in the main to the pre-war scene):

> The suburbs which once seemed to me so lovely with their freckled tennis girls and their youths in club blazers have spread so far in the wake of the motor car that there is little but suburb left. We are told that we live in the age of the common man. He would be better described as the suburban man. . . .
> . . . He is the explanation of such phenomena as plastic tea-cups, Tizer, light ale, quizzes, mystery tours, cafeterias, discussion groups, Chapels of Unity, station announcers . . . He is the Lowest Common Multiple, not even the Highest Common Factor. . . .[14]

There is a considerable similarity between the attitudes expressed here and those found in the following remarks by MacNeice from the later thirties:

> There is a natural culture which can subsist without comfort. And there is a sophisticated culture which depends upon comforts. But when the deserters from the former "gate-crash" the industrial world and try to live by its bread or its cake alone—its grand pianos, its club chairs, its blue underclothes—then one is presented with European man at his worst.[15]

MacNeice's feelings about the death of individuality and mass society are paralleled by Betjeman in poems like "Slough" (written in 1937):

> Come, friendly bombs, and fall on Slough!
> It isn't fit for humans now,
> There isn't grass to graze a cow.
>   Swarm over, Death!
>
> Come, bombs, and blow to smithereens
> Those air-conditioned, bright canteens,
> Tinned fruit, tinned meat, tinned milk, tinned beans
>   Tinned minds, tinned breath.
>
> Mess up the mess they call a town—
> A house for ninety-seven down
> And once a week a half a crown
>   For twenty years, . . .

As was the case with Evelyn Waugh, there is in Betjema[n's] writings a good deal of snobbishness mixed in with brillia[nt] and well-directed satire—plus an admixture of nastiness. T[he] nastiness is not vicious, as in the case of Waugh; though there is something decidedly unpleasant and unhealthy in the conjunction of an admiration for "strapping" girls and a nostalgia for childhood and adolescence in poems like "Pot Pourri from a Surrey Garden", "Myfanwy" and "A Subaltern's Love Song". However, there is a certain unity to Betjeman's cultural preoccupations. An essay of 1937 is entitled "Anti-quarian Prejudice". In this essay he attacks the false tradi-tionalism that values things by their antiquity. This leads not only to a hopelessly sentimentalised valuation of the medieval and Elizabethan (as opposed to a true aesthetic valuation), but also results in architecturally excellent Victorian buildings being despised. From this flows Betjeman's championing of London railway stations and nineteenth-century Non-Conformist chapels—classes of architecture almost automatic-ally rejected by most people. His dislike of "antiquarianism" also fits in with his criticisms of the suburbia of the thirties: the brick box with imitation Jacobean gables, fake half-timbered front and leaded light effects on full pane windows—the vulgar, bogus and cheap preferred to an attempt to make a pleasing production out of what a building genuinely is. No doubt there is a good deal of snobbishness in Betjeman's attitude to suburbia; and "How to Get on in Society" is an instance of this, though not a very serious instance, as it is a "stunt" poem. In defence of Betjeman's snobbishness it has to be remembered that modern England is the homeland of meretricious vulgarity in every type of domestic artifact. His book, *Ghastly Good Taste* (1933), is a history of the decline of English architecture, and is a combination of brilliance and good sense, rather than a display of snobbishness. Betjeman's positive interest in suburbia, on the other hand, does reflect an awareness that this is the setting for the lives and emotions of most English people; and the originality of his sensibility lies in the fact that he can realise this while rejecting what is rubbishy in the setting itself.

Betjeman's style has unusual antecedents, mainly in light verse:

G

Tennyson, the Reverend Robert Stephen Hawker, late eighteenth-century pastoral poets, Cowper and Thompson, and Crabbe, and the 'nineties willowy kind of poets like Dowson and later Aldous Huxley, and the Sitwells and Eliot, and, oh yes . . . Hardy.[16]

To these Betjeman might have added Praed and Locker Lampson. Betjeman is, of course, one of the most brilliant writers of light verse of his period; but his interest in it has little to do with the populist aspirations of the left-wing poets. Betjeman's individual combination of the flippant and the nostalgic is more an inheritance from the twenties.

It has been suggested that there is a problem of tone in reading Betjeman's poetry.[17] This is perhaps an accurate characterisation of the reader's predicament with some of the poems, though it is not necessarily a criticism of them. It may be a measure of their subtlety. "Love in the Valley" is a poem that leaves the reader doubtful of the tone:

> Take me, Lieutenant, to that Surrey homestead!
> Red comes the winter and your rakish car,
> Red among the hawthorns, redder than the hawberries
> Or trails of old man's nuisance, and noisier far.
> Far, far below me roll the Coulsdon woodlands,
> White down the valley curves the living rail,*
> Tall, tall, above me, olive spike the pinewoods,
> Olive against blueblack, moving in the gale.

The poem, as its title indicates, is an imitation of Meredith's poem of the same name, and uses the same strongly rhythmic form. The quoted stanza has a footnote to line six: "* Southern Electric 25 mins." Does this mean that the feelings expressed in the poem are being satirised? Is Betjeman refusing to take the poem seriously? It ends on what seems undoubtedly a sad note:

> Portable Lieutenant! they carry you to China
> And me to lonely shopping in a brilliant arcade;
> Firm hand, fond hand, switch the giddy engine!
> So for us a last time is bright light made.

Is there an uncertainty of tone? On the face of it, there might seem to be. Certainly, one aspect of the poem is its playfulness; and Betjeman's playfulness (perhaps a protection against taking himself too seriously) does at times get out of hand. The notion of form implied by the poem seems to be the reverse of "organic form": the traditional stanza sets up a pronounced rhythm that seems to work independently of the meaning. The "bounce" and the slightly exaggerated nostalgia in fact combine with the footnote to "place" the feeling: the nostalgia and sadness are given full play—this is human sadness, the only sadness we know: but this is Surrey—only Surrey. There is a deliberately contrived double vision—a character-istic twentieth-century irony—that is a feature of a great deal of Betjeman's work. (The double vision is made baldly explicit —a little too baldly explicit—in "In a Bath Teashop".) Betjeman's satirical writing about suburbia has a sadness and a sympathy (alongside the disgust) that is not there in William Plomer's satires of the same parts of English society.

It has to be admitted that Betjeman's own account of his interest in suburbia as a subject for poetry is not, as first sight, entirely in harmony with this conception of his poetry. In his essay, "Topographical Verse", he remonstrated:

> I see no harm in trying to describe overbuilt Surrey in verse. But when I do so I am not being satirical but topographical. . . . The suburbs, thanks to *Punch* which caters for them, are now con-sidered "funny". . . . I love suburbs and gas-lights and Pont Street and Gothic Revival churches and mineral railways, provincial towns and Garden cities. They are, many of them, part of my background. From them I try to create an atmosphere which will be remembered by those who have a similar back-ground, when England is all council houses and trunk roads and steel and glass factory blocks in the New Europe after the War.[18]

The gift for capturing the essential poetry of modern suburban life—a gift shared with Auden and MacNeice—made a definite contribution to the expansion of the scope of English poetry. However, the topographical, antiquarian nostalgia confessed to, while an obvious element in Betjeman's poetry, does not exhaust the effects that his poetry obtains.

Betjeman is one of the most powerful poets of death in his

generation, and his duality of vision is intrinsic to the impact of his poems on death. Later pieces, such as "Devonshire Street W.1." and "Variation on a Theme of Newbolt", get their power, not merely from firmly placing death in the local and the trivial, but also from their realisation of the fact that this greatest event is associated with what is otherwise trivial, and that the minutiae of life are seen to go on in spite of death. A similar effect is achieved in earlier poems like "Croydon" and "Oxford: Sudden Illness at the Bus-Stop".

> . . . What forks since then have been slammed in places?
> What peas turned out from how many a tin?
> From plate-glass windows how many faces
> Have watched professors come hobbling in?
>
> Too much, too many! so fetch the doctor,
> This dress has grown such a heavier load
> Since Jack was only a Junior Proctor,
> And rents were lower in Rawlinson Road.

Betjeman is not being merely nostalgic about Rawlinson Road, nor directly satirical about tinned peas. A line from Wallace Stevens's "Sunday Morning" comes to mind: "These are the measures destined for her soul". Death is sad because it is a passing of human life, of human happiness; and the average human life is bound up with things like tinned peas, and these trivia make up the setting of human happiness. In "Croydon", Croydon is a measure of the life that has disappeared—a suburban life; but the sadness of death is also a measure of what Croydon is in some human lives.

> In a house like that
> Your Uncle Dick was born;
> Satchel on back he walked to Whitgift
> Every weekday morn.
>
> Boys together in Coulsdon woodlands,
> Bramble-berried and steep,
> He and his pals would look for spadgers
> Hidden deep.

The laurels are speckled in Marchmont Avenue
  Just as they were before,
But the steps are dirty [dusty*] that still lead up to
  Your Uncle Dick's front door.

Pear and apple in Croydon gardens
  Bud and blossom and fall,
But your Uncle Dick has left his Croydon
  Once for all.

The poem is very telling in its directness, in the way in which it brings out the pathos of the death by constantly presenting images of youth and fruitfulness and renewal, in the sure handling of rhythm and in the effect attained by the under-playing of emotion. It is interesting to reflect that this poem and Betjeman's "Death of King George V" are among the most humanly touching poems of death from the thirties. They avoid the ultimately self-defeating rhetoric of poems like Auden's "In Memory of W. B. Yeats" and of many of the poems of the Spanish Civil War.

Reading Betjeman's *Collected Poems*, one cannot help thinking of Housman: not because both poets wrote well of death; but because both of them, read extensively, are much less good than they appear in selection. Housman, with his dying boys, seems continually to be going through the same poses of lachrymose stoicism. Betjeman, for all his excellence and individuality in his best poems, is too often, in his own phrase, "Summoned by Bells".

MacNeice and Betjeman have more in common than just the fact that each celebrates the ordinary. Neither of them attempted to assimilate the actual to an organised vision of their own (as did many other poets of the period), though elements of fable and fantasy were important in MacNeice's work. In MacNeice's case, in particular, it is the unostentatious humility of his acceptance of limited goals for his poetry that makes his poetry at once so engaging and so acceptable.

* *Collected Poems.*

Chapter 9

THE CENTRE OF THE STAGE

Acceptance of the New Poetry – *Scrutiny*, F. R. Leavis and other critics

IN THE CASE of most poetic revolutions, the legend develops of the early volumes "bursting" on a surprised but fascinated public. In fact, such legends are frequently the projection back of later literary quarrels and salutes. Many epoch-making volumes have not even been lucky enough to get abusive reviews. They have past unnoticed or been dismissed with faint praise, except in the writer's own circle.

The volumes of poetry discussed in this book that were published prior to 1932 seem to have received little notice. It was only after the publication of *New Signatures* that "the Auden group" became better known. The acceptance by the dominant in-group (presumably represented by publication in *The Criterion* or by Faber and Faber or the Woolfs' Hogarth Press), in which F. R. Leavis found the seeds of the undoing of these writers, had in fact taken place before 1932; though this was not in any great measure responsible for the success of *New Signatures*, which went through a number of impressions before the end of 1935. By the end of that year, various things had combined to make Auden, and some of his friends, well known to the poetry-reading public, small though it was. The growth of the Popular Front movement after that time brought them an even wider public, and also made them public figures as literary spokesmen of the Left.

Two anthologies published in 1936 marked the acceptance of the new poets as established writers. One was *The Faber Book of Modern Verse*, Michael Roberts's major venture in anthologising. Here Empson, Eberhart, Auden, Day Lewis and Spender from *New Signatures* and Charles Madge from *New Country* appear along with Hopkins, Yeats, Eliot, Pound. Also included were Louis MacNeice, George Barker, Dylan Thomas, David Gascoyne and James Reeves.

A similar list of younger poets is to be found in Yeats's notorious *The Oxford Book of Modern Verse*, the other well known anthology of modern poetry published in 1936. Yeats, who in a broadcast of the same year, characterised the early poets of the twentieth century as believing that "Tristram and Isoult were not a more suitable theme than Paddington Railway Station",[1] had included a more than adequate representation of the poetry of his own friends, but had been very scant in his choice of poems by Eliot and his contemporaries. The result was hardly a volume representative of "modern poetry" in 1936. However, Yeats found Auden and the poets of his generation more congenial. He included poems by Michael Roberts, William Plomer, Day Lewis, MacNeice, Auden, Spender, Julian Bell, Charles Madge and George Barker. The inclusion of these writers in an anthology in the series of Oxford Books of Verse at once put them on every library shelf.

Another collection produced in 1936, but published in January, 1937, was a special British number of *Poetry*, edited by W. H. Auden and Michael Roberts. It included a survey by Roberts, reviews by Auden, Day Lewis and Empson, and poems by a very mixed bag of authors, including Auden, Dylan Thomas, Bottrall, Edwin Muir, George Barker, Lilian Bowes Lyon, Richard Church and Roger Roughton. By this time Roberts had moved away from his *New Country* position. In his survey in *Poetry* he remarked: ". . . the poet is never a good party man";[2] and his long introduction to *The Faber Book of Modern Verse*—one of the best essays of its length on modern poetry—makes no mention of the *New Signatures/New Country* poets as a group. The discussion is conducted in terms reminiscent of Eliot and Richards rather than of the critical thinking of the thirties.

1937 saw an even more public recognition of the new poetry in the award of the King's Gold Medal for poetry to Auden. It is a measure of the esteem in which Auden was held in younger literary circles that this award did not break him as a poetic leader.

II

The rapid literary success of Auden and his friends was naturally enough associated with an equal fierceness of criticism from some who did not approve of them. One of these was Robert Graves. Graves's view of Auden was put succinctly in the dismissal of him in *The Long Week-end*: "Auden was a synthetic writer, and perhaps never wrote an original line. . . ."[3] Graves seems to have been extraordinarily sensitive on this subject. He wrote a long letter to *Left Review* because one of its articles suggested that Auden's interest in nursery rhymes might have something to do with Graves's earlier writings on them. Graves's opinions died hard—or rather, not at all. They were expressed again in 1956 in *The Crowning Privilege*; and, in the sixties, James Reeves, a friend and admirer of Graves, found Auden to be "an extremely accomplished verse journalist".[4]

More formidable than the Gravesian sniping was the extended attack of *Scrutiny*, especially in view of the wide cultural influence of that periodical after its decease. Readers of Leavis's "The Progress of Poesy" in *The Common Pursuit* may be surprised to know that Auden contributed six reviews to *Scrutiny* between 1932 and 1936. *Scrutiny*'s all out attack on anything and everything produced by Auden and his friends dates from their established acclaim in the middle thirties and the concurrent prevalence of simplistic left-wing ideas in the period of the Popular Front.

Auden was always spoken of in *Scrutiny* as having "talent"; though he is not mentioned in the original edition of *New Bearings in English Poetry* in 1932, Empson and Bottrall then being Leavis's choice among the new poets. By 1934, however, Empson and Bottrall appeared less promising, and "Auden's strength" seemed to be "to have just what Mr Empson appears to lack: a profound inner disturbance . . ."[5]

A review by Leavis, as was so frequently the case, established the *Scrutiny* attitude to the new poets. It was "This Poetical Renascence", of June, 1933. The position stated there is almost too well known to need quoting:

> Favourable reviews and a reputation are no substitute for the conditions represented by the existence of an intelligent public—the give-and-take that is necessary for self-realisation, the pressure that, resisted or yielded to, determines direction, the intercourse that is collaboration. . . .

The result is "a confusion, very natural where the Group counts for so much and is the only certain audience . . ."[6]

In 1934, Auden and Bottrall are still ". . . indubitable talents, capable, on a convincing measure of proof, of expressing sensibilities of our time in poetry".[7] However, neither has come up to expectation; and, in the case of Bottrall, the effect is seen as the work of one of *Scrutiny*'s recurrent enemies—"sophistication". "Sophistication"—the metropolitan, public-school, Oxonian veneer—was also responsible for damaging Auden's talents.

The early reviews are, on the whole, excellent criticism; but, after 1936, *Scrutiny* reviewers just let loose at Auden and his friends. *Scrutiny*'s weakness in dealing with contemporary poetry was that its orientation was too sociological. There was continual talk of critical reputations and critical positions. *Scrutiny* was concerned with holding before its public what it felt to be the right critical standards; and in doing this it made a contribution of the highest value to the cultural life of the period. It saw its public mission to be the upholding of these standards; and no judgement might be allowed that seemed to imply any deviation from these standards. Poets were measured and found wanting—or, rather, tested and found "unsound"—in terms of a conception of poetry that showed little openness to modification by the experience of reading new poetry. Like all puritans, the *Scrutiny* critics preferred the dull that is not tainted, to the brilliant and lively that is impure.

Where the British penchant for "soundness", as manifested in *Scrutiny*, can lead one is shown by the contemporary poets that the periodical published. *Scrutiny* sponsored two modern British poets, Ronald Bottrall and C. H. Peacock. The deadness of Bottrall's work has already been remarked upon. Three poems by Peacock were published in *Scrutiny*, two of them in the first and second numbers. They were unexceptionable and conventional. Peacock was a "sound" poet, but dull, as the following passage (praised by Geoffrey Walton at the expense of MacNeice's *The Earth Compels* in June, 1938) will show:

> I would not have life whittled to an hour
> Of sifted essence, and all memories creep
> Round one small orbit while the visual power

Becomes not means to gain but keep.
Better to leave all legacy behind
Than sign acceptance in terms of sleep.[8]

Of course, *Scrutiny* was in good measure right about the decline of cultural standards in the thirties, especially in matters affected by politics. However, it tended to be right partly for the wrong reasons. In the first place, its editor was not "posh", and it had a rooted dislike for anything that was; and this dislike attached itself to the left-wing, public school poets and to Bloomsbury and metropolitan literary circles. (It never attacked *Left Review*, much direr by *Scrutiny* standards than the Auden-*New Writing* group, but some of whose contributors were old friends from *The Calendar of Modern Letters*, *Scrutiny*'s distinguished ancestor.) More importantly, its real enemy was technology and the vulgarity of the new England with its middlebrow public. Its critical ideas were associated with a nostalgia for a past that never existed—a past which it located in seventeenth-century England. In that age "soundness" blossomed with full delicacy. In the twentieth century "soundness" could only be cultivated by excessive weeding and pruning. In the end, *Scrutiny* did not approve of any new flowers at all.

Chapter 10

NEW VERSE

New Verse – Geoffrey Grigson – Norman Cameron –
Bernard Spencer – Kenneth Allott

UNDOUBTEDLY THE MOST important periodical in the
history of poetry in the nineteen-thirties was *New Verse*. It
was conceived one winter evening in 1932 by Geoffrey Grigson
and his friend Hugh Ross Williamson, who had recently
written the first full-length book on T. S. Eliot. It appeared
first in January, 1933, and ran through thirty-four numbers,
closing at the beginning of the war in 1939. It cost sixpence—
"the price of ten Players or a brief library borrowing of *Angel
Pavement* or a 'bus fare from Piccadilly Circus to Golders
Green" (*NV*, 1 (Jan., 1933) 2), as the first number explained.
For his sixpence, the subscriber generally got about twenty
pages of poetry and reviews, with occasionally squibs thrown
at those members of the literary establishment that the editor
at the moment most disliked. The circulation was around a
thousand.

Grigson edited *New Verse* from start to finish, and wrote the
bulk of the reviews. He had a very decided notion of what
poetry should be, and even more decided notions of what it
should not be. This was the great strength of *New Verse*; and,
apart from the high quality of many of the contributions, is
what makes it still satisfyingly readable for its own sake after
thirty years. By example in what it chose to publish, and by
precept in its reviews, *New Verse* performed a valuable critical
rôle in the thirties.

Unlike many of the periodicals of the later thirties, *New
Verse* did not stand for any particular extra-poetic position.
The second number announced: "If there must be attitudes, a
reasoned attitude of toryism is welcomed no less than a
communist attitude" (*NV*, 2 (Mar., 1933) 1); though, typically
of the period, *New Verse* ran a special double number on
"Commitments", which contained no verse. (Indeed, six of

the thirty-four numbers contained virtually no verse at all.) However, Grigson favoured a particular attitude to poetry, and this attitude could be related to a definite attitude towards the world. Grigson in fact made this connection in the anthology, *New Verse*, in which, in 1939, he collected together the poems he most valued of those he had published. A selection of remarks from this preface will bring out as clearly as anything what Grigson, in retrospect, saw *New Verse* as standing for:

> It is a fact that both an epic and a limerick are poems. You cannot suppose a divine or an inspired origin for one against a secular or a rational origin for the other. You can only distinguish in them differences of effect and quality.
>
> It is this fact which is accepted by the best of those poets who have written for *New Verse*. . . . It prevents them from too much vagueness and subjectivity of illustration in their poems, and encourages them to write in terms and images commonly understood. It drives them outward on to natural facts and forms. It encourages them to observe well, and—it is Auden's terminology—to be good reporters.
>
> It is a very good thing for writers to be subjecting themselves in this way to a discipline of objects, and events. They deal once more with an explicable, if not with a calculable and an orderly, universe. . . .[1]

As a result of this discipline, poets are "very much better off . . . than they were, say, twenty-five years ago . . ."[2] Auden and Louis MacNeice are the best poets in England, after Yeats and Eliot: "Both are champions of common sense."[3] They do not "set up . . . Pure Poetry or Surrealism . . ."[4] Outside this beneficial situation, a poet like Stephen Spender would very likely be as bad as Grigson found Rupert Brooke to be. The criterion by which Grigson selected poems was that of whether they were "genuine".[5]

This one word, "genuine", perhaps sums up most succinctly what *New Verse* stood for. (Its name was carefully chosen: *New Verse*; "poetry" being a slightly suspect word in its vocabularly.) "Genuine" meant "something actual has happened to the writers, something has been sensed, imagined, understood, and the poems present the commotion set up in that way".[6]

New Verse reflected in its shortcomings what it positively stood for: if, as a whole, it might be criticised for anything, it would be that it preferred the well realised trivial poem to the more ambitious poem marred by pretentiousness or portentousness. It would be kinder to the epigrams of Geoffrey Taylor than to the poetry of George Barker:

> Sally, having swallowed cheese,
> Directs down holes the scented breeze,
> Enticing thus with baited breath
> Nice mice to an untimely death.
>
> ("Cruel Clever Cat")

This poem by Taylor was included in the *New Verse* anthology.

New Verse made its positions much plainer by attack than by positive assertion. A poem like Edgar Foxall's "A Note on Working Class Solidarity" was at once a performance in the *New Verse* manner and an attack on the simplifications and falsities of doctrinaire left-wing policy:

> There will be no festivities when we lay down these tools,
> For we are the massed grooves of grease-smooth systems.
> The Communist measures the future, the Elect fear the past,
> But we are those ribless polyps that nature insures
> Against thought by routines, against triumph by tolerance
> Against life by the sense of mechanical footbeats,
> Against protest by cant, extinction by syphilis,
> And the glory of crucifixion by the price of timber.
>
> (*NV*, 5 (Oct., 1933) 5)

New Verse consistently sniped at Day Lewis, not, as it explained, "for an excess of Communist loyalty", but "as a bad poet, a muddled writer distinctly respectable, bourgeois and ordinary in his way of writing, which differs altogether from his no doubt sincere political ideology" (*NV*, 23 (Christmas, 1936) 24). These attacks culminated two issues later in "Day Lewis Joins Up"—an announcement and a denunciation of his joining the selection committee of the Book Society:

> The Book Society is a Limited Company pimping to the mass bourgeois mind and employing "distinguished" members of the literary underworld, . . . On this Committee, Mr. Day Lewis no doubt will be Change, Revolution, Youth, the Rising Genera-

tion. But this ends his stance as the Poet writing thrillers . . . We can get along without him. (*NV*, 25 (May, 1937) 23–4)

The reviewing was often equally lively. Here is the greater part of a review of Hugh Macdiarmid's *Second Hymn To Lenin*:

> We would respect Mr. Hugh Macdiarmid if we could. He has written 8 books of verse, 2 of fiction, 1 of politics, $2\frac{1}{2}$ of criticism, $\frac{1}{2}$ a book of agriculture, and he has edited two anthologies. He has a name, he has contributed to *The Criterion*, he is always mentioned in books about Scotland, he dislikes Mr. St. John Ervine. And yet, here are these 77 pages of unvarying twitter. You expected a bulbul, you find—and don't need fieldglasses to make sure—a moulting, maundering chiff-chaff. In these poems there is just a little virtue. The sentiment is sometimes neat. Bathos is just avoided. Great authors have been read and respected. . . . We would sooner have a quick one, of course, with Mr. Macdiarmid than with Mr. Humbert Wolfe, but even the greasy ripples of Mr. Wolfe get nearer than these high-brow doggerels to good verse.
>
> (*NV*, 19 (Feb.–March, 1936) 19)

A frequent feature was the reprinting of snippets from other periodicals, intended to show their authors up as asses. Always under attack in this way were Michael Roberts and Edith Sitwell ("The Old Jane"):

> F. C. Boden   *A Derbyshire Tragedy*
> "A work of lasting importance."—Michael Roberts.
> *Publisher's Advertisement*
> (*NV*, 16 (Aug.–Sept., 1935) 22)
>
> *Spare Parts*
> ". . . my senses are like those of primitive peoples, at once acute and uncovered—and they are interchangeable."
> The Old Jane
> (*NV*, 22 (Aug–Sept., 1936) 19)

The sniping of "Old Jane" was so popular that, after the dedication to his first volume of poems, Grigson wrote: "And on second thoughts / also for my publicity manager, / *Edith Sitwell* / with love and thanks." "Michael the Mountaineer" was guilty of "that nauseating concern for *poetry*". "Mr Michael Roberts, an unremarkable stodge, a Pecuchet who has taken up mathematics, poetry (modern), and mountaineering, has put *himself* between the *Faber Book of Modern Verse* and those who may want to read it" (*NV*, 20 (Apr.–May, 1936) 26).

Michael Roberts was, of course, a rival *doyen* of the new poetry. However, *New Verse* attacked both its friends and its enemies if it felt that they were being shabby, false, or had lapsed in any way. The "Commitments" double number contained "In Memoriam T. S. E.[liot]" by Charles Madge. Many of the most biting comments contained a lot of good sense. "If *Scrutiny* is not to be the perfect body-builder for prigs it must change its formula. To risk a few bad plants from a few seeds is better than to water all the garden with weed-killer" (*NV*, 4 (June, 1933) 2). *Scrutiny*'s gradually hardening preoccupation with "soundness" is very acutely "placed" by the last remark.

The example of the type of poem it chose to publish was, even more than its comments, the way in which *New Verse* made its mark on the poetry of the thirties. Only an anthology, such as Grigson's own anthology of 1939, could make clear fully the nature of that example. However, a good deal may be gathered from the examination of the poems of the editors, Grigson, Bernard Spencer, and Kenneth Allott, and of that regular and exemplary contributor, Norman Cameron.

II

Grigson's own poems might be seen as a demonstration of the things that *New Verse* stood for. The first poem by Grigson to be published in *New Verse* under his own name ("Several Observations") reads like a manifesto, in that it is quite deliberately nothing but a list of things noticed:

> The hours of the public place:
> In the morning hour the old
> Man with his nurse meets
> The child with her nurse, between
>
> The rosebed and the violas.
> At three the students with
> Their theodolites and red
> And white and black poles

> Measure the known heights,
> And the scarlet and the green
> Footballers pattern their knees
> In the wind, by the black wood
>
> Where the caterpillars spin.
> And the evening hour, when
> The purple mallards are
> Saying ach ach on the pond,
>
> When the man dressed in ochre
> Spikes the silver paper, and
> The sweaty lover squirms
> Under the lime tree.
>   (*NV*, 20 (Apr.–May, 1936) 8)

It is easy to dismiss such a poem as trivial and to miss a great deal that is original in the poem. Grigson has become known as an art critic, and has a predilection for clearly realised images, as his criticisms of George Barker and Dylan Thomas show.[7] The position is a rather limiting one, and derives ultimately from Imagist doctrines. The title of Grigson's poem (which he used as the title of his first book) was meant to recall Eliot's *Prufrock and other Observations*, and the poem conceived as a series of observations without comment derives from Eliot's "Preludes". The deliberate, almost aggressive, avoidance of comment—moral or otherwise—is in line with Grigson's editorial dislike of the pretentious and the portentous.

These are negative features, and involve only the meaning and the imagery of the poem. A more positive rationale for Grigson's poetry is to be found in his statement in the double number of *New Verse* on commitments:

> Look for objects: the only poets who can go beyond them are those who have seen them, and checked and criticised the impression they have made upon them . . . The use of ideas . . . depends upon this fidelity to objects, and objects include language, but not "poetry". (*NV*, 31–2 (Autumn, 1938) 17)

Read in the context of its original publication in *New Verse*, the poem stands out as having a new, if muted and self-effacing, type of music. Francis Scarfe pointed out how Grigson carefully ends his lines with unresolved parts of speech, and how his poems are completely altered if these parts of speech are moved from the ends of lines to the beginnings of following lines.[8] The reason for this is that adjectives, for instance, require their following noun before a unit of sense is formed, so that, by placing "old" at the end of the second line, the poet presses the reader to move over the natural pause of the line end. This was a trick to be found in Rilke's poetry. The continued use of this device results in a poem where the form does not assert itself, and where there is no feeling that the meaning falls into line or stanza units. This effect is reinforced by the handling of rhythm. The free verse is not syllabic, nor is it, like Eliot's verse, a variation on a regular metrical pattern. There is a basic measure of three stresses to the line, from which the poet varies a little; but there is never any sense of the verse falling into feet. It comes very close to prose that has a fairly regular placing of stress. It is to be noted, too, that there is not a single metaphor or simile (or even a phrase that calls attention to itself) in the poem. The images are not "imagery" in the sense that Spender's images often are—oblique ways of conveying meaning or working on the reader. The images are a series of things noticed, and are included in the poem in their own right. The diction is such as to be as nearly transparent as possible in presentation of the images.

All these things are more surprising than they may at first thought seem. Auden, MacNeice and Spender all write poetry in which the reader is clearly intended to relish the poet's virtuosity in the handling of the language. They also use language in an overtly figurative way. The way in which Grigson writes marks a considerable change in approach to language. Nevertheless, Grigson's poem has very obvious limitations. It seems to stem partly from the British tendency to place a high valuation on sensitive observation for its own sake. Grigson grew up in Cornwall, and his most lasting attachment seems to have been to the flora and fauna of that area.

The "list" poem can be a bore, if it appears in the company of a large number of its own kind. *Several Observations* opens with the poem "Around Cadbury Castle". The poem, which will be found to consist of one sentence without a main verb, concludes in a series of dots. The effect is of observation cut

out of the thread of life. But why did he stop where he did?
And, in what sense is such a list a poem? In addition if the
poet is not in top form, the "list" poem may consist of nothing
but the conventional poetic furniture of the period in which
it was written:

> . . . Over boarded panes of a broken house, a notice
>   begging recruits,
> And lamps murder the moon, the dead king lies
> Under a lid, heart-failures vanish from cafés, . . .
>   "About Life" (*NV*, 22 (Aug.–Sept., 1936) 6)

The list poem may, on the other hand, add up to something
that comes very near to a moral message, as in "Knowledge
of This Knowledge", another poem without a main verb,
where the poet lists things he knows he knows, but in an
order that crescendos into quite a fierce perspective on all
the things listed.

Not all of Grigson's poems of the thirties are written to
prescription. One of the disappointing aspects of his first
book, *Several Observations*, is a lack of stylistic unity, when
compared with his second book, *Under the Cliff*, of 1943. This
arises partly from the inclusion of several early poems. Also,
there are some overtly political poems: "In Munich, City
of Art" (occasioned by seeing Hitler's exhibition of Degenerate
Art) and "The Non-Interveners". The most successful poem
in the book is "And forgetful of Europe", in which the fact
of turning his back on a troubled Europe into a scene of
personal delight gives a structure and framework to the
"observations" that fill the poem:

> Think now about all the things which made up
> That place: you noticed first
> Under the plane tree, where the gay [*NV*: "red"]
> And white canoes were, the green peppers
> And the black figs on the stall: the countess then
> (slightly red when we came close
> Between the brown of her body
> And her white bathing dress),
> Her blonde hair pulling off her smart
> Old face, her crimson nails, and not

A quiver in the guarded bust, as she rose
With Bull-dog Drummond from her wicker
Chair: then from the Countess
To the chapel, under the pink and the white
Oleanders, up the path between the white walls
And the soft agrimony: the orchard with
Scarlet pomegranate flowers, the very deep
Stream full of light in its curved
Silk-stocking-coloured limestone bed.
A sulphur wagtail balanced, where it moved
Under the mill-house.

                    (*NV*, 30 (Summer, 1938) 6–7)

The poem is too long to give in full. A comparison of the description of the Countess with a similar description in *Places of the Mind* (1949) shows the extent to which *Several Observations* were "observations".

III

In many respects, the poet who exemplified most what *New Verse* stood for was Norman Cameron, in spite of the fact that he had no part in any of the "movements" of the thirties. A friend and admirer of Robert Graves, "he could not", as Graves put it, "abide . . . pretentiousness and insincerity".[9] Dylan Thomas, whom Cameron befriended when he came to London, used to tell the story that Cameron had bought up and burned a number of copies of George Barker's first book, because he didn't want anyone to read such bad poems. He described himself as "a part-time poet"; and, whatever one may feel about the quality of his poetry, the pattern of his career bears this out. He was a contemporary of Auden at Oxford, though completely uninfluenced by Auden and his friends. Of the sixty poems in his *Collected Poems*, at least nine were written when he was an undergraduate, and appeared in *Oxford Poetry*. After a short period in Nigeria, he settled for a while with Graves and Laura Riding in Majorca, where he evidently wrote many of the poems that appeared in *New Verse*. He returned to London to become an advertising copy writer. The latter part of the thirties was a less prolific period for him: by 1936 he had written nearly two-thirds of the poems in *Collected Poems*, though he remained active as a translator. By 1950 his health was breaking, and he was psycho-analysed and became a Catholic shortly afterwards. He died in 1953.

His brief and sparse career shows little development. "The Voyage to Secrecy", which appeared in *Oxford Poetry* for 1928, is an entirely characteristic poem, and shows a fully developed control of his personal idiom:

> The morn of his departure, men could say
> "Either by such a way or such a way,"
> And, a week later, still, by plotting out
> The course of all the roadways round about,
> "In these same score of places he may be."
> How many days the voyage to secrecy?
> Always the milestones by the road hark back
> To whence he came, and those in idleness
> Can bound his range with map and compasses.
>
> When shall their compasses strain wide and crack,
> And alien milestones, with strange figures,
> Baffle the sagest geographers?

The poem is decidedly Gravesian, and this was to remain true of Cameron's poetry, despite its complete naturalness. The form of poem that responded to the pressures from which Cameron wrote was one that told a story or presented a scene that mirrored a psychological conflict in the poet. It was this, no doubt, that attracted him to Graves and made Graves his model throughout his career. Graves's own poetry can be seen as an attempt to accommodate his unconscious, to deal with emotional strains, and particularly those associated with sex. Graves's poetry is full of words of strain and tension, and a phrase in Cameron's poem that recalls Graves is "their compasses strain wide and crack".

However, Cameron's poems do not have the punch or the resonance of the best of Graves's poetry. Graves's rhythms have more muscularity and variety, his diction more tang, and he makes his details work harder, getting a greater fullness of suggestion behind them.

A revealing poem by Cameron in this connection is "The Compassionate Fool":

My enemy had bidden me as guest.
His table all set out with wine and cake,
His ordered chairs, he to beguile me dressed
So neatly, moved my pity for his sake.

I knew it was an ambush, but could not
Leave him to eat his cake up by himself
And put his unused glasses on the shelf.
I made pretence of falling in his plot,

And trembled when in his anxiety
He bared it too absurdly to my view;
And even as he stabbed me through and through
I pitied him for his small strategy.

(*NV*, 9 (June, 1934) 3)

Approached as an attempt to write like Graves, this poem seems rhythmically thin and muted in detail. Its story, too, seems lacking in depth and richness of suggestion. The theme, however, is a puritan Christian one: the middle-class virtue of consideration for others, together with the Christian virtue of turning the other cheek, are carried to the point of self-parody. When one notices this, one then begins to see that the individuality of the poem lies in its muteness and sparseness. It is not only the setting that suggests the poetry of George Herbert—in this case "Love"—but also the chastity of manner. The poetic virtues that give Cameron an individual voice as a poet are those one would associate with Herbert: simplicity that hides a sophisticated understanding of the medium; control and lack of ostentation.

Though Cameron was not a political poet, this was not due to lack of concern. In reply to a *New Verse* enquiry, he wrote:

> I believe that Communism is necessary and good, but I'm not eager for it. To act, from a feeling of moral compulsion, as if I were eager for it would be hysterical. (*NV*, 11 (Oct., 1934) 15)

The honesty and dignity of the answer is characteristic, and more maturely moral than the attitude of the tub thumpers. A mature self-effacement is revealed in his explanation of why he wrote poetry: "I write a poem because I think it wants to be written" (*NV*, 11 (Oct., 1934) 15). Those who rank maturity high should rank Cameron high. Certainly his unpretentious virtues might have been a salutary example to many writers of the thirties. Perhaps these are not the virtues that make for stature in poetry. The powerfully individual poetic voice is that of the man who needs to assert his vision of reality in the face of reality, to impose himself on the medium and on others. Cameron, in his "epitaph", seems to have recognised in himself this lack of pressure to go at full stretch:

> Forgive me, sire, for cheating your intent,
> That I, who should command a regiment,
> Do amble amiably here, O God,
> One of the neat ones in your awkward squad.
> (*NV*, 16 (Aug.–Sept., 1935) 9)

IV

Bernard Spencer was, for a time, co-editor of *New Verse*, and many of his poems appeared there between 1934 and 1937. As an undergraduate he had been, along with Richard Goodman, an editor of *Oxford Poetry*, and a comparison of two poems written at the beginning and at the end of his career as an undergraduate give an insight into what sort of poet he was. In 1929 he was represented in *Oxford Poetry* by a poem "Festa":

> Because it was the Queen's birthday
> we had all run up our spirits' pennons to the top of our
>   flagposts
> and skimmed about on the surface of our lives
> like little flies on water:
> No one knew what to do
> but they were all sure they were doing it: . . .

The celebration of the surface of life, the "carnival" imagery and the free verse remind one that Spencer was a friend of Louis MacNeice. Eliot and the poets of his generation must have been the poetic idols of the early 1930s in Oxford, and one would have expected Spencer to develop the colourful vein of "Festa". However, this was not the direction in which he went. In *Oxford Poetry* for 1932 there appeared his best undergraduate poem:

For seeing whole I had been too near my friends:
When we drank or drove I came near to one,
Near to another in speaking of a woman:
What could I hold back, using their blood, their brain?

In part only I saw them. Then in the train
I crossed fields that had never known their fire;
An evening country turning, hedges and trees
Not leaved with their words and laughter, as those were.

The brow of Summer matched against their quickness
Made them seem far and overshadowed them.
They must spill apart and change whom I thought firm;
I saw them draw like green things to their time.

He had moved away from the ostentatious and modish manner of the earlier poem to develop a self-effacing and meditative style reminiscent of Hardy and Edward Thomas. The poem is not particularly remarkable in its control; nevertheless, as is the case with Edward Thomas, it is easy to overlook the way in which the verse is handled to give variations of pace in harmony with the mood. The rhythm is used to suggest a particular tone of voice.

"Ill" is one of Spencer's best poems from the thirties, and shows what an effective model Hardy could be for those who could see him clear of his often incongruous diction:

Expectant at the country gate the lantern. On the night
Its silks of light strained. Lighted upper window.
"Is it you who sent for me?" The two go in
To where the woman lies ill, upstairs, out of sight.

I hear sky softly smother to earth in rain,
As I sit by the controls and the car's burning dials.
And always the main-road traffic searching, searching the
    horizons.
Then those sounds knifed by the woman's Ah! of pain.

Who dreamed this; the dark folding murderer's hands round
    the lamps?
The rain blowing growth to rot? Lives passed beneath a
    ritual
That tears men's ghosts and bodies; the few healers
With their weak charms, moving here and there among the
    lamps?

(*NV*, 24 (Feb.–Mar., 1937) 10)

The story poem with a bitter twist is brought up to date. The unassuming manner, the controlled movement of the poem, reflect the careful meditative attitude of the poet. It is not a poem by someone who is writing what he thinks a poem should be, out of a theory of poetry; though it is certainly a poem by someone who has thought about how a poem should be written. Its rhetoric is at the service of what lies behind it. Particularly effective is the way in which the woman's cry of pain leads the poet off into a vision of universal unhappiness— a vision rendered in terms of the scene in which he finds himself.

This unpretentious poem shows much more feeling for suffering, and a more mature understanding of its nature, than do most of the "committed" poems of the period. Spencer had a good appreciation of Auden's talent. In the *New Verse* double number on Auden he wrote of Auden "brutalising his thought and language to the level from which important poetry proceeds" (*NV*, 26–7 (Nov., 1937) 27). However, when Spencer deals with a theme that constantly preoccupied Auden and his contemporaries—the relation between personal feeling and public commitment—he shows a greater sensitivity than they in his recognition of human limitation and of the touch of megalomania in those who pretend to carry the world's woes. "A Cold Night", from which this passage is taken, reminds one of Edward Thomas's "The Owl". Indoors, the poet thinks of those out in the cold, while he is by a fire:

> I turn my back to my fire. Which I must.
> I am not God or a crazed woman.
> And one needs time too to sit in peace
> Opposite one's girl, with food, fire, light,
>
> And do the work one's own blood heats,
> Or talk, and forget about the winter
> —This season, this century—and not be always
> Opening one's doors on the pitiful streets
>
> Of Europe, not always think of winter, winter, like a
>   hammering rhyme
> For then everything is drowned by the rising wind,
>   everything is done against Time.
>
>   (*NV*, 24 (Feb.–Mar., 1937) 8–9)

Spencer seldom wrote with direct political concern, though the political situation is not ignored in his poetry. His best poem from the thirties is "Allotments: April", which Kenneth Allott said, "might very well represent the kind of poem for which *New Verse* stood: straightforward but unpedestrian language, feeling expressed through observation, intelligence reflecting on observation and awake to the implications of feeling".[10]

> Cobbled with rough stone which rings my tread
> The path twists through the squared allotments.
> Blinking to glimpse the lark in the warming sun,
> In what sense am I joining in
> Such a hallooing, rousing April day,
> Now that the hedges are so gracious and
> Stick out at me moist buds, small hands, their
>   opening scrolls and fans?
>   (*NV*, 21 (June–July, 1936) 4)

The poem is a meditation on what April means to the modern secular man like himself. Something deeper than prettiness, yet not something that will "deny and conceal" "The Worry about money, the eyeless work / Of those who do not believe real poverty, / The sour doorways of the poor . . . Rather it adds / What more I am; excites the deep glands / And warms my animal bones . . ." The poem characteristically attempts no grand or simple resolution.

Spencer's *Collected Poems* occupy less than a hundred pages. Coming, in that short space on so much that is sensitive, mature and well achieved, one regrets that there are no poems that display that absolute surety of touch that makes one feel that what has been done could not have been done any other way, and not better—the mark of poetry of the first order.

v

Kenneth Allott, the other co-editor, while not appreciably younger than Grigson and Spencer, belonged to a different "generation" from that of Day Lewis and Auden. Born in 1912, he came to maturity in the thirties, and started writing in the period when the intellectual life of the universities was dominated by the political clubs. Allott began to contribute to *New Verse* in 1935, when he was still co-editor of the Oxford undergraduate periodical, *Programme*. His early work is not political; but rather its dandyism may be seen as a reaction to the overbearing political atmosphere of the time. The first poem by Allott to appear in *New Verse* echoes a writer evidently very congenial to Allott both then and later: Jules Laforgue.

> . . . Desperate, feign a yawn, hint weariness,
> run through the bag of tricks without success.
> *(NV,* 16 (Aug.–Sept., 1935) 10)

It was only natural that a poet who admired Laforgue should be attracted to surrealism when it came into vogue in England in 1936. Allott contributed a number of poems to the surrealist *Contemporary Poetry and Prose*, and his poems in *New Verse* during 1936 and 1937 have a markedly surrealist flavour. Once again, the element of fantasy was well fitted to satire, and some of Allott's most effective surrealist poems are satirical:

> Will you take a seat?
>   The War will soon be over.
> The state requires
>   my wedding ring and my apostle spoons
>   my sons.
> There will be a special service in the cathedral
> after which the clergy will be disbanded
> and the fane profaned and put to immediate service
> to manufacture wooden legs for heroes
> with a profitable side-line in glass-eyes
> and employment found for over two hundred widows . . .
> *(NV,* 20 (Apr.–May, 1936) 6–7)

Throughout Allott's surrealist poems there is a controlled thread of sense or narrative. Perhaps the most effective of his poems of this period is "Lullaby"—a poem about falling asleep, where the surrealistic manner is evocative of the experience described:

> . . . Say goodnight and close the door behind you
> the wireless keeps on playing to the room
> and if a gesture like the boyhood of Raleigh
> and if a word who is there left to listen?
> the timid footsteps dropping so far behind you . . .
>
> (*NV*, 19 (Feb.–Mar., 1936) 6)

The broken syntax is in fact very guilefully handled to evoke the sense of discontinuity of experience; and "a gesture like the boyhood of Raleigh" (referring to a picture whose reproduction appeared in many middle-class homes) reminds one what a witty poet, in a Laforguean sense, Allott was.

At the end of 1936, Allott seems to have undergone a change of feeling concerning poetry and politics. His most effective political poem was the long "Men Walk Upright", which appeared in the July, 1938, issue of *Twentieth Century Verse*. The theme is the clash between private and public, coupled with a feeling that life as the poet knows it is doomed. The first theme is presented, as it was frequently in the poetry of the period, in terms of a sense of guilt that the things the poet most values in middle-class life and culture are economically dependent on social injustice:

> . . . Who can bear this? Who can face without wincing
> The noseless in the mean alley, the fellowship
> Of the loud saloon, the housewife losing a sixpence
>   And hopelessly crying?
>
> Knowing that this is the groundwork of that same freedom
> We so much boast: the right to accumulate
> Dust on library shelves, to be proud of an accent,
>   To decide in no question . . .
>
> (*Twentieth Century Verse*, 11 (July, 1938) 61)

Like Auden's "Spain", which is also, in part, a farewell to a whole way of life, the poem gets its power from the broad sweep of things mentioned in it. As in "Spain", too, the central feelings of the poem are very simple; and, again as in "Spain", one feels how the overpowering menace of fascism is imposing a growingly crude simplicity on political thought and feeling.

Allott explained his position regarding politics and poetry in his long contribution to the *New Verse* double number on commitments (*NV*, 31–2 (Autumn, 1938) 4–5):

It is hysterical to pretend to have the same feelings about social evils, slums, malnutrition, bad working conditions, as one has about the immediate disagreeable experiences which happen everyday.

His attitude is very similar to that of Bernard Spencer. In the same statement he wrote:

> What machines have been sufficiently identified with ourselves for the production of poetry about them? We have anthropomorphic ideas certainly about railways and automobiles. . . . The photographer with his bulb, his black cloth and his imaginary bird is a powerful image to me. . . .

The last remark refers, of course, to "Lament for a Cricket Eleven". The group of remarks as a whole points very well to one of the main concerns of the poets of Allott's age-group—the imaginative absorption of the contemporary scene. These ideas are also connected with the surrealist aim to free man imaginatively from the sense that the world is "other" and imposes limitations.

Allott's writing is witty and urbane. Like Grigson and like other poets of his own age-group, he is not, apart from his wit, a "phrase maker", as were Auden and Spender, for instance. The language is used flatly as a means of mentioning "things", which do not appear figuratively (though often symbolically) in the poetry. It is from the things mentioned (and from his wit) that his poetry derives its colour. The poetry has sparkle—but often a slightly dandyish, precious sparkle. Allott's precocious virtuosity seems too easily attained. After producing two books of poems—*Poems*, 1938, and *The Ventriloquist's Doll*, 1943—he appears to have ceased publishing poetry.

VI

Looking back on *New Verse*, Grigson wrote:

> If I can bear to look into old notebooks, it is rather more than I can bear to look now in old numbers of *New Verse*. My own fault. Many of the poems I published in it were good, many bad.

They are not the reason. But the public assault to which younger poets were treated in those days by such men as St. John Ervine and Ivor Brown and many of the hacks of Fleet Street with less talent and many of the bloodless followers of the *London Mercury* were an irritant to a reply in kind, to a slash with the billhook, which was far too much my weapon and which I endeavoured to keep sharp, wiping off the blood from time to time—when it happened, that is, to catch someone in whom any blood was flowing. But the tactic was wrong. It was worse than wrong. I had not grown up enough to discover those lines by Dryden and to realize that the neck of a beheaded fool grows three more foolish heads. The fun and the slaughter now make me, if I recall them, rather sick. They covered up too little in me of a positive affection, too little of a viable desire. The tactic was too uncharitable, and dust lies down sooner or later of its own accord.[11]

Reviewing his life in 1950, in *The Crest on the Silver*, Grigson saw the thirties, from the time of his discovery of Eliot while an undergraduate, as a period of unfaithfulness to the garden of the Cornish vicarage in which he grew up; and his work as a whole since 1940 gives the impression that he approaches the arts with a naturalist's eye. It is the criterion of the clearly visualised image that unites the taste of *New Verse* with the concerns of his later criticism: the poetry of Grigson, Allott, Kathleen Raine and of many other contributors to *New Verse* was marked by the visual clarity that Grigson admired in painters like Fuseli. A lack of visual clarity was one of the faults for which he assailed Dylan Thomas and George Barker in the forties. To those who disliked *New Verse*, *New Verse* stood for the cult of the "object-image". In so far as this was a fair characterisation, it implied a limiting attitude towards language in the editorial policy—what Henry Treece called "faith in the bare name".[12] The criteria for poetry implied by Grigson's tastes are perhaps adequate for the minor poets whom he has done so much to bring back to public attention: Rochester; William Diaper; Christopher Smart; John Clare; William Barnes; William Allingham; R. W. Dixon. However, they are insufficient to do justice to the greatest poetry or to poetry that takes hold of language in the most elemental way.

Chapter 11

PARTON STREET

Parton Street – Surrealism – *Contemporary Poetry and Prose*

PARTON STREET (which no longer exists) was a short but run-down Georgian crescent, adjoining Red Lion Square in Holborn. Number One, Parton Street, was "The Arts Café", where one might have seen David Gascoyne, John Pudney, George Barker, Dylan Thomas, John Cornford, at various times in the middle thirties. Opposite, at Number Four, was the literary heart of Parton Street, David Archer's bookshop. Next door to it, at Number Two, were the offices of Lawrence and Wishart, who published official Communist literature, and, in its latter days, the periodical, *Left Review*.

Archer, the son of a general, had started his bookshop when he came down from Cambridge in 1932. He is now little remembered, but he was one of the more remarkable people in the literary world of the thirties. His bookshop, which was anything but commercial, was a gathering place for young writers, who often borrowed Archer's stock. Archer was strongly Left in his political views. From his shop the review, *Twentieth Century* (the Journal of the Promethean Society), was published. Among its contributors in the early thirties were Auden and Spender. Archer's Parton Press produced the first books of poetry by George Barker (*Thirty Preliminary Poems*, 1933) and Dylan Thomas (*Eighteen Poems*, 1934); and David Gascoyne's *Man's Life is this Meat* (1936). In 1934, Archer's partner took control of the shop, and poetry gave place to politics as its main concern.

George Barker has given a celebrated and frequently quoted description of Archer and Parton Street, and it cannot be bettered:

I called one clear and sunny morning, at about eleven o'clock, and entered a showroom in which bright books on Marxism and

bright books of verse were unneatly displayed everywhere. Up
a ladder in a corner the tall and elegant figure of a character
who might have stepped equally well out of Wodehouse or
Proust . . . turned to me with a look of despair and relief as I
entered. Then it addressed me: "Be an angel," it said, "hand me
that hammer." This was Archer . . . whose insight into contemporary verse helped to form the poetic opinion of a generation.
He invited me to take coffee. We went across the street into a
cafe full of overcoated poets and truant schoolboys. There was an
atmosphere of industrious conspiracy and illegal enthusiasms. Mr.
David Archer was looking for a young poet to publish. Mr.
Grigson, like a feline mandarin in shadows, was preparing his
first or second issue of blood, entitled *New Verse*. A dark young
horse was pointed out to me as the bright hope of the new poetry;
he had a sad ingratiating face and bore his responsibility with
deliberation. This was Mr. Charles Madge, most gracious of
poets. . . . I can never remember whether David Gascoyne
really spoke only in French at this time, or whether he merely
happened to give this impression. . . .

John Cornford, filthy and consumed with a ferocity of nervous
energy, ashamed and delighted when it was disclosed that he
had written the two beautiful poems published in the *Listener*
under a Welsh pseudonym . . . a small, thin Dylan Thomas with
a dirty wool scarf wound around himself like an old love affair,
looking liker to a runaway schoolboy than Esmond Romilly, who
really was one. . . .

I do not know how many juvenile revolutionaries were tempor-
arily harboured on the top floor of this bookshop, but they came
and went like a rotation of furious tiger moths, always at night.
Mothers arrived, weeping, in taxicabs. Did all the conspirators
die, I wonder, in Spain?[1]

Parton Street was as much a political centre as a literary one,
and attracted young men with revolutionary ideas like John
Cornford and Esmond Romilly, as Barker mentions. Romilly
was the nephew of Winston Churchill, and ran away from
Wellington and published from Parton Street a subversive
magazine, attacking the public schools, called *Out of Bounds*.

Indeed, it is surprising how much historic if unnoticed
publication was done in Parton Street. In addition to the
periodicals already mentioned, the regionalist little literary
magazine, *Wales*, was published from Number Four. The
surrealist *Contemporary Poetry and Prose* was published by the

young Roger Roughton from Number One. Many of the young poets who gathered at "The Arts Café" combined left-wing political views with an interest in surrealism. Parton Street was thus the centre for one of the few British flirtations with any of the continental "isms" of the twentieth century. David Gascoyne, an habitué of the café, is perhaps the only notable British poet whose work was markedly influenced by surrealism.

II

Confined from early childhood in a world that almost everything he ever hears or reads will tell him is the one and only *real* world and that, as almost no one, on the contrary, will point out to him, is a prison, man—l'homme moyen sensuel—bound hand and foot not only by those economic chains of whose existence he is becoming ever more and more aware, but also by chains of second-hand and second-rate *ideas*, the preconceptions and prejudices that help to bind together the system known . . . by the name of "civilisation", is for ever barred except in sleep from that other plane of existence where stones fall upwards and the sun shines by night, if it chooses . . . a world to which the entrance has generally been supposed, up till now, to be the sole privilege of poets and other madmen.[2]

These are the opening words of David Gascoyne's *A Short Survey of Surrealism*, one of the first expositions of the subject in English, published in 1935. To bring "freedom" to men was the surrealists' aim—freedom, that is, as they conceived it. The shackles from which they intended to release humanity were those that chained it to "reality", or its conception of reality, with the attendant conceptions of limitation and contradiction. As André Breton wrote, in the *Second Surrealist Manifesto* of 1929:

There is every reason to believe that there exists a certain point in the mind at which life and death, real and imaginary, past and future, communicable and incommunicable, high and low, cease to be perceived in terms of contradiction. Surrealist activity would be searched in vain for a motive other than the hope to determine this point.[3]

These two sentences are the key to understanding what the surrealists hoped to achieve. As Breton had written in the *First Surrealist Manifesto* of 1924: "I believe in the future resolution of these two states—outwardly so contradictory—which are dream and reality, into a sort of absolute reality, a *surreality*, so to speak. I am aiming for its conquest, certain that I myself shall not attain it, but too indifferent to my death not to calculate the joys of such possession."[4] The freedom sought was to be attained, not merely by practising surrealism in art, but by practising it in life.

What was this practice? The *First Manifesto* gives the following definition of surrealism:

> SURREALISM, noun, masc., Pure psychic automatism by which it is intended to express, either verbally or in writing, the true function of thought. Thought dictated in the absence of all control exerted by reason, and outside all aesthetic and moral preoccupations.[5]

Freud's discoveries concerning the significance of dreams had a central importance for the surrealists. Like the Romantics before them, they found madness an interesting and significant condition, akin to inspiration. Louis Aragon and André Breton produced a piece called "The Quinquagenary of Hysteria"; Salvador Dali evolved a method called "paranoiac-critical activity", in which the subject induced in himself a frame of mind in which he imposed his own predilections on reality in defiance of the pressures of reality itself.

Surrealism has its roots in the Romantic movement, and its methods are implicit in the work of some of its heroes—Baudelaire, Lautreamont and Rimbaud. The movement originated from the group who directed the review *Littérature* from 1919 to 1924—Louis Aragon, André Breton and Philippe Soupault. Tristan Tzara, the Dadaist, was associated with *Littérature* after his arrival in Paris; but Breton and his friends were not negative like the Dadaists, even if they shared their iconoclasm, and, in 1922, Breton broke with Tzara. In 1924 he produced *Le Manifeste du Surréalisme* (*First Surrealist Manifesto*). The name of the movement came from the then dead Guillaume Apollinaire, though Breton and his friends used the word for their own new method of expression.

H

The surrealist review from 1924 to 1929 was *La Révolution Surréaliste*; after 1929 it was superseded by *Le Surréalisme au Service de la Révolution*, which ran until 1933. In the *Second Surrealist Manifesto* Breton declared the surrealists' "support [of] the principal of historical materialism".[6] This resulted in a rather one-sided wooing: the surrealists contended that their efforts to free mankind were in harmony with Communism; the Communists on the whole rejected them with the contention that, if one was a Communist, there was no need to be a surrealist.

Surrealism, in fact, was one of those movements more impressive in their rationale than in their achievement. A reading of any quantity of surrealist writing is extremely boring. Although surrealism was in origin a literary movement, surrealist painting was much more effective than surrealist writing. The painted image is fully realised on the canvas; and the juxtaposition of any set of images in a picture creates a world—often a dreamlike landscape. The surrealist poem tends to read like an Imagist poem gone mad. Too frequently the bizarre flow of images is not realised in the mind of the reader: the jarring sequence itself tends to inhibit realisation; and the result is an unfocused flow of suggestion. In the case of Paul Eluard, the surrealist method is often effective. An unconscious unifying principle seems to be at work, giving his poems a distinctive tone and producing something that might effectively be called "pure" poetry. However, many surrealist poems read like material for the psychoanalyst rather than the result of an artistic use of the methods of psychoanalysis. The preponderance of excrement, blood and putrefaction, and of things repulsive to the senses is easily spotted as a feature of surrealism. David Gascoyne gives a sample sequence from the surrealist film *The Andalousian Dog*:

> The following pass across the screen: first, a cork, then a melon, then two teachers from a church school, and finally two magnificent grand pianos. The pianos are filled with the carcasses of donkeys, their legs, tails, hind-quarters and excrement sticking out of the piano-cases. As one piano passes across the screen, a huge donkey's head is seen resting on its keyboard.[7]

This sort of thing has its rationale for the surrealist: images of sexuality, excrement and blood all have a significance for the Freudian, because of their instinctual and developmental associations. However, in practice, the repetition of such images gives the impression of morbid preoccupation.

It was the shock element in surrealism that gave it its public vogue in the thirties. The "International Surrealist Exhibition" at New Burlington Galleries in June, 1936, marked the arrival of surrealism in England. It was attended by very fashionable viewers, and was widely attacked in the popular press—both important factors in the success by scandal achieved by the exhibition. Nevertheless, surrealism cannot be considered an important literary movement in England. In its pure form it was confined to the work of a few writers, the most notable being Hugh Sykes Davies and David Gascoyne, and to the periodical, *Contemporary Poetry and Prose*.

III

Contemporary Poetry and Prose was published from May, 1936, to autumn, 1937, from Number One, Parton Street, the site of "The Arts Café" (Lunches and Suppers; Open 9 a.m to 10 p.m.; Home-made Cakes; Morning Coffee). Its editor Roger Roughton was nineteen. It began as a monthly, but became a quarterly for its last two issues.

Roughton did not produce a manifesto for the first (or any) issue. The few editorials were largely concerned with politics. However, there could be no doubt about the magazine's policy, which was to publish surrealist verse and prose. The second issue, for June, 1936, was a double surrealist number, and was made up largely of translations of work by Eluard, Breton, Dali and other continental surrealists. Indeed, translation was to occupy a good deal of the space in *Contemporary Poetry and Prose*. The foreign writers almost outnumber the writers in English. Translations included work by Picasso, Lorca and Lautreamont. The value of the periodical perhaps lay most in the foreign authors it introduced to its small public.

In its statements of policy, *Contemporary Poetry and Prose* was aggressive and political. Reviewing *Surrealism*, edited by Herbert Read, and evidently published in connection with the 1936 surrealist exhibition, Humphrey Jennings accused Read and Sykes Davies of attempting to kidnap surrealism as a form of Romanticism, and of thus imposing limitations on it. The first editorial (in the fourth issue) was entitled "Surrealism and Communism". Here, too, Herbert Read comes under attack for suggesting that surrealists were more consistent Communists than many who made compromises with capitalist culture. *Contemporary Poetry and Prose* comments: "This Trotskyist 'more communist than the communists' attitude must be carefully guarded against" (*CPP*, Aug.–Sept., 1936, p. 74). Roughton was always firmly Communist in statement, and the issue for November, 1936, contained a Declaration, "ARMS for the People of Spain".

After the inclusion of translations, prose and traditional ballads (which presumably illustrated the incipient surrealism in popular culture) there was not much space for poetry in English. The only contributors who could be called "regular" were Roughton himself, Kenneth Allott, David Gascoyne, Dylan Thomas, Francis Scarfe and Humphrey Jennings. Jennings's contributions were in prose, as were some of those by Dylan Thomas. All these poets were new to the literary scene, and considerably younger than Auden and his friends.

Roger Roughton's "Watch this Space" is fairly typical of the magazine's English contributions, and of English surrealist poetry at its best:

> Under the christian tree the horse and cart
> Are waiting for the second vision,
> And the valley river fondles indecision
> Stagnant in a pastoral estate;
>
> Lovers painted on the wall
> Are gazing at imperfect faces
> By the worn mozaic meeting-places
> Of the weevil and the necrophil . . .
>
> (*CPP*, May, 1936, p. 7)

The poem not only has unity of mood, but there is an element of control and unity in the rhyme and rhythm of the traditional form. In this it contrasts with the wordy and portentous free-verse "Fragments from The Symptomatic World" of David Gascoyne. Roughton's poem also has a wholesomeness not found, for instance, in Francis Scarfe's "Billet-Doux", a poem he said he wrote in five minutes:

Looking through the blue key-hole of your eye
into your lawn, the tall tree walks towards me
hurls me fat fruit eats me with caterpillars
I am devoured by ants by hedgehogs by the owl's nostalgia,
for love is hard, so very hard to forgive.
Your spirit crawls to me across the grass
takes me with tentacles and buries me alive
inside your heart: I write with your best blood.

(CPP, Aug.–Sept., 1936, p. 89)

The clichés that obtrude into this largely freshly written poem
illustrate the way in which surrealist poetry, the literature of
spontaneity, easily became the victim of its own highly stylised
rhetoric. The most effective poetry produced under the surrealist impulse was poetry where the free association was
combined within some narrative or discursive framework, as
in this poem by Edgar Foxall:

Shift your ground and say you are unhappy,
space weighs on your shoulders in the dark,
the crooner and his lily white boys make hay
through the partition where the thin bells chime,
and the tallest tremor is waiting on the stair,
waiting for you to tell you the time.

(CPP, Autumn, 1937, p. 26)

Again, the formality of the music of the poem makes an effective
counterpoint with the freedom of the images. Surrealism also
merged effectively into the satire of fantasy that was common
among the poets of the thirties. Here is a passage from "Abra-
cadabra" by Kenneth Allott:

It is wise to say the least to send your daughter
to an expensive school where they teach pianoforte
at a moderate charge and the cuisine is excellent
where the bootboys are dismissed every twenty-four hours.

Games are an excellent training for the after-life
but I suggest Havelock Ellis on wet afternoons
and trips to the sea at least every other fortnight
because as you know the sea is our birthright
and these are the things which count.

(CPP, July, 1936, p. 51)

Other poets who appeared in *Contemporary Poetry and Prose* included William Empson, Wallace Stevens and e. e. cummings. The work of Stevens, in particular, was little known then in England. The prose contributions were rather less interesting than those in verse. They included "collages" by Roughton and by Humphrey Jennings. Roughton's "Final Night of the Bath" was "assembled from passages in the *Evening Standard* of June 6, 1936". Humphrey Jennings was a believer in the "discovered" image. The poet was not to invent images, because poetry had to do with historical and collective reality. Jennings published collages that he called "Reports":

> The conditions for this race, the most important of the Classic races for three-year-old fillies, were ideal, for the weather was fine and cool. About one o'clock the Aurora again appeared over the hills in a south direction presenting a brilliant mass of light. Once again Captain Allison made a perfect start, for the field was sent away well for the first time that they approached the tapes. It was always evident that the most attenuated light of the Aurora sensibly dimmed the stars, like a thin veil drawn over them. We frequently listened for any sound proceeding from this phenomenon, but never heard any.
>
> <div align="right">(<i>CPP</i>, June, 1936, p. 93)</div>

Contemporary Poetry and Prose closed quite abruptly with its second quarterly number. It contained an announcement: "This is the last Number of Contemporary Poetry and Prose, as the Editor is going abroad for some time (*CPP*, Autumn, 1937, p. 2). Roughton committed suicide in Dublin in 1941.

Chapter 12

MAN'S LIFE IS THIS MEAT

David Gascoyne – George Barker – Philip O'Connor

ONE OF THE most precocious of all the young poets to be met in Parton Street was David Gascoyne. His first book of poems, *Roman Balcony*, appeared in 1932, when he was sixteen. By the end of 1936, his twentieth year, he had produced another volume of poems, *Man's Life is This Meat* (1936), an autobiographical work of fiction, *Opening Day* (1933), a collection of translations of twenty poems by Benjamin Peret, *Remove Your Hat* (1936) (done with Humphrey Jennings), and the still very readable and informative *A Short Survey of Surrealism* (1935). Gascoyne's father was a bank clerk, and Gascoyne's education was at Salisbury Cathedral School, with only the addition of some time at Regent Street Polytechnic after that. Yet Gascoyne was evidently, by the age of twenty, not only fluently conversant with contemporary French poetry, but was one of the few English writers of his generation to absorb into his work developments in French poetry since the time of Appollinaire. Indeed, he was one of the few English writers of this century (as opposed to Americans, like Pound and Eliot) to be influenced significantly by French literature; and *Man's Life is This Meat* is one of the very small number of surrealist works by an English writer. During the latter part of the decade Gascoyne came under the influence of Pierre Jean Jouve, translated poems by Jouve, and wrote poems in French in the manner of Jouve.

The poems in *Roman Balcony* are more up to date but less interesting than those written by Dylan Thomas at the same age in his notebooks. Gascoyne's poems have a bright, clear, imagistic quality, but little to startle one, except for such urbanity and competence in the work of so young an author.

The garden is cold.
Winds stir

over the green hollow of the lawn.
Faded roses
tumble delicately over the old brick wall.
Marigolds burn
on the margin of the green.
Here is colour,
but behind the darkling trees
clouds rear,
dark and ominous, rain-burdened,
like shreds of an old dream
which tumbles out of its chilly case
when the door of the mind
is opened by memory.

("Rain Clouds")

Gascoyne's second book of poems, *Man's Life is This Meat*, was published in February, 1936; and, between its publication and that of *Roman Balcony*, surrealism had clearly become the dominant influence in his work. Some of the earliest poems in *Man's Life is This Meat* are from 1933, and are in the imagistic manner of *Roman Balcony*. However, one of the most decidedly surrealist poems in the book, "The Last Dream is the Dream of Isis"—a longer poem, with lists of images with no logical connection, was also first published in 1933. Its second section is typical of surrealist poetry in its imagery, with the customary conjunction of flowers, meat, disease, sex and excrement.

there is an explosion of geraniums in the ballroom of the
    hotel
there is an extremely unpleasant odour of decaying meat
arising from the depetalled flower growing out of her ear
her arms are like pieces of sandpaper
or wings of leprous birds in taxis
and when she sings her hair stands on end
and lights itself with a million little lamps like
    glowworms
you must always write the last two letters of her
    christian name
upside down with a blue pencil

she was standing at the window clothed only in a ribbon
she was burning the eyes of snails in a candle
she was eating the excrement of dogs and horses
she was writing a letter to the president of france

This type of poetry is very monotonous and, consequently, boring, and Gascoyne seems early to have moved on from it. A good deal of the poetry in *Man's Life is This Meat* is lyrical, the surrealistic touch being in the daring and free choice of metaphor. The best of the pure surrealist poems is the one chosen by Michael Roberts for inclusion in the *Faber Book of Modern Verse*—"Salvador Dali":

> The face of the precipice is black with lovers;
> The sun above them is a bag of nails; the spring's
> First rivers hide among their hair.
> Goliath plunges his hand into the poisoned well
> And bows his head and feels my feet walk through his brain.
> The children chasing butterflies turn round and see him
>   there
> With his hand in the well and my body growing from his
>   head,
> And are afraid. They drop their nets and walk into the
>   wall like smoke.

Quite apart from its thread of pseudo-narrative, the poem has a well defined musical shape and makes a pattern of recurring images, features which give it a unity lacking in many surrealist poems.

There is little in the book directly to suggest the equation between surrealistic dislocation of images and the Communist image of a sick or broken society, though Gascoyne evidently made that equation in the middle thirties. A frequent theme— and one which connects the book with Gascoyne's work of the late thirties and subsequently—is that of anguish and guilt, as in "The Cage" or "Lost Wisdom" or "Purified Disgust". These are not surrealist poems at all, in that the choice of images is not left to the working of the unconscious, but is rather made in a loose, impressionistic way to evoke the often nightmare quality of the feeling behind the poem.

> An impure sky
> A heartless and impure breathing
> The fevered breath of logic
> And a great bird broke loose
> Flapping into the silence with strident cries
> A great bird with cruel claws

Beyond that savage pretence of knowledge
Beyond that posture of oblivious dream
Into the divided terrain of anguish
Where one walks with bound hands
Where one walks with knotted hair
With eyes searching the zenith
Where one walks like Sebastian

Heavy flesh invokes the voice of penitence
Seated at the stone tables
Seated at a banquet of the carnal lusts
Behind our putrid masks we snicker
Our men's heads behind our masks
Twisted from innocence to insolence

And there the pointing finger says and there
The pointing finger demonstrates
The accuser struggles with his accusation
The accused writhes and blusters
The finger points to the chosen victim
The victim embraces his victimization
The accused belches defiance

How could we teach that carrion?
A sudden spasm saves us
A pure disgust illumines us
The music of the spheres is silent
Our hands lie still upon the counterpane
And the herds come home.

("Purified Disgust")

In the October, 1934, issue of *New Verse*, in answer to Grigson's "Enquiry", Gascoyne wrote:

I have never been directly influenced by Freud in my poetry, but I have been indirectly influenced by him through the Surrealists. To give oneself up at any time to writing poems without the control of the reason is, I imagine, to have in a way come under the influence of Freud. I no longer find this navel-gazing activity at all satisfying. The Surrealists themselves have a definite justification for writing in this way, but for an English poet with continually growing political convictions it must soon become impossible.[1]

This might be taken to indicate an abandonment of surrealism, or, at least, a recognition of its limitations, a position not entirely in harmony with the impression created by *Man's Life is This Meat*. *New Verse* for June, 1935, contains the poem "Baptism", which has a bald, Marxist conclusion: "Statement: | *If you are with us you are red*"; while *Man's Life is This Meat* itself has as epigraph a translation of Paul Eluard's Marxist poem, "Critique of Poetry".

There seemed, of course, to the surrealists, no clash between surrealism and Marxism, a point that Gascoyne makes clear in *A Short Survey of Surrealism*; so that the tone of the remarks in *New Verse* is therefore surprising. Even after the publication of his second book of poetry, surrealist poems by Gascoyne continued to appear in *Contemporary Poetry and Prose*, up to the end of 1936. The October and November issues contain parts of a long poem, "Fragments from The Symptomatic World"; a poem which, as much as any by Gascoyne, reminds one of the poem by Tristan Tzara that Gascoyne described as "one of the finest achievements of surrealist poetry",[2] "The Approximate Man". It seems likely that, in 1934, Gascoyne had become disillusioned with the automatic aspect of surrealist writing, and had begun to write the more controlled poems in *Man's Life is This Meat*—poems a little reminiscent of the work of Eluard. His enthusiasm for pure surrealist poetry may have revived with the writing of *A Short Survey of Surrealism* (1935) and with the advent of the surrealist exhibition and of *Contemporary Poetry and Prose* in 1936. Gascoyne's last surrealist poem was the long "Phantasmagoria", first collected in 1942, though written earlier.

The change in outlook was, by 1942, far in the past. After the end of 1936, hardly any poems by Gascoyne are to be found in periodicals until the second world war begins. Stephen Spender recounts, in *World Within World*, how he was taken by surprise to hear Gascoyne's voice come over a loud speaker in Barcelona while he was in Spain in 1937. Gascoyne must have gone early to join the Republican side. In the last years of the decade, he seems to have been in Paris. Kathleen Raine states that he was given psychological help by the wife of Pierre Jean Jouve.[3] It is certainly true that a great change takes place in Gascoyne's poetry after 1937, and that the influence of

Jouve is strongly felt in Gascoyne's third collection of original poems, *Poems, 1937-42*.

Jouve was a Freudian who was also a Catholic. His poetry therefore showed the way to make the transition from surrealism to Marxism to Christianity. The influence of Jouve seems to have been behind Gascoyne's book of 1937, *Hölderlin's Madness*—a collection of adaptations of poems by Hölderlin, with four original poems by Gascoyne built into the sequence. At the end of the introduction to the book Gascoyne expresses his debt to Jouve's translation of the poems of Hölderlin's madness. Hölderlin has appealed to modern, and especially surrealist, poets just because he went mad. Discussing the freedom of the poet and its relation to the Marxist condition that freedom is the knowledge of necessity, Gascoyne makes a distinction that is very like the distinction between the Marxist notion of freedom and the surrealist conception of the sort of freedom that the inner liberation of man can bring:

> But is not freedom "the knowledge of necessity"? Yes, if we are speaking of human freedom, of the only freedom, that is to say, to which mortals can expect to attain here on earth. But the freedom towards which the poet aspires, the "free" Freedom of Paradise, is, on the contrary, the non-knowledge of necessity, a state in which necessity does not exist.[4]

However, Gascoyne says of Hölderlin that he belonged with those poets who "believed the poet to be capable of penetrating to a secret world and of receiving the dictation of a transcendental inner voice".[5] It is with such a secret world that Gascoyne evidently felt his poetry to belong after 1937.

The changed conception of poetry is reflected in the style of the four poems by Gascoyne himself included in *Hölderlin's Madness*. The deliberate illogicality of the surrealist poems is gone, and is replaced by a prophetic tone. This was to be the manner of most of the poems in the first two sections of Gascoyne's *Poems, 1937-42*, "Miserere" and "Metaphysical Poems". Many of these poems were written in the early forties, though "The Open Tomb", which was to have been the title poem of an ensemble of poems of 1937 to 1939, is from the thirties and is typical of the poems from this group:

Vibrant with silence is the last sealed room
That fever-quickened breathing cannot break:
Magnetic silence and unshakably doomed breath
Hung like a screen of ice
Between the cavern and the closing eyes,
Between the last day and the final scene
Of death, unwitnessed save by one:

By Omega! the angel whose dark wind
Of wings and trumpet lips
Stirs with disruptive storm the clinging folds
Of stalagmatic foliage lachrymose [sic]
Hung from the lofty crypt, where endlessly
The phalanx passes, two by three, with all
The hypnotising fall of stairs.

Their faces are unraised as yet from sleep;
The pace is slow, and down the steep descent
Their carried candles eddy like a stream;
While on each side, through windows in the rock,
Beyond the tunnelled grottoes there are seen
Serene the sunless but how dazzling plains
Where like a sea resounds our open tomb.

These poems, like the original poems in *Hölderlin's Madness*, constitute a return, stylistically, to Romantic poetry, widely maligned during the thirties, owing to the influence of Eliot's criticism. However, they have little in common with the limpid, delicate poetry of *Hölderlin*. They are reminiscent of Shelley at his most portentous. "The Open Tomb", with its flaccid rhythms, its ineffectual, self-important phrases—"Magnetic silence and unshakably doomed breath", "stalagmatic [sic] foliage lachrymose", and its clichés—"eddy like a stream" and "dazzling plains", is typical of the religious and quasi-religious poems by Gascoyne from this period. The poems in the section "Miserere"—evidently from the early forties—are overtly Christian, though it is the Christianity of "Christ of Revolution and of Poetry", as one of these poems ("Ecce Home") makes clear.

The change of sensibility was evidently the result of an acute personal crisis. Section IV of *Poems, 1937–42*, "Personal",

has as epigraph a quotation from *Monsieur Godeau Intime* by
Marcel Jouhandeau that concludes:

> "O suffoquer ainsi dans cette obscurité sans une lueur, sans
> enthousiasme, sans être entendu de personne. Le mur était si
> épais. Dieu, son Dieu ne pouvait pas l'entendre. N'était-ce pas
> l'Enfer: cette solitude continuelle de la vie?"

The unbearableness of the self abandoned by God is implicit in
many of the poems of this section, most of which seem to have
been written in Paris between 1937 and the outbreak of war:

> One who has wandered long
> Through labyrinths of his own brain
> More solitary and obscure
> Than any maze of stone
> Pavement and lamplit walls
> Now stops beside the Seine
> And leaning down to peer
> Into the swirling gloom
> Of swollen waters, says:
> *What day can ever end*
> *The night of those from whom*
> *God turns away His face,*
> *Or what ray's finger pierce*
> *The depths wherein they drown?*
> *Exhaustion brings no peace*
> *To the lost soul . . .*
>
> > ("Noctambules")

There is an uncertainty of style in this whole group of poems.
The brightness and "stylishness" of the surrealistic poems is no
longer Gascoyne's goal; and in the effort to reach a desired
plainness, he seems to be groping stylistically. The poem
quoted from above recalls the manner of the early T. S. Eliot.

By far the best and most assured stylistically of the poems in
the 1942 volume are those in the final section, "Time and
Place". Nearly all of them were written after the outbreak of
war and are truly poems of the forties. However, the first of
them, "Snow in Europe", was one of the few poems by Gascoyne
to appear in a periodical between the end of 1936 and the
outbreak of war.

Out of their slumber Europeans spun
Dense dreams: appeasement, miracle, glimpsed flash
Of a new golden era; but could not restrain
The vertical white weight that fell last night
And made their continent a blank.

Hush, says the sameness of the snow
The Ural and the Jura now rejoin
The furthest Arctic's desolation. All is one
Sheer monotone: plain, mountain; country, town:
Contours and boundaries no longer show.

The warring flags hang colourless a while;
Now midnight's icy zero feigns a truce
Between the signs and seasons, and fades out
All shots and cries. But when the great thaw comes,
How red shall be the melting snow, how loud the drums!
("Snow in Europe")

This poem appeared in *New Writing* for spring, 1939, and shows
how close Gascoyne had moved stylistically, in his occasional
poems, towards the manner associated with poets favoured by
that periodical. The poetic stance is a surprisingly urbane and
detached one, considering the manner of the religious poems
Gascoyne was writing at that time. "A Wartime Dawn" and
"The Gravel-pit Field" had a similar manner, and must be
among Gascoyne's finest poems. They are, however, from 1940
and 1941 respectively. There is one poem from 1940 that does
belong with any discussion of the poetry of the thirties, and that
is Gascoyne's valedictory "Farewell Chorus".

There are few poems that capture so well the quality of the
decade or the sense of helpless stillness that descended on those
who had been involved in its ideological struggles when the
expected war finally came. Gascoyne's poem gets its power of
evocation from its choice of detail:

And so! the long black pullman is at last departing now,
After those undermining years of angry waiting and cold tea;
And all your small grey faces and wet hankies slide away
Backwards into the station's cave of cloud. And so Good-bye
To our home-town, so foreign now its lights no longer show;
And to old lives already indistinct as a dull play
We saw while staying somewhere in the Midlands long ago.

The poem speaks with a plainness that is neither superior nor sneering of the misguided idealism of the age. Even if one is unable to feel sympathy with the religious conclusion, one cannot help but welcome the modesty of the author's stance in an age where that virtue was singularly absent in political writings. Where Gascoyne does reach for the stagey clichés of the era, their inclusion in the poem only seems to add to the authenticity of its flavour.

The poems in *Man's Life is This Meat*, together with Gascoyne's contributions to *Contemporary Poetry and Prose*, offer a poetic experience almost unique in English. There have been few poets in our language who have gone whole hog for the irrational and with such brilliance as did Gascoyne. Yet one can hardly imagine anyone going back to *Man's Life is This Meat* as one might to parts of *Poems, 1937–42*. The surrealist poems have a sameness which is the shortcoming of most surrealist writing. They also have a looseness that one associates with surrealist poetry, but which is, in fact, frequently a feature of Gascoyne's later work. Most importantly, and once again like most surrealist poetry, Gascoyne's poems of the middle thirties have a disembodied quality. They give a startling experience, but they do not make connection with or illuminate the main body of our experiences, as the poems in his later books were to do.

II

Like David Gascoyne (and Dylan Thomas also) George Barker came from the lower middle class and had little education beyond school. (He too was at the Regent Street Polytechnic.) Like Gascoyne and Thomas, he was associated with Parton Street; and, like them, he was precocious in publication, producing two books of poems and a poetic novel by the time he was twenty-three. In his early work, he had, in common with Thomas and Gascoyne, an apparent lack of social concern, and used images that were traditionally poetic, rather than the imagery of the industrial landscape used by Auden, Spender and Day Lewis. He was more fortunate than Gascoyne and Thomas in the publishers who took him up. His first book of poems, *Thirty Preliminary Poems* (1933), like Gascoyne's *Man's Life is This Meat* and Thomas's *Eighteen Poems*, was published by David Archer's Parton Press, as was his novel, *Alanna Autumnal* (1933). However, his second book of poems, *Poems* (1935), was included in the then prestigious list of poets published by Faber and Faber, who have continued to publish his work. All this led to Barker's being regarded as an important poet and as a rival of Dylan Thomas. In fact, Barker's poetry is only superficially similar to that of Thomas, and he is not a writer in Thomas's class at all. His use of language and imagery is rhetorical in the most limiting sense of the word, and his touch is uncertain to the point of being ham-fisted. His poetry is consistently marred by pretentiousness.

Thirty Preliminary Poems gives a valuable insight into Barker's poetry, because some of the poems in that book seem to have been written before he had learned some of his more pretentious tricks.

> Dark dreadful death I dread your approach:
> Knowing as I know you roll nearer every hour
> Fear of your fearful embrace spreads great folds
> Of coldness like an ocean over me; I cry, How
> How can I withstand, stand up, repel
> The ever invading eternal wave whose swell
> Beginning at birth, declines into what afterwards,
> Reaching its crested height at the second the heart
> Sick of resistance, sinks to succumb like a stone
> Marking the moment buoyant life departed.
> Not beaten, not beaten, but utterly fatigued
> These four limbs fall deaf to the word defeat:
> Aware by divine kindness that this descent
> Through cubic nothingness resembles supine rest.
> ("Sonnet": Evening of Monday, 25th June, 1933)

In language, imagery and sentiment this poem is very ordinary and undistinguished, and has none of the individuality that Thomas's earliest poetry had. This is true of quite a large proportion of poems in the book, including "Sequence of Ten Sonnets". The poems that are most attractive and that display the greatest surety of touch are the few lighter poems, such as "Verses for a Nursery Wall".

In reviewing *Thirty Preliminary Poems* in *New Verse*, Stephen Spender picked "Ode" as the most immediately appealing.[6] In sentiment and imagery it is indebted to Spender's poetry of the period; and the influence of Spender is also felt in "On First Hearing Beethoven" and in "No Feeble Dream":

> No feeble dream is as good as to act
> Vigorously across pellucid air;
> Elude the illusion of the aspiration
> But violently keep on the move, your direction
> Directs the deviation, Bethlehem star.

The similarity between these poems and those of Spender is not merely one of subject matter, diction or imagery. Barker also copies Spender's trick of distorting the syntax in such a way as to make certain words occupy positions of maximum effect and in such a way as to hold back the completion of the meaning so that attention is drawn to the words themselves.

"No Feeble Dream" is one of the poems from *Thirty Preliminary Poems* that Barker chose to include in his second book of poetry, *Poems* (1935). Its first stanza contains one of the more nauseating examples of Barker's taste for ringing changes on the sound of words. *Poems* offers other examples of this proclivity:

> Wandering one, too wonderful
> No wandering of one's wondering when
> Watching your wandering . . .
>   ("The Constellation")

In this volume playing with words and distortion of syntax have become Barker's favourite devices—and very dubious devices too. The first line of "Daedalus" gets an effect of portentousness from the incomplete and uncertain syntax, which creates an air of mystery: "Like the enormous liner of his limbs and fell." There are combinations of word play and distorted syntax that produce near nonsense:

> His perennial
> Superbly manual
> Like the firm bands

> Of a working wheel
> And insuperable hands
> Love's neutrality reveal.
>   ("His Perennial")

It is altogether surprising that anyone should write such bad lines, let alone print them, when he was capable of writing the occasional poem of limpidity and delicacy like "The Crystal", a poem that uses the same devices, but in a subdued and controlled manner.

> With burning fervour
> I am forever
> Turning in my hand
> The crystal, this moment
>
> Whose spatial glitter
> Travelling erratically
> Forward
>
> Touches with permanent
> Disturbance the pavements
> The faked walls the crevices
> Of futurity.
>
> Sooner than darken
> This crystal miracle
> With a hand's
> Vagary
>
> One would dissever
> This wrist this hand,
> Or remove the eyelid
> To see the end.

Barker's involuted dickering with words is associated in his early poetry with equally involuted themes. *Poems* contains three "Narcissus" poems, the first of which appeared in *Thirty Preliminary Poems* as "Poem on a Dream":

> My tired lips received that morning
> Their first kiss, so stirred the mind
> Cannot subside for days for weeks or months.
> That slim mouth on my mouth held firm complete
>   pressure,

Keep mine for the unimaginable period
Between meeting and meeting in mouth with an
    unknown person . . .

Travelling through a fine evening in a car
The delineation of my own face was at intervals
    caught
From the sunlight in outline—the chin's framed curve
Lips, jaws asseveration—on the windscreen
The reproduction on the reality through
I know no longer wander wondering who.

In spite of some unfortunate Barkerisms, this is a poem of definite individuality, both of theme and technique. The neurotic preoccupation with identity emerges in his prose writing of this time:

Momentarily overcome, I spring to the mirror and gaze deeply into those eyes. They stare back at me, dumb with absolute despair, that we two can approach no nearer. I am not here concerned with *myself*: within the confines of that long mirror lives entombed a person wavering between the feminine and masculine, whom I adore.[7] (*Janus* [1934])

However, this is far from being Barker's predominant theme, even in the early work. Barker was a lapsed Catholic, and of the Irish puritanical tradition, too. Throughout his writing he makes the association of sex, sin, birth and death.

We begin, genetic in the womb with stupendous life, from death; which I visualize the Perfection. From this we proceed into degenerative life. We live, shedding death, until, having exhausted life, death resumes its complete possession. This possession is the single absolute perfection of which I am aware. Perfect because it is absolute, utter, entire. Whereas there is not present in death the most infinitesimal microcosm of what life is, life has its only magnificent values as degrees from the centrality, death.[8] (*Alanna Autumnal* [1933])

Love is the terrible aboriginal calamity.[9]
(*The Dead Seagull* [1950])

The act of human procreation,
—O crown and flower, O culmination

Of perfect love throughout creation—
  What can I compare it to?
O eternal butterflies in the belly,
O trembling of the heavenly jelly,
O miracle of birth! Really
  We are excreted, like shit.
   (*The True Confession of George Barker* [1950])

The vulgarity of the last passage is a measure of how compulsive
and ill-focused this theme is for Barker. His prose works
Alanna Autumnal (1933), *Janus* (1934), and *The Dead Seagull*
(1950) are all lurid. *Alanna Autumnal* illustrates very well the
Poeian compulsion that the association of sex and guilt has for
Barker. It is the story of a young man who ends up feeling
guilty because he believes that he could have saved the life of his
sister, whose husband had deserted her, by sleeping with her
when she was eight months' pregnant.

    The association of sex, sin, birth and death is the theme of
Barker's third book of poetry, *Calamiterror* (1937), a long poem
occasioned by the death of his son, Albert Gordon Barker. This
long-winded, meditative poem opens with a stanza of over-
realised, surrealistic writing that is typical of it:

What when born upward breaking from heaven downward
It is my bare bloodred babe, with beauty
Branching from armpit, maypole at thigh, world flying
Like fairboats around, the axis of existence.
The bud beginning, the burning salamander
Suspended in his breast, the shambles in the bowels,
The tall tree spine supporting vertical
The crucified to life bare body blood.

                                       (I, 1)

In its egotistical visionary manner and in the way in which the
actual and the visionary are rudely jostled together, *Calimiterror*
reminds one of Whitman in his bad moments, and he may have
been the inspiration for attempting this kind of poem. After a
vision of William Blake "on Sunday the 12th of April",
Barker "achieved apocalypse", and the poem concludes by
connecting the death of his son, and sex, sin and death, with
the evils of the international situation, and especially the Civil
War in Spain:

Continually the women weeping in Irun's ruins
Call in distress with voices like swans;
I hear that cry which breaks the womb or room
Wherever I stand, and forces me to go.
The swan my world with the myriad at her breast,
The foaming human struggling, I hear their cry;
The feminine weeping and the masculine agony
Meet at the throat and make the swan's song.

(IX, 7)

Calamiterror must be one of the worst poems of the decade, if
only because it is so extravagantly bad and at such length.

In the later thirties, Barker wrote a number of visionary social
poems, shorter and more palatable than *Calamiterror*. One that
appeared in *Left Review* in 1937 has never been republished and
is short enough to give in full:

1. North is nothing where the axle point abuts
   Haunted by Amundsen and the Gothic figures of grief
   Which wail and chase in the winds, and these are whom
   Cold has killed not here but in the black Hell
   The Dowlais or the Derbyshire fell starved, here ·
   Having the ice at their gut-pipes, having died, dwell.

2. South is the shark in the seas and the flowery reef,
   Plenitude of proud food and extravagance of habits,
   Here in duck suits the managers float in the gloom
   Obediently observing the obvious Maugham verb
   Like marionettes in Mandalay hitched to work from here:
   South it souses in the scents of the lotus herb.

3. West is where the wanderers go with double fear.
   First fear is failure in the American money gluts.
   Second is fear of the American Aphrodite, from
   The foam of the war welter risen; she is no wife,
   She like inverted volcano swallows me whole,
   I fear to disappear in the glory hole.

4. East is tundra and steppes echoing thunder from
   The terrible engines manufacturing the future like glass.
   East is two hundred million daubing the Shelley dome,
   East is militant for man and has guns of years,
   East is sunrise where the Russo-Japanese sun
   Toils in the double fury remaining one.

5. Fifth is the hand's fingers that can squeeze grief
   Like sponge from heart or hunger from the guts
   With gifts of love of labour for all or any.
   Fifth is vertical, meaning mountains here
   Or the heavenly valleys as our home.
   Not that it matters, for both are the same.
   ("5 Stanzas on the 5 Pointed Star", *Left Review*, III, 4
   (May, 1937) 214)

In conception, the poem is original, in that it attempts to combine a controlled visionary symbolism with a presentation of the politico-economic situation as it was. One is left wishing that the poem were successful, as there are too few such poems in English; but there are too many Barkerisms and too many bathetic lapses.

These visionary social poems seem to have been written under the influence of Robert Owen. ("Sermon on May Day" (*Seven*, Spring, 1940) is an article on Owen, while the October, 1939, issue of *Wales* contains a poem "To Robert Owen".) They attempt to apply the methods of the English romantic poets to contemporary material. This is done most strikingly in "Vision of England '38", where the model seems to have been Shelley's "Triumph of Time":

Not sleeping not dreaming I saw the imperial procession
Flicker past my foot in postures of triumph or violence;
Some moved in shapes of gluttony or envy, others
Rode pride like lions, and some bore their own flowers.

I heard voices that whispered and voices that sang,
'Death is no glory', or 'I shun not the fire'.
Three women came screaming, wringing hands, flying,
With crowns on their brows, the last of them Victoria.

Behind them, randy as the angry beast who craves
Dominion for its ball and sceptre, loped the Disraelian lion.
The three queens with its scions in their loins
Flew forward screaming, hunting for their graves.

In "Resolution of Dependence", he meets Wordsworth among the Saturday crowd, and the conjunction gives a strong sense of the emotional impoverishment of most people's lives at the time:

> I encountered the crowd returning from amusements,
> The Bournemouth Pavilion, or the marvellous gardens,
> The Palace of Solace, the Empyrean Cinema: and saw
> William Wordsworth was one, tawdrily conspicuous,
> Obviously emulating the old man of the mountain-moor,
> Traipsing along on the outskirts of the noisy crowd.

The possibilities in this situation are not realised. Indeed, there is no true resolution in the poem, and it falls apart in its pretentiousness and vapid generalisation.

These visionary social poems are brought together in Barker's fourth book of poems, *Lament and Triumph* (1940). The remarkable thing about *Lament and Triumph* is that it would be impossible to read more than a page, even if taken at random, without realising that it was by Barker and without carrying away an almost indelible sense of the book's style; and yet it would be equally impossible to read as much as a page without encountering an example of execrable writing. There are passages which have a promise and an individual quality that make one wish that one could wholeheartedly endorse the poem in which they are found. Most of the failures of the book are associated with Barker's besetting failure, his pretentiousness; while the imagery is monotonous, being a mixture of over-worked conventional images like "birds", "flowers", "hearts", "eyes", and repetitive imagery of decay. Very often the images are little more than an assortment of images made commonplace by surrealist poetry.

Lament and Triumph is not dull. Is is astonishing in its energy, and, where it is dreadful, it is dreadful with panache. It justifies Dylan Thomas's remark, in a letter of December, 1938 (to Vernon Watkins): ". . . a new paper should give—(say)— Barker a rest: he must be very tired".[10] There are a few good things: "Elegy for Spain", and the delicately nostalgic opening of "Battersea Park":

> Now it is November and mist wreathes the trees,
> The horses cough their white blooms in the street,
> Dogs shiver and boys run; the barges on the Thames
> Lie like leviathans in the fog; and I meet
> A world of lost wonders as I loiter in the haze
> Where fog and sorrow cross my April days.

Such poems remind one how much better a poet Barker was to become in his next book, *Eros in Dogma* (1944). "Battersea Park" has something of the tone of the marvellous poem to his mother in the later volume.

In his attempts to write a visionary style of poetry, and in his conception of poetry as an esoteric mode of understanding, Barker had something in common with David Gascoyne, Vernon Watkins and Kathleen Raine. In one of his statements about poetry, "The Miracle of Images", written in 1947, Barker said: "The image is what the imagination ascertains about the hitherto unimaginable";[11] and ". . . to glorify the unknowable is the predominant responsibility and the functional purpose of the poem".[12] However, more revealing was one of his answers to the *New Verse* "Enquiry" in 1934: "I find myself very powerfully conscious of the purely verbal origin of a poem. . . ."[13] Barker, in his early poetry, had a Swinburnian infatuation with words without Swinburne's distinctive talent. His fondness for puns and play on words and his rather unpleasant verbal doodling with a limited set of words of unpleasant association is more than a manifestation of innate vulgarity. In Barker's poetry the conflicts are frequently not explained or resolved, but are, in fact, relished. Such poetry can offer little mature satisfaction, because it is too often the occasion for covert indulgence of unpleasant tendencies on the part of the author.

III

A poet whose work might seem at first sight as strongly surrealistic as any poetry in English is Philip O'Connor, best known for his autobiography, *Memoirs of a Public Baby*. In fact O'Connor is very much his own animal. An unusual temperament and a weird upbringing disqualified him from seeing the world in the way in which one should if one is ever successfully to fit into it.

> Grown-ups, to me, are recognisably the result of . . . educational antics; they are made men, formed in a hard enamel scribbled with personal advertisements, like baked beans; and quaking within, no doubt, like myself without.
> . . . Education makes for order, and society is, basically, without true order; it is marshalled, but it isn't an organism;

that's to say, there's no organic unity, no integration between what
one does, work, and what one gets, culture—and culture fundamentally includes money. Ethics taught at school, as all the
world knows, have no application outside for anyone unwilling
to be a passive employee-robot for the rest of his days, so that
the connection between spirit, initiative and delinquency is
logically a close one.[14]

After his own outlook was formed, he came into contact with
surrealism, and adopted some of its attitudes; but, as he himself
remarked, the real resemblance was to Céline—". . . but with
. . . less bravura and less inverted 'faith' . . ."[15]

In his late teens he persuaded his guardian to support him
for a year while he became a writer, though he does not appear
to have given much time to poetry to begin with. His appearance in poetry periodicals, according to O'Connor, dated from
his being put into a mental hospital, and he gives a characteristically iconoclastic account of his entry into the poetry world:

> In the hospital I'd written a long poem . . . and an editor inter-
> ested in the labours of the mad had seen and printed it in his
> *avant-garde* magazine. . . . To me my poems are the mess of my
> having collided with my head against the brick wall of society's
> guardians. . . . I spent no longer than the time required to
> write them out twice, sometimes once—about half an hour on
> each. My aim . . . was to write as a communist, in the Maya-
> kovsky manner; but my writing persisted in its "decadent"
> manner, beyond my control.

He adds the footnote: "Secure in a minority of one, I can now
reverse this opinion."[16]

His poems are not written in accordance with the surrealistic
formula of an unconscious association of images, though they do
achieve a disorientation of accepted attitudes by means of
startling or shocking collocations of images or ideas. Like the
surrealists, O'Connor was an enemy of middle-class idealism;
but the viewpoint is O'Connor's own strange "unschooled"
vision, rather than the doctrine surrealist one:

> The clock ticks on; the wild-fingered hand
> on a dark wet evening strokes the face
> and combs the hair out-of-doors,

and traffic and expressions are woof and warp
of a cruelly-clear understanding. The people drag a train of
  ancient monsters,
cumbrous shadows with banners
of factory hours and weekly wage.

                    (*New Verse*, 28 (January, 1938), 5)

O'Connor gives a brief elucidation in his autobiography of one
passage of poetry, bringing out his particular orientation:

> Down the shute whose sides
> are black with feathers squealing with the
>   fright of my dream
> goes the bundled heart
> to a white bulb blooming on the bottom
>
> gather in your robes
> streaming like hair in the bitter drafts
> rolling deliriously in the flight of your fall
>
> bind your limbs to you be a helpless thing
> falling to this bulb and fundamental
>
> laughing like the spilling of wine
> bathing in my shrieking skin I impinge upon
> the air down to the glowing light's node.

Apart from vogue-cry the meaning is clear enough; erotic
passivity was, I anti-freudianly think, a corollary, or re-agent.
"Fundamental" meant "low", associated with decadence. All
elevation was into a sky of lies aerially inhabited by middle
class angels.[17]

O'Connor's career as a poet seems to have begun with the
publication of "several poems" in the February–March, 1937,
number of *New Verse*. (These could be the long piece transmitted
from the mental hospital.) In spite of O'Connor's reportedly
cynical attitude to his poems, he succeeded in being published
in nearly all the avant-garde poetry magazines, including the
chauvinistic *Wales*. Nevertheless, although his small number of
poems of the period are startling and individual (and, in many
respects, very salutary) they suffer from a limited range of
tone, and often seem the raw material for poems rather than
finished works. However, it would seem that this was probably
part of the intended effect.

Chapter 13

THE RIMBAUD OF CWMDONKIN DRIVE

Swansea – Notebooks – *Eighteen Poems* – *Twenty-Five Poems* – The art of the early poetry

THE MOST STARTLING of the new young poets associated with Parton Street was Dylan Thomas, whose first book, *Eighteen Poems*, was published by David Archer in 1934, and who achieved one of the notable publishing successes of the poetry of the decade with his *Twenty-Five Poems* two years later. Thomas came from Swansea. He is the only significant poet of the thirties not to have been associated in his education with the English public schools, Oxford, Cambridge or London. In background he was in every respect provincial; though this does not mean, as has been suggested more recently, that there was anything provincial about his outlook or his art. It would be wrong to think of Thomas as being culturally deprived in the Swansea of his day. It was the place of his boyhood friendship with Daniel Jones, described in *Portrait of the Artist as a Young Dog*. Later he knew the painter, Alfred Janes, and, more importantly, Vernon Watkins.

Thomas's education ("which critics say I do not have")[1] ended at the age of sixteen at the grammar school where his father taught. In subjects other than English, it may be said never to have begun, as Thomas showed a complete unwillingness or inability to work at what did not interest him. However, the poets whom he had read (taking the evidence of his boyhood writings and his early letters) and the poems he had written in his notebooks from the age of sixteen on, indicate a sophisticated precocious knowledge of literature.

Some people who knew Thomas when he first came to London in 1934 have suggested that he was indeed provincial in his tastes and a little behind the times. Geoffrey Grigson, older than Thomas, who helped Thomas when he was first in London, has said that the poets frequently mentioned then by Thomas included Rossetti, Francis Thompson, and James Thomson

(B.V.).[2] In writing to Henry Treece in 1938, Thomas commented: "Sometimes, I think, the influence of Swinburne is more obvious than that of Hopkins . . ."[3] However, whatever Thomas's predilections in poetry, they were not the product of ignorance. The poets to whom he refers in his early writings and letters include both fashionable and unfashionable ones. One of his first London publications was a poem in a style imitative of T. S. Eliot.[4] In his political opinions he was decidedly Left, but these opinions did not find their way into his poetry.

It is certainly true that Thomas felt ill-at-ease with the young poets whom he met in London. He was constantly afraid that they would find him out; and this was not surprising when he found himself in the presence of people who had been at Oxford and Cambridge and who knew modern and classical languages (which he did not know). This may have contributed to Thomas's characteristic defensiveness and his anti-intellectual stance. Yet his capacity to be outrageously funny, at times geared to his defensiveness, often covered a biting appraisal of works and writers he was funny about. His gift for parody showed a very clear and sophisticated critical awareness of other writers' poetry. The *Letters to Vernon Watkins* are documentary evidence of his sensitivity to the details of his craft.

II

Thomas's early work is impressively recorded in his notebooks, of which there are five extant—four containing poetry, and one (the "Red Notebook") containing ten early short stories. The notebooks containing poetry are from 1930, 1930–2, February, 1933 (to August, 1933), and August, 1933 (to August 1934). In addition there are a few poems published while Thomas was at school, and twenty poems from the period 1930 to 1934 extant in manuscript or typescript.

The most interesting notebooks are, naturally enough, those begun in February and August, 1933. The August notebook contains, in near final form, thirteen of the poems used in *Eighteen Poems*. To the February notebook Thomas returned when he was compiling *Twenty-Five Poems* in 1936; and, when getting together the poems and stories published in 1939 as *The Map of Love*, he turned to the "Red Notebook" and the first three poetry notebooks. The early notebooks thus become an important source book for Thomas's poetry of the middle and late thirties, and this is the obvious way to view them. Yet it is a way of viewing them imposed by hindsight. When Thomas put the poems in the notebooks, they were, in the main, completed or near completed poems, so far as he was concerned at the time. Some of them differ very little from the versions Thomas chose to print later: "Ears in the Turrets Hear" (from the July, 1933, Notebook) differs only by one word and a few commas from the version in *Twenty-Five Poems*.

If we regard the notebooks—and especially the February and August, 1933, notebooks—as books of poems, we form a very different picture of Thomas as a poet from that presented by his poetry as he published it. 1933 and 1934 are his great years— his nineteenth and twentieth years. During this period he wrote all the poems in *Eighteen Poems* and nearly all those in *Twenty-Five Poems*, together with versions of at least half of the sixteen poems included in *The Map of Love*. Among them were "And death shall have no dominion", "Why east wind chills", "The hand that signed the paper" and "Especially when the October wind" (not in the notebooks, but in an early type-script). Among the poetry written in 1933 was the following marvellous poem:

> We lying by seasand watching yellow
> And the grave sea, mock who deride
> Who follow the red rivers, hollow
> Alcove of words out of cicada shade,
> Navy blue bellies of the tribes,
> For in this yellow grave twixt sea and sand
> A calling for colour calls with the wind
> That's grave and gray as grave and sea
> Supine on either hand.
> Bound by the yellow strip, we lie,
> Watch yellow, wish for wind to blow away
> The strata of the shore and leave red rock.
> But wishes breed not, neither
> Can we fend off the sandy smother,
> Nor tear the spindwind from our breath,
> The seaweed from our chests,
> Lie, watching yellow, until the yellow mists
> Proclaim the last smother of death.
>
> > (*Notebook*, May, 1933)

This was expanded for inclusion in *The Map of Love* six years later; but nearly all of the original lines were used again with little alteration. As a poem in the February, 1933, notebook, it is an achievement in its own right.

An examination of some of Thomas's most famous poems as they stand in the notebooks gives an insight into his nature as a poet that the later versions do not give. One of his poems of consummate Blakean simplicity is "The hand that signed the paper", dated 17th August, 1933, in the *Notebooks*, and included in *Twenty-Five Poems*:

> The hand that signed the paper felled a city;
> Five sovereign [*sic*] fingers taxed the breath,
> Doubled the globe of dead and halved a country;
> These five kings did a king to death.
>
> The mighty hand leads to a sloping shoulder,
> The finger joints are cramped with chalk;
> A goose's quill has put an end to murder
> That put an end to talk.
>
> The hand that signed the treaty bred a fever,
> And famine grew, and locusts came;
> Great is the hand that holds dominion over
> Man by a scribbled name.
>
> The fingers count the dead but do not soften
> The crusted wounds nor pat the brow;
> The hand rules pity as a hand rules heaven;
> Hands have no tears to flow.
>
> [These five blind kings have quills for sceptres;
> Each has a parchment for his shield,
> Debates with vizier words what time he shatters
> The four walls of the world.]

To write with such simplicity and yet with such firmness, resonance and power at the age of nineteen was the mark of mastery. Yet there is something slightly crude about the poem as it stands. The last stanza spells out the message too much; and Thomas left it out when he printed the poem in 1936, leaving the first four stanzas virtually as in the original. The spelling out of the message was old-fashioned in 1933: the modern poem of the day did not do this.

A further example is another celebrated poem from *Twenty-Five Poems*, which appeared in the notebooks dated April, 1933, "And death shall have no dominion". The poem is blatantly committed to the statement in the first line, which it proceeds to "prove" or illustrate. In spite of the startling visual impression created by some of the lines, what remains in the mind is the powerful general statement of the first line—an uncompromising (and, in a sober light, unsupportable) philosophical generalisation. The gift for the moving general statement or exhortation was to remain with Thomas throughout his life: "After the first death, there is no other" ("A Refusal to Mourn . . ."); "Do not go gentle into that good night". In addition, in the early poems, this gift goes along with a practice of thinking in terms of abstractions which were the part of the normal stock of earlier poetry—"love", "death", etc. Thomas's liking for the sonorous, rotund phrase is to be associated with a taste slightly old-fashioned in 1935.

At this point in Thomas's career, the philosophical generalisations went along with certain clear philosophical and religious preoccupations. A poem illustrative of this is one dated May, 1933—never collected by Thomas into a book, but powerful, in spite of the fact that it consists almost entirely of general statements:

> No man believes who, when a star falls shot,
> Cries not aloud blind as a bat,
> Cries not in terror when a bird is drawn
> Into the quicksand feathers down,
> Who does not make a wound in faith
> When any light goes out, and life is death . . .

These religious preoccupations were a prelude to Thomas's development of his own "world picture", his "process" philosophy, which dominates the August, 1933, notebook and *Eighteen Poems*. The first fully explicit statement of this philosophy is to be found in "A Process in the Weather of the Heart", dated 2nd February, 1934, in the *Notebooks*, though it is implicit in poems of the preceding months:

> A process in the weather of the heart
> Turns damp to dry; the golden shot
> Storms in the freezing grave.

A weather in the quarter of the veins
Turns night to day; blood in their suns
Lights up the living worm . . .

In a letter of March, 1934, he speaks of his "preconceived symbolism derived . . . from the cosmic significance of the human anatomy".[5] The new symbolism may derive something from Blake, whom Thomas clearly admired at this time. The new "philosophy" evidently owed a great deal to "The Marriage of Heaven and Hell" as a whole, but two passages are particularly relevant:

1. Man has no Body distinct from his Soul; for that call'd Body is a portion of Soul discern'd by the five Senses, the chief inlets of Soul in this age.
2. Energy is the only life, and is from the Body; and Reason is the bound or outward circumference of Energy.
3. Energy is Eternal Delight.[6]

Without Contraries is no progression. Attraction and Repulsion, Reason and Energy, Love and Hate, are necessary to Human existence.[7]

In a long letter to Pamela Hansford Johnson at Christmas, 1933, he speaks of ". . . the divinity that is so near us and so longing to be nearer, in the staggering, bloody, starry wonder of the sky I can see above and the sky I can think of below".[8] The new outlook seems to spring from an altogether too acute sense of dichotomy between body and spirit that the poems set out to deny. This in turn seems to have arisen from sexual frustration and disillusionment (". . . so often the opportunity comes too late, the seed has soured, love has turned to lust . . .")[9] so that he finds himself apologising for his choice of imagery:

. . . I defend the diction, the perhaps wearisome succession of blood and bones, the never-ending similes of the streams in the veins and the lights in the eyes, by saying that, for the time at least, I realise that it is impossible for me to raise myself to the altitude of the stars, and that I am forced, therefore, to bring down the stars to my own level and to incorporate them in my own physical universe.[10]

There is undoubtedly something unhealthy about the imagery of "worms", "wombs", "tombs", "flesh", "blood", "bone", "seed", "hair", etc., which dominates the early poems. Thomas is said to have been preoccupied by the idea that he had tuberculosis and was to die of it; though whether he had the disease is not clear, and his attitude towards it has the appearance of being a morbid game. Along with this type of preoccupation went a liking for Webster, Beddoes and James Thomson (B.V.).

Nevertheless, the "process" philosophy provided an organising principle for poetry, and not merely a basic set of ideas. This is most clearly seen in the poem "In the beginning":

> In the beginning was the three-pointed star,
> One smile of light across the empty face;
> One bough of bone across the rooting air,
> The substance forked that marrowed the first sun;
> And, burning ciphers on the round of space,
> Heaven and hell mixed as they spun.
>
> In the beginning was the pale signature,
> Three-syllabled and starry as the smile;
> And after came the imprints on the water,
> Stamp of the minted face upon the moon;
> The blood that touched the crosstree and the grail
> Touched the first cloud and left a sign.
>
> In the beginning was the mounting fire
> That set alight the weathers from a spark,
> A three-eyed, red-eyed spark, blunt as a flower;
> Life rose and spouted from the rolling seas,
> Burst in the roots, pumped from the earth and rock
> The secret oils that drive the grass.
>
> In the beginning was the word, the word
> That from the solid bases of the light
> Abstracted all the letters of the void;
> And from the cloudy bases of the breath
> The word flowed up, translating to the heart
> First characters of birth and death.
>
> In the beginning was the secret brain.
> The brain was celled and soldered in the thought
> Before the pitch was forking to a sun;

Before the veins were shaking in their sieve,
Blood shot and scattered to the winds of light
The ribbed original of love.

(Eighteen Poems)

The "three-pointed star" is at once the trinity and the male sexual organ. The poem runs on two levels at once: it can be read as an account of the creation and as an account of the conception of the human child. There is at once the identification of the human being with the whole cosmos, and also the identification of the sexual impulse with the creative forces of the universe. The poem appears twice in the August, 1933, notebook, and the earlier version makes the sexual interpretation more obvious. The third stanza begins: "In the beginning was the three-eyed prick . . ." A further level of interpretation also seems to be implied: an analogy between the creation of the universe, the creation of the human being and the creation of the poem—together with the implication that the same driving force is behind them all.

"In the beginning" is one of the masterpieces among the early poems. One must, however, recognise that its life is in its imagery. For Thomas, poetry seems always to have been the unique way of grasping what he had to say: and if we pay attention to the diction of "In the Beginning"—especially to the verbs, we get the impression of pressures scarcely contained, and of pressures decidedly sexual: "rooting"; "forked"; "spun"; "mounting"; "rose"; "spouted"; "rolling"; "burst"; "pumped"; "shot"; "scattered". Not all the sexual suggestions are "contained" by the ostensible impulse of the poem: some other impulse is creeping in, and there is something decidedly vertiginous about the poem as a whole.

The fact that the life of the poems is in the imagery is only too clear in some of the more obscure poems in *Eighteen Poems*. Furthermore, a very definite difficulty of interpretation arises, because one is in a quandary as to what impulses are to be taken as dominating any particular poem. A case in point is the first section of the first poem in the book:

I see the boys of summer in their ruin
Lay the gold tithings barren,
Setting no store by harvest, freeze the soils;

There in their heat the winter floods
Of frozen loves they fetch their girls,
And drown the cargoed apples in their tides.

These boys of light are curdlers in their folly,
Sour the boiling honey;
The jacks of frost they finger in the hives;
There in the sun the frigid threads
Of doubt and dark they feed their nerves;
The signal moon is zero in their voids . . .

(Eighteen Poems)

Ralph Maud writes at great length about this poem, speaking of an "attempt to justify the ways of God to man", and seeing its basic idea as the "interdependence between life and death forces that Thomas is portraying . . ."[11] With its "jacks of frost", however, the poem gives a clear and simple reading as a poem about masturbation, with the hoary old notion that self-induced ejaculation is a waste. As such, of course, the poem might not recommend itself for its maturity and centrality of concern; and attention to what is actually talked about in the poems that make up *Eighteen Poems* (instead of attention to putative notions enshrined in them) may underline this impression.

The early poems are paradoxical creations, evoking in one and the same line adverse and applauding reactions. The verse, as Thomas himself admitted, tended to be rhythmically monotonous; yet, in his development of a style of loose syllabic verse, Thomas was very original. What cannot be denied the early poems is their verbal vitality—their taking hold of words in a decidedly unprosaic way to create poems of immense energy that are almost wholly lacking in cliché or poeticism. They are among the most original and lasting poems of the decade.

III

The first poem of Thomas's to be printed by a literary weekly was "And Death Shall Have No Dominion" in the *New English Weekly* in May, 1933. More important were three poems in the *Sunday Referee*, and "Light Breaks Where no Sun Shines" in the influential *The Listener* early in 1934.

The *Sunday Referee* was an unusual paper in that it ran a poet's corner for amateur poets, prizes being given for the best poems in a weekly competition, and a major prize, periodically, of the support of the publication of a book. "Poet's Corner" was run by an eccentric but colourful character, Victor Neuburg. Among the poets whose work appeared in the "Corner" were David Gascoyne, Laurie Lee, Julian Symons, Ruthven Todd—and Thomas. Thomas won the weekly prize with "The force that through the green fuse . . ."; and, in March, 1934, it was decided that he should be awarded a major prize. There proved to be difficulty in getting a publisher, and, in the end, Thomas asked David Archer to publish the book from the Parton Press. It eventually appeared in December, 1934. It was not widely reviewed, though it came to attract some attention in the right places, and was the means of Thomas's coming to know Vernon Watkins.

Eighteen Poems was brought to the attention of Richard Church, who at the time was editing a poetry series for Dent. Church asked Thomas for a book of poems, and this began Thomas's connection with the house that was to be his publisher until his death. Thomas sent off a collection of poems in October, 1935, and, although the obscurity of some of them caused Church to have doubts, he asked for further poems to fill out a volume. These Thomas sent to him in March, 1936.

In sending the additional poems to Church, Thomas commented on the inclusion of a number of "simple poems" that might be more acceptable to Church than some of his more recent poems, which were obscure, but which he felt were necessarily so. The "simple poems" were, in fact, poems from the Notebooks—mainly from the book started in February, 1933, so that they precede the work included in *Eighteen Poems*. Indeed, there seem to have been only six poems included in *Twenty-Five Poems* that were not based on pre-1935 versions: "I, in my intricate image"; "Hold hard, these ancient minutes in the cuckoo's month"; "A grief ago"; "How soon the servant sun"; "Now"; and the ten sonnets "Altarwise by Owl-light". As in *Eighteen Poems*, the poems appeared without titles.

The "simple poems" include some of his most celebrated: "The hand that signed the paper"; "I have longed to move away"; "This bread I break"; "Out of the sighs"; "Ears in the

turret hear"; and "And death shall have no dominion"—all
from 1933, except "Out of the sighs", which was extracted from
a poem written in 1932. All the additional poems sent to Church
in March, 1936, seem to have been from the notebooks,
and Thomas spent three months in Swansea revising them.
The more recent poems are a very different matter. While in
theme and style they may seem a continuation of the work in
Eighteen Poems, the resemblance is superficial. The "process"
philosophy no longer had the adequacy it had had for Thomas.
The poetry is extremely mannered, as in

> Now
> Say nay,
> Man dry man,
> Dry lover mine . . .

(a poem Vernon Watkins tried to persuade Thomas to leave
out). It is also extremely literary, both in the allusive imagery
and in the echoes of Hopkins ("Jack Christ") and Joyce ("That
Adam's wether in the flock of horns"). The imagery no longer
gets unity from the central philosophy, but seems applied and
contrived. The result is an acrostic style of poetry, most
exemplified by the "Altarwise by Owl-light" sonnets.

These sonnets have been much praised by critics, and seem
to have been among the poems that Edith Sitwell admired
when she reviewed *Twenty-Five Poems* on its appearance. If one
is prepared to pore over them, they will surrender a meaning;
though they do not become poems to which one can respond at
all spontaneously. Whether the meaning one finds in them has
anything to do with what the author thought the poems were
about before or after he wrote them is another matter. The
eighth sonnet may be taken as an example:

> This was the crucifixion on the mountain,
> Time's nerve in vinegar, the gallow grave
> As tarred with blood as the bright thorns I wept;
> The world's my wound, God's Mary in her grief,
> Bent like three trees and bird-papped through her shift,
> With pins for teardrops is the long wound's woman.
> This was the sky, Jack Christ, each minstrel angle
> Drove in the heaven-driven of the nails

Till the three-coloured rainbow from my nipples
From pole to pole leapt round the snail-waked world.
I by the tree of thieves, all glory's sawbones
Unsex the skeleton this mountain minute,
And by this blowclock witness of the sun
Suffer the heaven's children through my heartbeat.

Francis Scarfe wrote of it:

> In a sense this poem seems to symbolize the birth of love
> through the death of sex. Mary suffers the true punishment of
> Eve—not merely the pangs of child-birth, but the death of her
> offspring . . . The secret of death, and its horror, is that it is
> sexless.[12]

While Elder Olson concludes:

> In Sonnet VIII the Cross sets; this is the crucifixion, then,
> both of Christ and of man; he must die, like Christ, to nourish
> those who come after. There is no immortality, no redemption,
> only sacrifice . . .[13]

Both passages are only short extracts from the complex
discussions these two authors offer. It may be added in Thomas's
favour that, if asked the "meaning" of such poems, he could
only repeat extracts, or offer something equally metaphoric.

William Empson's remarks about these poems are a just
appraisal:

> There is a period of sag in his work, already just feelable perhaps
> in the second book of poetry, where the succession of thrilling
> magical lines, each practically a complete poem in itself, fails
> to add up. The sonnet sequence called "Altarwise by owl-light"
> in the collected edition is a fair example, because a lot of it is
> undoubtedly wonderful and yet one can't help feeling that the
> style has become a mannerism.[14]

Thomas himself, wrote to Pamela Hansford Johnson in May,
1934: "The old fertile days are gone and now a poem is the
hardest and most thankless act of creation . . . when the words
do come, I pick them so thoroughly of their *live* associations that
only the *death* in the words remains."[15] In a letter to Glyn
Jones of December, 1936, in which he discussed Jones's

review of *Twenty-Five Poems*, he speaks of parodying his own tricks of style in the sonnet sequence.

One cannot easily say why a man changes his style or outlook. Thomas had come to London; he was drinking more (at other people's expense); he had no regular work, and had started the hand-to-mouth existence of cadging and odd jobs which was to be his for the rest of the decade. When *Twenty-Five Poems* appeared, he was reviewing thrillers for Geoffrey Grigson for *The Morning Post*. Yet, although Thomas regretted the old days when a poem came easily, he liked his second book of poems better than his first, according to Vernon Watkins. At all events, the highly worked over, time-consuming mode of composition of the more recent poems was to stay with Thomas for the rest of his life, and the very mannered style was to characterise the few new poems that he wrote in the thirties.

If *Twenty-Five Poems* marked the end of a rich period in Thomas's production as a poet, it also marked the beginning of an expanded public reputation. This seems to have begun with Edith Sitwell's praise of the book in *The Sunday Times* in 1936. *Twenty-Five Poems* went into four impressions very rapidly and 3000 copies were sold. This was a good sale for a book of poems in the thirties.

IV

After the publication of *Twenty-Five Poems* Dylan Thomas had hoped that his publisher, Dent, would bring out a book of his early stories. However, the project was turned down, because some of the stories were felt to be obscene. A collection of sixteen stories, *The Burning Babe*, was then projected by the Europa Press of London and Paris, but fear of proceedings for obscenity led to this project being dropped too, and it was decided that Dent would bring out a selection of the stories. This appeared as *The Map of Love* in August, 1939. Also included were sixteen poems.

It was three years since Thomas's last book of poems had appeared, and five to six years since the August, 1933, notebook, which marked the end of his prolific, youthful period. Poems had no longer come easily to Thomas. Vernon Watkins described him as taking roughly a year to finish one of the poems in *The Map of Love* ("Poem to Caitlin"—"I make this in a warring absence"). He had become a friend of Watkins around the beginning of 1935; and, from 1937, he took to sending his poems to Watkins for criticism and to be typed. In the course of their correspondence there developed a classification for Thomas's poems: "exhausters" (Thomas's term, meaning the dense, intensely worked out poems that took up most of his creative energy); and "opossums" (Watkins's term for the simpler poems, coined in contrast to "opus", his term for the more ambitious poems). Most of the "opossums" were re-workings of poems from the notebooks. Only five of the poems in *The Map of Love* seem to be entirely new poems: "It is the sinners' dust-tongued bell"; "I make this in a warring absence"; "A saint about to fall"; "If my head hurt a hair's foot"; and "Because the pleasure-bird whistles". All except the last may properly be termed "exhausters". They were self-consciously "rhetorical" and densely over-written in the manner of "I, in my intricate image" and "Altarwise by Owl-light" in *Twenty-Five Poems*, though there is some relaxing of the obscurity and compression.

On one of these poems we have Thomas's own commentary, and it gives an insight into their mode of construction. This is "Poem for Caitlin", which Vernon Watkins recalled seeing in several versions, and which was first published in *Twentieth Century Verse* for January/February, 1938. It is one of the longest poems Thomas had written up to that time. The poem was evidently composed in the months before and after his marriage in July, 1937. [Thomas's commentary is continuous, and the poem is not contained in the letter from which the commentary is taken.]

> You say you want to know what the poem . . . is "about". There I *can* help you. I can give you a very rough idea of the "plot". But of course it's bound to be a most superficical, and perhaps misleading, idea because the "plot" is told in images, and the images *are* what they say, not what they stand for . . .
> The poem is, in the first place, supposed to be a document or narrative, of all the emotional events between the coming and going, the creation and dissipation, of jealousy, jealousy born from pride and killed by pride, between the absence and the return of the crucial character (or heroine) of the narrative, between the war of her absence and the armistice of her presence.

I make this in a warring absence when
Each ancient, stone-necked minute of love's season
Harbours my anchored tongue,
slips the quaystone,
When, praise is blessed, her
pride in mast and fountain
Sailed and set dazzling by the
handshaped ocean,
In that proud sailing tree with
branches driven
Through the last vault and vege-
table groyne,
And this weak house to marrow-
columned heaven,

The "I", the hero, begins his
narrative at the departure of the
heroine, . . . at the time he feels
that her pride in him and in
their proud sexual world has
been discarded.

Is corner-cast, breath's rag,
scrawled weed, a vain
And opium head, crow stalk,
puffed, cut, and blown,
Or like the tide-looped breast-
knot reefed again
Or rent ancestrally and roped
sea-hymen,
And, pride is last, is like a child
alone
By magnet winds to her blind
mother drawn,
Bread and milk mansion in a
toothless town.

All that keen pride seems, to
him, to have vanished, drawn
back, perhaps, to the blind
wound from which it came.

She makes for me a nettle's innocence
And a silk pigeon's guilt in her
proud absence,
In the molested rocks the shell of
virgins,
The frank, closed pearl, the sea-
girls' lineaments
Glint in the staved and siren-
printed caverns,
Is maiden in the shameful oak,
omen.

He sees her as a woman made of
contraries, innocent in guilt and
guilty in innocence, ravaged in
virginity,

Whalebed and bulldance, the
gold bush of lions,
Proud as a sucked stone and
huge as sandgrains.

These are her contraries: the   virgin in ravishment, and a
beast who follows   woman who, out of a weak
With priest's grave foot and   coldness, reduces to nothing the
hand of five assassins   great sexual strength,
Her molten flight up cinder-
nesting columns,
Calls the starved fire herd, is cast
in ice,
Lost in a limp-treed and un-
eating silence,
Who scales a hailing hill in her
cold flintsteps
Falls on a ring of summers and
locked noons.

I make a weapon of an ass's   heats and prides of the world.
skeleton   Crying his visions aloud he
And walk the warring sands by   makes war upon her absence,
the dead town,   attacks and kills her absent
Cudgel great air, wreck east, and heart, then falls, himself, into
topple sundown,   ruin at the moment of that
Storm her sped heart, hang with   murder of love. He falls into the
beheaded veins   grave:
Its wringing shell, and let her
eyelids fasten.
Destruction, picked by birds,
brays through the jaw-bone,

And, for that murder's sake,   in his shroud he lies, empty of
dark with contagion   visions and legends; he feels
Like an approaching wave I   undead love at his heart. The
sprawl to ruin.   surrounding dead in the grave
Ruin, the room of errors, one   describe to him one manner of
rood dropped   death and resurrection:
Down the stacked sea and water-
pillared shade,
Weighed in rock shroud, is my
proud pyramid;
Where, wound in emerald linen
and sharp wind,

The hero's head lies scraped of
    every legend,
Comes love's anatomist with
    sun-gloved hand
Who picks the live heart on a
    diamond.

"His mother's womb had a
    tongue that lapped up mud,"
Cried the topless, inchtaped lips
    from hank and hood
In that bright anchorground
    where I lay linened,
"A lizard darting with black
    venom's thread
Doubled, to fork him back,
    through the lockjaw bed
And the breath-white, curtained
    mouth of seed."
"See," drummed the taut masks,
    "how the dead ascend:
In the groin's endless coil a man
    is tangled."

the womb, the origin of love, forks its child down to the dark grave, dips it in dust, then forks it back into light again.

These once-blind eyes have
    breathed a wind of visions,
The cauldron's root through this
    once-rindless hand
Fumed like a tree, and tossed a
    burning bird;
With loud, torn tooth and tail
    and cobweb drum
The crumpled packs fled past
    this ghost in bloom,
And, mild as pardon from a
    cloud of pride,
The terrible world my brother
    bares his skin.

And once in the light, the resurrected hero sees the world with penetrating, altered eyes; the world that was wild is now mild to him, revenge has changed into pardon.

Now in the cloud's big breast lie
    quiet countries,
Delivered seas my love from her
    proud place
Walks with no wound, nor light-
    ning in her face,

He sees his love walk in the world, bearing none of the murderous wounds he gave her. Forgiven by her, he ends his narrative in forgiveness—but he sees and knows that all that has

A calm wind blows that raised
the trees like hair
Once where the soft snow's blood
was turned to ice.
And though my love pulls the
pale, nippled air,
Prides of to-morrow suckling in
her eyes,
Yet this I make in a forgiving
presence.

happened will happen again,
tomorrow and tomorrow.[16]

The poem works obliquely, dealing with the poet's psychological concerns imagistically or in terms of fantasy. For all its virtuosity, it does not touch the reader in the way in which the simple poems in the volume do. Several of these were from the February, 1933, notebook, and one from the 1930–1932 notebook. Touchingly direct and economical is "Once it was the Colour of Saying" (probably from a version of 1932).

On 24th October, 1938, Thomas sent Vernon Watkins a postcard. The twenty-seventh was Thomas's twenty-fourth birthday. The message on the postcard was a poem:

Birthday Poem

Twenty four years remind the tears of my eyes.
(Bury the dead for fear that they walk to the grave in labour).
In the groin of the natural doorway I crouched like a tailor
Sewing a shroud for a journey
By the light of the meat-eating sun.
Dressed to die, the sensual strut begun,
With my red veins full of money,
In the final direction of the elementary town
I advance for as long as forever is.

Vernon Watkins came to see this poem as a turning point for Thomas. Certainly it seems to have coincided with a crisis in his poetry, as the related poem "On no work of words now for three lean months . . ." (based loosely on a poem of 1933) seems to attest. Watkins associated the crisis with a change and expansion of Thomas's interest, which saw him writing, in the stories in *Portrait of the Artist as a Young Dog*, about people as they actually were (as opposed to the fantasy of earlier stories).[17]

The poem that most obviously marks the change of style is

"After the Funeral"—a poem "In memory of Ann Jones",
his aunt who lived at Fern Hill, the farm where Thomas spent
summers as a boy. It was one of his first poems about another
person. It began as a poem in his notebook in February, 1933:

> After the funeral mule praises, brays,
> Shaking of mule heads, betoken
> Grief at the going to the earth of man
> Or woman, at yet another long woe broken,
> Another theme to play on and surprise
> Fresh faults and till then hidden flaws
> Faded beyond ears and eyes,
> At [he or she], loved or else hated well,
> So far from love or hate [,] in a deep hole . . .

The extent to which he used this original poem merely as a
starting point only indicates his changing relationship to the
poems in the Notebooks. At the time of the original writing, he
had, with honesty, admitted that the death of his aunt did not
touch him deeply: he was nineteen.[18] In rewriting the poem,
he came to a realisation of what that death—and death
generally—involved, and he came to a knowledge of the grief
previously missed. Thomas rather groped his way to the final
poem (and its final resolution). According to Watkins, as first
sent to him in March, 1938, it ended at the line: "Round the
parched world of Wales and drowned each sun." In sending the
revised version to Watkins in February, 1939, Thomas's
comment (not quite consistent with Watkins's) was:

> Now here is the Anne Jones poem, & now I think it is more of a
> poem; will you type it for me? I knew it was feeble as it stood
> before, & the end of it—that is the part that becomes the new
> brackets—was too facile &, almost, grandiosely sentimental.[19]

The reference to the bracketing and the sentimentality is of
interest because of the stylistic quandary that it reveals Thomas
to have been in, and because of his solution of the quandary.
The passage in brackets in the final version is a comment on the
rhetoric through which he projects his grief in the early part of
the poem:

(Though this for her is a monstrous image blindly
Magnified out of praise; her death was a still drop;
She would not have me sinking in the holy
Flood of her heart's fame; she would lie dumb and deep
And need no druid of her broken body).
But I, Ann's bard on a raised hearth, call all
The seas to service that her wood-tongued virtue
Babble like a bellbuoy over the hymning heads,
Bow down the walls of the ferned and foxy woods
That her love sing and swing through a brown chapel
Bless her bent spirit with four, crossing birds.

The poem is strongly rhetorical, and in a deliberately artificial way, in parts; but this is contained by oscillations back into realism: rhetoric for the grief, which is, in a sense, beyond measure; realism for his aunt, an old woman pitifully reduced by sickness. The poem itself is spoken of as a rhetorical artifact: ". . . this monumental / Argument of the hewn voice, gesture and psalm . . ." It is as though the shortcomings of his style of the period were recognised, but had, for the moment, been contained and utilised. Thomas seems to have remained dissatisfied with the result; though the poem was, in its day, his most celebrated. Theodore Roethke recorded that Thomas felt that the poem creaked a bit at the beginning and that he had not put enough work into it.[20] It is at the beginning that the poem most follows the original.

The new accent on "subject" in Thomas's poems reminds one that there is more than one attestation that his favourite twentieth-century poet was Hardy—a seemingly unlikely preference. The turn towards actuality in his stories in *Portrait of the Artist as a Young Dog* may have been associated not merely with Joyce, who is recalled by the title, but also with another seemingly unlikely preference, Dickens, from whom Caitlin Thomas recalled him reading to her regularly in bed while they were in Laugharne in the late thirties. Thomas, in his stories, has Dickens's eye for the way in which ordinary people are so exotically commonplace.

In *Eighteen Poems* death was accommodated by the process philosophy; in *The Map of Love* it is tragic; in his late poems it is accepted in "unjudging love". The movement towards that attitude had begun in *Portrait*. It is also suggested in one of the new poems in *The Map of Love*:

> "Rest beyond choice in the dust-appointed grain,
> At the breast stored with seas. No return
> Through the waves of the fat streets nor the skeleton's thin ways.
> The grave and my calm body are shut to your coming as stone,
> And the endless beginning of prodigies suffers open."
>   ("If My Head Hurt a Hair's Foot")

v

The real difficulty in reading or discussing Thomas's early poetry is that of forming a sure sense of the idiom in which it was written. While it is untrue that Thomas was the old-fashioned poet unaware of contemporary developments that Geoffrey Grigson and Julian Symons have suggested he was, he was not a conscious experimenter with words in a doctrinaire fashion.

> . . . I'm not an experimentalist & and never will be. I write in the only way I can write, & and my warped, crabbed & cabinned stuff is not the result of theorising but of pure incapability to express my needless tortuities in any other way.[21]

At the time of the compilation of *Twenty-Five Poems*, Richard Church, the editor for the publisher, Dent, suggested that Thomas's poems were indebted to surrealism. Thomas's celebrated reply was very definite:

> I am not, never have been, never will be, or could be for that matter, a surrealist . . . I think I do know what some of the main faults of my writing are: Immature violence, rhythmic monotony, frequent muddleheadedness, and a very much overweighted imagery that leads too often to incoherence. But every line *is* meant to be understood; the reader *is* meant to understand every poem by thinking and feeling about it, and not by sucking it in through his pores, or whatever he is meant to do with surrealist writing.[22]

The letter is rather exaggerated, but it does reflect Thomas's attitude to surrealism throughout his life.

When asked later in life how he began to write poetry, Thomas replied that he "had fallen in love with words".[23] This accords with what Vernon Watkins said about the way Thomas got into a poem: "Dylan worked upon a symmetrical abstract with tactile delicacy; out of a lump of texture or nest of phrases he created music, testing everything by physical feeling, working from the concrete image outwards."[24] This suggests an exploratory approach to the materials of a poem— an approach where "meaning", if the word can be used at all, is discovered in the writing. Indeed, Thomas said to Watkins, about one of the poems in *Twenty-Five Poems*, that "so far as he knew it had no meaning at all".[25] In a letter to Pamela Hansford Johnson for 2nd May, 1934, he distinguished between two types of writers—those who, like Bennett, work *in the direction* of words, and those who, like Shelley, begin with the meaning and work *out of* words.[26] He would have put himself in the second class.

All of this suggests a characterisation of Thomas that has had some acceptance among his sophisticated admirers, and which has been used to reply to those detractors who contend that his poetry is worthless because it is senseless: that Thomas uses words or images at a level more fundamental than that at which the conventional notion of "meaning" applies. He thus gets literary respectablity as a "symbolist" (or "*symboliste*", for those who even bother to make the distinction)—a sort of Welsh Mallarmé *cum* Rimbaud.

It was in this spirit that Edith Sitwell evidently read *Twenty-Five Poems*, when she praised them at their first publication. Thomas was gratified by her praise, but he criticised her interpretation:

Edith Sitwell's analysis, in a letter to the *Times*, of the lines "The atlas-eater with a jaw for news/Bit out the mandrake with tomorrow's scream [,]" seems to me very vague and Sunday-journalish. She says the lines refer to "the violent speed and the sensation-loving, horror-loving craze of modern life." She doesn't take the literal meaning: that a world-devouring ghost creature bit out the horror of tomorrow from a gentleman's loins. A "jaw for news" is an obvious variation of a "nose for news", and means that the mouth of the creature can taste already the horror that has not yet come or can sense it coming . . . What is this creature? It's the dog among the fairies, the rip and cur among the myths, the snapper at demons, the scarer of ghosts, the wizard's heel-chaser. This poem is a particular incident in a particular adventure not a general, elliptical deprecation of this "horrible, crazy, speedy life".[27]

Thomas speaks up for "the literal meaning"; but the meaning he offers is as metaphorical as the poem itself. Of Thomas, more than of most poets, it seems true that his poetry was his only method of saying what he had to say. Henry Treece asked Thomas for analyses of poems for his book on Thomas. Thomas promised them, but put things off and put things off, eventually giving up.[28] Thomas's method of working is well known, and was described by Vernon Watkins:

> His method of composition was itself painfully slow. He used separate work-sheets for individual lines, sometimes a page or two being devoted to a single line, while the poem was gradually built up, phrase by phrase. He usually had beforehand an exact conception of the poem's length, and he would decide how many lines to allot to each part of its development. In spite of the care and power and symmetry of its construction, he recognized at all times that it was for the sake of divine accidents that a poem existed at all.[29]

He seems to have "built up" his poems out of phrases. In so doing, he appears not merely to have been working towards "meaning" but also towards a maximising of intensity. His approach, and even more, some aspects of the results, remind one of the work of his friend, William Empson. A passage by Empson that might have been by Thomas was quoted in Chapter 6. An early poem by Thomas shows Empson's "witty" type of obscurity:

> Incarnate devil in a talking snake,
> The central plains of Asia in his garden,
> In shaping-time the circle stung awake,
> In shapes of sin forked out the bearded apple,
> And God walked there who was a fiddling warden
> And played down pardon from the heavens' hill.

Comparison with the original version in the notebooks shows that it had been reworked in the direction of this type of obscurity. There is no question of influence, though Thomas evidently found Empson's idiom congenial, as his parody of Empson, published in *Horizon*, in 1940, shows:

> Not your winged lust but his must now change suit.
> The harp-waked Casanova rakes no range.
> The worm is (pin-point) rational in the fruit . . .

Empson's analytic remarks on "The force that through the green fuse" read like a note to one of his own poems, but they clearly get the spirit and the letter of Thomas's poem.

> It centres on comparing the blood-stream of the child Dylan to the sea-cloud-river cycle by which water moves round this planet, and he is united with the planet, also personally guilty of murder whenever a murderer is hanged, and so forth. The mining term "vein" for a line of ore was naturally a crucial pun for the early Dylan, because of his central desire to identify events inside his own skin with the two main things outside it, the entire physical world and also the relations with that of other men.[30]

In reading Empson's poems, it is necessary to grasp the single and often highly specialised aspect of a metaphor that is literally meant and to ignore the rest: then the poem becomes comprehensible. Some of the suggestions of his figures and images must be suppressed; others are clearly manipulated to support the literal sense; and yet others introduce implications of which the poet seems not fully aware. These remarks might be applied to Thomas's poetry. His obscurity is not that of someone who is trying to use language in a consciously non-literal manner, such as Hart Crane, whose poetry Norman Cameron thought Thomas's work resembled.[31]

Thomas insisted that simplicity (like literalness) was a virtue in poetry, yet obscurity might be unavoidable; and he felt his own obscurity to be unavoidable, just because it was necessary to the literal presentation of what he wanted to present. He told Vernon Watkins that working on *Twenty-Five Poems* was "very like plumbing: getting things in the right position so that they function properly".[32] In his letters to Watkins, he often discussed the choice of particular words, and generally in terms of their local (and often musical) effect.

However, if Thomas's choice of words was often dictated by the need to get the word that was as literally right as possible at the particular point in the poem, he does not seem to have been strongly aware of general pressures operating in his choice of words. He kept lists of favourite words, and his friends criticised him from time to time for using them too much. His fondness in his early poems for words that delineate his preoccupation with birth, sex, death, disease and decay has been pointed out; and there seems to be a pressure, legitimate and understandable, to go for such words in these poems. It is surprising, however, to find Thomas reacting strongly to a rejection of an early poem because of the sexual suggestions of the vocabulary:

> . . . the B.B.C. have banned my poetry. After my poem in the *Listener* (Light Breaks Where No Sun Shines) the editor received a host of letters, all complaining of the disgusting obscenity in two of the verses. One of the bits they made a fuss about was:
>
> > 'Nor fenced, nor staked, the *gushers* of the sky
> > *Spout* to the *rod* divining in a smile
> > The *oil* of tears.'
>
> The little smut-hounds thought I was writing a copulatory anthem. In reality, of course, it was a metaphysical image of rain and grief.[33]

The protest is understandable; but so was the misunderstanding. The stanza immediately before the quoted passage begins: "A candle in the thighs" and ends "Where no wax is, the candle shows its hairs." The poem and Thomas's comment are a good illustration of the way in which he seems to have expected his imagery to be taken rather specifically, and reaction to it not to be controlled by the imagery of its context. In his letters to Vernon Watkins he seems more concerned with local clashes of association or with the way that words fit musically than with the larger orchestration of imagery. This larger orchestration is there in later poems like "A Winter's Tale", "Poem in October" or "Fern Hill". His famous statement to Henry Treece suggests that, in the earlier poems, the relationship of images was an associative step-by-step relationship:

> . . . the *life* in any poem of mine cannot move concentrically round a central image; the life must come out of the centre; an image must be born and die in another; . . . Out of the

inevitable conflict of images . . . I try to make that momentary peace which is a poem.[34]

In answering the *New Verse* "Enquiry" in 1934, he went for the same strongly verbal conception of a poem:

The writing of a poem is, to me, the physical and mental task of constructing a formally watertight compartment of words, preferably with a main moving column (i.e., narrative) to hold a little of the real causes and forces of the creative brain and body. The causes and forces are always there, and always need a concrete expression.[35]

However, he described what the poem does for the poet in very different terms:

Poetry, recording the stripping of the individual darkness, must, inevitably, cast light upon what has been hidden for too long, and, by so doing, make clean the naked exposure.[36]

In the contrast between the two answers we see exemplified the paradoxical combination of acuteness and vagueness that characterised Thomas's talk and writing about poetry: the acumen in criticising the craftsmanship of his own and other people's poetry; and the sentimental, defensive vagueness about the writing of poetry generally. The contrast corresponds to that between the incredibly witty (and often acutely critical) introducer of poems for reading, and the gong-like voice in which they are intoned. Thomas's mixed, confused stance concerning the writing of poetry—witty, perceptive, sentimental and truculent—is caught most perfectly in a letter to Charles Fisher written in 1935:

You asked me to tell you about my theory of poetry. Really I haven't got one. I like things that are difficult to write and difficult to understand; I like "redeeming the contraries" with secretive images; I like contradicting my images, saying two things at once in one word, four in two and one in six . . . Poetry, heavy in tare though nimble, should be as orgiastic and organic as copulation, dividing and unifying, personal but not private, propagating the individual in the mass and the mass in the individual. I think it should work from words from the substance of words and the rhythm of substantial words set together, not towards words. Poetry is a medium, not a stigmata on paper. Men should be two tooled, and a poet's middle leg is his pencil.[37]

Chapter 14

IMAGINATION AND THE WORLD

The nature of the Imagination – J. Bronowski,
Humphrey Jennings, Charles Madge, *Mass Observation*
– Kathleen Raine – *Wales*, Vernon Watkins

THE RADICAL, SOCIAL poetry of Auden, Day Lewis,
Spender and Lehmann had considerable variety; but, behind
it all, there was the notion that poetry, while not the slave of
political doctrine, should absorb revolutionary political ideas,
either by acclimatising them to some mythology of social
renewal, or by making them part of the poet's response to his
experience of society. However, there were other writers who
saw the relationship of poetry to society and social renewal in
different terms. Among these were, of course, the surrealists,
who believed one aim of the Arts to be the imaginative liberation of human beings from reality. Others, like Humphrey
Jennings, one of the editors of *Experiment* at Cambridge,
rejected the surrealist dream of liberating the imagination from
reality, believing that the poet must come to grips as fully as
possible with the actual world. In this connection Jennings
developed the notion of the "found image"—the image that had
actually been observed, as opposed to an imagined one.

The great radical poet of the interplay of the imagination
and the world is Blake: he knew how the imagination could
liberate as well as how the imagination could be enchained by
thought and circumstance. Blake had a considerable influence
on some of the poets of the thirties. He was one of the "healers"
admired by Auden as a young man; he seems to have had an
influence on the early poetry of Dylan Thomas; and he was to
be one of George Barker's models in the development of his
visionary social poetry in the latter part of the decade. Randall
Swingler wrote admiringly of Blake in *Left Review*: "The Songs
of Experience are the discovery of that potentiality in Man
enchained by economic necessity . . . and by religion, the
weapon of the property owners."[1] His influence is felt in the

work of four writers who had been at Cambridge around 1930: Vernon Watkins; Kathleen Raine; and Humphrey Jennings and Jakob Bronowski, fellow editors of *Experiment*.

The concept of the "image" was a dominant critical idea in the period between the two World Wars. The most widely held notion of it was one that showed the influence of the Imagist poets and of Freud. For the Imagists, the image was the most natural rhetorical device for poetry, the means of attaining maximum sensory impact. Freud, in *The Interpretation of Dreams*, explained the images of dreams as the mode of expression of the unconscious. These two notions combined to produce the notion of the poetic image as an *expressive* device. This seems to be the way it is basically conceived by Louis MacNeice in *Modern Poetry* (1938), by Cecil Day Lewis in *A Hope for Poetry* (1934), by William Empson, in *Seven Types of Ambiguity* (1930), by the editors of *New Verse*, and by Dylan Thomas. A different conception was held by Kathleen Raine, Vernon Watkins, David Gascoyne, and George Barker. They held a more Romantic view of the image as a special mode of insight as well as of expression; or as something akin to Yeats's notion of the image, as giving one access to a collective human memory.

II

In 1943, Bronowski met Jennings, whom he had not seen for ten years. They found that they had each independently come to see Blake as the radical poet of the industrial landscape of nineteenth-century England.[2] This is Bronowski's thesis in his book on Blake, *William Blake: A Man Without a Mask* (1942). Blake, as a social critic, ". . . saw the machine grow larger than man, to make him stunted, ignorant, and beastly".[3] It is a criticism of industrial capitalism more embracing than that of Marx, yet consonant with it:

> The bourgeoisie, wherever it has got the upper hand, has put an end to all feudal, patriarchal, idyllic relations. It has pitilessly torn asunder the motley feudal ties that bound man to his "natural superiors", and has left no other nexus between man and man than naked self-interest, than callous "cash payment". . . . It has resolved personal worth into exchange value, and in place of the numberless indefeasible chartered freedoms, has

set up that single, unconscionable freedom—Free Trade.[4]

(Manifesto of the Communist Party)

Bronowski gives no evidence of sympathy for doctrinaire Marxism. A scientist, he rejects a "materialist" psychological explanation of the poetic process, and criticises Coleridge for having anything to do with one. In *The Poet's Defence*, he stated: "I believe in ideal truth . . . The mind of man has a knowledge of truth beyond the near-truths of science and society. I believe that poetry tells this truth."[5]

Humphrey Jennings's conception of poetry seems to have been close to that of Bronowski, and to the practice of Blake as Bronowski saw it. Jennings, who was killed accidentally in 1948 while filming in Greece, was one of I. A. Richards's two most brilliant students in the late twenties, the other being William Empson. Jennings was best known as a film producer, though he seems to have thought of himself above all as a painter. His friend Kathleen Raine, who knew him at Cambridge, epitomised his career in an introduction to his one collection of poetry, *Poems*, published posthumously in 1951, and containing fourteen pieces:

> He early became a member of the Surrealist group, and his early work shows the influence of the ideas formulated by his friends Breton, Eluard, and Marcel Duchamp. In particular the surrealist preoccupation with the image interested Jennings; but with this difference, that for him the image was always a public and objective, never a private and subjective, symbol . . .
> . . . the image must never be invented. Rather it must be sought for, visually, or in literature, or history. The locomotive is such an image of the Industrial Revolution, with which is contrasted the horse, its natural antithesis; the plough, symbol of agriculture, is another. The very phrase "I see London" deliberately echoes Blake's "I behold London, a human awful wonder of God", and the comparison, in the same poem, of the dome of St. Paul's to the forehead of Darwin is a condensed statement about the relation of Wren's architecture to Newtonian science, that had its fulfilment in the work of Darwin.[6]

Poems contains a number of Jennings's "Reports", which were written when he was most under the influence of surrealism in 1936 and 1937, and which were discussed and quoted in Chapter

11. (He collaborated with David Gascoyne in a volume of translations of twenty poems by Benjamin Peret, *Remove Your Hat*, in 1936.) The Blakean poems referred to by Kathleen Raine were written in the second year of the war:

> I see London
> I see the dome of Saint Paul's like the forehead of
> Darwin
> I see London stretching away North and North-East,
> along dockside roads and balloon-haunted allotments
> Where the black plumes of the horses precede and
> the white helmets of the rescue-squad follow.
> I see London
> I see the grey waters of Thames, like a loving nurse,
> unchanged, unruffled, flooding between bridges and
> washing up wharf steps—an endlessly flowing eternity
> that smoothes away the sorrows of beautiful churches—
> the pains of time—the wrecks of artistry along her
> divine banks—to whom the strongest towers are but a
> moment's mark and the deepest-cleaving bomb an untold
> regret.
>
> ("I See London", I)

Jennings also left behind him a long work called *Pandemonium*: it was a compilation of eighteenth- and nineteenth-century material that was intended as an imaginative exploration of industrialism and its impact on the human imagination.

It was his interest in exploring the popular imagination and the English scene as the storehouse of the products of the English imagination that led Jennings to cooperate with Charles Madge in his project, Mass-Observation, which Madge started with Tom Hopkinson in November, 1936. During the thirties, Madge was married to Kathleen Raine, who has quite rightly pointed out that the aims of Mass-Observation have been misunderstood:

> Charles Madge originally envisaged "Mass-Observation" as a technique for recording the subliminal stirrings of the collective mind of the nation; through the images thrown up in such things as advertisements, popular songs, themes in the press, the objects with which people surround themselves (have on their mantel-piece, for example). This idea was akin to (perhaps in part determined by) the surrealist *"objet trouvé"* . . . For Charles Madge

and Humphrey Jennings the movement had more to do with the nature of the imagination (and the functioning of a collective imagination) than with those Gallup-polls and trade-surveys which have since become commonplace.[7]

Kathleen Raine's characterisation of the movement may, in retrospect, have been coloured by her later predilections. However, it is clear that the interests of its founders were more than sociological, and that their techniques were intended to transcend those of the public-opinion poll. Mass-Observation recruited untrained observers, who, in collaboration with trained observers, contributed to surveys of smoking, pub-going, dance halls, astrology, football pools and other aspects of popular culture. "Day-Surveys" were conducted, in which a large number of observers contributed their observations of a single day. Among other things, the observer was "to ask himself at the end of each day what image has been dominant in it".

> This image should, if possible, be one which has forced itself on him and which has confirmed its importance by recurrence of some kind. . . . Such a test is going to throw light on such questions as: Is there an image typical of a certain day, of a certain area, of a certain class, etc.? The reactions of individuals when plotted on a map may turn out to form a mass-picture, just as many separate barometer-readings go to make a weather-map.[8]

An interesting by-product of Mass-Observation was the Oxford collective poem. Twelve undergraduates at Oxford collected for three weeks the images that each day were predominant in their minds. The six most frequent images were taken, and each participant composed a pentameter line around each image. The best six lines were then chosen. Each member wrote a poem of twelve to eighteen lines around these six lines. Finally, after the poems had been passed round among all the participants for correction, a vote was taken on the best one. The resulting poem went as follows:

> Believe the iron saints who stride the floods,
> Lying in red and labouring for the dawn:
> Steeples repeat their warnings; along the roads

Memorials stand, of children force has slain;
Expostulating with the winds they hear
Stone kings irresolute on a marble stair.

The tongues of torn boots flapping on the cobbles,
Their epitaphs, clack to the crawling hour.
The clock grows old inside the hollow tower;
It ticks and stops, and waits for me to tick,
And on the edges of the town redoubles
Thunder, announcing war's climacteric.

The hill has its death like us; the ravens gather;
Trees with their corpses lean towards the sky.
Christ's corn is mildewed and the wine gives out.
Smoke rises from the pipes whose smokers die.
And on our heads the crimes of our buried fathers
Burst in a hurricane and the rebels shout.

The process of composition resembles that used in the surrealist game, "the exquisite corpse", where a poem is composed word by word by a group, each of whom contributes a word on the basis of the suggestion of previous words. The rationale behind the experiment was that a writer's style contained "social fantasy representative of his class environment". The collective poets "produced what is virtually a 'landscape' for their Oxford environment". It was felt to show "the sense of decay and imminent doom which characterises contemporary Oxford".[9] The experiment was not repeated. Mass-Observation itself seems to have been brought to an end, within two years of its launching, by the war.

Madge was the poet pointed out to George Barker in Parton Street in 1933 as the young hope of English poetry. Madge, like Jennings and Empson, had been a pupil of I. A. Richards. In 1933, at the age of twenty-one, he had poems in *New Country, New Verse* and *The Listener*; and along with David Gascoyne, Dylan Thomas and George Barker, he was one of the five poets under twenty-five included in Michael Roberts's *Faber Book of Modern Verse* in 1936. The following poem of 1933 gives an idea of his early quality:

The sun, of whose terrain we creatures are,
Is the director of all human love,
Unit of time, and circle round the earth

And we are the commotion born of love
And slanted rays of that illustrious star
Peregrine of the crowded fields of birth,

The crowded lanes, the market and the tower
Like sight in pictures, real at remove,
Such is our motion on dimensional earth.

Down by the river, where the ragged are,
Continuous the cries and noise of birth,
While to the muddy edge dark fishes move

And over all, like death, or sloping hill,
Is nature, which is larger and more still.

                              ("Solar Creation")

His first book, *The Disappearing Castle* (1937), has no uniform manner and no uniform standard, though the later poems are duller than the earlier ones, which admittedly have a quality that makes Madge's early reputation understandable. His second book, *The Father Found* (1941), confirms the impression made by the first one, and is not as good. It contains one poem that is of interest because it is clearly connected with the Mass-Observation "Worktown" surveys, and gives an idea of the imaginative approach to their material:

Not from imagination I am drawing
This landscape (Lancs), this plate of tripe and onions,
But, like the Nag's Head barmaid, I am drawing
(Towards imagination) gills of mild,
The industrial drink, in which my dreams and theirs
Find common ground. I hear the clattering clogs,
I see the many-footed smoke, the dance
Of this dull sky. And I perceive (the beer
Helping) a dialect of dirty swans
And Persil ads, along White Lion Brow.
But a new generation, now the sun
Throws coats off, in the park lays on the ground
The emaciated man, short-haired, thin-jowled,
And warms him with this girl, whose curious smile
Hangs, secret as heaven, on his mill-made fears.
(The accordion in the vault forces a smile.)
So night falls and the Bank of England opens
And in this hour are crowded all men's lives,

> For, as they drink, they drown. So final night
> Falls, like a pack of cards, each one of which
> Is fate, the film-star and the penny pool.
> You sit there waiting for the spell to break.
>
> ("Drinking in Bolton")

It was indeed to be in Mass-Observation rather than in poetry that Madge's imagination was to show its brilliance.

III

Kathleen Raine, who was the wife of Charles Madge, had been a student of biology at Cambridge, and had contributed to *Experiment*. However, she never felt at home in Cambridge. Though she could not then articulate her feelings, she felt out of tune with the positivism of Russell and Wittgenstein, which she came later to see as being the basis for the view of poetry put forward by William Empson and many of his contemporaries.

> I had assumed, when I reached that long-vanished Cambridge of the late twenties, that others who spoke of poetry and who wrote verse must understand it as I did . . . When I met these writers of my generation, some of whom have since become famous, I assumed that when they made pronouncements upon poetry that they and I were discussing the same thing. I did not like their poems any more than they liked mine . . . but those of William Empson were of a brilliance I could not but admire; so that my own preference for Yeats (he was not fashionable at the time), for Keats and Shelley (who were despised) and even for Walter de la Mare I attributed to my ignorance, and kept very quiet.
>
> Yet to me it seemed strange that a poem about love should begin "And now she cleans her teeth into the lake" . . . I had not read Plato, nor Plotinus, nor the Vedantic literature, nor Berkeley, nor *A Vision*, nor Coomaraswamy; nor any of the books I needed in order to discover the first principles of the kind of poetry I instinctively recognized as such . . . I have since had to undergo the double process of discovering the underlying assumptions of the *avant-garde* in which at Cambridge I found myself; of discovering that I could not accept these . . . and then, after years of search, discovering the discredited and neglected writings which constitute the learning of the imagination.[10]

She came to discover a "mode of thought" entirely different from that of science or logic; and she went on to see the world as embodying a language of archetypal signs that give to the imagination access to a timeless world of all that is eternal and unchanging in human experience. Her admirations include Blake and Yeats. She subscribes to Jung's notion of the collective unconscious, and to the Yeatsian idea of *Spiritus Mundi*. However uncongenial such conceptions may be to logic, her collection of essays, *Defending Ancient Springs* (1967), constitutes one of the most cogent and persuasive expositions of them to appear since Yeats.

Her first book, *Stone and Flower* (1943), was written in Northumbria in the early part of World War II. It contains few of her poems of the thirties, and one is led to suppose that her poems of that decade pre-dated her full discovery of what she feels to be the true sources of poetry. Of the poems in *Stone and Flower* that are from the thirties, "Maternal Grief" is perhaps the best. It first appeared in *New Verse* for April–May, 1936.

> I am not human,
> I am not human,
> Nor am I divine.

> To whom,
> To whom can I cry
> "I am thine"?

> I have picked my grandsire's corpse to the bone,
> I have found no ghost in brisket or chine.

> I shed the blood of my female kin,
> But they never return to speak again.

>> I am not human,
>> I am not human,
>> How shall I feed my hungry children?

> I make the porridge of meal and wine
> And pour it out in the troughs for swine.

> And ghosts are hungry, the ghosts are divine,
> But the pigs eat the meal, the priests drink the wine.

The poem is typical of her writing of the period in its combination of a sparse directness with an archetypal visionary quality.

There seems to be a steadfast avoidance of the actual and contemporary. The most attractive aspect of her poetry of the period is its limpid visual quality. This clear visual quality is what must have made her welcome in the pages of *New Verse*, to which she contributed throughout its publication, even though this home of the "object-image" was committed to a conception of poetry almost completely opposite to her own.

In some of her poems of the thirties there is an explicit suggestion of her imaginative orientation:

> The voice of nature is
> one of the dead languages
> the alphabet of birds
> frames obsolete words
> of love the nightingales
> and swallows no true tales.
>
> yet admirably how restored each leafy page
> in hieroglyphic of a golden age!
>
> > (*NV*, (June, 1934) 5)

Towards the end of the decade, political questions obtrude into at least two of her poems: "Fata Morgana", where she thinks of Spain; and "Advice to a Gentleman", which contains writing almost fierce enough for *Left Review* (*NV*, N.S. 1,2 (May, 1939) 44–5):

> It saves time, it saves time
> to circumscribe catastrophe in rhyme.
> Go fascist—peace will harvest every time
> out of your flowering bomb and pregnant mine.

This poem was not included in *Stone and Flower*; but, placed beside some of the poems that were, it shows up Kathleen Raine's characteristic shortcomings.

There is a trance-like monotony about the rhythm of her simple lyric poems. The language, for all its directness and clarity, is not used in a way that makes us sit up and take notice; and, in the end, we begin to long for something ordinary like a brick or a bus among all the archetypal seas, trees, voices, birds, etc. Her poetry illustrates the dangers that there are for writers who have a visionary and archetypal conception of poetry. The archetypal in its naked form is deprived of the particular and local to which human emotion tends to attach itself; and the poet of vision tends to forget that it is only by an individual handling of words that the poem interests us and affects us. Kathleen Raine's poems do not live up to the expectations to which her critical writings give rise.

IV

The career of Vernon Watkins as a poet in the thirties is one of the most unusual of the period. To most readers he became known during the forties, with his first book *The Ballad of the Mari Lwyd* appearing in 1941. In fact he was thirty-five when this book appeared, and had been writing poetry for over fifteen years. Born in the same year as William Empson, he was at Cambridge at the same college as Empson, but left after a term or two in 1925, because he was evidently so out of sympathy with the positivistic intellectual atmosphere of the Cambridge of those days. The immediate occasion of his departure was a revelation concerning the temporal and the eternal. He went back to Swansea, and took a job with Lloyds Bank, where he remained as a cashier until he retired.

In spite of this act of poetic integrity, Watkins did not make himself felt as a poet in the decade that followed. This was not due to his writing little: by the time he met Dylan Thomas in 1934 he had written a thousand poems. Thomas was to help him to cut out what was derivative, and, eventually, to encourage him to get his poems published. Watkins did not work steadily on one particular poem, but worked at a body of poems over the years. ("Ballad of the Rough Sea" was published in *Life and Letters* in 1940, but was not collected in a book until it appeared in *The Death Bell* in 1954.) Watkins's first poem to be published was "Griefs of the Sea", which appeared, along with another poem by Watkins, in the first issue of *Wales* in 1936. The publication of the two poems by Watkins was evidently arranged by Thomas, and it came close to disillusioning Watkins with publication at the first shot, as Thomas inadvertently submitted a version of the poem on which he himself had been making suggested improvements. Watkins's work, however, continued to come out in *Wales*; and in 1939 his poems started to appear in *Life and Letters*, edited by Robert Herring, whom Watkins met in the early part of that year. Appearance in these periodicals seems to have been the extent of Watkins's publication during the thirties—in total fifteen poems.

It is tempting to think of Watkins, Dylan Thomas and the poets who appeared in *Wales* as a "Welsh school". *Wales* published work by Watkins and Thomas, and by younger or less well known Welsh poets, such as Keidrych Rhys (its editor), Idris Davies and Lynette Roberts, the wife of Rhys. The invitation to subscribe contained in the first number was a manifesto:

> British culture is a fact, but the English contribution to it is very small. McDiarmid told the Scots that they could gain nothing by joining forces with the English and aping their mannerisms.
>
> There is actually no such thing as "English" culture: a few individuals may be highly cultured, but the people as a whole are crass.
>
> Welsh literature is carried on, not by a clique of moneyed dilletantes, but by the small shopkeepers, the blacksmiths, the non-conformist ministers, by the miners, quarrymen, and the railwaymen.
>
> The Kelt's heritage is clear as sunlight, yet the burden of English literature has also fallen upon him. The greatest of present-day poets are Kelts.
>
> We publish this journal in English so that it may spread far beyond the frontiers of Wales, and because we realise the beauty of the English language better than the English themselves, who have so shamefully misused it.
>
> We are beyond the bigotry of unintelligent fascist nationalism.
>
> In case the English should claim our contribution for their own, we produce this pamphlet, calling it "Wales" in defiance of parasitical adoption.
>
> Though we write in English, we are rooted in Wales. [*Wales*, 1]

A regular feature was a series of bibliographies of Welsh authors, and a regular policy was ridicule of the exponents of pseudo-Welshness. However, *Wales* does not leave one with the impression of achievement that is distinctively Welsh. The contributions by Welsh poets other than Thomas and Watkins are rather characterless. *Wales* first ran for eleven numbers (including two double numbers) from 1937 to 1940, and fizzled out in the lone issue of a one-page "Wartime Broadsheet". Its main achievement was the publication of five of the sixteen poems that appeared in Dylan Thomas's *The Map of Love* in 1939, and the publication of twelve poems by Watkins. (It also published several stories by Thomas.)

A concentration on Watkins's Welshness would be a missing of his central quality. His father was an ardent student of Welsh poetry, but Watkins could not speak Welsh. As Kathleen Raine has pointed out: ". . . a characteristic of Watkins's poetry is the presence of some organizing idea which can only be apprehended poetically, some true cosmic or metaphysical apprehension of what Coleridge calls 'the eternal in and through the temporal' ".[11] The phrase of Coleridge comes from his definition of "symbol", and it would be easy to exaggerate the symbolic nature of Watkins's poetry. Nevertheless, he captures the timeless quality of all he writes about, and suggests a depth of inherited experience in so much that he handles poetically.

> Inert he lies on the saltgold sand
> And sees through his lids the scarlet sky.
> The sea will run back if he breathes a sigh.
> He can hide the sun with a roselit hand . . .
>
> The sun, the sea and the wind are three
> But he narrows them down with a dreaming eye.
> With his hands at rest and his drawn-up thigh
> He can imagine the sacred tree.
>
> For a point of light has seeded all
> And the beautiful seed has come to rest
> For a sunblown moment in his breast,
> A tree where the leaves will never fall . . .
> ["The Sunbather", *Wales*, 2, August, 1937, 63–4]

An awareness of the centrality of this timeless quality is explicit in his poetry:

From my loitering as a child
In paving-square and field
And from my stone-still tongue
Time is unsealed.

The ages are unstrung
By water from a Triton flung
And the world finds its heart
Which was not always young.

I cannot tell what art
Set the grave spring to start
In whose old pipe and stop
Time plays no part.
["From my Loitering", *Wales*, 4, March, 1938, 148–9]

Before he left Cambridge, he destroyed all his early poetry
because of its involvement with the temporal; and later, he
said: ". . . I could never write a poem dominated by time . . ."[12]
One of his earlier poems is called "A Prayer Against Time"
and concludes:

I have been luckier than
All others in one thing,
Devoted secret time
To one love, one alone;
Found then that dying man
Exulting in new rhyme:
The river standing,
All but miracle gone.

Watkins's professed simplicity of impulse is an attainment
rather than a mark of naïvety. He was in fact a learned poet.
He translated Heine's "The North Sea" and poems by Valéry,
the limpid quality of whose poetry was shared not only by his
translation of poems such as "Cantique des Colonnes", but also
by Watkins's own lyrics. He also translated poems by Rilke,
with whom he shared a sense of the mysteriousness of *things* in
themselves. His poem "Thames Forest" is in sapphics.

The poet whom he read continuously and with admiration
throughout the thirties, and by whom he felt himself to have

been strongly influenced, was Yeats. His admiration for Yeats
led to his visiting him towards the end of Yeats's life—a visit
that he recorded in "Yeats in Dublin", first published in *Life
and Letters* in April, 1939. The poem pays homage to Yeats in its
style:

> Words and the flight of images,
> That unerring dance,
> Passionate love of wisdom,
> Hatred of ignorance.
> Words laid on silence.
> The tragic utterance.

The effect is one of talented but not very assured imitation.
When he attempts Yeats's magnificent simplicity, Watkins is
only prosaic:

> The Psychical Research Society
> Lately has found
> It can experimentally
> Foresee that resting-ground
> A second before the fall of space
> And the death of sound.

Only Watkins, perhaps, could have said all that he learnt from
Yeats; but to the reader of Watkins's poetry, the influence of
Yeats does not seem to have been a very salutary one. The
influence is felt in Watkins's second book of poems, *The Lamp
and the Veil* (1945)—not only in "Yeats in Dublin", but also in
the other two long poems that make up the volume: they are
unduly diffuse. However, the object lesson lies in Watkins's
attempt at Yeats's simplicity. Yeats was simple, but with a
public voice, and his extreme plainness was carried by his
magnificent and self-consciously rhetorical rhythms. The
simplicity of Watkins is different. It is a simplicity limpid and
subdued: his rhythms, the rhythms of the inner ear.

> I must go back to Winter,
> The dark, confiding tree,
> The sunflower's eaten centre
> That waved so tenderly;

Go back, break fellowship
With bud and leaf,
Break the loud branch and strip
The stillborn grief . . .
["Two Decisions"]

Of Heine, whose sequence "The North Sea" he translated, he
said: "The key to the apparent triteness of some poems is in the
cadence, which is the reverse of trite";[13] and, of himself; "I
worked from music and cadence towards the density of physical
shape".[14]

It is not surprising that the contemporary scene enters little
into Watkins's poetry. That is not to say that he was unmoved
by the problems of the thirties. When he does write about that
period, as in "Pit Boy" or "Elegy on a Heroine of Childhood",
one is left wishing that he had written more often on these
themes. "The Collier" has Watkins's wonderful simplicity: it
also has a learned inner structure, with its references to Blake's
"The Chimney Sweeper" and to the story of Joseph. It is one
of the most moving and the most balanced presentations to be
found in the poetry of the thirties of the emotional deprivation
that poverty and oppressive work bring with them.

When I was born on Amman hill
    A dark bird crossed the sun.
Sharp on the floor the shadow fell;
    I was the youngest son.

And when I went to the County School
    I worked in a shaft of light.
In the wood of the desk I cut my name:
    Dai for Dynamite.

The tall black hills my brothers stood;
    Their lessons all were done.
From the door of the school when I ran out
    They frowned to watch me run.

The slow grey bells they rung a chime
    Surly with grief or age.
Clever or clumsy, lad or lout,
    All would look for a wage.

I learnt the valley flowers' names
   And the rough bark knew my knees.
I brought home trout from the river
   And spotted eggs from the trees.

A coloured coat I was given to wear
   Where the lights of the rough land shone.
Still jealous of my favour
   The tall black hills looked on.

They dipped my coat in the blood of a kid
   And they cast me down a pit,
And although I crossed with strangers
   There was no way up from it.

Soon as I went from the County School
   I worked in a shaft. Said Jim,
"You will get your chain of gold, my lad,
   But not for a likely time."

And one said, "Jack was not raised up
   When the wind blew out the light
Though he interpreted their dreams
   And guessed their fears by night."

And Tom, he shivered his leper's lamp
   For the stain that round him grew;
And I heard mouths pray in the after-damp
   When the picks would not break through.

They changed words there in darkness
   And still through my head they run,
And white on my limbs is the linen sheet
   And gold on my neck the sun.
        [*Wales*, 6/7, March, 1939, 205–6]

Sometime in the thirties, Dylan Thomas told Kathleen Raine that Watkins ". . . was probably the finest poet . . . writing in Britain . . ."[15] In the final retrospect, the purity of diction and impulse, the absence of modishness or concern with problems of the day, may well ensure that Watkins's poetry wears better than that of many of his contemporaries. However, although Watkins wrote prolifically throughout the decade, he did not begin to publish poems until the middle of 1937, and then almost entirely in the minor periodical, *Wales*. Indeed, he scarcely enters the history of English poetry until the nineteen-forties, the decade with which he is most associated.

Chapter 15

POPULAR ARTS

Highbrow literature and a popular audience – Verse
Drama – Light Verse – Letters from Iceland – William
Plomer – Literature and Reporting

... I am primarily concerned with the "highbrow" literature of
young English Communists. This is not in any sense proletarian:
it is advance-guard experimental writing imbued with Communist
ideology. I am thinking here particularly of some of Auden's
poems (for example, of *The Dance of Death*), of the anthologies
New Signatures and *New Country*, and in particular of Edward
Upward's two short stories in *New Country*.[1]

THESE WORDS OF Stephen Spender, from *The Destructive
Element* (1935), give an accurate characterisation of the works
he mentions, but also one which must have been, at the time,
a painful one. Throughout the thirties it remained true that
the majority of poetry of leftist sympathy—and certainly nearly
all such poetry of any value—was in some measure highbrow
and of interest only to a limited intellectual audience. The
poets of the thirties had based their art on a highbrow art that
accepted its appeal to a very small public; yet they had come
themselves to accept political and social ideals that demanded
that their poetry should have the widest possible accessibility.

In the middle of the decade, this contradiction gave rise to a
widespread concern with popular poetry and the popular arts
in general. This concern with clearer and more popular forms
had behind it a more critical pressure from writers of the
extreme Left. The literary idols of the new poets—Proust,
Joyce, Eliot, even Lawrence—were doomed, according to
Marxist doctrine, because they did not understand and portray
the forces of destruction within bourgeois society. Outside of
England, political pressures had led to the abandonment of
difficult and esoteric "modern" art: in Russia Revolutionary
Dynamism had given place to Socialist Realism.

As a result, in the middle thirties, we find poets trying to write poetry that is simpler and clearer; experimenting with forms of poetry that are lighter and more popular, such as the popular song; and attempting to adapt poetry for use in other media, such as the theatre and the radio and the film.

II

One means whereby poetry might reach a wider audience was the drama. A club, called the Group Theatre, was formed, and it staged Auden's *The Dance of Death* in 1933, all three of the plays by Auden and Isherwood—*The Dog Beneath the Skin* (1935), *The Ascent of F6* (1936, produced 1937) and *On the Frontier* (1938), Louis MacNeice's *Out of the Picture* (1937) and Stephen Spender's *Trial of a Judge* (1938). All these plays were produced by Rupert Doone, whose ideas dominated the Group Theatre, and who worked with Auden and Isherwood on their first two plays. He believed that drama was an art of the body, and that the plays of the Group should be in a form analogous to musical comedy or to folk plays of the period that preceded an organised theatre. *The Dance of Death* was clearly written to that prescription, and in the programme of its production Auden included some remarks that echo Doone's ideas. He also held that the drama should not be documentary but should take familiar stories for its themes.

The first two plays by Auden and Isherwood seem loosely to follow the prescription. *The Dog Beneath the Skin* has its musical comedy quest theme, which is trivial as drama, and its choruses, which are, at times, marvellous as poetry.

> The Summer holds: upon its glittering lake
> Lie Europe and the islands; many rivers
> Wrinkling its surface like a ploughman's palm.
> Under the bellies of the grazing horses
> On the far side of posts and bridges
> The vigorous shadows dwindle; nothing wavers.
> Calm at this moment the Dutch sea so shallow
> That sunk St Paul's would ever show its golden cross
> And still the deep water that divides us still from
> Norway.

The Ascent of F6 is better as a play, though its development is rather obvious. Its hero, Michael Ransom, a brilliant mountaineer and a self-confessed prig—a monkish Michael Roberts—gets the opportunity to climb F6, the mountain he has always dreamed of conquering. He is surrounded by a group who have various peculiar reasons for being climbers. He is asked to undertake the climb for reasons of national prestige and colonial policy by his brother who is in government: their relationship to the undertaking mirrors that of their childhood, and Michael is only persuaded to undertake the climb by his mother. At the foot of the mountain he has a session of spiritual exploration with the abbot of a monastery. During the climb he loses all but one of his party. At the summit he is tried in the phantom presence of other characters of the play, and finally encounters the figure of his mother, at whose feet he falls dead.

Auden's brother was in fact a mountaineer. Ransom, another of Auden's thwarted questors, is clearly a revival of Isherwood's "Truly Strong Man", and F6 is "The Test". Isherwood has said that Ransom was modelled on T. E. Lawrence.[2] Ransom has been made strong by his mother's deliberately depriving him of her love (and herself of his). Ransom is at once strong and neurotic, with an Oedipal attachment to his mother and his mother's admiration, for which F6 and its ascent is a symbol. He undertakes his ultimately fatal action because his mother tells him to, as does Seth in "Paid on Both Sides"; but, in *The Ascent of F6*, the "Truly Strong Man" image has been Freudianised. Early in the play, when Ransom refuses to attempt the climb because it is involved with politics, he reminds one of Thomas, in *Murder in the Cathedral*, shunning the temptation to do the right deed for the wrong reason. Eliot's play had appeared in 1935, and its influence no doubt accounts for the inconclusive soul-searching and the temptations that are supposed to surround Ransom's climb. However, behind Ransom's actions lurks the old Freudian dichotomy that seems to have haunted Auden—strength and sensitivity. Sensitivity is associated with weakness and neurosis; the strong man is unreflectingly normal—ultimately a fascist conception.

The Freudianism of the play is rather disturbingly glib and knowing. At the climax of the play, when Ransom is faced by his phantom accusers at the summit, there is a pause in the action, while the chorus speaks:

> At last the secret is out, as it always must come in
> the end,
> The delicious story is ripe to tell to the intimate friend;
> Over the tea-cups and in the square the tongue has its
> desire;
> Still waters run deep, my dear, there's never smoke
> without fire. . . .
>
> For the clear voice suddenly singing, high up in the
> convent wall,
> The scent of the elder bushes, the sporting prints in
> the hall,
> The croquet matches in summer, the handshake, the
> cough, the kiss,
> There is always a wicked secret, a private reason
> for this.

It is the best piece of verse in the play, and one of Auden's best light poems; but it is light, it is "knowing" in a snickering way, and mars the scene.

There is, in fact, less poetry in *The Ascent of F6* than there had been in *The Dog Beneath the Skin*, though there is more attempt to integrate it into the play. At what is intended to be the play's grandest moment, the verse lapses into imitation Shakespeare in the manner of *King Lear*:

> O senseless hurricanes,
> That waste yourselves upon the unvexed rock
> Find some employment proper to your powers,
> Press on the neck of Man your murdering thumbs
> And earn real gratitude!

A good deal of verse is given to Mr and Mrs A., who sit listening to reports of the ascent read by the radio announcer. Their vaguely choric role is evidently intended to give a dimension of social significance to what is an almost totally Freudian play. In fact, Mr and Mrs A. only reinforce one's awareness that Auden did not understand ordinary people.

On the Frontier is a further improvement dramatically on *The Ascent of F6;* but it hardly qualifies as a verse drama at all, as the little verse in it is almost wholly confined to rather humdrum commentary on the main scenes, which are done in prose. It is a very superficial play on the theme that politicians—especially fascist politicians—are the tools of big business.

Even more superficial is Louis MacNeice's play, *Out of the Picture*, of which MacNeice himself confessed that he was "trying to write as Wystan did, without bothering too much with finesse . . ."[3] The comic theme is nothing but flippant, and not particularly funny. Auden's device of the announcer is copied, though for more farcical purposes. A few of the lyrics are good, and look impressive enough reprinted side by side; but the play, as a whole, is nothing.

Stephen Spender's *The Trial of a Judge* is the one attempt by Auden and his friends to write a full-length play that is wholly in verse. It presents the dilemma of a liberal judge called on to condemn fascist thugs for the murder of a Communist and to impose the death penalty on Communists for carrying arms. He is brought under pressure by the government to pardon the fascists; his ideal of "abstract justice" tells him to pardon the Communists. The play concludes in favour of a recognition of the power of the forces of history and a rejection of an ineffectual abstract justice.

Unfortunately—or fortunately—Spender's heart was with the liberal judge, whose position is the one sympathetic one in the play, and the production of *Trial of a Judge* was ill received by orthodox Communists. The play has two main faults. The poetry, even at its best, is too intense in the manner of lyric or meditative poetry to be effective on the stage:

> Your tragedy
> Is not a Beethoven symphony where the hidden silence
> Of the deaf genius becomes the terrible core
> Of all his sound, and symbol
> Of suffering humanity.
> There is no suffering humanity
> In whom your death will be the multifoliate rose
> Of a Christian sunrise
> Speared on the eternal mountain snows.

The ineptness and straining of this passage needs no comment. The other main fault of the play is that the characters, groups of fascists, groups of Communists, the judge's wife and friends, are merely mouthpieces for attitudes whose conflict is the judge's dilemma. Everything is very abstract and there is no dramatic action.

A verse drama of the period, never performed, was C. Day Lewis's *Noah and the Waters* (1936). Of it, Day Lewis only reprinted choruses in his *Collected Poems* of 1954. However, *Noah and the Waters* is by no means so objectionable as parts of the Auden and Isherwood plays, nor as other things Day Lewis was writing during the middle thirties. Though it might not have been suitable for the stage, its short length, simplicity and clarity of plot, and its swiftness of movement could have made it a good radio play.

It offers a reinterpretation of the story of Noah. The flood is the revolution; the waters the proletariat; those who are destroyed by the flood are the bourgeoisie who exploit the waters. Noah's position is made plain by a quotation from *The Communist Manifesto* that stands as an epigraph:

> Finally, when the class war is about to be fought to a finish, disintegration of the ruling class and the old order of society becomes so active, so acute, that a small part of the ruling class breaks away to make common cause with the revolutionary class, the class which holds the future in its hands. . . .

While this fits the Noah story to an extent, it puts Noah in a very peculiar position; and, understandably, *Left Review* asked, "Who is this Noah?"[4] The waters of England, a not very flattering symbol of the revolutionary proletariat, will presumably subside someday, to leave Noah to inherit the earth. Furthermore, the bourgeois Noah has merely to ride out the revolution by accepting the forces of history in the shape of the flood. The play is only effective, in fact, until Noah actually speaks towards the end.

The verse is largely confined to the choruses, which are done in the long line of "A Time to Dance", and which are effective, except for some blatant imitations of Auden, the usual Day Lewis clichés, and a few infelicitous "modern" images, such as "These hills were grown up, to the sky happily married". The best part of the play is the address of the burgess to the waters of England. It captures very bitingly the sort of arguments concerning poverty presented in political speeches of the day. In this *Noah and the Waters* also shows the influence of

Murder in the Cathedral, where a startling effect is produced by giving the Knights' anachronistic speeches in the manner of Shaw.

In all, the ventures into verse drama by the left-wing poets of the thirties were not very successful, and were in no sense in the class of Eliot's plays of the period. In addition, these plays never attained to anything like a popular appeal. As Julian Symons summed it up: "It was a gesture made by middle-class radicals to a middle-class liberal audience."[5]

III

Another way in which it was felt that poetry might make a wider appeal and serve a social function was through its use in conjunction with popular art forms, such as the radio or the cinema, or through the use of popular forms, such as the popular song or light verse. Light verse in particular was tried by many of the poets of the thirties; and, under Auden's patronage, gained a new respectability. In 1935, Auden, with John Garrett, produced an anthology, *The Poet's Tongue*, in which every type of poem from *Piers Plowman* to the limerick was represented. In 1938, Auden edited *The Oxford Book of Light Verse*.

There were, it seems clear, a number of reasons why light verse appealed to Auden. In the first place, he was adept at it. Secondly, it fitted in with the anti-romantic stance adopted by Auden after he had abandoned the submerged but tormenting preoccupations of his earliest work. In addition, the notion that poetry did not deal only with elevated subjects was one of the more aggressively accepted canons of modern poetic taste in the twenties and thirties. However, the most pressing and explicit reason for Auden's interest in light verse was undoubtedly the "gap between what is commonly called 'highbrow' and 'lowbrow' taste", as he puts it in the introduction to *The Poets' Tongue*. The concern with this gap was partly political, and partly a concern that "universal art can only be the product of a community united in sympathy, sense of worth, and aspiration; . . . it is improbable that the artist can do his best except in such a society".[6] He expands this point in the introduction to *The Oxford Book of Light Verse*:

When the things in which the poet is interested, the things which he sees about him, are much the same as those of his audience, and that audience is a fairly general one, he will not be conscious of himself as an unusual person, and his language will be straightforward and close to ordinary speech. . . . In such a society [a true democracy], and in such alone, will it be possible for the poet, without sacrificing any of his subtleties of sensibility or his integrity, to write poetry which is simple, clear, and gay.[7]

Light verse is to be found among Auden's work from the beginning. *The Dance of Death* contained parodies of popular songs. In *Another Time* (1940), Part II is headed "Lighter Poems", and collects together much of Auden's light verse from the later thirties. Some of these poems have a high reputation. Among them are "Four Cabaret Songs for Miss Hedli Anderson" (who later married Louis MacNeice). The word "cabaret" suggests the limitations of the songs. The kind of song Auden evidently knew best was the kind to be found in intimate revue.

> Does it look like a pair of pyjamas
>   Or the ham in a temperance hotel,
> Does its odour remind one of llamas
>   Or has it a comforting smell?

goes the second song, "O Tell Me the Truth About Love". The song is not exactly a parody of popular songs; though, as in the case of the songs in *The Dance of Death*, one would not like to be positive. It has the tone of clever self-parody, and would not appeal to those who liked the popular songs of the day. As a writer of sophisticated lyrics for popular music, Auden is not in the class of Cole Porter. Indeed everything suggests that his contact with popular music was limited. The two blues, "Refugee Blues" and "Roman Wall Blues", included in *Another Time*, do not give evidence of much familiarity with, or feeling for, this well defined, traditional folk form.

These light poems in *Another Time* do not indeed have the mastery shown in some of the light poems in Auden's other volumes, such as "It's no use raising a shout" (*Poems*, 2nd ed: IX) or "Master and Botswain" ("The Sea and the Mirror").

To find that type of virtuosity in Auden's light verse of the thirties, one has to turn to "Letter to Lord Byron", in *Letters from Iceland* (1937), or to poems like "Law" and "Hell is neither here nor there", where the tone is light, but Auden is "off duty" and not competing with the writers of cabaret lyrics.

Louis MacNeice was at first more successful than Auden in his adaptation of popular forms. His "Bagpipe Music" is perhaps the most famous light poem of the period. Behind its surrealistic flippancy, there is a serious feeling, the obverse of the sense that the period is moving towards a dark end and that all must take responsibility in the face of this. The poem is a release from this feeling, and an expression of a feeling of helplessness, along with a desire to throw everything over and accept the innate absurdity of things.

> John MacDonald found a corpse, put it under the sofa,
> Waited till it came to life and hit it with a poker,
> Sold its eyes for souvenirs, sold its blood for whiskey,
> Kept its bones for dumb-bells to use when he was fifty.
>
> .   .   .
>
> It's no go the picture palace, it's no go the stadium,
> It's no go the country cot with a pot of pink geraniums.
> It's no go the Government grants, it's no go the elections,
> Sit on your arse for fifty years and hang your hat on a pension.
>
> It's no go my honey love, it's no go my poppet;
> Work your hands from day to day, the winds will blow the
>   profit.
> The glass is falling hour by hour, the glass will fall
>   for ever,
> But if you break the bloody glass you won't hold up the
>   weather.
>
> (from *I Crossed the Minch*)

Almost equally successful with this is the adaptation of a popular form in a poem of spring, 1939, which uses the type of jingle associated with games of prediction to suggest (and, by its lightness, heighten) the feeling of impending disaster.

> Good-bye, Winter,
> The days are getting longer,
> The tea-leaf in the teacup
> Is herald of a stranger.

> Will he bring me business
> Or will he bring me gladness
> Or will he come for cure
> Of his own sickness?
>
> .   .   .
>
> Will his name be Love
> And all his talk be crazy?
> Or will his name be Death
> And his message easy?
>
>   ("Prognosis")

Later, in *Springboard* (1944) particularly, MacNeice was to become too fond of adapting popular forms, especially with refrains, using them for the chatty seriousness that was one of his vices as a poet.

A number of Auden's lighter pieces involved the use of verse in conjunction with another medium. John Pudney has described how, when he was with the B.B.C., Auden wrote a programme for broadcast from Newcastle around the theme of the Roman Wall. Auden insisted on music by Benjamin Britten, who had followed Auden and Pudney at their old school, Gresham's School, Holt. From this programme came the already mentioned "Roman Wall Blues".[8]

It was in collaboration with Britten that Auden worked on two films made with the G.P.O. Film Unit, *Coal Face* and *Night Mail*. From the former came the delightful short lyric "O lurcher-loving collier, black as night . . ." (entitled "Madrigal" in *Another Time*); from the other came the longer "Night Mail".

IV

Among the social "applications" of poetry in the thirties might be listed the travel books produced by Auden and MacNeice. The first was *Letters from Iceland*, published in 1937, and done by them in collaboration. The second, *I Crossed the Minch* (1938), a book about a tour of the Western Isles, was done by MacNeice alone. He counted it, along with the more trivial *Zoo* (1938), as a money-making project. The third travel book was *Journey to a War*, produced by Auden and

Isherwood in 1939. Of the three books, it alone reads well as a travel book today. The other books are too filled out with extraneous material, and are to be valued today for the poetry they contain. MacNeice included most of his poems from these books in *The Earth Compels*.

The journey to Iceland was made in the summer of 1936. Auden was there longer than MacNeice. The book was produced in a hurry; and, though recommended by the Book Society, it might, as a travel book, be regarded as mainly "padding". It contains a chapter of information for tourists; an anthology of passages from Icelandic writing "addressed to John Betjeman"; a diary addressed as a letter from W. H. A[uden] to E. M. A[uden] (Erika Mann, the daughter of Thomas Mann, whom Auden had recently married—though he had never seen her—to give her a British passport); a burlesque letter "Hetty to Nancy", purporting to be by a garrulous woman traveller, but actually by MacNeice; a retrospective letter to an Icelander, Kristian Andriersson; and two co-operative verse letters, one to R. H. S. Crossman, later famous in politics, and the other to the painter, William Coldstream. The book concludes with a further co-operative poem, "Last Will and Testament", in which Auden and MacNeice send up or graciously flatter almost everyone they have ever heard of by making suitable bequests:

> We leave to Stanley Baldwin, our beloved P.M.,
> The false front of Lincoln Cathedral, and a school
> Of Empire poets.

"Last Will and Testament" is the truly "in-group" performance, and the writers seem very much at home in it.

There are a number of poems by Auden and MacNeice scattered throughout the book. Some are trivial, like MacNeice's epistle "To Graham and Anna". Perhaps the most substantial serious piece of poetry in the book is his "Eclogue from Iceland". The most important and individual poetic contribution is, however, the poem that runs through the whole book and is arranged in five chapters, Auden's brilliant "Letter to Lord Byron".

The poem, though written in rhyme royal and not in the ottava rima of *Don Juan*, nevertheless takes Byron's poem as a model. As Auden remarked of *Don Juan* in 1941, ". . . the hero is . . . a device enabling Byron to get down to the business for which his talents were really suited, a satirical panorama of the ruling classes of his time".[9] Auden's aim is similar, though he has no hero. In the introduction to *The Oxford Book of Light Verse*, Auden was to call Byron ". . . the first writer of Light Verse in the modern sense".[10] Auden is interested in writing verse in which one may say anything and adopt any tone. He is chatty, serious, witty, silly and deliberately banal, as well as ostentatiously brilliant, without destroying the tone of the poem. The form of *Don Juan* protected Byron from his tendency to stagey self-dramatisation, as in *Childe Harold*, because an essential part of *Don Juan* is Byron's pose of not taking his poem entirely seriously. In the same way, the form of "Letter to Lord Byron" protects Auden from the lapses and uncertainty of tone that mar a great deal of his poetry, because the lapse of tone becomes one of the rhetorical devices of the poem, which never has the air of taking its tone wholly seriously. Auden's tendency to be dogmatic and to adopt "The preacher's loose, immodest tone", is quite in place in this causerie:

> . . . To me Art's subject is the human clay,
> And landscape but a background to a torso;
>   All Cézanne's apples I would give away
>   For one small Goya or a Daumier . . .
>
> Art, if it doesn't start there, at least ends,
>   Whether aesthetics like the thought or not,
> In an attempt to entertain our friends; . . .

His love for the witty, but shallow comparison, so glibly manifest in his poetry in the later thirties ("Here war is simple like a monument . . .") is brilliantly in place in "Letter to Lord Byron": "This letter that's already far too long, / Just like the Prelude or the Great North Road; . . ." Throughout, the poem is marked by Auden's panache and inventive ridicule:

> "Lord Byron at the head of his storm-troopers!"
>   Nothing, says science, is impossible:
> The Pope may quit to join the Oxford Groupers,

Nuffield may leave one farthing in his Will,
   There may be someone who trusts Baldwin still,
Someone may think that Empire wines are nice,
There may be people who hear Tauber twice.

Even at its most pedestrian, the poem has pace and manages to be interesting and engaging; so that, despite its extreme topicality, it remains one of Auden's most congenial poems and his major achievement in light verse.

v

A poet who made his most distinctive contribution in light verse was William Plomer. He is rightly best known for his novels and short stories and for his two volumes of autobiography, *Double Lives* (1943) and *At Home* (1958). However, he has remarked: "I am not a prolific poet, but since I began to write I have never found prose the only possible medium".[11] His poetry, with its decidedly "prose" virtues of directness and clarity of observation, might be characterised by the title under which Auden reviewed a volume of Plomer's poetry in 1937: "A Novelist's Poems".[12] However, it is poetry that is more than the by-product of writing fiction; and in one form, the ballad, Plomer has the distinction of being an innovator.

Plomer's early life was a varied one; and this, together with the fact that he was slightly older than Auden and his friends, contributed to his having a more detached attitude to the political alignments of the thirties. He was born of English parents who emigrated to South Africa. He went to school at Marlborough, but did not go on to university. He went instead to work as an apprentice to a trader in Africa in a situation similar to that described in his famous short story "A Child of Queen Victoria". His first poems were poems of Africa. On something of an impulse he took ship to Japan, where he stayed for three years, travelling thence to England across Russia on the Trans-Siberian Railway. In the early thirties he was in Berlin and later in Greece. His poetry reflects all these changes of scene, but the settings of his most effective poems were the suburbs and countryside around London.

Plomer was one of the contributors to *New Signatures* and to

New Country, though in *New Country* his contribution was a short story. In *New Signatures* he had two poems: "The Russian Lover" and "Epitaph for a Contemporary". The first of these has nothing to do with politics, and presumably sprang from Plomer's Trans-Siberian journey. "Epitaph for a Contemporary" is an odd poem, considering the company in *New Signatures*. It is a narrative poem about a young man who was "brought . . . up a gentleman" and found himself a misfit in the violent modern world. He is killed by accident in the revolution:

> A cold wind blows around the corners of this world;
> It blew upon the corpse of a young man
> Lying in the street with his head in the gutter
> Where he fell, shot by a revolutionary sniper.

The firmness and definition of diction, with no aura of suggestion, is characteristic of Plomer's poetry. The four-line stanza without rhyme, but with its broken and shifting ryhthms, is ideally suited to modern narrative. It moves the poem along steadily, without the feeling of things being rounded into certainties that resolved rhymes and regular ryhthms give. The combination of violence and commonplace narrative looks forward to Plomer's later ballads.

The subject of the poem and its handling are certainly deflationary of revolutionary aspirations. This was not because Plomer was indifferent to politics or entirely cynical of them. Indeed, he has expressed the opinion that it was in response to the violence of his times that he developed the pattern of poem original to him, the short ballad of violence, such as "Murder on the Downs" or the poems collected in *The Dorking Thigh* in 1945.

Plomer has given an extensive account of how he came to write this type of poem and what he feels to be its character:

> In a volume called *Visiting the Caves* . . . published in 1936, there is a piece called "Murder on the Downs". When confronted with this, as soon as it had been completed, I felt a mingled suprise and uneasiness, as if I were being impersonated. Somebody else seemed to have written it, not the self with which I thought myself acquainted . . .

The poem is about an erotic murder committed in daylight, in fine weather, on the Sussex Downs . . . the victim of the crime, in her last words, declares, quite unprotestingly, that it is what she expected; and there is no room for doubt that such an end is what she half invited and half desired.

. . . the mood of the murderer and his victim seems to me the prevailing mood of the period. Compulsive violence unchecked by religious scruples or humaneness was matched with compulsive, unreasoning surrender: there was no effort to avert what seemed invited, desired, and inevitable.

. . . I have once or twice been reproached with "cruelty" and a choice of sordid themes. No defence seems necessary. The themes brought themselves forward. In so far as they are what used to be called "unpleasant" they reflect an age for which unpleasant would be a very mild term.[13]

"The Murder on the Downs", the first of these poems, bears out very well Plomer's remarks. The two lovers go for a walk on the downs, and then, like lovers, lie down in the bracken.

> Jennifer, in sitting touches
> With her hand an agaric,
> Like a bulb of rotten rubber
> Soft and thick,
>
> Screams, withdraws, and sees its colour
> Like a leper's liver,
> Leans on Bert so he can feel her
> Shiver.
>
> Over there the morning ocean,
> Frayed around the edges, sighs,
> At the same time gaily twinkles,
> Conniving with a million eyes
>
> At Bert whose free hand slowly pulls
> A rayon stocking from his coat,
> Twists it quickly, twists it neatly,
> Round her throat.
>
> "Ah, I knew that this would happen!"
> Her last words: and not displeased
> Jenniver relaxed, still smiling
> While he squeezed.

> Under a sky without a cloud
> Lay the still unruffled sea,
> And in the bracken like a bed
> The murderee.

A great deal of the success of the poem comes from the use of unpleasant or dehumanised images—"Like a leper's liver", "Dissolving in his frank blue eyes / All her hope, like aspirin"— with a tone of complete indifference. The wit and the extreme economy of words give the poem rapidity and pungency. The very plainness with which the horrible details are presented makes them stand out all the more starkly. It is interesting that, in speaking of his early reading, Plomer recalls that, "The successive volumes of *Georgian Poetry*, breaking in upon the post-Victorian twilight, had been quickening to many readers of my generation".[14] John Lehmann had made a similar remark, connecting the study of the Georgians with the diction of his poetry. A firm, unliterary diction was not to be associated with the study of Eliot and Pound.

Plomer's remarks about violence are borne out by many of the other poems in *Visiting the Caves* (1936), such as "The Silent Sunday", "Tatooed" and "In the Night", all of which touch on the violence beneath the ordinary. However, as a "straight" poet, Plomer is less successful than in his light verse, and is apt to be diffuse, and by turns prosy and literary. The gift for narrative shown in the ballads is there in non-satirical narratives; and at times Plomer can write with a lyric delicacy that is reinforced by his peculiar clarity of language, as in the opening of "Thoughts on the Japanese Invasion of China, 1938":

> Taut paper and clean wood enclose
>   A neat, sweet domestic place
> Where slant sun and magic snows
>   Alter the shadow on a well-loved face.
>
> Warm wine in a little cup,
>   A red leaf fell, a white sleeve fluttered,
> Morning smoke was wafted up,
>   More, more was felt than uttered.

In a special British number of *Poetry* (January, 1937) W. H. Auden reviewed Plomer's *Visiting the Caves*, and remarked favourably on his gift for narrative and on "The Murder on the Downs". In the summer of 1937, while staying with Stephen Spender, Auden wrote two of the notorious ballads that appear in *Another Time*—"Miss Gee" and "Victor", both of which appeared in *New Writing* for autumn, 1937. It is reasonable to think that Auden got the idea for these poems from reading "The Murder on the Downs". Auden's ballads are also marked by economy and speed, in contrast with his use of the form in the epilogue to *The Orators* and in poem VI of *Look Stranger!* ("O what is that sound . . ."), where the element of refrain suggests an affinity with traditional ballads. Auden's two ballads are also violent. However, his violence has a cruelty and nastiness that has often been remarked upon, and to which Plomer's apologia will not apply. His small-time victims, "Miss Gee" and "Victor"—victims of cancer and of a puritanical naïvety—are sneered at from a Freudian height. The unpleasantness is not in the subject, but in the author himself. It is a pity that this is so. Auden showed elsewhere that he could write with a mordant directness in this ballad form:

> O plunge your hands in the water,
> Plunge them up to the wrist;
> Stare, stare in the basin
> And wonder what you've missed.
> *(Another Time*, XXVII)

VI

"I cannot believe . . . that any artist can be good who is not more than a bit of a reporting journalist," Auden wrote in 1936.[15] In the atmosphere of social concern, the notion of the writer as reporter was a natural and pervasive one. *Left Review* had working-class writers describing their jobs; *New Writing* presented its material under headings like "Island View" that suggested that the contributions had a documentary value; Unity Theatre, the left-Wing theatre, put on pieces under the title "Living Newspaper". A "reporting" attitude to his materials seems implied by Christopher Isherwood's handling of the sketches that make up *Goodbye to Berlin* (1939), incomparably his best book, and one of the most typical works of the period.

The notion of the poet as reporter fades into the notion of the poet as sensitive to social change and social events. The imaginative rationale of Mass-Observation made it something rather different from the opinion polls with which it is sometimes confused; nevertheless, it was only in the thirties that something so decidedly sociological could have been conceived of as an adjunct to poetic activity.

Behind the notion of the writer as reporter and behind the actual "reporting" done by writers of the thirties there was a desire to get the writer out of his highbrow, remote setting into work that had a social function, and a social function that was popular, like that of the newspaper. In some types of writing, such as in light verse, something valuable and original came out of that impulse. In other instances, the notion of the poet as social commentator or popular entertainer only led to sloppy writing.

Chapter 16

POPULAR FRONT

The Popular Front movement – *Left Review* – *New Writing* – *The Left Book Club* – Idris Davies, Julius Lipton and proletarian poetry – Christopher Caudwell

1936 WAS THE year of Popular Front governments in France and Spain. In the face of the growing power of fascism in Europe, the Communist International had decided that, for the defence of the Soviet Union, it was necessary to make common cause with other radical movements, instead of denouncing them as reactionary. Liberal ideals of liberty and justice were no longer to be despised. Affiliation was to be sought with trade unions and radical political parties. There was to be co-operation with intellectuals and intellectual bodies of progressive tendency. All such moves on the part of the C.P.G.B. were, however, rejected by the Labour Party and the Trades Union Congress; and in the face of the impossibility of official co-operation with the main left-wing movements in England, the Communists gave their support to the notion of a "People's Front"—a grand, popular coalition of all people of progressive inclination.

International events seemed to many to be moving rapidly towards war. The National Government did not have to face an election again until 1940. It might not have to even then, if war came before. The idea of co-operation against fascism found tremendous support from people who might have termed themselves "men of goodwill" of all walks and persuasions. Though it was not possible for the Communists to appear on the same platform as members of the Labour Party, they could still address meetings alongside intellectuals and public figures who were genuinely concerned with the international situation and were against the government's handling of it by non-intervention, placation and waiting to see.

How did the movement come to have such a strong appeal? First of all, the Labour Party had not recovered from the discredit that followed the co-operation of some of its most revered leaders in the National Government. Then there was the feeling that, after the Hoare-Laval plan of 1936, the League of Nations was no longer an effective means of dealing with the warlike actions of the fascist powers. The despair in the face of this was strengthened by the National Government's support of non-intervention in the Spanish Civil War, in spite of the flagrant breaches of this policy by Germany and Italy. It was widely felt that only firm co-operative action on the part of all opponents of fascism could prevent a Second World War. On the other hand, there was widespread pacifism: by 1937 the Peace Pledge Union had 130,000 members. Pacifism was strengthened by memories of the Great War and disillusionment concerning it; while the advances in air bombardment—minor at the time—led people to believe that a further war would be the end of civilisation. Their feelings, often muddled and conflicting, but ardent, were strengthened by the example of the struggle of the Spanish people against fascist reaction, and by the treatment of the Jews by the Nazis.

It is possible that those who participated in the "People's Front" were dupes of the Communists. This charge has been made against the intellectuals concerned. They certainly fell in with Communist intentions. However, the central intention, to combat fascism, was one that should have been adopted wholeheartedly without any provocation from the Left. A more damaging criticism of left-wing intellectuals of the period was that they were armchair revolutionaries, glib with words and phrases like "revolution", "dictatorship of the proletariat", "the workers", but having little conception of what these words stood for. However, in the earlier thirties, and up to the time of the inception of the movement for a popular front, failures of perception are understandable. As John Lehmann pointed out, "In the future lay the Trials, the new terror . . . , the betrayal of the Spanish Civil war and the Nazi-Soviet Pact . . ."[1] It must be admitted that, when the darker side of Communism grew increasingly blatant, many of the intellectuals of the Left accepted too easily the Communist rationale for the Party's actions. However, in the case of the poets dealt with in this book, in so far as they went along with Communism at all, the adoption of doctrines of political necessity did not last for long; and most of these writers had parted with Communism by 1939, if not before.

What effect did the movement for a Popular Front have on the poets and poetry of the period? It must have increased the audience for that poetry, and, at the same time, enhanced its influence. However, under the pressure of the Popular Front ideal of co-operation against fascism, political notions became increasingly simplified, to the point of emotional crassness. This could only be harmful to poetry; so that the best political poems of the decade are those written by Spender and Lehmann at its beginning. Indeed, the years most productive of directly political poetry are from 1931 to 1934, particularly if we ignore the poems on the Spanish Civil War. While the movement for a Popular Front led to increased political activity on the part of Day Lewis, Spender, Rex Warner, John Lehmann, there are only a handful of overtly political poems by them after 1935 not concerned with Spain: a few by Day Lewis, one or two each by Spender and Warner; while Lehmann seems virtually to have stopped writing poetry during this time.

II

The left-wing literary periodical with the largest circulation in the late thirties was *Left Review*. It ante-dated slightly the period of demand for a Popular Front. It began in 1934 as *Viewpoint* and changed its name to *Left Review* after the first issue. Its forthright and doctrinaire policy was stated at its commencement:

> *Viewpoint* stands for militant communism and against individualism and metaphysics in the arts. It declares that the work of art is an organic individual creation and that it can only exist in its integrity in a classless society, in a completely communistic state; that art must become the production and the property of all.[2]

These principles, with their antagonism to individualism, were to be followed throughout its publication monthly from 1934 to 1938, when it closed down because of financial difficulties (presented officially as a closing down to make way for a new monthly review that would be the organ of "a people's culture"). Offering sixty to eighty pages for sixpence, it was competitively priced with commercial periodicals of the period, and was far cheaper, page for page, than *Scrutiny*, *The Criterion* and *New Verse*.

Its cut and dried doctrinaire policy seems strange in the light of its origins. Edgell Rickword, who edited *Left Review* for nearly half its life, had previously edited *The Calendar of Modern Letters*, which appeared from 1925 to 1927. *The Calendar* is often thought of as the predecessor of *Scrutiny*, and the title of a selection from it edited by F. R. Leavis, "Towards Standards of Criticism", suggests the nature of the relationship; yet many old contributors to *The Calendar* appeared in *Left Review*.

The first issue of *Left Review* contains a report of a meeting held at the Conway Hall in February, 1934, which established a British Section of the Writers' International. The executive committee consisted of John Strachey, Ralph Fox and Michael Davidson. Edgell Rickword was treasurer, and Tom Wintringham, secretary. Wintringham was one of the original editors of *Left Review*, along with Montagu Slater and Annabel Williams-Ellis (Mrs John Strachey). Early contributors included Hugh MacDiarmid, Alec Brown, Sylvia Townsend Warner, Montagu Slater, Hamilton Fyfe (one-time editor of *The Daily Herald*), Storm Jameson, Osbert Sitwell, Naomi Mitchison and Siegfried Sassoon.

Most of these people had been a part of left-wing intellectual life in the twenties, and had come to the Party through an interest in politics which had finally led them to Communism. It was this which distinguished these earlier intellectuals from Day Lewis, Spender and poets of their generation. The poets of the early thirties had been largely a-political until 1931, when the collapse of Labour and the impact of the depression had made them look further Left. They took up Communism from positions, in most cases, of political naïvety, when Communism was becoming fashionable. In this they in turn differ from slightly younger intellectuals like John Cornford and Philip Toynbee, who matured when Communism was becoming established on the university political scene. The editors of *Left Review* and its contributors were not so notably Left because they were of working-class origin. Wintringham, Fox, Strachey, Montagu Slater and Rickword had been at Oxford. Coming to Communism in the twenties out of a mature political conviction, they had stayed with the Party and changed with it. The change, however, so far as literary judgement was concerned, was largely for the worse.

A good deal of attention was given in early issues of *Left Review* to aims. In January, 1936, in the second year of publication, the editorship was taken over by Edgell Rickword, and this began the period when the magazine had the most interesting contributions. More space was given to literature, and foreign contributions were more frequent. The beginning of Rickword's editorship more of less coincided with the movement to create a Popular Front. *Left Review* of course strongly urged this, and began to include contributions of a strictly political nature by non-Communists. Indeed, in a special number in October, 1936, it made great play of publishing statements supporting the Popular Front from people who should have been restrained from doing so by the Labour Party's embargo. Articles and poems appeared by C. Day Lewis, Rex Warner and Stephen Spender, and it was announced in the special People's Front issue that Day Lewis and Spender would become regular contributors. Spender in fact contributed only about half a dozen minor pieces.

It is hard to give the exact character of *Left Review* to those who have not seen it. It contained cartoons that were strikingly pungent. It contained, by present day standards, an inordinate amount of politics and information about political goings-on for a literary periodical. Many of its prose pieces seem unduly short—a page or a page and a half; while, on the other hand, half an issue might be given up to a report on a writers' conference. The most rewarding pieces today are the articles on literary subjects by Douglas Garman, who had been with *The Calendar of Modern Letters*. Even at its best, under Rickword's editorship, *Left Review* did not contain much memorable fiction. In the period after July, 1937, when Randall Swingler, a doctrinaire Communist of the younger generation, took over the editorship, contributions to *Left Review* showed an increasing tendency to simplify actuality to fit dogma. The *Review* could hardly be called a literary periodical at all in its last stages, with its special China number and its Soviet Anniversary number and an increasing amount of space being devoted to political matters.

So far as one can judge, *Left Review* published poems by only one working-class writer, Idris Davies. Two of his poems in all were published; though *Left Review* must have included, on average, about one poem per issue. The majority of poets who contributed (like the majority of contributors generally) seem to have been left-wing intellectuals who came to Communism in the twenties. Many of the poems, like the stories, are written from a simplified, dogmatic point of view, assumed rather than established, and not in tension with any alternative attitude:

> I had a job in a laundry
> I had a job in a shop
> My hands were caught in a factory
> Till I thought that I should drop.
>
> Get out into the fields,
> Get into the clean air,
> Take a day in the country
> Where spring buds, and there's no despair.
> (Maurice Carpenter, "A Welsh Girl":
> *LR*, III, 6 (July, 1937) 340)

It is hard to decide whether over-simplified attitudes made such poets bad poets, or whether it was their lack of talent led them into thinking that poetry and politics could have such a simplistic relationship.

There were not many doctrinaire Communists of the thirties who were good poets. *Left Review* published a poem by the young Communist, John Cornford, after his death in Spain. It also included one or two poems by the young poet who was the last of its editors, Randall Swingler. Swingler resembles Day Lewis, whose poetry he sometimes imitated, in writing political poems of rather generalised aspiration. The theme to which he responds best is that of the temptation to ignore the need for change and struggle, the recurrent poetic theme of middle-class intellectuals of the period, and a theme that can be dramatised independently of the political position of the poet:

> This is my weakness and my pain alone;
> To long still for the whole scene again
> For the cold hills and the moveless deer,

The intimate isolation, easy and secure,
The slow looks across the room and the music flowing,
Signal of an understanding which was not really there . . .

Now that which grows wrestles with that which stays
Untouched by change, the hidden wall
Hovering about me, always ready to close
When I retreat defeated by history's ways.
For lapsing, our lives into early chaos fall
And the coffin is the last inhibition of all . . .
("Sussex in Winter": *Life & Letters* 52–3)

One of the poetic "sports" of the period was poetry written for mass declamation, which was developed by Jack Lindsay, and whose "On Guard for Spain" was evidently declaimed with considerable effect at mass meetings. Lindsay's poems were longer than most poems written at that time, running for four or five pages. They are an object lesson in how inanity of feeling goes along with inanity of rhetoric:

I rose from the bed of my wife's young body
at the call of Liberty.
O feed with my blood our flag's red flame.
Comrades, remember me.

The fascists shot my children first,
they made me stand and see.
O dip the flag in my heart's blood.
Comrades, remember me.

Spain rose up in the morning,
roused by the bluster of bullets.

Unbreakfasted, the people
put the fascists to rout.
Spain rose up in the morning,
Spain rose up in the morning,
Spain rose up in the morning,
and drove the fascists out.
("On Guard for Spain": *LR* III, 2 (Mar., 1937) 83–4)

Looking back on *Left Review*, Edgell Rickword gave this estimate of its achievement:

The real triumphs of the socially conscious literature of the time were not individual achievements. True, there was fine work by Ralph Bates, *The Olive Field* and *Lean Men*; of Welsh working-class life by Lewis Jones, *Cwm Mardy* and another; plays and reportage by Montagu Slater; reportage and short stories by John Sommerfield; a totally new break-through by Jack Lindsay in verse declamations—a thing that could have come off only in a time of exceptional emotional intensity. The real triumph was the drawing into the cultural ambit of a significant number of men and women who were barricaded out from participation in what was regarded as a middle-class preserve. Our aim was a political one, to eradicate Fascism, and this could only be done by the fullest co-operation of the masses. Fascism in Germany had succeeded by giving them the fake dignity of a uniform and a death-wish. We hoped they would find their way to self-expression and a life wish.[3]

This may have been so. In addition, he might have added that many of the comments in *Left Review* on fascism and on current events remain valid in retrospect. *Left Review* is certainly an important periodical for anyone who wants to understand the thirties. Even its ability to remain steadily oblivious to defects in the Soviet Union while it constantly unearthed the same defects in Nazi Germany is instructive. As a source of literature —and particularly poetry—to be read for its own worth, it has little to offer.

III

New Writing is the periodical that gives most completely the flavour of the later thirties and of the period of the Popular Front in literature. It included contributions from European as well as British writers, and it published work from working-class and educated contributors. Of all the periodicals of the thirties, it is the one that can be read with the most pleasure today. Indeed, the excellence of some of its contributions was such that they have become and remain familiar to most readers, so that one is unsurprised on meeting them, and the tendency is to overlook the editorial achievement of being the first to publish them. Orwell's "Shooting an Elephant"; V. S. Pritchett's "Sense of Humour"; several sections of what became Isherwood's *Goodbye to Berlin*.

The idea of a periodical had been in John Lehmann's mind since the publication of *New Signatures* and *New Country* when he was with the Woolfs' Hogarth Press. *New Writing* may be seen as a continuation of the movement begun by these two anthologies. One of the notions fixed upon was that of providing space for short stories longer than most periodicals would take. Partly to accommodate such contributions, it was decided to produce *New Writing* as a hard-cover miscellany of 150 to 200 pages every six months; and, as such, it ran through eight issues under its original name, starting in spring of 1936. The first number contained a "Manifesto":

> NEW WRITING will appear twice yearly, and will be devoted to imaginative writing, mainly of young authors. It does not intend to concern itself with literary theory, or the criticism of contemporaries.
> NEW WRITING aims at providing an outlet for those prose writers, among others, whose work is too unorthodox in length or style to be suitable for the established monthly and quarterly magazines. While prose will form the main bulk of the contributions, poetry will also be included.
> NEW WRITING is first and foremost interested in literature, and though it does not intend to open its pages to writers of reactionary or Fascist sentiments, it is independent of any political party.
> NEW WRITING also hopes to represent the work of writers from colonial and foreign countries.

This statement gives an accurate picture of what *New Writing* turned out to be.

Lehmann's friends and fellow contributors to *New Signatures* and *New Country* provided the backbone of contributions. This was particularly the case with the poetry. Except for the second number, which contained no poetry, all the issues of *New Writing* contained poems by contributors to the earlier anthologies. Some of the most distinguished prose contributions by Lehmann's friends have already been mentioned; and it was the stories and the reporting that determined the character of *New Writing*, if only because they formed the bulk of each issue.

Apart from publishing fiction by writers of his own group— Christopher Isherwood, William Plomer, Edward Upward, Rex Warner—Lehmann sought out stories and reporting by two important classes of writers: foreign writers and proletarian

L

writers. Of the foreign writers, several were from Georgia, which Lehmann had visited. Among the European writers to appear in *New Writing* were André Chamson, Jean Giono, Jean Paul Sartre, Ignazio Silone, Anna Seghers and André Kantorowitz.

No writer better exemplifies the quality of *New Writing* than André Chamson. His stories still make powerful reading, and the way in which he is now largely forgotten in England is hard to understand. He came from the mountainous south-east of France, and he wrote of the peasants of that area with a fierce sense of local individuality. His stories are not overtly political, but get their radical flavour from his sympathy with the individual inhabitants of what is a linguistically separate and minority region.

Lehmann evidently went to a great deal of trouble to encourage working-class and lower middle-class writers, but the results were not as gratifying as his account in his auto-biography, *The Whispering Gallery*, would lead one to expect. The nearest he came to publishing poetry by a "worker" of British origin was in the issue for autumn, 1938, which contained poems by Albert Brown, a former sales clerk and soldier, at the time helping run the family fish and chip shop.

Because *New Verse* existed when *New Writing* began, Lehmann deliberately adopted a policy of favouring prose rather than poetry. A list of the poetry he published certainly contains the names of many famous poems—Auden's "Lay Your Sleeping Head" and "Palais des Beaux Arts" (and about a dozen others by him) and MacNeice's "June Thunder", "Trilogy for 'X' " and "Meeting Point". There was only a little poetry by European writers, presumably because of the difficulty of translation; though Pasternak's "1905" and poems by Lorca and other Spanish poets were included. In addition, as the decade progressed, poems by younger writers in English appeared. The issue for autumn, 1938, has a section "Seven Poets", containing one poem each by H. B. Mallalieu, David Gascoyne, R. P. Hewett, Geoffrey Parsons, Clifford Dyment, Kenneth Allott and Robert Waller.

The fact that many poets were represented by one or two poems in the whole eight issues, coupled with the fact that each half-yearly volume contained perhaps a dozen poems in all (and sometimes less), meant that *New Writing* could not be an important force in the development of poetry in the late thirties, because it could not establish an image of the type of poetry it stood for, even though poets may have been eager for the sort of recognition that inclusion in its pages implied. Furthermore, although it published poems of high quality by Auden, MacNeice, Spender and Day Lewis, these writers were well established by 1936, though this had not been the case when *New Verse* started in 1933.

These remarks apply in some measure to *New Writing* as a whole. *Left Review* recommended *New Writing*, but remarked on the lack of a clear editorial policy. Lehmann's deliberate eclecticism, bringing in what he felt to be the best and most advanced writing from many countries, did not result in a periodical that gave the impression of standing for a particular type of writing, as did *New Verse*, even though this eclecticism and openness to a variety of types of writing of real quality is what makes *New Writing* still so readable today. If any tendency can be observed, it is probably one that the editor was not fully aware of: a liking for writing that captures the quality of a particular place or scene.

"Reporting" might have been the thirties' word for this. Christopher Isherwood's Berlin pieces come close to this conception of reporting, with their lack of a "story" and their presentation of character through dialogue. Some of the more distinguished pieces in *New Writing* are pure reporting, such as T. C. Worsley's moving "Malaga has Fallen". However, one cannot call writing like André Chamson's "Metamorphoses of the Snow" or some of the Soviet and Georgian stories "reporting". One feels that they are stories that have their *raison d'être* in giving the experience of a particular place or area; and it is the flavour given by this type of writing that one comes away with from *New Writing*.

In autumn, 1938, a new series began. Stephen Spender and Christopher Isherwood now joined as advisory editors. Literary and theatre criticisms and social commentary were included for the first time. The original series had run for five numbers: the new series ran for three, the last issue appearing in autumn, 1939, when war had already broken out. After that *New Writing* went two ways. In its original format, it appeared intermittently as *Folios of New Writing*, and then amalgamated with another project to become *New Writing and Daylight*. At the same time, Lehmann began, in 1940, to produce selections from *New Writing* in paper covers for Penguin Books, under the title *Penguin New Writing*. Very soon, this had become an independent periodical publishing original material. At one point its circulation reached the unbelievable figure (for its time) of 100,000. It ran until 1950.

IV

The most characteristic publishing venture of the period of the movement for a Popular Front was Victor Gollancz's *Left Book Club*. It offered a book a month to its members at a price of two shillings and sixpence. It began in March, 1936, and its success was immediate and astounding. Within eighteen months its membership was 50,000. It had its own house magazine, *Left News*, and there was an ancillary publication, *Poetry and the People*, produced by the Poetry Group of the Club. A Readers' and Writers' Group was formed, with the aim of enabling writers to meet their public and discuss mutual problems. An important feature of the Club was local study groups, sometimes consisting of numbers of poor or unemployed people who clubbed together to purchase the monthly choice.

The aim of the *Left Book Club* was to promote the idea of a Popular Front; and, although the Labour Party rejected an invitation to co-operate unless its official line was represented on the selection committee, the Club was the institution that came nearest in England to achieving the ideals of the Popular Front. The idea of the Club took form at a meeting between Gollancz and John Strachey. Strachey suggested talking to Harold Laski, the great socialist professor at the London School of Economics. The three formed a selection committee: Laski for Labour; Strachey for Communism; and Gollancz for "Men of Good Will". Their selections included books which have since become classics, like Orwell's *Road to Wigan Pier* and Malraux's *Days of Contempt*. Among the books chosen was Spender's *Forward from Liberalism*, a characteristic document of the liberal mind accommodating itself to Communism. Books of a variety of left-wing persuasions were put out, including C. R. Attlee's *The Labour Party in Perspective*. However, the Communist influence dominated—as it did in most Popular Front movements—and a large number of the books issued were by Communists or advocated Communist policies or provided a Communist commentary on contemporary events.

The public demand for social and political commentary, associated with the feeling of helplessness in the face of approaching war, was realised by Allen Lane, who had started Penguin Books in 1936. In 1937 he began "Penguin Specials". The aim was to produce new books on immediately current themes, and to bring these books up to date edition by edition if necessary. One of the first books commissioned for the series, G. T. Garratt's *Mussolini's Roman Empire*, sold 120,000 copies in two months. Titles published by 1939 included Norman Angell and Dorothy Buxton's *You and the Refugee*, *Britain* by Mass-Observation, Stefan Lorant's *I was Hitler's Prisoner* and P. E. P. report on *Britain's Health*. Social and political documentation, with a leftish pressure, rather than dialectic and polemic, was what Penguin Specials offered. Editions were always in 50,000s.

Another unusual venture in the field of social documentation was *Fact*. Started by a group that included Margaret Cole, Lancelot Hogben, Stephen Spender and Raymond Postgate, it offered "A Monograph a Month". Titles included *Writing in Revolt*, *Why Pacifists should be Socialists* (by George Lansbury), *Portrait of a Mining Town*, *I Joined the Army* (by Private XYZ), and *Japan's War on China*.

One effect of this popular demand for left-wing publications was similar to that of the Popular Front Movement as a whole. Writers sympathetic to the Left found an increased audience for their writings; but they also found an increased opportunity to do their bit in addressing meetings or in writing directly on politics in a popular vein; and were thus involved, inevitably, in the world of slogans and rhetoric. Such an atmosphere, with its temptations to opt for the emotional comfort of simplistic positions, was not conducive to the writing of good poetry.

v

The one writer who might be exhibited as a proletarian poet of the period was Idris Davies. Davies was born in 1905, the son of a mineworker, in Rhymney in Monmouthshire, and he went to work in the pits at the age of fourteen. After seven years at the coal face, he found himself idle in the long strike of the mineworkers that took place at the time of the General Strike in 1926. He never went back to the mines, going first to a teachers' college and then to Nottingham University. In 1928 he became a school teacher in the East End of London.

All his poetry dates from the time after he became a school teacher, though the bulk of it looks back on his days in the mining valleys. He published four books of poems: *Gwalia Deserta* (1938); *Angry Summer* (1943); *Tonypandy* (1945); and *Selected Poems* (1953). *Gwalia Deserta* and *Angry Summer* are both sequences of poems about the mining valleys of Wales.

Davies was at his best and most typical when he wrote directly about the valleys as he knew them; though what he gained from first-hand experience was frequently spoiled by its being presented in the hackneyed rhetoric of protest.

> There are countless tons of rock above his head,
> And gases wait in secret corners for a spark;
> And his lamp shows dimly in the dust.
> His leather belt is warm and moist with sweat,
> And he crouches against the hanging coal,
> And the pick swings to and fro,
> And many beads of salty sweat play about his lips
> And trickle down the blackened skin
> To the hairy tangle on the chest.
> The rats squeak and scamper among the unused props,
> And the fungus waxes strong.
> And Dai pauses and wipes his sticky brow,
> And suddenly wonders if his baby
> Shall grow up to crawl in the local Hell,
> And if to-morrow's ticket will buy enough food for six
>   days,
> And for the Sabbath created for pulpits and bowler hats,
> When the under-manager cleans a dirty tongue
> And walks with the curate's maiden aunt to church. . . .
>
> Again the pick resumes the swing of toil,
> And Dai forgets the world where merchants walk in
>   morning streets,
> And where the great sun smiles on pithead and pub and
>   church-steeple.
>   (*Gwalia Deserta*, 4–5, VII)

There is some good observation—the gift of someone who knows what he is writing about. The criticism to be brought against the poem is not that it presents a one-sided propagandist case. (Anyone who knows the history of the coal industry in South Wales or who has read official reports of mining disasters could not be blamed for feeling that there is only one side.) It is that the material gains so little from the poet's putting into it verse.

The only book of poetry of the period by a writer who was proletarian in the sense that he was employed in a working-class occupation at the time of its publication (so far as it has been possible to trace) is *Poems of Strife* by Julius Lipton, published by Lawrence and Wishart in 1935. Lipton was evidently a Jewish tailor, and a prose sketch by him had appeared in "Nine Workers on Their Jobs" in *Left Review* for March, 1935. In some respects, this makes him hardly a typical worker, as the Jewish tailors of the East End were, by tradition, politically intellectual.

Poems of Strife is not only uneven in quality: it has no consistent style. Most of the poems are written in accordance with a naïve traditional conception of poetry:

> Oh worthy comrade! Oh thou mighty wave
> That hath washed and shaped the cliffs of history! . . .

Lipton's political attitudes may have been developed in contact with the realities of work, but they cannot be distinguished from the most over-simplified attitudes to be found in the poetry of *Left Review*:

> Rebel Worker, hero fighter,
>   Red Front Greetings embrace your stand,
> You've toiled bravely, daring smiter,
>   For the workers in every land. . . .

There are some passages in the book that suggest some talent. They occur mainly when Lipton is looking at the particular and forgets his formulated attitudes:

> She is forever sniffing the air like a hungry wolf,
> Crazily fighting round noxious food stalls;
> She suckles the love-child with milk-starved breast,
> Wasting waning strength on a germ-ridden house,
> And exchanges the bloom of youth for the cloak of a drudge . . .

Lipton's poems, apart from their naïvety of tone, are restricted ultimately by the fact that they are the poems of a man who has too completely made up his mind about things.

The only periodical of the thirties that might be described as publishing proletarian poems was *Poetry and the People*, the organ of the Poetry Group of the Left Book Club, which began publication in the summer of 1938, and appeared more or less monthly until the summer of 1940, after which it became *Our Time*, a broader and more interesting literary periodical. Even in the case of *Poetry and the People*, the amount of poetry of working-class origin may not be large. There were a number of names familiar from *Left Review* among the contributors from the beginning. The magazine appeared first in mimeographed form for threepence; but, after the war began, it appeared in printed form, and the price rose to sixpence. After the change to print, the contributions became more sophisticated, and people like Edgell Rickword and Douglas Garman from *Left Review* appeared in it. As *Left Review* closed just before the war, it is not fanciful to see *Poetry and the People* as being taken over as an alternative outlet. *Left Review*, of course, had contained virtually no working-class poetry.

The average poem in *Poetry and the People* by someone whose name is totally unfamiliar is conventionally rhetorical in the worst sense; so that, whatever the writer may have had to offer in the way of experience, is completely obscured by hackneyed poeticisms.

> Awake, awake, the Spring is here at last,
> And dawns in life and work its greatest day.
> Awake, awake, the call rings from the past,
> Keep faith with us—it is the First of May.
> (J. R. Walker: "The First of May", *P & P* 11, May, 1939)

Only the occasional poem stands out as succeeding in reflecting the real experiences that left-wing theory was supposed to arise from:

> I was one who delighted on Sunday mornings
> To walk in the public gardens with my children,
> Lounge in the sun, smoke,

Follow the motions of the playing children.
But the masters forced me to idle in parks
                    and gardens
Not one but each day of seven.
And, shadowed by black and nightmare wings
Of bombing planes, the sun grew cold and colder,
And the children, the beautiful limber children,
Had shrivelled faces of old men,
And rarely danced now on rickets and empty
                    bellies.

Wherefore to change this world grown dark
With dearth and buzzard wings of death
Myself I change.
Sometimes I dream
Still of the lawns, the flowers and lazing in
                    the sun.
But that is Tomorrow's grace. Today reveals me,
One stub of candle lit, my children hunger-
                    stilled in dream,
Sitting in the kitchen, reading, reading,
Till my eyes ache, and so much the dictionary
                    thumbed
It seems I read an alien tongue; in the mornings
Striving for hope and courage in the Bureau queue;
Speaking at corners of the streets
Through kniving winds and grating of Saturday-
                    night trams;
At demonstrations facing the batons of the
                    gallant mounted police;
Learning, thinking, fighting . . .
I did not choose the fight; but challenged I
were maniac to turn a blind or coward eye.

                    (*P & P* 10, April, 1939)

The poem had a note beneath it:

(As this poem was not marked with a name we are unable to
state the author. We shall be pleased to do so if he or she will
write in.)

VI

A writer whose work may be seen as a product of the movement for a Popular Front is Christopher Caudwell, who became

a Communist in 1935. Caudwell's output as a writer has the
air of being prodigious. He left school at the age of fifteen in
1922. Between then and his death in 1937 he had been a
reporter and editor, founded an aeronautical publishing
company and written eight thrillers and five books on aviation
under his real name, Christopher St John Sprigg.

Had he died in 1935, he would not be remembered. Under
the impact of Marxism he produced the books that made him
famous—*Studies in a Dying Culture* (1938), *Further Studies in a
Dying Culture* (1949), *The Crisis in Physics* (1939), and, the most
celebrated of them all, *Illusion and Reality* (1937)—subtitled
"A Study of the Sources of Poetry". None of these books was
published in his lifetime; and they must, along with most of his
poems, have been written over a period of less than two years.

The most notable thing about Caudwell's work is that it
constitutes one body of literary work of the thirties by an
orthodox Communist that is still well worth reading. *Studies in
a Dying Culture* and *Illusion and Reality* are stimulating today,
despite the fact that the author's convictions concerning the
proletariat and its place in history have not been borne out by
events. The epigraph in *Illusion and Reality* is a quotation from
Engels: "Freedom is the recognition of necessity". This
statement is the starting point for Caudwell's writing in
Studies in a Dying Culture, and for a great deal of *Illusion and
Reality*.

The essays in *Studies* consist of critiques of Shaw, T. E.
Lawrence, D. H. Lawrence, H. G. Wells and Freud as upholders
of the bourgeois conception of freedom, together with essays on
"Love", "Liberty" and "Pacificism and Violence". Bourgeois
culture, Caudwell contends, is dying because "it cannot rid
itself of the basic bourgeois illusion. . . ."

> This illusion is that man is naturally free—"naturally" in this
> sense, that all the organisations of society are held to limit and
> cripple his free instincts, and furnish restraints which he must
> endure and minimise as best he may. From which it follows that
> man is at his best and noblest when freely working out his own
> desires.[4]

This position is a very effective one for criticising Freud, for
instance. The Rousseauistic notion that there is a "normal"

condition that consists in the absence of inhibition of "natural" drives is endemic to psychoanalytic thought, even though very much qualified and hedged round with notions like "adjustment" and the "Reality Principle".

The accent on the autonomy and freedom of the individual consciousness found in the heyday of bourgeois society is quite obviously the expected concomitant of the expanding capitalism, the geographical exploration and the growing democratic institutions of that era. Caudwell discusses his five figures in terms of this historical explanation, and again there are some telling insights. He sees T. E. Lawrence as the hero of the decline of the middle class, tragically aware of his own dividedness and incapacity, and longing for a society based on more real relationships, which he finds among the Bedouins and in the ranks in the Air Force. Take away Caudwell's suggestion that Lawrence ought to have seen that he longed for the classless society, and the essay is highly convincing. The main trouble with it is the way in which it is convincing. There is little reference to anything known about Lawrence. One does not imagine Caudwell as ignorant of the subject, but the facts that are mentioned are the two or three facts that anyone who had heard of Lawrence knows. The essay works by arguing that Lawrence must, of necessity, have been a particular type of person—the sort of person whom he is known generally to have been. This is the method of all the essays in *Studies*; and it is, of course, their weakness. When we compare them with Orwell's essays, which are also left-wing and sociological in interpretation, we become aware of how much Caudwell's views are applied to his subjects rather than arising out of them.

The abstractness and lack of reference to the subject as a thing in itself demanding that we come to terms with it in discussing it, is a feature of *Illusion and Reality*. Admittedly the book is about the *sources* of poetry. Nevertheless, there is a noticeable lack of particularised reference to poetry—as though the nature of poetic activity was not a subject full of subtle difficulty. We see in *Illusion and Reality* what is the obverse of Caudwell's notable gift for clarity—his encyclopedic tendencies. He takes on everything and puts everything in its place. W. H. Auden, reviewing *Illusion and Reality* in *New Verse* for May, 1937, said of it: "This is the most important book on poetry since the books of Dr Richards, and, in my opinion, provides a more satisfactory answer to the many problems which poetry raises".[5] It has the same remoteness from poetry as does *Principles* of *Literary Criticism*. The appeal that the book would have to Auden is obvious. He was, at the time, strongly involved with Marx and Freud. In addition he has always had both the interest in the motive for poetry and the tendency to schematise shown by Caudwell. The diagram of the historical development of poetry in *Illusion and Reality* is reminiscent of the diagram in Auden's slightly earlier essay, "Psychology and the Arts Today". However, if we compare *Illusion and Reality* with *The Enchafèd Flood* or *The Dyer's Hand*, we see the difference between a man theorising about his subject and one intimately involved with its subtleties.

It is as a poet that Caudwell has a place in this book, and it is not surprising that he does not turn out to be a very interesting one. His *Collected Poems* were published posthumously in 1939. Of the seventy-eight pages of poetry, four are Juvenilia, and forty are occupied by a dramatic poem, *Orestes*. For all his trenchant revolutionary statements, Caudwell is a rather old-fashioned literary poet. Although he took the customary dubious line about Auden, Spender and Day Lewis, seeing them as still entrapped by their liberal upbringing, he frequently wrote like Day Lewis when the latter was off form:

> In Nature's factory not laggard workers
> We've yet produced no trophy of our skill
> And she may well dismiss us both as shirkers
> Barren by no misfortune but ill-will.

This is from a sequence of sonnets called "Twenty Sonnets of Wm Smith". The blurb on the dust cover of *Collected Poems* says: "Had Donne been faced with the problems of the modern world he might have written poems not unlike these." Caudwell in fact shows the way in which someone who had read Donne and whose poetic impulses were strongly tinged by his reading might write. Nearly all the poems are marked by archaic features. Even at his most felicitous, Caudwell shows that the inspiration of his poetry comes as much from literature as from experience. *Collected Poems* contains one poem in which Caudwell seems to be himself and which one can read with pleasure today, "The Progress of Poetry":

I saw a Gardener with a watering can
Sprinkling dejectedly the heads of men
Buried up to their necks in the wet clay.

I saw a Bishop born in sober black
With a bewildered look on his small face
Being rocked in a cradle by a grey-haired woman.

I saw a man, with an air of painful duty
Binding his privates up with bunches of ribbon.
The woman who helped him was decently veiled in white.

I said to the Gardener: "When I was a younger poet
At least my reference to death had some sonority.
I sang the danger and the deep of love.

"Is the world poxy with a fresh disease?
Or is this a maggot I feel here, gnawing my breast
And wrinkling my five senses like a walnut's kernel?"

The Gardener answered: "I am more vexed by the lichen
Upon my walls. I scraped it off with a spade.
As I did so I heard a very human scream.

"In evening's sacred cool, among my bushes
A Figure was wont to walk. I deemed it angel.
But look at the footprint. There's hair between the toes!"

If this poem is the best to be found in Caudwell, then it is a fair measure of his stature as a poet. Had he only written poetry, he would be remembered only by historians of the Spanish Civil War.

Caudwell, with a characteristic through-goingness, went to Spain to fight on the Republican side in December, 1936. He was killed in action against Franco's Moors in February, 1937. It was his first day of action, a fact that underlines the double heroism of his death and that of all the sketchily trained men who fought on the Republican side against a professional army. His death was undoubtedly a loss to English intellectual life— though not, perhaps, as great as some have suggested. It cannot with any confidence be said that England missed a poet of any note.

Chapter 17

SPAIN

The Spanish Civil War – Its impact in Britain –
The war and the literary Left – John Cornford –
W. H. Auden, C. Day Lewis, Stephen Spender,
George Barker – Retrospect

ON THE FIFTH of July, 1936, a rising occurred throughout
Spain among the officers of its armed forces. Though it had
been under secret discussion for some time, it was expected by
those taking part in it that it would have a swift success. In
North Africa and in parts of southern and north-central Spain,
it did. Wherever there was success, all who had resisted were
executed, along with anyone of radical political leanings or of
any prominence in trade union organisations. It was stopped
partly by certain elements of the army and administration, and
partly by the arming of popular organisations, such as the
trade unions, especially in Madrid. The revolt was not successful
on the Basque north coast, nor in Catalonia, another culturally
separate region, which contained the important industrial port
of Barcelona, a key centre of Anarchism in Spain.

Political disturbance was not new to Spain, and the period
immediately preceding the war had seen both change and
disturbance. The long dictatorship of Primo de Rivera had
come to an end in 1930, and with the removal of the monarchy
came the establishment of the second Republic in 1931. During
the few following years of democratic rule, there were distur-
bances both on the Left and on the Right. In February, 1936, a
Popular Front Government was elected. Reforms affecting
both the landowners and the Church were brought forward.
Further violence ensued, and the forces of the Right, by no
means united, decided to strike.

The leader of the army revolt, Franco, was a shrewd and not
very idealistic man. In the period when the revolt was being
planned, he was confined to the island of Teneriffe. On the eve
of the revolt, he flew to Las Palmas, and soon found himself in

control of Spanish North Africa. However, the insurgents did not at that time control the seas—far from it; so that Franco was cut off from the areas in Spain where the revolt had succeeded. At that point he received one of several key pieces of aid from Germany. By the end of September nearly 20,000 troops (many of them Moors) had been airlifted (mainly in Junkers 52s) to southern Spain. From there Franco was able very rapidly to subdue south-west Spain and link up with his fellow insurgents in the north.

The result of the arming of the people had been to give an opening to radical and regionalistic tendencies in loyalist Spain. Basque and Catalan nationalism became a fact of administration. In Barcelona the Anarchists were dominant; and throughout Spain there was a great and popular uprising. The collectivisation of agriculture and the democratisation of industry occurred rapidly in many places. Churches were closed or burned; priests were removed, imprisoned or executed. George Orwell was struck by the revolutionary aspect of Barcelona when he first arrived there in December, 1936.

The fact of civil war in Spain was bound to make an impact on a Europe apprehensive of another general war. Under British inspiration, a Non-Intervention Agreement was drawn up and a Non-Intervention Committee set up by September, 1936. The Germans and Italians were soon happy to join in, thus providing themselves with a cover for their own participation on Franco's side. Very soon there were 50,000 Italian soldiers in Spain, along with significant German aid. The effect of the Non-Intervention Agreement was principally to prevent supplies reaching the Republican government across the French border, a key restriction when the insurgents gained control of the seas.

The Soviet Union was the only large European power to give military aid to the Republican government. The Comintern early conceived the idea of International Brigades, not ostensibly Communist, to be recruited in all countries where there were people sympathetic to the Republican cause. These brigades played a key rôle in the war, the first important contingents going into action in the November battles that saved Madrid. The result of these battles would not have been the same without the brigades; though they had had little time for training, they contained some men who knew how to handle a rifle or a machine gun before coming to Spain. It was in these battles that many of the British literary intellectuals who fought in Spain took part, and it was in these battles that several lost their lives: Boadilla; the defence of University City; the battle of the Jarama.

Because the Soviet Union was the supplier of arms to the Republic, the Communists became increasingly dominant in loyalist Spain. Originally the Republican side had been a loose agglomeration of organisations. The militia in Catalonia was part Anarchist. The group joined by John Cornford and George Orwell (the P.O.U.M. Militia) was Trotskyite. In the early days tactical decisions might be the result of majority decision. In the reforming of the army, it was inevitable that centralisation should occur and the authority of rank be reintroduced. It is not surprising that such reorganisation should favour the Communists, nor that increasing centralisation and governmental crises should result in a strengthening of their hand. It would be disingenuous to contend that the Communists did not make the most of their opportunities; though it seems doubtful whether Comintern policy favoured anything beyond preventing defeat for the Republican cause. One event along the line towards Communist dominance was the putting down of the P.O.U.M. in Barcelona in May and June, 1937, described at first hand in George Orwell's *Homage to Catalonia* (1938). Another feature of the growing rigidity of organisation was discontent in some of the International Brigades. Esmond Romilly, who fought at Boadilla, decided to go home afterwards. After 1936, there was no more coming out for three months and returning home. A separate peace was now desertion; and, at the same time, many of the volunteers objected to being returned to the lines after heavy fighting in which there had been casualties of the order of seventy-five per cent. The facts of war as much as the facts of Communism were disillusioning.

The Communists were the dominant political force in Republican Spain by the end of 1937. In the meantime, Madrid had been held, but the Basques in the north had been overrun. On 15th April, 1938, Franco's troops reached the Mediterranean between Barcelona and Valencia, thus dividing the Republic in two. Even then, Franco might not have been able to defeat the Republic quickly, had his opponents not launched an offensive on the Ebro in September, 1938, in which they lost many men and a high percentage of their irreplaceable military equipment in Catalonia. In addition Franco again received German aid, in the form of military supplies, at a key time. The war ended in the unconditional defeat of the Republic on 31st March, 1939, just five months before a second world war might have led to English and French alignment with the Republic.

In the meantime, the English and French had come to terms with Hitler and Mussolini in October, 1938, at Munich, giving Hitler part of Czechoslovakia. An alternative to the agreement would have been to make common cause with the U.S.S.R. Despairing now of making international ties in opposition to Hitler, the Comintern began to modify its policy and move towards friendship with Hitler as the best defence of the Soviet Union. A consequence of this was agreement to withdraw the International Brigades. Many of their members were killed on the Ebro before this could take place. Many preferred to remain in Spain. Perhaps 40,000 had gone to Spain in all, though the Brigades never totalled more than 18,000. A large number were dead. The losses of the British battalion were over 500 killed, with 1200 wounded, out of 2000 volunteers. The departure of the brigades was the end of the left-wing hope that the spontaneous will and heroism of the people might avert an international disaster precipitated by the Right.

II

"Never since the French Revolution had there been a foreign question that so divided intelligent British opinion as this,"[1] wrote Robert Graves and Alan Hodge in 1940. For those of the Left the war seemed to be the beginning of the final confrontation with fascism that would end with the triumph of the proletariat. The arming of the people and the transformation of Republican Spain that followed gave the war the appearance of a class struggle—which in part it was. In particular, the war altered completely the orientation of the British Labour movement. The desire to avoid war was undoubtedly the strongest feeling with regard to international politics in Britain of the thirties. Pacifism was a growing movement and the Labour Party was traditionally pacifist. Yet the opening of the war saw the British government adopting a policy of non-intervention, while the Labour opposition clamoured for resolute and militant action.

The war provided an ideal meeting point for the various groups that supported the notion of the Popular Front. Spain was the great rallying issue for the movement, and a theme that brought distinguished speakers of no more than liberal outlook to the same platform as doctrinaire Communists. This was particularly true of the Spanish Medical Aid Committees. Large sums of money were collected, even in areas where very few people were at work, and many ambulances, with volunteer drivers, were sent off to Spain. It is easy for those who took part in these efforts to deride them today as cynical Communist front machinations; but they would not have had the scale of support they did if there had not been widespread spontaneous sympathy for the Republican cause, and if there had been nothing in that cause worthy of sympathy. However one may look at it, the Republican side in the Spanish Civil War presents a more attractive picture than Nazi Germany or the governments of Baldwin and his successor.

One of the things most striking about the war was the innocence of the reaction to it. In the film "The Spanish Earth", bomb demolition is shown with horror, yet of a scale that would have seemed negligible in any British city three years later, and a pin prick in Hamburg or Cologne in 1944. Guernica, where a few hundred people were systematically bombed in the market place in daylight by medium bombers, shocked the world. It is a pity today that we cannot regain some of that horror; though it is true to say that the alarming bombing casualties in Spain and the apprehension they caused regarding air-raids were largely due to the fact that the most elementary notions of taking cover were slow to develop there.

In the history of the thirties as a whole, the war did several things: it was a rallying point, but also a cemetery, of left-wing hopes of stopping fascism; it showed how unscrupulously willing the dictators were to take advantage of any agreement they entered into, though it took Munich to bring this lesson home; and it served to prepare the British public for the notions that the dictators could not be ignored, and that only by facing up to them could they be stopped. The intellectuals of the thirties have been criticised for seeing the Spanish Civil War as a confrontation with fascism, and for not seeing the complexity of its origins. They have also been criticised for not seeing the nature of the Communist attitudes and actions in the war. Yet Franco was a fascist, and it does not seem naïve today to see the war as one of many opportunities lost of halting the dictators on the road that led to World War II. The last twenty years have seen a lot of breast beating about Communism in the thirties. However devious the Comintern may have been in its propaganda and policies—and the war coincided with the Moscow trials—the Communists in Spain were always firm in their resistance to Franco and were the last group to continue to advocate resistance. As for atrocities, it would be hard to get into the class of the insurgents, who adopted a deliberate policy of terror and executions from the first day of their revolt.

III

Among British writers, support of the Republican cause was almost unanimous. A survey, *Authors Take Sides on the Spanish Civil War* (1937), found only five who supported Franco, with sixteen neutral and a hundred in favour of the Republic. Many wrote, spoke or worked for the Republican cause. Yet the notion that many British intellectuals fought or were killed in the Spanish Civil War turns out to be false. Most of the British recruits to the International Brigades were working-class men, which was not the case with the Americans. The list of British literary intellectuals who fought in Spain is short: John Cornford; Ralph Bates; Christopher Caudwell; Ralph Fox; John Sommerfield; Esmond Romilly; Charles Donnelly; Julian Bell; Tom Wintringham; and George Orwell. Cornford and Donnelly were men who had scarcely found their feet as writers; Romilly, apart from his editing *Out of Bounds* as a renegade public school boy, is remembered as a writer for *Boadilla*, the account of the major battle in which he fought. All these men, except Bell and Orwell, went out in the very early heroic days of the war. Cornford, Caudwell, Fox and

Donnelly were all dead by the end of February, 1937. They were involved in the battles of Boadilla and the Jarama that helped to save Madrid. The slaughter was enormous in these battles, presumably because untrained men were facing regular troops. In the Jarama battle, which so horrified Stephen Spender's friend, T. A. R. Hyndman, the British battalion under Tom Wintringham lost 225 of its 600 men, with nearly 300 wounded. Nor was much poetry produced by these writers out of the experience of battle. Wintringham wrote a few poems; Caudwell and Bell, none. Cornford's Spanish poems date from his period with the Trotskyite P.O.U.M. Militia outside Huesca on the then quiet Aragon front.

Nor did the war in fact produce all that much poetry in England. The anthology, *Poems for Spain*, produced by John Lehmann and Stephen Spender in 1939, has the air of being a selection of poems about the war. They note that they are unable to include Day Lewis's "Nabara" for copyright reasons. Evidently modesty prevented Spender from including all his poems on the war. (He wrote in all about a dozen, at least one of which, "The Town Shore at Barcelona", has never been collected.) However, a good deal has now been written on the literature of the war, and nobody has come up with more than a few poems by British poets other than those by Day Lewis and Spender and those included in *Poems for Spain*. Lehmann and Spender printed several poems by Spanish poets; and, with forty-three poems by twenty-nine authors, were clearly scraping the barrel, so far as poems by British writers were concerned.

Of non-combatants, Auden went to Spain for about three months as a stretcher-bearer; Spender went to look for his friend T. A. R. Hyndman, and later to a Writers' Congress; Louis MacNeice went as an observer. Spender records that David Gascoyne was working in Valencia when he was there. Auden wrote one poem on the war; Day Lewis, three. MacNeice recorded his impressions in *Autumn Journal*.

War seldom produces a plethora of poetry. The entire poetry of World War I, so celebrated for its war poetry, would not fill a large book. War taxes the human being too greatly for much creativity. This seems to have been the case in the Spanish Civil War. The poems by combatants are very few, though in some respects the most interesting to come out of the war.

Nearly all speak of death and the horror of war. One poem, found in the papers of a dead soldier, has the power one sometimes finds in the work of a naïve writer whose experience is so powerful that he takes hold of language in an unusually direct way:

> Eyes of men running, falling, screaming
> Eyes of men shouting, sweating, bleeding
> The eyes of the fearful, those of the sad
> The eyes of exhaustion, and those of the mad.
>
> Eyes of men thinking, hoping, waiting
> Eyes of men loving, cursing, hating
> The eyes of the wounded sodden in red
> The eyes of the dying and those of the dead.

"Jarama Front" by T. A. R. Hyndman similarly has the directness of authenticity, despite its nearly sentimentalised ending:

> I tried not to see,
> But heard his voice.
> How brown the earth
> And green the trees.
> One tree was his.
> He could not move.
> Wounded all over,
> He lay there moaning.
>
> I hardly knew:
> I tore his coat
> It was easy—
> Shrapnel had helped.
>
> But he was dying
> And the blanket sagged.
> "God bless you, comrades,
> He will thank you."
> That was all.
> No slogan,
> No clenched fist
> Except in pain.

A young Irish poet, Charles Donnelly, who had written for *Left Review*, was killed in the Jarama battle. His poem "The

Tolerance of Crows", one of the two he wrote in Spain, is more sophisticated formally than those already quoted, but it is a little mannered in the air of knowledgeability behind its choice of imagery:

> Death comes in quantity from solved
> Problems on maps, well-ordered dispositions,
> Angles of elevation and direction;
>
> Comes innocent from tools children might
> Love, retaining under pillows,
> Innocently impales on any flesh.
>
> And with flesh falls apart the mind
> That trails thought from the mind that cuts
> Thought clearly for a waiting purpose.
>
> Process of poison in the nerves and
> Discipline's collapse's halted. [sic]
> Body awaits the tolerance of crows.

Tom Wintringham, the commander of the British battalion, and one of the original editors of *Left Review*, wrote a number of poems about the war. Wintringham, who had fought in the Great War, knew war for what it was. He was later to write his reminiscences of the Spanish Civil War in *English Captain* (1939); and, later still, to sum up some of its lessons for World War II in an excellent little handbook for Penguin books, *New Ways in War* (1940). Unfortunately he was not a very good poet. His best piece is perhaps "Granien". It is a little too reminiscent of Wilfred Owen with its "thigh-proud", but the concluding image has the particularity of something fully experienced, and is one that sticks in the mind:

> Too many people are in love with death
> And he walks thigh-proud, never sleeps alone;
> Consider him neighbour and enemy, both
> Hated and usual, best avoided when
> Best known.
>
> Weep, weep, weep! say machine-gun bullets, stating
> Mosquito-like a sharper note near by;
> Hold steady the torch, the black, the torn flesh lighting,
> And the searching probe; carry the stretcher; wait,
> Eyes dry.

> Our enemies can praise death and adore death;
> For us endurance, the sun; and now in this night
> The electric torch, feeble, waning, but close-set,
> Follows the surgeon's fingers; we are allied with
> This light.

A poet who seems to have stayed longer in Spain than any of the British intellectuals was the Irish poet, Ewart Milne. He volunteered to do work with Medical Aid early in the war, and was still in Spain at the end of 1938. His poem "Sierran Vigil" appeared in *New Writing* for Spring, 1939;

> Where the lazy wall is down
> where the lemon leaf is poisoned
> where the road is holed: where gloom of
> cloud and sky is blessing: we
>
> Speaking no good word for war
> for heroics, for the kingly dust,
> exaulting not the self-evident murder,
> turn: not assuming hope: turn, offering hands.
>
> .   .   .
>
> Though no man here is hero, and we
> line up defending the unheroic unalterably!
> Who taught us war? This time
> those who did not begin will finish it. . . .
>
> .   .   .
>
> And where the lazy wall is down
> where the lemon leaf is poisoned
> where the road is holed, is trustless,
> here shall we grow the olive, and the orange blithely.

IV

John Cornford was not the most distinguished writer to be killed in Spain. He was one among several who died on the edge or in the midst of achievement. He wrote only three poems in Spain, and left behind only about a dozen written after his eighteenth birthday. Rupert John Cornford, he was named after Rupert Brooke, and, like Brooke, who wrote very few poems about the Great War, he was well suited to legend, and in many respects his life proves adequate to the minor legend that surrounds him. He was the great grandson of Charles Darwin and the son of Francis Cornford, the Cambridge translator of Plato, and of Frances Cornford, a minor poet. His gifts, both as a writer and as a leader in student political movements, were precocious, and made him nationally known before his death. He was the first Englishman to see action on the Republican side in Spain, and recruited a group that was to form a nucleus of the British battalion. He was at Boadilla, and he took part in the defence of the University in Madrid. He was killed on his twenty-first birthday, or on the day after.

As another writer has pointed out, what gives Cornford the air of legend is that his whole life was so involved in the left-wing movement of his day.[2] He has no other dimension in terms of which we can imagine what he might have been when the era with which he was identified had passed away. There is no *Illusion and Reality* or *Winter Movement*. He was a socialist at school, and close in thought to Communism by the time he left. He did not go immediately to Cambridge, but went instead to London, where he enrolled (rather casually) at the London School of Economics, and took rooms in Parton Street. This was in 1933 when Archer's bookshop was making the street a rendezvous for young radicals. Throughout that year he was fully engaged in political work, and joined the Young Communist League in March. From then until his death, all his activities were associated with the Party, which he joined in 1935.

He is one of that brilliant generation of university Communist organisers that included Philip Toynbee. They were very different from Auden and his generation. Auden, Spender, Day Lewis and Lehmann came to politics after they had left the university. When Cornford arrived back in Cambridge to enter Trinity College in 1933, left-wing activities were already flourishing in Cambridge. The intellectual Communism of the thirties was what he and his generation grew up with. They were consequently far more doctrinaire, far more politically accomplished than Auden and his friends; and they did not carry into their politics that hang-over from the twenties, the taste for "debunking".

Political organisation rather than the writing of poetry was Cornford's first devotion. Poetry he wrote only intermittently. Nevertheless, in this too, he was precocious. He started to write poetry in 1930, at the age of fifteen. By 1931 he had discovered Graves, Eliot and Auden—and, apparently, Day Lewis. It seems, in fact, to have been his most productive year as a poet, though there are a number of poems from his time in London and Cambridge.

Cornford tended to see his devotion to Communism as involving sacrifice, pain and courage. It is on the tension between these feelings and his exhilarating certainty that the struggle will lead to the triumph of his cause that his famous Spanish poem, "Full Moon at Tierz", is built:

> Though Communism was my waking time,
> Always before the lights of home
> Shone clear and steady and full in view—
> Here, if you fall, there's help for you—
> Now, with my Party, I stand quite alone.
>
> Then let my private battle with my nerves,
> The fear of pain whose pain survives,
> The love that tears me by the roots,
> The loneliness that claws my guts,
> Fuse in the welded front our fight preserves.

It is this tension that lies behind the Day Lewisish opening, with its depiction of time in terms of a glacier and a cataract. Cornford's theme here is historical inevitability, but it has none of the glib certainty that Day Lewis in his early days brought to such writing. Cornford's stanzas are full of words suggesting strain and near disaster: "gripped"; "crashes"; "Breaks down"; "that cross both ways". As Stephen Spender said, "Cornford's poems seem to be written by the will".[3] Spender's remark applies in another sense to the second section of the poem, with its bald statements about the Seventh Congress, Dimitrov and Maurice Thorez—statements that exemplify the directness that is one of the strengths of the poem. Once these particulars have established themselves as valid in the poem, however, they lend it particularity and strength. The last section of the poem is Audenesque in its sweep and in the way it clothes the actual with the serenity of the poet's achieved vision. The only blemish is the heavy reliance that the poet places on our response to the word "freedom", a response which is partly a stock response and not fully established by the poem.

Now the same night falls over Germany
And the impartial beauty of the stars
Lights from the unfeeling sky
Oranienburg and freedom's crooked scars.
We can do nothing to ease that pain
But prove the agony was not in vain.

England is silent under the same moon,
From Clydeside to the gutted pits of Wales.
The innocent mask conceals that soon
Here too our freedom's swaying in the scales.
Oh, understand before too late
Freedom was never held without a fight . . .

Nevertheless, the poem is Cornford's most individual poem; though, oddly enough, while singularly fitting to the death Cornford met, it is rather deflated by its own subtitle "Before the Storming of Huesca". Huesca never was stormed, and the front there remained quiet well after Cornford's death.

Cornford's most famous poem, and perhaps his best, is his poem to Margot Heinemann—not his last, but almost his last.

Heart of the heartless world,
Dear heart, the thought of you
Is the pain at my side,
The shadow that chills my view.

The wind rises in the evening,
Reminds that autumn is near,
I am afraid to lose you,
I am afraid of my fear.

On the last mile to Huesca,
The last fence for our pride.
Think so kindly, dear, that I
Sense you at my side.

And if bad luck should lay my strength
Into the shallow grave,
Remember all the good you can;
Don't forget my love.

The directness, the naturalness of the rhythms, the honesty that eschews any attempt to decorate the situation in a consolatory way, makes it perhaps the best English poem to come out of the

Spanish Civil War. The deliberate throw-away of the last line is a little too deliberate, but this is a minor blemish. The poem is similar to the less successful "Sad Poem", which he wrote on parting from Ray, the girl with whom he lived for two years, and by whom he had a child.

If these two personal poems are his best, it is as the poet of "Full Moon at Tierz" that he is remembered. It is not merely because it is part of his legend. It is also because it is one of those poems that give classic and definitive expression to a particular mood of a particular time; so that, even if we are critical of the mood, we would not be without the poem. Cornford gives us Spain of the early volunteers, with their belief that they were making the revolution. Though the hopes come to nothing and the mood seems naïve in the light of later events, it is still a mood to which we can respond and feel it worthwhile to do so.

v

Auden went to Spain in January, 1937, as a stretcher-bearer in the British Ambulance Unit. Accounts of his visit are all rather sketchy and somewhat contradictory. On return to England in March, he seemed unwilling to talk about his experiences. Later, in 1962, he said:

> I did not wish to talk about Spain when I returned because I was upset by many things I saw or heard about. Some of them were described better than I could ever have done by George Orwell, in *Homage to Catalonia*. Others were what I learned about the treatment of priests.[4]

The literary result of Auden's visit was *Spain*, published as a pamphlet in May, 1937, all royalties going to the British Medical Unit. In its day it was hailed as Auden's greatest poem: Auden himself subsequently called it "trash".[5] It was attacked by George Orwell who picked on the phrase "the necessary murder", interpreting it to mean that Auden accepted the idea of political murder.[6] However, Orwell seems to have construed the phrase "the necessary murder" in the light of his own disillusioning experience of political executions after the clash between the Trotskyites and the Communists in which he was involved in Barcelona. In fact the phrase "necessary murder" seems to be in tune with the basic attitude expressed in the poem—that all are implicated in a war and its injustices, that all are murderers. The defence of a just cause then becomes a "necessary murder". The notion of everyone's guilt before the fact of war is a Christian one, and Auden's Christianised mixture of Freudianism and Marxism provides the key idea of the poem.

Spain falls fairly clearly into three parts: yesterday, today, tomorrow. The first and third parts are impressive near lists of features of the past and future, through which runs the refrain, "But to-day the struggle". The middle part introduces us first to the poet, the scientist, and "the poor in their fireless lodgings" (rather like Mr and Mrs A. of *The Ascent of F.6*); all of whom call on "the life / That shapes the individual belly" to "descend as a dove or / A furious papa or a mild engineer". At this point the one clear Marxist idea in the poem appears, that men are made by what they do, and are not passive victims of the "life force":

> "Oh, no, I am not the mover . . .
> I am your choice, your decision. Yes, I am Spain."

Then we see those who have made the right choice, who have gone to fight in Spain; after which comes the intellectual climax of the poem:

> On that arid square, that fragment nipped off from hot
> Africa, soldered so crudely to inventive Europe;
>   On that tableland scored by rivers,
> Our thoughts have bodies; the menacing shapes of our fever
>
> Are precise and alive. For the fears which made us respond
> To the medicine ad. and the brochure of winter cruises
>   Have become invading battalions;
> And our faces, the institute-face, the chain-store, the ruin
>
> Are projecting their greed as the firing squad and the bomb.
> Madrid is the heart. Our moments of tenderness blossom
>   As the ambulance and the sandbag;
> Our hours of friendship into a people's army.

The last eight lines were cut out by Auden when he included the poem in *Another Time* in 1940. This would seem to indicate that he felt even then that he was overdoing things. Not merely is it brash to draw the psychoanalytic parallels between aspects of modern culture and events in Spain: the parallels are trite; and it is untrue, in the final analysis, that the war in Spain was either a manifestation of the sickness of Western Society, or a product of the evil in the heart of man. As in "September 1st, 1939", Auden commits his poem to an idea—and the poem is ruined because the idea is false. To this extent *Spain* is "trash". Trashy ideas generally give rise to trashy writing: "descend as a dove or / A furious papa or a mild engineer, but descend". The whole passage that culminates in these lines caricatures its subject: the lines themselves are ludicrously smart and superficial.

The contrast between the middle section and the first and last sections of *Spain* epitomises the embarrassment that the reader feels regarding a great deal of Auden's poetry in this period. The first section must be among the finest things he ever wrote, even if the voice is rather self-consciously public.

> Yesterday all the past. The language of size
> Spreading to China along the trade-routes; the diffusion
>   Of the counting-frame and the cromlech;
> Yesterday the shadow-reckoning in the sunny climates.
>
> Yesterday the assessment of insurance by cards,
> The divination of water; yesterday the invention
>   Of cartwheels and clocks, the taming of
> Horses. Yesterday the bustling world of the navigators . . .
>
> Yesterday the belief in the absolute value of Greece,
> The fall of the curtain upon the death of a hero;
>   Yesterday the prayer to the sunset
> And the adoration of madmen. But to-day the struggle.

The panoramic accumulation of detail was evidently suggested by memories of T. S. Eliot's translation of St John Perse's *Anabase*, which is echoed towards the conclusion of Auden's poem.[7] Auden's gift for evoking a place or an era by a significant, particularised image is brilliantly displayed in the first section. Much the same is true of the closing section:

To-morrow the exchanging of tips on the breedings of terriers,

.   .   .

To-morrow for the young the poets exploding like bombs,
The walks by the lake, the weeks of perfect communion;
    To-morrow the bicycle races
Through the suburbs on summer evenings. But to-day the
    struggle.

Here we see Auden's very engaging feeling for the everyday
pleasures of urban living, which contrasts so strongly with his
lack of feeling for "everyday" people shown in the middle
section. It would be idle to call the poetry of either the first or
the last section "trash": it is highly individual and deservedly
celebrated.

Spain was, before 1940, one of Auden's longest poems. Cecil
Day Lewis also produced a long poem about the civil war,
"Nabara", this time turning to straight narrative, as opposed to
the modified sequence of "A Time to Dance". The poem, based
on an episode in G. L. Steer's *The Tree of Guernika* (1938), tells
the story of the fight of a Republican armed trawler against a
rebel cruiser near the Basque coast. Day Lewis's handling of the
narrative keeps one interested, and because he is intent on
presenting a story that is in need neither of up-dating nor of
embellishment, his taste for poetic clichés is less in evidence than
in *A Time to Dance*.

For more than two hours they fought and at seven
They fired their last shell.

Of her officers all but one were dead. Of her engineers
All but one were dead. Of the fifty-two that had sailed
In her, all were dead but fourteen—and each of these half
    killed
With wounds. And the night-dew fell in a hush of ashen
    tears,
And *Nabara*'s tongue was stilled.
Southward the sheltering havens grew dark, the cliffs
    and the green
Shallows they knew; where their friends had watched them
    as evening wore

To a glowing end, who swore
Nabara must show a white flag now, but saw instead the
  fourteen
Climb into their matchwood boat and fainting pull for the
  shore.

The fight of the *Nabara* would bring to mind the last battle of
the *Revenge*, and, with it, Tennyson's magnificently banal
reciter's masterpiece on that subject. It clearly did for Day
Lewis, whose refrain-like phrase, "Men of the Basque Country",
echoes Tennyson's "Men of Bideford in Devon". The echoing
of Tennyson's stagey *tour de force* is not to the advantage of
Day Lewis's poem, particularly in the opening section, where
the "passage bird" seems to have been suggested by Tennyson's
marvellous simile, "a pinnace, like of flutter'd bird, came
flying from far away":

Freedom is more than a word, more than the base coinage
Of statesmen, the tyrant's dishonoured cheque, or the
  dreamer's mad
Inflated currency. She is mortal, we know, and made
In the image of simple men who have no taste for carnage
But sooner kill and are killed than see that image betrayed.
Mortal she is, yet rising always refreshed from her ashes:
She is bound to earth, yet she flies as high as a passage
  bird
To home wherever man's heart with seasonal warmth is
  stirred:
Innocent is her touch as the dawn's, but still it unleashes
The ravisher shades of envy. Freedom is more than a word.

The rather factitious rhetoric of this passage seems to negate its
sentiment, that "Freedom is more than a word".

After the publication of his *Forward from Liberalism* (1937),
Spender was invited by Harry Pollitt, the secretary of the
C.P.G.B., to join the Party, and also to go to Spain, though he
did not immediately take up the suggestion. It was through the
Party, however, that Spender eventually reached Spain, on a
wild goose chase for the crew of the Soviet ship *Komsomol*.
Spender by then had a pressing personal concern, because his
companion of some years, a former guardsman, T. A. R.
Hyndman (the Jimmy Younger of *World Within World*), had

enlisted in the Republican army when Spender got married in
1936. Hyndman was soon disillusioned with the experience of
war, and he deserted. Spender had to pull a lot of strings to
secure his release.

During this period, Spender visited the front, and saw
something of the war at first hand. Although he was strongly
sympathetic to the Republican cause, most of his poems
emphasise the tragic aspect of war, as does "Two Armies":

> Clean silence drops at night when a little walk
> Divides the sleeping armies, each
> Huddled in linen woven by remote hands.
> When the machines are stilled, a common suffering
> Whitens the air and breath and makes both one
> As though these enemies slept in each other's arms.

Some of these poems are among the most celebrated poems of
the war, though they do not remain especially rewarding
beyond their immediate impact:

> All the posters on the walls
> All the leaflets in the streets
> Are mutilated, destroyed or run in rain,
> Their words blotted out with tears,
> Skins peeling from their bodies
> In the victorious hurricane . . .
>   ("Fall of a City")

The phrase "words blotted out with tears" is both conventional
and exaggerated, and does nothing to focus the emotion of the
poem. The tendency of the imagery to diffuse the response to
the experience is exemplified by another well-known poem,
"Ultima Ratio Regum" (which is redolent of Wilfred Owen's
"Futility"):

> The guns spell money's ultimate reason
> In letters of lead on the spring hillside.
> But the boy lying dead under the olive trees
> Was too young and too silly
> To have been notable to their important eye.
> He was a better target for a kiss.

The imagery has a bright, carnival air that is out of tone with the experience of the poem, especially in the last line quoted. There are poems of a decided clarity and forcefulness among Spender's poems of the war—"A Stopwatch and an Ordnance Map" and "Thoughts during an Air Raid". However, there seems something artificial about all of them when placed beside the following poem, in which he remembers his friend in Spain, and in which the eye seems to be on the emotion and not on the need to make poetry out of it.

> The light in the window seemed perpetual
> Where you stayed in the high room for me;
> It flowered above the trees through leaves
> Like my certainty.
>
> The light is fallen and you are hidden
> In sunbright peninsulas of the sword:
> Torn like leaves through Europe is the peace
> Which through me flowed.
>
> Now I climb alone to the dark room
> Which hangs above the square
> Where among stones and roots the other
> Peaceful lovers are.
>   ("The Room above the Square")

Spender returned to Spain in the summer of 1937, to attend a Writers' Congress in Madrid, which was utilised by the Communists to attack André Gide, who had criticised the U.S.S.R. after his visit to it as a Communist supporter. Spender reported on the congress, but did not make clear the way in which it had been used to abuse Gide.[8] Years later he was to do so, holding up his earlier reporting as an example of the duplicity that an adherence to Communism made seem necessary and acceptable. The fact that he did omit things he knew to be true when he originally reported the congress would seem to show that he made no sharp break at that time with the Left or the Republican cause. Although his poems on the war are all anti-heroic, he does not himself seem to have seen this at the time as a symptom of disillusionment. In the foreword to *The Still Centre* in 1939, he wrote:

M

As I have decidedly supported one side—the Republican—in that conflict, perhaps I should explain why I do not strike a more heroic note. My reason is that a poet can only write about what is true to his own experience, not about what he would like to be true to his experience.

George Barker wrote three times about Spain. Once was in the conclusion of *Calimiterror* (1937) where he heard "Continually the women weeping in Irun's ruins . . ." His second piece was the sonnet "O Hero Akimbo on the Mountains of To-morrow", which is prototypical bad Barker, with its clashing images and its clumsy handling of rhythm and words. The third, "Elegy for Spain", is another matter. Its theme is that the future will blossom out of the death of heroes. It too has its bad moments, with Barker indulging his taste for word echoing or for moving around favourite words like "sun", "star" or "blood". However, its conclusion is remarkably effective in its comparative restraint that goes along with a devastating vividness:

> So close a moment that long open eye,
> Fly the flag low, and fold over those hands
> Cramped to a gun: gather the child's remains
> Staining the wall and cluttering the drains;
> Troop down the red to the black and the brown;
> Go homeward with tears to water the ground.
> All this builds a bigger plinth for glory,
> Story on story, on which triumph shall be found.

The same is true of the introductory stanzas, "Dedication to the photograph of a child killed in an air raid on Barcelona", that make a poem of their own:

> O ecstatic is this head of five-year joy—
> Captured its butterfly rapture on a paper:
> And not the rupture of the right eye may
> Make any less this prettier than a picture.
> O now, my minor moon, dead as meat
> Slapped on a negative plate, I hold
> The crime of the bloody time in my hand . . .

More directly human in its horror than anything on the war by Auden, Day Lewis or Spender, this passage, in spite of its Barkerisms, must be one of the most moving produced by the Spanish conflict.

It would be wrong, on the whole, to imagine that the experiences of the Spanish Civil War severely disillusioned British literary intellectuals, other than Auden and Orwell, with the Left. It is easy, of course, to write history as if these experiences did have such a result. *Homage to Catalonia* in 1938 revealed the true state of affairs to the British public, it might be argued; but *Homage to Catalonia* was too late. In ten years, only nine hundred of its original edition of fifteen hundred copies were sold. By 1938 the real cause of left-wing disillusionment had begun to operate; it was clear that no political action was going to stop Hitler, except a war. The left-wing intellectuals did not abandon the Left: history abandoned them.

In large measure, in fact, they were right about Spain. It was a key struggle against fascism, and non-intervention merely reinforced Hitler's feeling that he could get away with annexing whatever he wanted of Eastern Europe. There is no doubt that big business supported non-intervention, feeling that a Franco régime would be more sympathetic to its interest. The Catholic Church supported Franco and gave the Basque Bishops a cold shoulder when they came to Rome to ask for protest against Guernica; and the Catholic Church hailed Franco's victory as a Christian triumph. (Recently the Catholic Church in Spain has apologised for its attitudes.) In one other respect the left-wing intellectuals were right. Christopher Caudwell died covering the retreat of his company: the company commander was a Dalston busman. For once the dream of the Left was realised, intellectual and worker fighting side by side against fascism.

For many writers of the period, the war is still not over. Franco remains, the last of Hitler's friends whom nobody can ferret out. One can only echo the exemplary sentiments of John Lehmann concerning his friend, Julian Bell.

For me, it is as hard to forgive the killing of Julian as the killing of Lorca, wanton and deliberate as the murder of the young Spanish genius was compared with Julian's death; and I have been unable to find it in my heart to visit Spain as long as Franco's régime lasts.[9]

Chapter 18

NEWER SIGNATURES

The Newer Poets – *Twentieth Century Verse*, Ruthven Todd, H. B. Mallalieu, D. S. Savage, Julian Symons, Roy Fuller, Francis Scarfe – The Apocalypse Movement, J. F. Hendry, G. S. Fraser, Norman MacCaig, Tom Scott, Nicholas Moore, Henry Treece, Dorian Cooke – Laurie Lee, W. R. Rodgers, F. T. Prince, Henry Reed – Subsequent Careers

THE LATER THIRTIES saw the appearance of several new poets in *New Verse, New Writing* and other reviews. Some of them published their first books during the forties, and are associated with that period. Nevertheless, many of them were as old or older than Dylan Thomas, George Barker or David Gascoyne, but were not so precocious poetically; and their work was frequently a reaction to the "committed" or socially oriented poetry of writers slightly older than themselves. Some indeed began as imitators of Auden and his friends, and then moved away from their style of poetry. In their work there is an insistence, stated or implied, that the poet's business is with his personal vision, and not with ideologies or the reform of society. There is a rejection of the difficulty and intellectuality of much modern poetry in favour of the traditional, which is partly a reaction against the rejection of Romantic poetry by the leading critical spokesmen of early twentieth-century poetry. In line with this is the cultivation of the irrational elements in poetry, sometimes in direct continuation of the work of the surrealists, sometimes under the influence of Kafka, whose work was then appearing in the Muirs' translations. Most of these poets show an interest in fantasy, myth and dream, rather than in social reporting. In a time of doubt, like that immediately before World War II, myth gave form to the questionings and questings of those who were searching for something to believe in.

II

A group of new poets of the late thirties appeared in *Twentieth Century Verse*, a periodical of about twenty-four pages an issue, devoted mainly to poetry and reviews of poetry, which ran through eighteen numbers from January, 1937, to July, 1939. The editorial in the first number stated:

> Our chief object is to print the work of young poets who from one reason or another, the cut of their jacket or the colour of their tie, do not get much of a hearing elsewhere. [*TCV*, 1 (January, 1937) 2]

Twentieth Century Verse dissociated itself, in an early editorial [*TCV*, 2 (March, 1937) 22], from any particular political stance; and decided that surrealism "should be allowed to die quietly" [*TCV*, 3 (April/May, 1937) 42]. Its editor, Julian Symons, printed few of the well established poets of his day, the only ones being George Barker, Michael Roberts, Dylan Thomas, and Rex Warner. *Twentieth Century Verse* had, in fact, its own group, mainly friends of Symons, who seemed to share his aims. The nucleus was H. B. Mallalieu, D. S. Savage, Roy Fuller and Ruthven Todd. They were all regular contributors. The magazine had some connection with the Fortune Press; and in 1938 the press announced "The Fortune Poets", the first volumes of which included Symons's *Confusions about "X"* and Savage's *The Autumn World*. Later productions included Roy Fuller's *Poems* and *Inscapes* by Francis Scarfe (another contributor to *Twentieth Century Verse*) and the first anthology by the Apocalypse movement. These were the poets (apart from the Apocalypse movement) whom Symons may be said to have brought before his public; though they never presented themselves as a group, and never, until later, offered individual statements of aims, other than those set out in the early editorials.

Was there a typical *Twentieth Century Verse* poem? There was —more so than there was a typical *New Verse* poem. Ruthven Todd's "Northward the Islands" exemplifies much that was best in *Twentieth Century Verse*:

Northward the islands and the sullen shore,
The bald rocks where sulk the summer seas;
Distantly, as in a shell held to the ear,
I can remember their petulant noise
Quickening in winter to a sudden roar.

The leisurely seal fishing from the rock
And the otter trapped beside the burn,
The silver sand with network of brown wrack,
Were once my life, but I cannot return
To scythe the corn or build a stack.

The difference has grown in me,
The islands stay the same. No change
Is possible for me, who move so quickly
To strengthen my acquaintance with the strange.
Tomorrow someone else, but "I" today.

Where I am going and where I will end
Do not concern me for the present.
Nostalgia for the past I have, and find
It is the imminence of the future I resent,
Not my romantic leanings to the land.

[*TCV* 8 (January/February, 1938) 163]

The form of the poem is traditional and regular, bringing to mind a remark in Symons's first editorial: ". . . nor . . . are we much interested in such already outworn acrobatic parlour tricks as those of Mr. E. E. Cummings" [*TCV* 1 (January, 1937) 2]. The occasion of the poem is a personal experience rather than a public attitude; and, while one of the virtues of the poem is its directness and visual clarity, the poet is interested in the "images" of his poem as aspects of a place he has known, rather than as the isolated "object images" of some of the poets of *New Verse*. The diction is natural and unpretentious, as is the poet's attitude towards his experiences. Todd was one of the best of the regular contributors to *Twentieth Century Verse*.

There is one aspect, however, of the poetry of the group that is not illustrated by this poem, and that is the tendency to create private mythologies in their poetry, or to present experience in mythologised terms. One of the dangers of this type of writing is that the associations of the mythological elements may be excessively private, and not recreated within the poem. This is true of "Landscape 2' by D. S. Savage:

There where the river shrank past shack and shelter
I dug the iron earth and planted iron
For mutilated trees to drip all winter
Out of the itching of the dangerous sun.

I planted dragonteeth: and men of metal
Armoured with anger climbed from the sullen ground
Aching with pain to murder the maternal
And spill the running wax with which they groaned.

And where they paced the torn ramshackle circle
Of grief and sin the crippled shells of pain
Rose from the bed of sorrow with a manacle
Of splintered bone to ring the bursting sun.

There where the gasdrums hoisted through the city
I hacked a corpse of grass and fed with death
The mouth of seaweed in a ghastly pity,
And drove my martyred men again to earth.
                    [*TCV* 9 (March, 1938) 11]

The feeling that the poets were "talking to themselves" is also
evoked by a casualness—almost a confessional sloppiness—of
diction sometimes found in their writing: as though they no
longer felt it necessary to see the poem as a public object, but
took as their ideal a chatty communication with a member of
their group.

Nevertheless, the poems in *Twentieth Century Verse* did, on the
whole, have the virtues of directness and simplicity of vision and
of unpretentious personal feeling already noted. A fault too
common in them was an excess of plainness—a prosiness of
rhythm and of diction:

> Now that the dream no longer binds
> Our hope to everlasting winds,
> Or to eternal summer lands,
>   Need we assume
> That eastward all those birds have flown
> Whose song was love's one real renown,
> Whose flight was our expected boon
>   From Europe's tomb? . . .
>   ["Renewal", *TCV* 1 (January, 1937) 10]

There is a lack of inevitability about the imagery and other

rhetorical features of this poem that was characteristic of the
poetry of its author, H. B. Mallalieu; so that, in reading his
work, one is often left asking what, apart from a certain
urbanity and compression, the poems have to offer as poems.

The talents of the editor, Julian Symons, are, at first sight,
more impressive. His poetry is not flat, and it has an individual
theme, stated in the title of his first book of poems, *Confusions
about "X"*. The poems about *"X"* are an exploration of a
division within the poet that is described in terms of the poet as
"Stock-Exchange walker, record-breaker", as "the brooder",
and as "your humble", who "holds the two / In play
together . . ." In fact, the treatment of this theme is the least
attractive aspect of Symons's book. When he writes about *"X"*,
or explores his own personality, Symons is pretentious. He is
best when he is off duty as poetic intellectual, dealing directly
with a well delimited subject:

> Let us applaud this and the other evenings
> When twilight comes at about half-past seven
> And we look at the cars passing odd or even
> Without thinking of the particular end
>
> .   .   .
>
> Let the ambiguous heart accept whatever may happen
> As the child accepts the witches in the wood
> Or the other tales where everyone is good
> Let us accept hate as being in the pattern
>
> Let us make a pattern ourselves out of sunlight
> And the shallow leaves that continually spring green
> And the faces in the Square and whatever the eye has seen
> Like an eager camera travelling over light
>
> .   .   .
>
> Out of the shadow of the tired image
> Let us look at life as it looks now
> Dark as inside a cab or the first night of a marriage
> Or the childish darkness that fell down long ago.
> ["Poem (for W. E. L.)" *TCV* 14 (December, 1938) 128]

The one poet associated with *Twentieth Century Verse* who
has continued writing poetry steadily since the thirties is Roy
Fuller, whose *Collected Poems* appeared in 1962, and brought

together the contents of six other books. His work has maintained an even standard throughout his career, and, at first sight, his full achievement is impressive, as seemed his early talents. There is much that is brilliant in his first volume, *Poems* (1939), and he handles difficult forms like the sestina with ease; but the rhetorical features of the poetry frequently seem a product of facility, rather than of an emotional pressure.

In the following passage—the first eight lines of a sonnet—one feels that the rhetoric generates itself, and the unresolved syntax (a frequent bogus mannerism in the poetry of the thirties) is symptomatic of the fact that the elements of the poem are not linked by being the means of expression or resolution of an impulse from which the poem takes its life.

> Reaching the rarer atmosphere of change
> When the forecast even like an eclipse
> With dark disc, blocks our light, a fearful lapse
> No charm could conjure, minds unhinge,
> Protective masks that hamper gasping lungs
> With fumbling hands laid by and birds that lisp
> Their impersonal numbers tumble dead at last
> Like little stones to quiet grassy plains.
>   [*TCV* 5 (September, 1937) 94]

What the poem offers is a jumble of the literary stage properties of horror.

Readers of Fuller's *Collected Poems* will notice a considerable change after section I, which contains the pieces he has chosen to reprint from *Poems*. The wartime poems in succeeding sections are mostly based on actual events or on experiences set in the real world; while in many of the poems from his first book, a fantasy world is created. Auden's influence is strongly felt; but in the poems of fantasy the influence of Graves and Norman Cameron, with their gift for projecting a psychological landscape through fantasy, is seen. There is a decided fluency in some of these poems: the poem subsequently called "End of a City" is very powerful (IX):

> Somewhere between and out of time, a flare
> Will suddenly cast the shadow of a nose,
> Gone with disease, across the praying mouth.
> Those aquiline thrown lights will follow, gods

Dissolve like snowmen and the stiff pavement jerk
Its sharp plane upwards. Fragments of the thing ·
Brought down at first will after choke the outlets,
Force horror through the floor of private places.

There are not many poems with political themes in *Poems*,
though Fuller revealed very decided left-wing opinions in his
reviewing.

Francis Scarfe is perhaps best known to readers of modern
poetry for his book *Auden and After*, published in 1942, and still
one of the most congenial and perceptive books on its subject.
As a poet, he does not truly belong with the *Twentieth Century
Verse* group, though he contributed five poems and a review,
and his poetry was published by the Fortune Press. He became a
university teacher of French, and his first volume of poetry,
Inscapes (1940), contains a section of poems translated from
French. He was strongly influenced for a time by French
surrealist poetry. His style, after he gave up surrealism, was
close to that of the *Twentieth Century Verse* group, with a
simplicity of manner and personal themes; and the poems
Scarfe contributed to *Twentieth Century Verse* are as representative of his writing in the late thirties as any he wrote.

See that Satan pollarding a tree,
that geometric man straightening the road;
surely such passions are perverse and odd
that violate windows and set the north winds free.

No doubt to-morrow the world will be too straight,
five hundred knots an hour will churn our dreams
like surprised whales, when we lie a dead weight
in an ignorant sleep, and things will be what they seem.

To-morrow we will hear on the gramophone
the Music of the Spheres registered H. M. V.,
by a divorced contralto: we shall perhaps
meet Adam under glass in a museum
fleshless and most unlovely, complete with pedigree.

Or else, to-morrow, workers kings and crooks
will all have aeroplanes, and be fast friends,
in a world no longer divided by dividends,
where love will be almost as simple as it looks.

["Progression", *TCV* 10 (May, 1938) 31]

Summing up the achievement of *Twentieth Century Verse*, Julian Symons felt:

> This was limited by the fact that there seemed to be no point in printing the work of writers already well known like Auden, Spender, Day Lewis, MacNeice. They could appear in *New Verse*, *New Writing* and elsewhere: what was the point in trying to print them too? But this attitude meant nursing one's own ugly ducklings: and, as a friend said of Geoffrey Grigson's similar nursing in *New Verse*, the sad thing is that all the ugly ducklings turned out to be geese. Not quite all, however. I am pleased to have printed so many of Roy Fuller's early poems, and the first poems of Robert Conquest, and some of the poems written at this time by Kenneth Allott and Ruthven Todd. Pleased, too, to have printed Wallace Steven's work when he was barely a name in England, and to have published the work of half a dozen other American poets totally unknown here.[1]

Twentieth Century Verse's ducklings were uglier than those of *New Verse*, which could point in its brood to Cameron, Spencer and Allott. Indeed, as was the case with *Contemporary Poetry and Prose*, the peripheral achievements outshone the central attainment. Three of the best of the sixteen poems in Dylan Thomas's *The Map of Love* (1939) appeared first in *Twentieth Century Verse*. The poems in the double American number, along with Stevens's "The Man with the Blue Guitar", were the most important things that Symons published.

Twentieth Century Verse came to an end in the summer of 1939, as did *New Verse*. The editors, by then friends, were both feeling the financial pinch of running a literary magazine, and discussed amalgamation. There was insufficient in common, other than monetary need, and the discussions fizzled out. The literary scene was changing as war approached.

III

With the "Apocalypse" movement of the late thirties we make the final step from public school boy as left-wing intellectual to grammar school boy as unacknowledged legislator. The movement was as grandiose in aim as it was small in achievement. Its emergence was marked by the publication of an anthology, *The New Apocalypse*, produced by the Fortune Press in 1939, and edited by J. F. Hendry and Henry Treece. The other contributors were the poets Dorian Cooke, Norman MacCaig, Nicholas Moore, Philip O'Connor and Dylan Thomas, along with the painter and art critic, Robert Melville. (Dylan Thomas contributed a short story and one poem.) A second anthology, *The White Horseman*, published in 1941, was also edited by Treece and Hendry and included the same group of writers, with the omission of Thomas, O'Connor and Cooke, but with the addition of the poets G. S. Fraser, Tom Scott and Vernon Watkins. A third anthology edited by Treece and Hendry, *Crown and Sickle*, appeared in 1942, and contained poetry by a large number of poets, though only Treece, Hendry and Cooke were represented from the earlier anthologies. Thomas, Watkins and O'Connor had been writing and publishing for some time before the publication of the anthologies in which they appeared. The movement may therefore be considered as consisting of Treece, Hendry, MacCaig, Moore, Cooke, Fraser and Scott.

The movement stressed individualism and the importance of myth, disliked the type of poetry fostered by *New Verse*, and was generally more favourable to poetry of the Romantic period than had been poets of the early thirties. As a result, it has been seen as a reaction to the political concern of the poetry of the thirties; its origins are seen in periodicals like *Seven* and *Delta*; and it is generally regarded as a movement of the forties (during which decade it eventually faded into a branch of personalism). In fact, the thought of the Apocalyptic poets was, to begin with, clearly of a socially amelioristic type, and took as its starting points the doctrines of Marx, Freud and surrealism, so much a part of the ethos of the thirties.

J. F. Hendry was the thinker of the movement, and his contribution to *The White Horseman*, "Myth and Social Integration", gives the clearest exposition of what the movement stood for. The heart of Hendry's protest is in the phrase "the crucifixion of self on the cross of the object, of all that is not-self".[2] Freud, in particular, is seen as taking the world outside the individual as something given and fixed. Hendry stresses the importance of "myth"—along with "organic", a key word for the Apocalypse poets:

By myth, we mean the idea an individual has of himself, the sum of his aspirations and inspirations, the *incentive* to the sublimation discussed by Freud.[3]

One aim of the movement was the integration of social myths and patterns of society with individual myths. The result would be a truly "organic" society, one in which patterns were not impressed on human beings.

The poet's task was to create "his own organic myth", or to recreate myths with contemporary meaning. However, Hendry and Treece saw their doctrines as having other implications for poetry. They rejected both the notion of the image as an independent expressive entity—what they thought of as the "object image" of the Imagists and of *New Verse*—and also the surrealist notion of the image as something accepted uncritically from the subconscious. Both notions of the image were seen as allowing a limited interplay between the imagination and the outside world. The imagination was a means of creating an organic relationship between man and the world.

Hendry's "Myth and Social Integration" is still stimulating and fairly impressive: the poetry that went along with it in no way lives up to the aims of the movement. Hendry's poem "Apocalypse", from *The New Apocalypse*, is representatively dreadful:

> A cloud-skull strangling sun
> In spine-haired cannibal sky
> Stabs the blown heart green. Man
> Polared east of sex and west
> Of death crowns iron
> Orbits with a bone.

Norman MacCaig's poems differ little from bad surrealist poetry, except in so far as they seem to aim at a unity of imagery. G. S. Fraser's poems are urbane and literary, if not particularly impressive, and seem out of place in *The White Horseman*. Tom Scott's poems have little to distinguish them from those of Hendry and MacCaig. The only poets of anything like individual talent (at that time), who were associated with the movement, were Henry Treece and Nicholas Moore.

Treece contributed to *The New Apocalypse* poems from two

sequences that he had started work on in 1938: "The Never-ending Rosary" and "Towards a Personal Armageddon". The latter is a series of sonnets, clearly prompted by the ten sonnets that ended Thomas's *Twenty-five Poems*; and the sequence is a good demonstration of the way in which pretentiousness leaves a writer blind to bathos. Nevertheless, Treece could write poems that had a consistency of idiom and some rhythmic control and delicacy; but he was a much more conventional writer than his critical statements might suggest, and in *The White Horseman* he appears as a delicate if whimsical poet of myth reminiscent of the early Yeats:

> Brief months ago I loved a merry girl,
> Whose fingers wove with mine a merry game.
> While our flocks mingled, mingled was our tale
> Of faith, and fullness and the fire-lit home.
> ("The Shepherd Lad's Lament")

Nicholas Moore's poetry has a visual clarity and an individual lyricism that owe something to a slightly surrealistic freedom in the choice of images:

> The wind is a girl's heart,
> The wind is an apple in the spring,
> The wind is an horseshoe swinging on a gate.
>
> I offered her an orchard of trees hung with nails,
> I offered her a basket of deer.
> She took only the eye from my lap.
>
> But there's deer in the orchard,
> My apples are yours for the picking
> Dear, I only want the horseshoe and the simple truth.
> ("Song")

The main faults of poetry like this are prettiness and cosiness. Some of his poems have a chatty "in group" carelessness that marked the writing of the movement as a whole—the carelessness that goes along with self-importance.

Perhaps the most interesting thing about the Apocalypse movement was that it was a provincial, non-London-Oxford-Cambridge movement (though G. S. Fraser had gone from St Andrews to Cambridge, and represented *Seven* there).

It was also a Celtic movement. Hendry, Scott, Fraser and MacCaig were Scots; Treece was half Welsh. They associated themselves with two established Welsh writers, Dylan Thomas and Vernon Watkins, and Hendry was a friend of Keidrych Rhys, the editor of the regionalist periodical, *Wales*. In *Seven* (a periodical edited by Nicholas Moore, first from Taunton and then from Cambridge, from 1938 to 1940) they appear alongside writers of similar attitude but greater talent like Lawrence Durrell, Anias Nin and Henry Miller, and the result is an appearance of something more sober and acceptable than their own anthologies.

IV

Not every poet of the thirties had a book published during that decade or even appeared extensively in periodicals. Laurie Lee seems to have been writing poems for ten years before the publication of his first book, *The Sun My Monument*, in 1944. He was one of the poets—among them Dylan Thomas, David Gascoyne and Ruthven Todd—who appeared in the *Sunday Referee* poetry column around 1934. He spent some time in Spain before the Civil War, wandering from place to place and supporting himself by playing his violin.

While in Spain, he got to know the poetry of Lorca, whose influence seems to have been a congenial and enduring one in Lee's poetry. It shows in the use of traditional images that are simple and clear, almost to the point of quaintness:

> Now I am still and spent
> and lie in a whited sepulchre
> breathing dead
>
> but there will be
> no lifting of the damp swathes
> no return of blood
> no rolling away the stone
>
> till the cocks carve sharp
> gold scars in the morning
> and carry the stirring sun
> and the early dust to my ears.
> ("Words Asleep", Andalucia, 1936)

The telling use of clear, sharp but slightly over-realised metaphor is the most noticeable characteristic of Lee's better poetry. Lee was, indeed, most effective as a poet of sensation. When he explored feelings that are intense or complex, his poetry tended to be conventionally rhetorical and emotionally somewhat strained.

Though Lee has published only a small amount of poetry in his whole career as a writer, he has remained throughout that career a poet of decided and engaging individuality. In addition, he is one of the few poets of the thirties of working-class background. He grew up in a cottage in the Cotswolds; and, after leaving home in the middle of the decade, supported himself by playing the violin in the streets and as a builder's labourer. Apart from having a poem published in the *Sunday Referee*, his sole contact with the literary world during this period was meeting Philip O'Connor. Reading Lee's poetry, one would hardly suspect his origins, and he certainly does not fit the rôle of the worker poet. Yet he is the only poet of any talent in the thirties to have had nothing but elementary education or to have come from a working-class home.

Another poet who did not publish a book until the 1940s was W. R. Rodgers. Rodgers was in fact of the same generation as Auden, MacNeice and Spender, but had orginally taken orders as a Presbyterian minister in Ulster. He was around twenty-eight years old when he wrote his first poem. He later went to London to work for the B.B.C.

Rodgers is a rather rhetorical poet, and his writing sometimes reminds one of MacNeice's more contrived poems. In a poem entitled "Words", he writes:

> O for a world where words would always be
> The windows of feeling (and not mere blinds),
> Revealing and relieving living needs.
> And that I could,
> Looking from this between-times meeting, see
> The cumbered evening leave, bare morning come
> Leaping so clean, peeled clear of cloudy speech, . . .

Words are generally not "windows of feeling" in Rodgers's poetry, for all its apparent linguistic vitality. The writing is distinguished, stylish and controlled, but the figurative features of his use of language draw attention to themselves, rather than carrying us directly through to the feeling. His first volume, *Awake! and other Poems* (1941), was considered a very promising book when it first appeared. The poems in it have polish and individuality. Yet, although the manner is distinctive and remains with one as an emotional flavour, the book gives an overall impression of diffuseness, and there is no single memorable poem.

A poet who started to publish in periodicals in the later thirties, but who did not publish a book until the mid-forties, was Henry Reed. Reed came from Birmingham, and was a student at the university there when MacNeice was a lecturer in classics. Reed's only book of poems is *The Map of Verona*, published in 1945. A good deal of the poetry in it was, however, written during the thirties. The book shows a considerable interest in myth, both in the creation of situations and stories that have a mythological resonance, and in the reinterpretation of established myths. These reinterpretations, which make up about one-quarter of the book, seem to belong to the forties. They are preceded by a sequence of six poems called "The Desert", three sections of which appeared in *The Listener* in 1937, 1938 and 1939. These offer a variation on the thwarted quest theme. In spite of the urbanity with which both verse and diction are handled, there is a listlessness and confusion about the poems. Their relationship to one another is not clear, and the listlessness is connected with Reed's besetting failing as a poet, a tendency to spin things out, to conjure the appearance of subtlety out of playing with words. All this seems to be symptomatic of the fact that there is little pressure and conflict of feeling to be resolved. Reed's very finished talent, his delicate control of rhythm and diction that create the tone of an intimate speaking voice, are well displayed in the following short poem that also appeared in *The Listener* in 1939. This poem, too, has the slightly inane vacuity that marks so much of his writing. The details are brilliantly and impellingly realised, yet the poem as a whole seems an occasion for emotional doodling, in spite of the strong evocation of "atmosphere".

> Suddenly I knew that you were outside the house,
> The trees went silent you were prowling among,

The twig gave warning, snapped in the evening air,
And all the birds in the garden finished singing.
What have you come for? Have you come in peace?
Or have you come to blackmail, or just to know?

And after sunset must I be made to watch
The lawn and the lane, from the bed drawn to the window,
The winking glass on top of the garden wall,
The shadows relaxing and stiffening under the moon?
I am alone, but look, I have opened the doors,
And the house is filling with cold, the winds flow in.

A house so vulnerable and divided, with
A mutiny already inside its walls,
Cannot withstand a siege. I have opened the doors
In sign of surrender. The house is filling with cold.
Why will you stay out there? I am ready to answer.
The doors are open. Why will you not come in?

The South African poet, F. T. Prince, who was born in 1912 and came to Oxford in 1931, reminds one, in his early virtuosity, of Reed. Prince's *Poems* (1938) was one of the few books of poetry by a new poet to get any praise from *Scrutiny* in the thirties. The poems in this first book had remarkable polish, even if it was in places the polish of an accomplished imitation —often of Yeats. There are poems in which the poise and control that go along with this kind of accomplishment harmonise with a delicacy of feeling to produce touching and delightful poetry; but Prince's gift for handling adopted styles is, in fact, a symptom of the very literary nature of his inspiration. The best-known piece from *Poems* is perhaps "An Epistle to a Patron":

   ... I have acquired a knowledge
  Of the habits of numbers and of various tempers and skill in
     setting
  Firm sets of pure bare members which will rise, hanging
     together
  Like an argument, with beams, ties and sistering pilasters:
  The lintels and windows with mouldings as round as a girl's
     chin; thresholds
  To libraries; halls that cannot be entered without a sensa-
     tion as of myrrh

By your vermilion officers, your sages and dancers. There
  will be chambers
Like the recovery of a sick man, your closet waiting not
Less suitably shadowed than the heart, and the coffers of a
  ceiling
To reflect your diplomatic taciturnities. . . .

In this poem Prince's virtuosity reminds one of Henry Reed's
in a further respect, namely, in the tendency to spin things out,
to parade the virtuosity for its own sake. Though much of the
detail of the poem must have been derived from reading, it is
evoked with startling vividness: yet the total effect of the passage
quoted is not one either of visual clarity or of clarification of
feeling. The syntax of the poem is handled with accomplishment, but with an accomplishment that is not a servant of
subtlety of feeling, but which rather works to suggest a subtlety
that is, in fact, not there. One of the personae of Prince's poems
asks, "Shall I weep?" ("Chaka"). The phrase epitomises
Prince's usual emotional stance in *Poems*: for all the brilliance
of some of the writing, the poet is not engaged by the feelings
he writes about, but rather stands back from them, tasting,
relishing.

v

In 1939 the Hogarth Press published *Poets of Tomorrow:
First Series*. The poets included were H. P. Mallalieu and
Ruthven Todd, along with two even less well known poets,
Peter Hewett and Robert Waller. Two other selections followed,
one in 1940 from Cambridge, and another in 1942—the last
including poetry by Laurie Lee and David Gascoyne. The
title today seems strongly ironic: hardly any of the poets
included in the three selections had a poetic future. Yet the
title was true to the fact that these poets were of a generation
quite distinct from that of Auden and his friends.
  Some of these younger poets came, like Auden and Empson
and their generation, from Oxford or Cambridge. At
Cambridge G. S. Fraser represented the periodical *Seven*,

associated with the Apocalypse movement; and at Oxford there was *Programme*, edited at one time by Kenneth Allott and Alan Hodge. However, the intellectual life of the universities was by this time very much coloured by the dogmatic attitudes of the left-wing political clubs. It is not surprising that many of the poets of new outlook came from provincial universities or had not been to universities at all. Perhaps more significant is the fact that few of them were public school boys: the new poets were not "posh", as the intellectual literary Left had been on the whole.

Julian Symons, in presenting himself as "in some ways, a standard Thirties model", notes as "oddities": "non-public school, non-University".[4] Francis Scarfe grew up in a naval orphanage; Henry Treece was from Birmingham University, as was Henry Reed; Roy Fuller was articled to a solicitor at 16; Ruthven Todd studied painting at the Edinburgh College of Art; Laurie Lee's childhood in the Cotswolds is well known from his *Cider with Rosie*; Tom Scott was at one time a stone-mason. The traditionalist leaning of some of the new writers, along with their insistence on simplicity and immediacy, may have been partly a reaction against the tone of unconscious superiority in the work of the poets of the Auden generation.

Many of the new poets came from regions remote from the centres of metropolitan culture, and tended to identify themselves with the culture of the region from which they came. Evidence for the strength of cultural regionalism in the late thirties can be seen in the magazines like *Wales*. The Apocalypse movement included some poets who were Scots or Welsh, and they associated their brand of Romanticism with the fact that they were Celts.

There can have been few groups of poets so unfortunate in their poetic destinies as those discussed in this chapter. Their talents were not, to begin with, remarkable; and this may have been due in part to the fact that they grew up in a period of uncertain (or sometimes all too certain and crude) critical values, and under the shadow of writers of the virtuosity of Auden or Dylan Thomas, who seemed to have cornered the contemporary scene. Before they had had time to develop their individualities, the war brought the world of the thirties to a dramatic end, and, in its turn, brought new and pressing demands. Almost as dramatically as it closed the thirties, the war itself ended to reveal in Britain an emerging welfare state in a period of austerity under the menace of the atom bomb.

Chapter 19

OVERTURES TO DEATH

Left-wing disillusionment – The Coming of War

> When Auden and I left for China in January 1938 our departure
> inspired no one. The emotional climate had changed. The
> Spanish Civil War had become overcrowded with celebrities.
> The Chinese War, as viewed from England, seemed very far
> away, politically confused and quite lacking in glamour. If we
> had died . . . it would have been just another occupational
> accident to two amateur war correspondents.
>
> We returned to England that July and went to work on our
> Chinese travel-book, *Journey to a War*. We also finished our third
> and last play, *On the Frontier*. It was produced in October. In
> January 1939 we left for the United States.[1]

THIS TERSE, FLAT account of the year 1938 by Christopher
Isherwood reflects accurately enough the running down of
left-wing hopes at the end of the decade. It would not be true to
say that intellectuals increasingly saw through the activities of
the Communists. Certainly the change in atmosphere in
Republican Spain from the anarchistic idealism of the early
days of the war to the increasing rigidity and narrowness that
went along with growing Communist domination had something to do with the changing attitudes of intellectuals, as did
reports of the Moscow trials and of Communist ruthlessness in
Spain; but 1938 was the year in which it became clearer and
clearer that war was not to be avoided. Even after the Munich
agreement of September, there were still people in England
who believed there might not be a war, and there were still
those who advocated appeasement. However, except for the
most doctrinaire Communists, it became clear that the confrontation with fascism was not to be in terms of radical
political action but was to take the form of a major war. No
pamphlets, rallies, poems, speeches, or even People's Armies
could any longer avert this. As Stephen Spender put it:

The epoch ended with the collapse of the hope that the inter-vention by certain groups, and even by individuals, could decide the fate of the first half of the twentieth century.[2]

The imminence of war or its coming seemed to bring into focus the life of the thirties in a kind of accepting valedictory: "September 1st, 1939", for Auden; *Autumn Journal* for MacNeice; and, in the last issue of *New Writing*, which appeared after the outbreak of war in the autumn of 1939, A. S. J. Tessimond's "England".

> Plush bees above a bed of dahlias;
>   Leisurely, timeless garden teas;
> Brown bread and honey; scent of mowing;
>   The still green light below tall trees.
>
> The ancient custom of deception;
>   A Press that seldom stoops to lies—
> Merely suppresses truth and twists it,
>   Blandly corrupt and slyly wise.
>
> The Common Man; his mask of laughter;
>   His back-chat while the roof falls in;
> Minorities' long losing battles
>   Fought that the sons of sons may win . . .
>
> England of clever fool, mad genius,
>   Timorous lion and arrogant sheep,
> Half-hearted snob and shamefaced bully,
>   Of hands that wake and eyes that sleep . . .
> England the snail that's shod with lightning . . .
>   Shall we laugh or shall we weep?

War came as something of a loosening of tension in a world that had known for too long that it was coming. In August, 1939, Louis MacNeice was in Ireland. The impressions of that time of waiting for the war to begin are recorded in the ten poems (later reduced to seven) called "The Coming of War". No poem captures so well the stillness, the sadness, the bewilder-ment when the feared event has finally struck, as does the last of these poems.

> Why, now it has happened,
> Should the clock go on striking to the firedogs

And why should the rooks be blown upon the evening
Like burnt paper in a chimney?

And why should the sea maintain its turbulence,
    Its elegance,
And draw a film of muslin down the sand
With each receding wave?
And why, now it has happened,
Should the atlas still be full of the maps of countries
We never shall see again?

And why, now it has happened,
And doom all night is lapping at the door,
Should I remember that I ever met you—
Once in another world?

Nearly all the important poets of the period produced a volume of poetry in 1939 or 1940—volumes that often had a valedictory quality, and were certainly the final collections of poetry for the thirties. Day Lewis's *Overtures to Death* appeared in October, 1938; Spender's *The Still Centre*, in May, 1939; Thomas's *The Map of Love*, in August; Barker's *Lament and Triumph*, in March, 1940; Auden's *Another Time* in June; and Empson's *The Gathering Storm*, in September of that year. A collection by MacNeice, *Poems 1925–1940*, was published in America. Geoffrey Grigson's first book, *Several Observations*, appeared the day war broke out. For some of the poets of the period their wartime books were indeed to be *final* collections: Charles Madge's *The Father Found* (1941) and Kenneth Allott's *The Ventriloquist's Doll* (1943) marked the end of their public careers as poets; though Vernon Watkins's *The Ballad of the Mari Lwyd* (1941) was his first volume.

In collecting his poems in 1940, Louis MacNeice wrote a saddened and a broken valedictory for all the writers of the thirties who felt so strongly that their world had come to an end:

When a man collects his poems, people think he is dead. I am collecting mine not because I am dead, but because my past life is. Like most other people in the British Isles I have little idea what will happen next. I shall go on writing, but my writing will presumably be different.[3]

Chapter 20

CONCLUSION

IT IS NOT always possible, reviewing the poetry of a decade, to isolate one or two common qualities for which we value it—to sum up its achievement in a few sentences. Where this is possible, it is generally because a dominant conception of the rôle of poetry held in common by a group of poets gives a unity to their achievement. In the thirties there was such a dominant and widely held view of the rôle of poetry: that it should concern itself with political issues. Yet, while there are fine political poems from the period, such as Spender's early work, they do not make up the core of the poems of the period to which one wishes to return, even though the poetry of the period would not be the same without them. There is no "Easter, 1916"; and, considering the amount of bad or mediocre political poetry produced in the thirties, it can hardly be maintained that the political concern provided a basis for what was best in the poetry as a whole. It might better be argued that Auden's *Look Stranger!*, for instance, derives a great deal of its power from the political ethos, even when it is not overtly political; though it is unfortunate for the poetry of the period that many of Auden's directly political poems seem blemished or to have involved him in dubious poetical strategies. Much more obviously, political concern obtruded in an unfortunate way in the work of poets whose poetry, one must feel, would have been better without it. The work of C. Day Lewis is a case in point. Finally, of course, one must remember poets such as Dylan Thomas whose poetry seems only lightly touched by social concern.

One of the surprising facts about the left-wing poetry of the thirties is that so much of it was written by upper-middle-class poets and virtually none by poets of working-class background. Indeed, of the poets discussed at any length in this book, nearly all are public school, Oxford or Cambridge educated. This was true of virtually all the poets of the 1904 to 1914 age group. It was the poetry of these upper-middle-class, public school, university poets—and particularly that of the group associated with *New Signatures*, *New Country* and *New Writing*—that gave its particular tone to the poetry of the decade; though this tone was not an unqualifiedly left-wing political one. The political concern of these writers sprang in part from their horror at the gap between their way of life and the way of life of those whose work made middle-class life possible; yet everything that these poets most valued in the culture they had inherited was in some way associated with the economic position of the class from which they came. This was true even of their liberalism, so often criticised by doctrinaire Communists. The feeling of guilt engendered by their ambivalent attitude to their material and ideological heritage is a theme of some of their best poetry. They lived in the declining years of their class, and their social protest frequently mingled Marxism with a decidedly conservative criticism of the meritricious culture of the new Britain, with its ribbon development, cinemas, dog tracks and the appalling acres of semi-detached mock Elizabethan villas. These were the years during which the radio, the motor car and the aeroplane became widespread phenomena. They appeared in the new poetry in association with the forces of renewal in the early part of the decade and were a noted aspect of its "social realism"; but by the end of the period they had come to be associated with the malaise of society. Indeed, though these poets began in revolt against the decadence of Victorian puritanism, they came increasingly to write with nostalgia for the England that was passing.

The most striking common quality of the poetry that gives the immediate feeling that it could have been produced at no other time—the work of Auden, MacNeice, Spender, Day Lewis, Lehmann, and, to a lesser degree, of Betjeman and Grigson—is a capacity to give the quality of English life and to elucidate the English experience of the decade. This is what characteristically so much English fiction has done, and the capacity emerges in the thirties strongly in poetry.

It was suggested earlier that the poets of the thirties belonged to the first generation of writers in England to develop under the influence of the great makers of modern thought and literature —of Eliot, Lawrence, Freud and Marx particularly. This is of course true, but it is a view that must be qualified by an appreciation of the strong conservatism and insularity in artistic matters shown by the poets of the period. Indeed, they were quite consciously far from being whole-hearted continuers of the revolution in poetry created by Eliot and his contemporaries, in spite of the fact that Eliot had such an influence on the sensibility of the period. An essay of 1937 by Louis MacNeice is called "Subject in Modern Poetry":[1] its claims should be constrasted with the emphasis placed on "treatment" by the writers of the previous generation. The dichotomy is of poor critical validity; but it is true to say that the poets of the thirties tended to write poems *about* things, and that they did not, at times, mind being didactic. This goes for their good poetry as well as for their bad, and contrasts strongly with the conception of the poem as a construct rather than a communicative device that lies behind the practice of Eliot, Pound and the Imagists.

While the poetry of the thirties used the language and rhythm of ordinary speech, in other more formal characteristics it differed from that of the early modern period. Traditional forms, such as the sonnet and the lyric, were reintroduced by Auden, Empson, Day Lewis and several others, and rhyme was the common practice. Most of the poets of the period used regular syntax, whereas bogus, distorted or fragmentary syntax was one of the stylistic devices of Eliot and Pound—a device exploited by Stephen Spender and by George Barker at times. In the work of William Empson and Dylan Thomas, the syntax is contorted, but usually logical and grammatically complete.

One respect in which the poetry of the thirties continued the revolution of the great poets of the previous generation was in the preoccupation with imagery as a central device in poetry. A great deal of the obscurity of twentieth-century poetry arises from the avoidance of general statements and the substitution for them of particularised images.

Some of the poetry of the thirties has the same startling visual impact as that of Eliot and Pound, even though the approach to the poem is different. However, as has been seen, the conceptions of the rôle of the image associated with this effect varied widely. Dylan Thomas and William Empson tended to use imagery in the way in which it was used by Eliot, Pound and the

Imagists—as a sensory translation of general statements. George Barker came close to this, though he seems to have shared the Yeatsian notion of Kathleen Raine and Vernon Watkins that images give access to an unchanging world of arcane knowledge. For Geoffrey Grigson, whose ideas about poetry exerted a considerable influence through the editorial policy of *New Verse*, a key criterion of poetic judgement seems to have been the use of hard, clear images—one of the criteria of the Imagists, though in Grigson's case it went along with an insistence on "subject", on the primacy of *things*. Finally, for David Gascoyne in his earlier work, the image was the surrealist image—the liberating image from the uncensored unconscious.

In discussing the influence of the "modernist" revolution, two important observations must be made. The work of David Gascoyne, George Barker and Dylan Thomas seems to have been more open to "modernist" influences than that of Auden, Spender, Day Lewis, MacNeice, Betjeman, Plomer and Lehmann; and it is interesting that these poets were not public school or university educated, were younger than the upper-middle-class poets, and their poetry had much less social orientation.

In addition, one has to bear in mind the almost blatant absence of influence of continental poetry on the poetry of the thirties in England. This is seen markedly in the way in which the impact of surrealism on English poetry appears as an isolated event in the decade—a moment of startling interest but superficial influence. The influence of Rilke is another exception. There is no doubt that most of the poets of the period could read French. Their provincialism was evidently either characteristically English or else deliberate. In the case of Auden it was deliberate—an aspect of his poetic conservatism.

The unwillingness or incapacity to learn effectively from French poetry has been endemic to British writing since the 1880s at least. The poets of the nineties knew the work of Baudelaire, Verlaine and Mallarmé; but what they made of this is a measure of their smallness when we make comparison with what T. S. Eliot got from the same examples. It has been argued that the whole experimental movement in modern poetry is American, and that it never caught on very well in

England.[2] Certainly, a great deal of what is best in British poetry from 1930 to 1960 is heavily indebted stylistically to conservative features of the English tradition. A further admission might be suggested: that all the great poets in English since the time of Hardy and Hopkins have not been British. The great flowering of American poetry in the first quarter of the century has already been remarked upon. Yeats was rootedly Irish. The rosta of British poets is impressive, but not great: Edward Thomas, Owen, Lawrence, Graves, Sitwell, Muir, the poets of the thirties. And after the thirties came the forties.

Indeed, the English middle-class ethos of the late nineteenth and early twentieth centuries offered an environment debilitating if not hostile to the arts—not merely because of its outright philistinism. The intensity of concern that is the mark of the dedicated artist could not easily be harmonised with the attitudes appropriate to a gentleman—the avoidance of any sort of fuss, the distaste for discussion of religion and politics, the insistence on amateurism. Even too great an emphasis on decency can be inhibiting to the life of the imagination. Certainly, the type of character idealised by the public schools, and productive of the classifications "hearties" and "aesthetes", was uncongenial to an easy commerce with the Arts. The concern for the in-group, the coterie jokes, often cited as shortcomings of the poets of the thirties, can be seen as by-products of the difficulty of accommodating the vocation of the artist to a British middle-class upbringing—an obvious defence in the face of the embarrassment and hostility with which the Arts were often greeted in England if they were anything more than a decoration.

A related fault frequently found with some of the poets of the thirties is that they were immature; and it has to be remembered here how literally immature some of them were. By the end of the decade, Dylan Thomas was only twenty-five. Maturity is seldom a virtue of young writers in rebellion; and the more socially oriented poets of the period were in revolt against all that was most solid in their culture. New ideas, as opposed to traditional wisdom, were very much in vogue in the thirties; and the temptation to callow pontification is considerable when art is seen as having an immediate and important political mission—especially in an atmosphere like that of the years of the Popular Front.

The obscurity of modern poetry becomes almost a necessary ingredient for some of its admirers; and this obscurity was involved in the separation of middle-brow and high-brow art in the period—a separation encouraging the new poet to regard only the tastes of the self-elected élite who like his kind of poetry. The horrifyingly meretricious tastes of middle-class readers of the period served to reinforce this tendency.

An aspect of English poetry in the nineteen-thirties that seems not to have been remarked upon is the decline in subtlety of rhythm. Undoubtedly Auden's poetry startled with the newness and firmness of its rhythms; and, in so far as the poets of the period used traditional forms, they did better than in free verse. However, there is a decided monotony in the rhythm of Dylan Thomas's early poetry, to which he admitted; and in the work of Stephen Spender there is a growing lack of rhythmic tautness as the decade proceeds. George Barker, David Gascoyne, and others of the younger poets, show a frequent insensitivity in their rhythms. The rhythm of poetry is a manifestation of the deepest impulses behind it, and this insensitivity can be seen as another symptom of a vulgarisation of sensibility that became more manifest in the forties.

In terms of its "modernism" as well as in terms of its emphasis on political ideology (though not in other respects) the thirties may be regarded as something of a diversion in the development of English poetry. The apparent unity of concern of many of the older poets disappeared with the end of the decade and the dramatic changes in political and economic climate. Some of them ceased to publish poetry. This was true of nearly all the poets who appeared at the end of the decade. Some of the older poets survived the decade as poets for careers very different from what might have been predicted in the thirties. Auden remained an outstanding literary figure, though he became a Christian, left England, and grew into a sounder, but, in the opinion of many, a duller poet. Cecil Day Lewis, after abandoning his political activities, seemed to find himself as a poet of personal themes in *World Over All* (1943), only to become increasingly conventional, ending as Poet Laureate. Stephen Spender, after writing some moving introspective poems in the forties, wrote less and less poetry. For Empson, Warner, Cameron, Allott, and Madge, the end of the decade saw a decline or a virtual cessation in their publication of poetry.

It is perhaps too early to assess how fruitful the example of the poetry of the thirties has been in the work of later poets. Stylistically, the poetry of the forties was very much a continuation of the previous decade, except for some rejection of political themes, and in spite of a favouring of more traditional diction and imagery. The first important new manifestation of poetic style after *New Signatures* is *New Lines*—a fact recognised both in the title and in the introduction to the newer anthology. There are important debts of the poetry of the fifties to that of the thirties—particularly in its Englishness and its poetic conservatism. The accommodation of everyday life to poetry owes a lot to the work of Auden, MacNeice and Betjeman—a debt recognised by Philip Larkin. The ease with which the poets of the fifties combined traditional forms with a relaxed, highly colloquial diction derives from the work of the thirties; while the urbanity, wit and readiness to deal directly with ideas found in *New Lines* is another inheritance.

The writers of the fifties were also dissatisfied with what Britain had become, and were in revolt against false traditionalism, snobbery and the establishment. As with the poets of the thirties, many of them were university men, and a number had known one another at Oxford—Larkin, Amis, Wain. Left-wing in inclination, they were perhaps more effective enemies of the bogus than were the poets of the thirties, from whom they were separated by the social revolution of World War II—something that made it much easier for them to dissociate themselves from the stance of the class in which they had been brought up or educated. Deflation was the stock-in-trade of much of the writing of the fifties, and was the acknowledged stance of the anthology *New Lines* (1956); but it did not go along with hopes concerning revolutionary change, as it had in the thirties. In *New Lines* the apocalyptic was one of the targets for deflation. The difference between the two groups is a measure of the social and political changes in Britain and its position in the world that had taken place in the forties.

In terms of a belief in the value of revolutionary action and in a hope of implementing a better society through it, the sixties in America resembled the thirties in Britain more than did the British fifties. Once again university students identified themselves with left-wing ideologies in opposition to the class in which they had grown up. Once again there was a distrust of the processes of liberal democracy and a demand that revolutionary action be resorted to in their place. People who had little idea of what wholesale revolution might mean talked about it glibly, just as the young men in the thirties with expensive educations had done. The students of the sixties admittedly tried their hands at civil disruption (though they had no Spanish Civil War to go to, but only a war in Vietnam to stay away from); but, as in the thirties, there was little recognition on anyone's part that, in a sense, the revolutionary behaviour was a measure of the capacity and willingness to tolerate deviance that was a feature of the affluent and liberal society against which they revolted. In this respect both the British thirties and the American sixties resembled the British nineties: the idealisation of the useless in the nineties can be seen as a luxury product of Victorian materialism, just as the existence of a left-wing educated élite in the thirties and sixties could be seen as a measure of the degree of ideological accommodation that the societies could afford. As in the thirties, the radical activities of the sixties were associated with a revolt against puritanism, and the new society was seen in terms of a renewal that would be a product of the wiping out of puritanical restrictions. In this connection, the sixties in America differed rather markedly from the thirties in Britain: the culture hero was not the worker, but the bum and the drop-out, the hipster and the addict. The down-trodden proletariat had disappeared, to be replaced as objects of social concern by outsiders and minority groups.

When we come to evaluate the poetic achievement of the thirties, we must acknowledge one that is decidedly blemished. The number of new poets of individuality is startling, and one could not call the poetry of the era dull. One would not want to be without nearly all the poetry of the period by Auden, MacNeice, Betjeman, Thomas or Watkins; and Spender's *Poems*, Lehmann's *The Noise of History* and Empson's *Poems* have a quality and individuality that one would not want to miss. There were other very good poets besides these—C. Day Lewis (at times), William Plomer, Norman Cameron, Bernard Spencer, Geoffrey Grigson, David Gascoyne, Laurie Lee—and even George Barker, at his best. There are many excellent poems—but there are few, if any, great ones. Speculation can never get very far in explaining such a situation. The overtly political poetry of the period is too often theoretical; and the overpowering feeling that a writer should be political or concerned with the issues of the day may often have diverted the true impulses of poetry. In the case of Auden's work, certainly, one frequently feels a gap between the manifest concerns of the poem and pressures beneath its surface. The way in which some careers changed with the end of the decade could attest to a similar situation for other poets. For the great poet, the pressures of his inner life are harmonised with his perceptions of the world to produce a unified vision of experience. While the poetry of many writers of the thirties is immediately identifiable by its individuality, it never attains to this power of vision. It may be said, also, that there are too few poems in which experience is nakedly faced, and in which the poet meets its challenge by moulding his form to the individuality of that experience. Nevertheless, art that is not great art can offer an individuality of experience that makes it irreplaceable. It is to that category, it is suggested, that the poetry of the thirties worthily belongs; and it belongs, too, as contemporary poetry makes us increasingly aware, to the mainstream of English poetic development. It played a key rôle in elucidating the experiences of its period both to the period and to those who came after. To make alive and understandable our past—to arouse recognition of what we have known or of where we have come from (as does the best poetry of the thirties) —is surely one of the central functions of poetry.

N

BIBLIOGRAPHY

BIBLIOGRAPHY

A FULL BIBLIOGRAPHY of all books and articles referred to or quoted in this book would not be a full bibliography of all works relevant to the subject of the book and would contain many writings of marginal interest. Similarly, a full list of all books by all authors discussed in this book would include more works from outside the thirties than from within them. Indeed, an attempt at a full bibliography of every publication during the thirties by all such authors would require additional research comparable in extent to the research that has gone into the writing of this book, as the compilation of such a bibliography would involve the searching of periodicals for uncollected material and for material collected in different versions from those originally published. A full listing of books of poetry published in the thirties by authors discussed in this book is given, together with a selection of other material.

A standard reference text for biographical and bibliographical information is *Contemporary Poets* (London: St James, 1970).

The following bibliographies deal comprehensively with their subjects:

Bloomfield, B. C. and Mendelson, E. *W. H. Auden: A Bibliography* (Charlottesville: University of Virginia, 2nd ed., 1972)

Maude, R. "Chronology of Composition" in *Entrances to Dylan Thomas* (Pittsburgh, 1963)

Lowbridge, P. "An Empson Bibliography" in *The Review* 6 and 7 (June, 1963)

Handley-Taylor, G. and T. D'Arch Smith. *C. Day Lewis: A Bibliography* (London: St James, 1968)

Tolley, A. T. *The Early Published Poems of Stephen Spender* (Ottawa: Carleton, 1967)

A helpful listing of works by most of the poets of the thirties is contained in Spender, S., *Poetry Since 1939* (London: Longmans (for the British Council) 1946). Louis MacNeice's *Poems, 1925–1940* (New York: Random, 1940) gives a date for every poem included in it. The dating is presumably the author's own dating.

A list of books that provide a starting point for a general reading of the literature of the period is contained in *New Writing in Europe* by John Lehmann (London: Penguin, 1940)—unfortunately rather rare. The book gives a good picture of the literary activities of the period as they appeared to a participant at its close. A retrospective view by another participant is given in Julian Symons's *The Thirties* (London: Cresset, 1960). A contemporary survey of the poetry of the period by one of its younger poets is Francis Scarfe's *Auden and After* (London: Routledge, 1942)—also, unfortunately, rather rare.

The important anthologies and periodicals of the period are discussed in the book. The anthologies are:

Oxford Poetry (Oxford: Blackwell, 1925 to 1932 and annually)
Cambridge Poetry (London: Hogarth, 1929 and 1930)
New Signatures ed. M. Roberts (London: Hogarth, 1932)
New Country ed. M. Roberts (London: Hogarth, 1933)
Poems of Tomorrow ed. J. A. Smith (London: Chatto, 1935)
The Faber Book of Modern Verse ed. M. Roberts (London: Faber, 1936)
Poems for Spain ed. S. Spender and J. Lehmann (London: Hogarth, 1939)
New Verse ed. G. Grigson (London: Faber, 1939)
The New Apocalypse ed. J. F. Hendry and H. Treece (London: Fortune, 1940)
The White Horseman ed. J. F. Hendry and H. Treece (London: Routledge, 1941)
The Crown and Sickle ed. J. F. Hendry and H. Treece (London: King, 1944)
Poets of Tomorrow 1st Series (London: Hogarth, 1939)
　　　　　　　　　　2nd Series (London: Hogarth, 1940)
　　　　　　　　　　3rd Series (London: Hogarth, 1942)

In addition, the following symposia are important and representative:

The Arts Today ed. G. Grigson (London: Lane, 1935)
The Mind in Chains ed. C. Day Lewis (London: Muller, 1937)
In Letters of Red ed. E. A. Osborne (London: Joseph, 1937)

The following is a list of important periodicals of the thirties:

Experiment (Cambridge: ed. J. Bronowski, H. S. Davies, W. Empson, Lord Ennismore, H. Jennings. 1928–31)
Venture (Cambridge: ed. M. Redgrave, R. Fedden, A. Blunt. 1928–30)
The Twentieth Century (The Journal of the Promethean Society) (London: ed. D. Archer. 1931–4)

New Verse (London: ed. G. Grigson. 1933–9)
Left Review (London: ed. T. Wintringham, M. Slater, A. Williams Ellis; E. Rickword; and R. Swingler. 1934–8)
Contemporary Poetry and Prose (London: ed. R. Roughton. 1936–7)
New Writing (London: ed. J. Lehmann. 1936–9)
Programme (Oxford: ed. K. Allot and A. Hodge. 1935–6)
Wales (Llangadock: ed. K. Rhys. 1937–40)
Twentieth Century Verse (London: ed. J. Symons. 1937–9)
Seven (Taunton and Cambridge: ed. N. Moore and others. 1938–40)
Poetry and the People (Published by the Poetry Group of the Left Book Club. 1938–40)

Life and Letters Today, which in 1939 absorbed *The London Mercury*, came under the editorship of Robert Herring in 1935.

Two older periodicals are important: T. S. Eliot's *The Criterion* (1922–39); and *Scrutiny* (1932–53), edited from Cambridge by F. R. Leavis and his colleagues. The contribution of *Scrutiny* is best understood in the light of Leavis's *New Bearings in English Poetry* (London: Chatto, 1932) and the "Retrospect" he wrote for later editions.

A considerable amount of the poetry of the thirties appeared first in the *Listener*, published by the British Broadcasting Corporation from 1929 on. Janet Adam Smith (Mrs M. Roberts) was assistant editor during the early part of the decade.

There are autobiographies by the following poets of the period. (Details are given under the main entries for the poets.)

John Betjeman, Cecil Day Lewis, Geoffrey Grigson, Laurie Lee, John Lehmann, Louis MacNeice, Philip O'Connor, William Plomer and Stephen Spender

The following memoirs are also of value:

Davidson, M. *The World, the Flesh and Myself* (London: Barker, 1962)
Heppenstall, R. *Four Absentees* (London: Barrie, 1960)
Isherwood, C. *Lions and Shadows* (London: Hogarth, 1938)
Pudney, J. *Home and Away* (London: Joseph, 1960)
Toynbee, P. *Friends Apart* (London: MacGibbon, 1954)

Isherwood's book is perhaps the most important memoir of the period, especially as it was written (like MacNeice's autobiography) during the period.

Stephen Spender's *Forward from Liberalism* (London: Gollancz, 1937) and "Remembering Eliot" (*Encounter*, XXIV, 4 (April,

1965)) both contain valuable biographical information, as does Louis MacNeice's *Modern Poetry* (London: Oxford, 1938), three chapters of which deal with aspects of his development not dealt with in his autobiography.

March, R. and Tambimuttu (eds.), *T. S. Eliot: A Symposium* (London: Poetry London, 1948) contains contributions by William Empson, Louis MacNeice, Kathleen Raine and James Reeves that are mainly autobiographical, together with an article by Neville Coghill in which he recalls Auden at Oxford. The series "Coming to London" published in the *London Magazine* was collected as a book, *Coming to London* (London: Phoenix, 1957). The contributions by George Barker, Geoffrey Grigson and William Sansom are of special interest. Interviews with the following poets are contained in *The Poet Speaks*, ed. P. Orr (London: Routledge, 1966): Ronald Bottrall; Roy Fuller; John Lehmann; Charles Madge; William Plomer; James Reeves; W. R. Rodgers; Bernard Spencer; Stephen Spender; Rex Warner; and Vernon Watkins. Reminiscences concerning their schools by W. H. Auden, William Plomer and Stephen Spender are contained in *The Old School*, ed. Graham Greene (London: Cape, 1934). To these should be added the title essay of George Orwell's *Such, Such Were the Joys* (New York: Harcourt, 1953).

Fitzgibbon, P., *The Life of Dylan Thomas* (London: Dent, 1965) is a very full biography of Dylan Thomas. Everything fit to be printed concerning Julian Bell and John Cornford is contained in *Journey to the Frontier* by P. Stansky and W. Abrahams (London: Constable, 1966). *Vernon Watkins, 1906–1967*, ed. L. Norris (London: Faber, 1970), contains many reminiscences of Vernon Watkins. A similar volume devoted to George Barker is *Homage to George Barker*, ed. J. Heath-Stubbs and M. Green (London: Brian and O'Keefe, 1973). M. K. Spears in his *The Poetry of W. H. Auden* (New York: Oxford, 1963) tabulates the facts of W. H. Auden's life, while "Background to a Poet" by E. R. Dodds in *Shenandoah*, XVIII, 2 (Winter, 1967) gives information concerning Auden not elsewhere available. The introductory passages in Christopher Isherwood's *Exhumations* (London: Methuen, 1966) contain information about himself, Auden, Spender and others. T. W. Eason contributes a biographical article to *A Portrait of Michael Roberts*, ed. T. W. Eason and R. Hamilton (London: College of St Mark and St John, 1949). Information on Idris Davies is contained in *The Dragon has Two Tongues* by G. Jones (London: Dent, 1968).

One of the most valuable sources of biographical information is *The Penguin Book of Contemporary Verse*, edited by Kenneth Allott, which has gone through at least three editions. In the case of those poets too uncelebrated to be mentioned in standard library reference works, this book is often the only source of biographical information.

Two critical books by Cyril Connolly help to enhance understanding of the thirties literary scene: *Enemies of Promise* (London: Routledge, 1938) and *The Condemned Playground* (London: Routledge, 1945). In addition, the following novels of the thirties contribute considerably to an understanding of the period and its poetry:

Isherwood, C. *All the Conspirators* (London: Cape, 1928)
       The Memorial (London: Hogarth, 1932)
       Mr. Norris Changes Trains (London: Hogarth, 1935)
       Goodbye to Berlin (London: Hogarth, 1939)
Upward, E. *Journey to the Border* (London: Hogarth, 1938)
Warner, R. *The Wild Goose Chase* (London: Lane, 1937)

The following is a bibliography of the poets of the period, author by author. All volumes of poetry published in the period are listed, together with any other volumes that bring together poems of the period for the first time. "Collected Poems" are listed only when the collections present the poems generally as they were originally written and in such a format as to give some idea of the groupings in the original volumes or of the chronology of the poems. Relevant works of prose are also listed.

No attempt is made to review books and articles about individual authors. The literature on W. H. Auden and Dylan Thomas is voluminous and far exceeds all other secondary writing on the literature of the period, so that a review of the material concerning these authors would unbalance the bibliography. A good deal of the writing about Auden treats his work of the thirties only peripherally; while a large part of the writing about Thomas appeared before the *Notebooks* were available.

Individual Poets

Allot, K. (b. 1912)
 Poetry   *Poems* (London: Hogarth, 1938)
           The Ventriloquist's Doll (London: Cresset, 1943)
Assistant editor of *New Verse*
Auden, W. H. (1907–1973)
 Poetry   *Poems* (1928) (S.H.S., 1928; facsimile reprint, U. of Cincinnati, 1964)

	Poems (1930) (London: Faber, 1930) (1st. ed.)
	The Orators (London: Faber, 1932) (1st. ed.) (2nd ed., little changed, 1934)
	Poems (London: Faber, 1933) (2nd ed. with change of contents)
	Look Stranger! (*On this Island*) (London: Faber, 1936)
	Spain (London: Faber, 1937)
	Another Time (London: Faber, 1940)
Travel(including poetry)	*Letters from Iceland* (with Louis MacNeice) (London: Faber, 1937)
	Journey to a War (with Christopher Isherwood) (London: Faber, 1939)
Verse Drama (all with Christopher Isherwood except *Dance*)	*The Dance of Death* (London: Faber, 1933)
	The Dog Beneath the Skin (London: Faber, 1934)
	The Ascent of F.6 (London: Faber, 1936)
	On the Frontier (London: Faber, 1939)
Films	*Coal Face* (G.P.O. Film Unit)
	Night Mail (G.P.O. Film Unit)
Prose	"The Good Life" in *Christianity and the Social Revolution*, ed. J. Lewis et al. (London: Gollancz, 1935)
	"Psychology and Art Today" in *The Arts Today* ed. G. Grigson (London: Lane, 1935)
	"Psychology and Criticism", *New Verse*, 20 (April–May, 1936)
	Review of *Visiting the Caves* by W. Plomer, *Poetry*, 49 (Jan., 1937)
	Review of *Illusion and Reality* by C. Caudwell, *New Verse*, 25 (May, 1937)
	"Jehovah Housman and Satan Housman" *New Verse*, 28 (Jan., 1938)
	"A Literary Transferance", *Southern Review* VI (1940)
	"Byron" in *Fifteen Poets* (Oxford, 1941)

"Yeats as Example", *Kenyon Review*, X, 2 (Spring, 1948)

The Dyer's Hand (New York: Random House, 1962)

Editor   *The Poet's Tongue* (with J. Garratt), (London: Bell, 1935)

The Oxford Book of Light Verse (London: Oxford, 1938)

(It is necessary to read Auden's poems of the thirties in the original volumes, as many of them have been eliminated or rewritten by Auden when he made collections.)

Barker, G. (b. 1913)

Poetry   *Thirty Preliminary Poems* (London: Parton, 1933)

Poems (London: Faber, 1935)

Calamiterror (London: Faber, 1937)

Lament and Triumph (London: Faber, 1940)

The True Confessions of George Barker (London: Fore, 1950)

Collected Poems (London: Faber, 1957)

Prose   *Alanna Autumnal* (London: Parton, 1933)

Janus (London: Faber, 1935)

"The Miracle of Images" in *Orpheus*, II (1949)

The Dead Seagull (London: Lehmann, 1950)

"Coming to London" in *London Magazine*, 3, 1 (Jan., 1956) 49–54

Essays (London: MacGibbon and Kee, 1970)

Bell, J. (1908–1937)

Poetry   *Winter Movement* (London: Chatto, 1930)

Work for the Winter (London: Hogarth, 1936)

Collection   *Essays, Poems and Letters*, ed. Q. Bell (London: Hogarth, 1938)

Betjeman, J. (b. 1906)

Poetry   *Mount Zion* (London: James, 1931)

Continual Dew (London: Murray, 1937)

Old Lights for New Chancels (London: Murray, 1940)
Collected Poems (London: Murray, 1958)
Summoned by Bells (London: Murray, 1960) (Verse Autobiography)

Prose

Ghastly Good Taste (London: Chapman, 1933)
Antiquarian Prejudice (London: Hogarth, 1939)
"Topographical Verse" in *Slick but not Streamlined* (New York: Doubleday, 1947)
First and Last Loves (London: Murray, 1952)

Bottrall, R. (b. 1906)
Poetry

The Loosening and Other Poems (Cambridge: Heffer, 1931)
Festivals of Fire (London: Faber, 1934)
The Turning Path (London: Miles, 1939)
Collected Poems (London: Sidgwick, 1961)

Bronowski, J. (1908–1975)
Prose

The Poet's Defence (Cambridge, 1939)
William Blake (London: Secker, 1943; 2nd ed. London: Penguin, 1954)
"Recollections of Humphrey Jennings", *Twentieth Century*, CLXV, 983 (Jan., 1959)

Cameron, N. (1905–1953)
Poetry

The Winter House (London: Dent, 1935)
Selected Verse Poems of Arthur Rimbaud (London: Hogarth, 1942) (Translation)
(with R. Graves and A. Hodge) *Work in Hand* (London: Hogarth, 1942)
Forgive Me Sire (London: Fore, 1950
Collected Poems (London: Hogarth, 1957)

Caudwell, C. [Sprigg, Christopher St John] (1907–1937)

Poetry — *Poems* (London: Lawrence and Wishart, 1939)

Prose — *Illusion and Reality* (London: Macmillan, 1937)
Studies in a Dying Culture (London: Lane, 1938)
Further Studies in a Dying Culture (London: Bodley, 1949)

Cornford, J. (1915–1936)

Collection — *John Cornford: a memoir*, ed. P. A. Sloan (London: Cape, 1938)

Davies, Idris (1905–1953)

Poetry — *Gwalia Deserta* (London: Dent, 1938)
Angry Summer (London: Faber, 1943)
Tonypandy (London: Faber, 1945)
Selected Poems (London: Faber, 1953)

Day Lewis, C. (1904–1972)

Poetry — *A Beechen Vigil* (London: Fortune, 1925)
Country Comets (London: Hopkinson, 1928)
Transitional Poem (London: Hogarth, 1929)
From Feathers to Iron (London: Hogarth, 1931)
The Magnetic Mountain (London: Hogarth, 1933)
Collected Poems, 1929–1933 (London: Hogarth, 1935)
A Time to Dance (London: Hogarth, 1935)
Overtures to Death (London: Cape, 1938)
The Georgics of Virgil (London: Cape, 1940) (Translation)
Poems in Wartime (London: Cape, 1940)
Collected Poems (London: Cape, 1954)

Verse Drama — *Noah and the Waters* (London: Hogarth, 1936)

Prose — *A Hope for Poetry* (Oxford: Blackwell, 1934; 2nd ed., 1936)

Revolution in Writing (London: Ho-
garth, 1935)
"Foreword" to *The Aeneid of Virgil*
(London: Hogarth, 1952)
The Buried Day (London: Chatto,
1960)

Editor   *The Mind in Chains* (London: Muller,
1937)

Empson, W. (b. 1906)
Poetry   *Poems* (London: Chatto, 1935)
The Gathering Storm (London: Faber,
1940)
Collected Poems (London: Chatto,
1955)
Prose   *Seven Types of Ambiguity* (London:
Chatto, 1930)
Some Versions of Pastoral (London:
Chatto, 1935)
"Donne the Spaceman", *Kenyon Re-
view*, XIX, 3 (Summer, 1957)
Interview   *The Review*, 6 and 7 (June, 1963)

Ewart, G. (b. 1916)
Poetry   *Poems and Songs* (London: Fortune,
1939)

Fraser, G. S. (b. 1915)
Poetry   *The Fatal Landscape* (London: Poetry
London, 1941)

Fuller, R. (b. 1912)
Poetry   *Poems* (London: Fortune, 1939)
Collected Poems (London: Deutsch,
1962)

Gascoyne, D. (b. 1916)
Poetry   *Roman Balcony* (London: Temple Bar,
1932)
Man's Life is this Meat (London,
Parton, 1934)
(with H. Jennings) *Poems* by Benjamin Peret (London: Contemporary
Poetry and Prose, 1936) (Translation)
Hölderlin's Madness (London: Dent,
1938) (Translation)
Poems 1937–42 (London: Poetry London, 1943)

Collected Poems (London: Oxford, 1965)

Collected Verse Translations (London: Oxford, 1970)

Prose   *Opening Day* (London: Cobden-Sanderson, 1933) (Novel)

A Short Survey of Surrealism (London: Cobden-Sanderson, 1935)

Grigson, G. (b. 1905)

Poetry   *Several Observations* (London: Cresset, 1939)

Prose   *The Harp of Aeolus* (London: Routledge, 1948) (Essays)

Places of the Mind (London: Routledge, 1949)

The Crest on the Silver (London: Cresset, 1950) (Autobiography)

Poems and Poets (London: Macmillan, 1969)

Editor   *The Arts Today* (London: Lane, 1935)

New Verse (London: Faber, 1940) (Anthology with introduction)

Editor of *New Verse*

Hendry, J. F. (b. 1912)

Poetry   *The Bombed Happiness* (London: Routledge, 1942)

The Orchestral Mountain (London: Routledge, 1943)

Editor (with H. Treece)   *The New Apocalypse* (London: Fortune, 1940)

The White Horseman (London: Routledge, 1941)

Crown and Sickle (London: King, 1944)

Jennings, H. (1907–1948)

Poetry   (with D. Gascoyne) *Poems* by Benjamin Peret (London: Contemporary Poetry and Prose, 1936) (Translation)

Poems (New York: Weekend Press, 1951)

(See also works on Mass Observation)

Lee, L. (b. 1914)
Poetry   *The Sun My Monument* (London: Hogarth, 1944)
Prose   *Cider with Rosie* (London: Hogarth, 1959) (Autobiography)
                                As I walked out one Midsummer's Morning (London: Deutsch, 1969) (Autobiography)

Lehmann, J. (b. 1907)
Poetry   *A Garden Revisited* (London: Hogarth, 1931)
                                The Noise of History (London: Hogarth, 1934)
                                Forty Poems (London: Hogarth, 1942)
                                Collected Poems (London: Eyre, 1963)
Prose   *Prometheus and the Bolsheviks* (London: Cresset, 1937)
                                Evil was Abroad (London: Cresset, 1938)
                                Down River (London: Cresset, 1939)
                                New Writing in Europe (London: Penguin, 1940)
                                The Whispering Gallery (London: Longmans, 1955) (Autobiography)
Editor (with Stephen   *Poems for Spain* (London: Hogarth, 1939)
  Spender)
Editor of *New Writing*
Lipton, J. (No information)
Poetry   *Poems of Strife* (London: Lawrence and Wishart, 1935)

MacNeice, L. (1907–1963)
Poetry   *Blind Fireworks* (London: Gollancz, 1929)
                                Poems (London: Faber, 1935)
                                The Earth Compels (London: Faber, 1938)
                                Autumn Journal (London: Faber, 1939)
                                The Last Ditch (Dublin: Cuala, 1940)
                                Poems, 1925–1940 (New York: Random House, 1941)
                                Plant and Phantom (London: Faber, 1941)
                                Collected Poems (London: Faber, 1966)

Travel (including poetry)   *Letters from Iceland* (with W. H. Auden) (London: Faber, 1937)

I Crossed the Minch (London: Longman, 1938)

Verse Drama   *The Agamemnon of Aeschylus* (London: Faber, 1936) (Translation)

Out of the Picture (London: Faber, 1937)

Prose   "Poetry Today" in *The Arts Today*, ed. G. Grigson (London: Lane, 1935)

"Subject in Modern Poetry" in *Essays and Studies*, XXII (Oxford: Clarendon, 1937)

Modern Poetry (London: Oxford, 1938)

The Poetry of W. B. Yeats (London: Oxford, 1941)

"Experience with Images" in *Orpheus*, II (1949)

The Strings are False (London: Faber, 1965) (Autobiography)

Madge, C. (b. 1912)
  Poetry   *The Disappearing Castle* (London: Faber, 1937)

The Father Found (London: Faber, 1941)

(See also works on Mass Observation)

Mallalieu, H. B. (b. 1914)
  Poetry   *Letter in Wartime* (London: Fortune, 1940)

McCaig, N. (b. 1910)
  Poetry   *Far Cry* (London: Routledge, 1943)

Moore, N. (b. 1918)
  Poetry   *A Wish in Season* (London: Fortune, 1941)

  Editor of *Seven*

O'Connor, P. (b. 1916)
  Poetry   *Selected Poems* (London: Cape, 1968)

  Prose   *Memoirs of a Public Baby* (London: Faber, 1958) (Autobiography)

Plomer, W. (b. 1903)
  Poetry   *Notes for Poems* (London: Hogarth, 1928)

The Family Tree (London: Hogarth, 1929)

The Fivefold Screen (London: Hogarth, 1932)

Visiting the Caves (London: Cape, 1936)

Selected Poems (London: Hogarth, 1940)

The Dorking Thigh (London: Cape, 1945)

Prose   Double Lives (London: Cape, 1943) (Autobiography)

At Home (London: Cape, 1958) (Autobiography)

Prince, F. T. (b. 1912)
Poetry   Poems (London: Faber, 1938)

Raine, K. (b. 1908)
Poetry   Stone and Flower (London: Nicholson & Watson, 1943)

Prose   Defending Ancient Springs (London: Oxford, 1967)

Reed, H. (b. 1914)
Poetry   A Map of Verona (London: Cape, 1946)

Prose   "The End of an Impulse", New Writing and Daylight, 3 (Summer, 1943), 113–123

Reeves, J. (b. 1909)
Poetry   The Natural Need (London: Seizin, 1936)

Interview   The Review, 11–12 (1965)

Rhys, K. (b. 1915)
Poetry   The Van Pool, and Other Poems (London: Routledge, 1942)

Editor of Wales

Roberts, M. (1902–1948)
Poetry   Poems (London: Cape, 1936)

Orion Marches (London: Faber, 1939)

Collected Poems (London: Faber, 1958)

Prose   Critique of Poetry (London: Cape, 1934)

The Modern Mind (London: Faber, 1937)

T. E. Hulme (London: Faber, 1938)

"Notes on English Poets", *Poetry*, 39 (Feb., 1932)

"Aspects of English Poetry", *Poetry*, XLIX, 4 (Jan., 1937)

Editor   *New Signatures* (London: Hogarth, 1932)

New Country (London: Hogarth, 1933)

The Faber Book of Modern Verse (London: Faber, 1936)

Rodgers, W. R.

Poetry   *Awake! and other poems* (London: Secker, 1941)

Savage, D. S. (b. 1917)

Poetry   *Don Quixote and other poems* (London: Right Review, 1939)

The Autumn World (London: Fortune, 1939)

Time to Mourn (London: Routledge, 1943)

Prose   *The Personal Principle* (London: Routledge, 1944)

Scarfe, F. (b. 1911)

Poetry   *Inscapes* (London: Fortune, 1940)

Prose   *Auden and After* (London: Routledge, 1942)

Spencer, B. (1909–1963)

Poetry   *The Aegean Islands* (London: Poetry London, 1946)

Collected Poems (London: Ross, 1965)

Assistant editor of *New Verse*

Spender, S. (b. 1909)

Poetry   *Nine Experiments* (S.H.S., 1928) (facsimile reprint, U. of Cincinnati, 1964)

Twenty Poems (Oxford: Blackwell, 1930)

Peoms (London: Faber, 1933) (1st ed.) (2nd ed., with change of contents, 1934)

Vienna (London: Faber, 1934)

The Still Centre (London: Faber, 1939)

Verse Drama   *Trial of a Judge* (London: Faber, 1938)

Prose

The Destructive Element (London: Cape, 1935) (Criticism)

The Burning Cactus (London; Faber, 1936) (Stories)

Forward from Liberalism (London: Gollancz, 1937)

Life and the Poet (London: Secker, 1942)

World Within World (London: Hamilton, 1951) (Autobiography)

"The Theme of Political Orthodoxy in the 'Thirties" in *The Creative Element* (London: Hamilton, 1953)

"The Making of a Poem" in *The Making of a Poem* (London: Hamilton, 1955)

"W. H. Auden and his Poetry", *Atlantic Monthly*, CXCII (1953)

Editor

(with J. Lehmann) *Poems for Spain* (London: Hogarth, 1939)

N.B. The Poems in *Collected Poems* (London: Faber, 1955) have many of them been considerably rewritten from the versions of the thirties.

Symons, J. (b. 1912)

Poetry

Confusions About "X" (London: Fortune, 1939)

Prose

The Thirties (London: Cresset, 1960)

"A Glimpse of Thirties Sunlight", *Times Literary Supplement*, 3, 504 (24th April, 1969)

Interview

The Review, 11–12 (1965)

Editor of *Twentieth Century Verse*

Tessimond, A. S. J.
(1902–1962)

Poetry

The Walls of Glass (London: Methuen, 1934)

Voices in a Giant City (London: Heinemann, 1947)

Selection (London: Putnam, 1959)

Thomas, D. (1914–1953)

Poetry

Eighteen Poems (London: Parton, 1934) (Later editions from Fortune Press)

	Twenty-five Poems (London: Dent, 1936)
	Collected Poems (London: Dent, 1952)
Poems and Stories	*The Map of Love* (London: Dent, 1939)
Notebooks	*The Notebooks of Dylan Thomas* (New York: New Directions, 1967)
Prose	*Portrait of the Artist as a Young Dog* (London: Dent, 1940)
	Quite Early One Morning (London: Dent, 1954)
	A Prospect of the Sea (London: Dent, 1955)
	Adventures in the Skin Trade (London: Dent, 1955)
	"I am going to read aloud", *London Magazine*, 3, 9 (Sept., 1956)
	"Notes on the Art of Poetry" in *Modern Poetics*, ed. J. Scully (New York: McGraw, 1965)
Letters	*Letters to Vernon Watkins* (London: Dent, 1957)
	Selected Letters (London: Dent, 1966)

Todd, R. (b. 1914)

| Poetry | *Until Now* (London: Fortune, 1942) |

Treece, H. (b. 1912)

Poetry	*Thirty-eight Poems* (London: Fortune, 1940)
	Towards a Personal Armageddon (Illinois: Decker, 1941)
	Invitation and Warning (London: Faber, 1942)
	Collected Poems (New York: Knopf, 1946)
Prose	*How I See Apocalypse* (London: Drummond, 1946)

Editor (with J. F. Hendry) *The New Apocalypse* (London: Fortune, 1940)

The White Horseman (London: Routledge, 1941)

The Crown and Sickle (London: King, 1944)

Warner, R. (b. 1905)
   Poetry   *Poems* (London: Boriswood, 1937)
   Prose   *The Wild Goose Chase* (London. Boriswood, 1937) (Novel)

Watkins, V. (1906–1967)
   Poetry   *The Ballad of the Mari Lwyd* (London: Faber, 1941)
                              The Lamp and the Veil (London: Faber, 1945)
   Prose   Introduction to *Adventures in the Skin Trade* by D. Thomas (London: Dent, 1955)
                              Introduction to *Letters to Vernon Watkins* by D. Thomas (London: Dent, 1957)

NON-LITERARY BACKGROUND

The events of the nineteen-thirties leading to World War II are described in *The Origins of the Second World War* by A. J. P. Taylor (London: Hamilton, 1961). Two full histories of Britain in the early twentieth century are:

Taylor, A. J. P. *English History: 1914–1945* (Oxford: Clarendon, 1965)
Mowat, C. L. *Britain Between the Wars* (London: Methuen, 1955)

The social history of the inter-war period is covered in the very readable *The Long Week-end* by R. Graves and A. Hodge (London: Faber, 1940). The thirties themselves are given a full but excoriatory treatment in *The Thirties* by M. Muggeridge (London: Hamilton, 1940); while J. Symons, *The Thirties* (London: Cresset, 1960), gives most fully the flavour of the decade. *The Baldwin Years*, ed. J. Raymond (London: Eyre, 1960), and *The Age of Illusion* by Ronald Blythe (London: Hamilton, 1963) are of interest on the topics they choose to cover.

The relationship between the Communist Party and the literary intellectuals of the period has been little written about, though *Today the Struggle: Literature and Politics in England During the Spanish Civil War* by Katherine Bail Hoskins (Austin: U. of Texas, 1968) gives an extended treatment of its subject. *Poets of the Thirties* by D. E. S. Maxwell (London: Routledge, 1969) is about six of the more politically concerned poets of the period—Caudwell, Cornford, MacNeice, Spender, Day Lewis and Auden. *Communism and British Intellectuals* by N. M. Wood (New York: Columbia, 1959) is too short and wide-ranging to provide much insight into its subject. Brevity is a shortcoming of *The British Communist Party* by H. Pelling (London: Black, 1958). Since *The God that Failed*, ed. R. H. S. Crossman (New York: Harper, 1949), there has been a good supply of breast-beating books by former Communist intellectuals, though these books tend to give unreliable accounts of the earlier motives of their authors. Among them may be mentioned *I Believed* by D. Hyde (New York: Putnam, 1950). A book that gives a picture of the real activities of the Communist Party in Britain is *The Communist Technique in Britain* by B. [C. H. D.] Darke (London: Penguin, 1952). A history of the development of Comintern policies is given in *Comintern and World Revolution* by K. McKenzie (New York: Columbia, 1964). The supporting documents are contained in *The Communist International, 1919–1934: Documents*, ed. J. Degras (London: Oxford, 1965). Valuable representative left-wing statements from the thirties are:

Strachey, J. *The Coming Struggle for Power* (London: Gollancz, 1932)
Spender, S. *Forward from Liberalism* (London: Gollancz, 1937)
Lewis, J. *et al.* (eds.) *Christianity and the Social Revolution* (London: Gollancz, 1935)
Day Lewis, C. (ed.) *The Mind in Chains* (London: Muller, 1937)

The following books by George Orwell provide an independent critical inside view of the Left and of the decade as a whole:

Down and Out in Paris and London (London: Secker, 1933)
The Road to Wigan Pier (London: Gollancz, 1937)
Inside the Whale (London: Gollancz, 1940)
The Lion and the Unicorn (London: Secker, 1941)
Collected Essays (London: Secker, 2nd ed., 1961)

A full and fascinating account of the Spanish Civil War is given by H. Thomas in *The Spanish Civil War* (London: Penguin, 2nd ed., 1965). The war was widely written about in the thirties, and continues to attract writers. The book that best gives an impression of the war is *L'Espoir* by André Malraux. Almost equally valuable is the film of the same name made by Malraux. Another important film is *The Spanish Earth*. *Poems for Spain* ed. J. Lehmann and S. Spender (London: Hogarth, 1939) brings together nearly all the poetry of any importance written in Britain about the war. George Orwell's *Homage to Catalonia* (London: Secker, 1938) gives an eye-witness critical account of the activities of the Communists in Barcelona in the earlier part of the war. *Boadilla* by E. Romilly (London: Hamilton, 1937) tells the story of one of the early battles in which the author participated. The following are recent books on the literature of the war:

Ford, H. D. *A Poet's War* (Philadelphia: Pennsylvania, 1965)
Muste, J. D. *Say that We Saw Spain Die* (Seattle: U. of Washington, 1966)
Weintraub, S. *The Last Great Cause* (New York: Weybright, 1968)

A well illustrated account of surrealism is given in *Surrealism* by P. Waldberg (London: Thames and Hudson, 1965), which reprints many of the original documents. David Gascoyne's *A Short Survey of Surrealism* (London: Cobden, 1935) remains very readable.

The main documents of Mass Observation are:

Madge, C. and T. Harrison. *Mass-observation* (London: Muller, 1937)
Jennings, H. and others (eds.) *May the Twelfth: Mass-observation day surveys 1937* (London: Faber, 1937)
Madge, C. and T. Harrison. *Britain, by Mass-Observation* (London: Penguin, 1939)
Madge, C. and T. Harrison (eds.) *First year's work, 1937–38* (London: Drummond, 1938).

REFERENCES

REFERENCES

Chapter 1

1 Degras, J. (ed.) *The Communist International, 1919–1934: Documents* (London: Oxford, 1965) 361
2 Auden, W. H. *The Orators* (3rd edition) (London: Faber & Faber, 1966) 7
3 Crossman, R. *The God that Failed* (New York: Bantam, 1952) 5
4 Day Lewis, C. *The Buried Day* (London: Chatto, 1960) 209
5 Plomer, W. *At Home* (London: Cape, 1958) 120–1
6 Isherwood, C. *Exhumations* (London: Methuen, 1966) 13
7 Day Lewis, C. *Hope for Poetry* (Oxford: Blackwell, 1935) 3
8 Spender, S. "Remembering Eliot", *Encounter*, XXIV, 4 (April, 1965) 6

Chapter 2

1 Day Lewis, C. *The Buried Day* (London: Chatto, 1960) 177
2 *The Buried Day*, 174
3 "A Literary Transference", *Southern Review*, VI (1940); reprinted in *Hardy: A Collection of Critical Essays* (New Jersey: Prentice-Hall, 1963) 135–42
4 *Lions and Shadows* (London: Hogarth, 1938) 186–8; and *New Verse*, 26–7 (Nov., 1937) 4–9
5 *Lions and Shadows*, 191
6 "A Literary Transference"
7 *Lions and Shadows*, 192
8 Coghill, N. "Sweeney Agonistes", in *T. S. Eliot: A Symposium*, ed. R. March and Tambimuttu (London: Editions Poetry London, 1948) 82
9 *New Verse*, 26–7 (Nov., 1937) 6
10 *Lions and Shadows*, 190–1
11 *Lions and Shadows*, 192–3
12 Isherwood, C. *Exhumations* (London: Methuen, 1966) 5
13 MacNeice, L. *The Strings are False* (London: Faber, 1965) 114

14 "A Literary Transference"
15 Auden, W. H. "Louis MacNeice", *Encounter*, XXI, 5 (Nov., 1963) 48–9
16 *The Strings are False*, 113
17 *The Strings are False*, 113
18 MacNeice, L. *Modern Poetry* (Oxford, 1938) 55–6
19 *Modern Poetry*, 56–7
20 MacNeice, L. "Experience with Images", *Orpheus*, II (1949)
21 "Experience with Images"
22 *Lions and Shadows*, 281
23 *World Within World* (London: Hamish Hamilton, 1951) 68
24 *World Within World*, 46–9 and 57–9
25 *World Within World*, 48
26 *World Within World*, 60–4
27 *World Within World*, 56
28 *New Verse*, 26–7 (Nov., 1937) 9
29 *T. S. Eliot: A Symposium*, 146–51

Chapter 3

1 Reeves, J. "Cambridge Twenty Years Ago" in March, R. and Tambimuttu (eds.) *T. S. Eliot: A Symposium* (London: Editions Poetry London, 1948) 38
2 Raine, K. J. "The Poet of Our Time", March, 78
3 Reeves, J. March, 38
4 Quoted in Eberhart, R. "How I Write Poetry" in Nemerov, H. (ed.) *Contemporary American Poetry* (Voice of America: No Date) 27
5 Roberts, M. "Notes on English Poets", *Poetry*, 39 (Feb., 1932) 223–4
6 Leavis, F. R. *New Bearings in English Poetry* (London: Chatto, 1932) 201
7 Orr, P. (ed.) *The Poet Speaks* (London: Routledge, 1966) 39
8 Orr, 41
9 Leavis, 202
10 Leavis, 209
11 *Festivals of Fire* (London: Faber & Faber, 1934)
12 Lehmann, J. *The Whispering Gallery* (London: Longmans, 1955) 142
13 Bell, J. "A Brief View of Poetic Obscurity", *The Venture*, June, 1930. (Quoted in Stansky, P. and W. Abrahams—*Journey to the Frontier* (London: Constable, 1966) 53. Stansky and Abrahams give a different title for this piece on p. 62.)

14 Bell, J. *Letter to New Statesman and Nation* (9th Dec., 1933) 731–2. (Quoted in Stansky and Abrahams, 109.)

15 Lehmann, 147

16 Lehmann, 137–8

17 "Donne the Spaceman" in *Kenyon Review*, XIX, 3 (Summer, 1957) 337

18 *Kenyon Review*, XIX, 3, 361–2

19 *Kenyon Review*, XIX, 3, 370

20 Hamilton, I. "A girl can't go on laughing all the time", *The Review*, 6 and 7 (June, 1963) 37–8

21 "William Empson in Conversation with Christopher Ricks", *The Review*, 6 and 7 (June, 1963) 28

Chapter 4

1 Isherwood, C. *Lions and Shadows* (London: Hogarth, 1938) *passim*

2 *Lions and Shadows*, 192–3

3 Printed in *New Directions 11* (New York: New Directions, 1949) 84–116

4 *Lions and Shadows*, 75–6

5 *Lions and Shadows*, 207

6 *Lions and Shadows*, 300–1

7 Auden, W. H. in *Modern Canterbury Pilgrims* (ed. J. A. Pike) (New York, 1956). (Passage quoted in *The Poetry of W. H. Auden* by M. K. Spears (New York: Oxford, 1963) 174)

8 *Lions and Shadows*, 302

9 Spender, S. *World Within World* (London: Hamilton, 1951) 102

10 Spears, M. K. *The Poetry of W. H. Auden* (New York: Oxford, 1963) 20

11 Auden, W. H. and MacNeice, L. *Letters from Iceland* (London: Faber, 1937) 119

12 *Lions and Shadows*, 192–3

13 Hamilton, G. Rostrevor, *The Tell-tale Article* (London: Heinemann, 1949)

14 *The Times Literary Supplement*, 1520 (19th Mar., 1931) 221

15 Preface to *Collected Poetry* (New York: Random House, 1945)

16 Beach, J. W. *The Making of the Auden Canon* (U. of Minnesota, 1957) 19

17 *Exhumations*, 12. (See also Fuller, J. *A Reader's Guide to W. H. Auden* (London: Thames and Hudson, 1970) 79–90)

Chapter 5

1 Lehmann, J. *The Whispering Gallery* (London Longmans:) 1955, 173

2 *Granta* (9th Mar., 1928) 340. Quoted in "Some Ambiguous Relations", J. Jensen, *Criticism* 8 (1966) 357

3 Raine, K. "Michael Roberts and the Hero Myth", *Penguin New Writing* 39

Chapter 6

1 Isherwood, C. *Exhumations* (London: Methuen, 1966) 61

2 "Sketch Book III" (University of Buffalo manuscript). (For information on this see Tolley, A. T. *The Early Published Poems of Stephen Spender* (Ottawa: Carleton, 1967))

3 Spender, S. *Forward from Liberalism* (London: Gollancz, 1937) 183–5

4 *Forward from Liberalism*, 34

5 *The Destructive Element*, 221

6 Spender, S. *World Within World* (London: Hamilton, 1951) 147

7 *World Within World*, 171

8 Orr, P. (ed.) *The Poet Speaks* (London: Routledge, 1966) 239

9 Spender, S. *The Creative Element* (London: Hamilton, 1953) 63

10 Spender, S. *The Still Centre* (London: Faber, 1939) 10–11

11 *World Within World*, 331–2

12 Lehmann, J. "Author's Note" in *The Noise of History* (London: Hogarth, 1934)

13 Lehmann, J. *The Whispering Gallery* (London: Longmans, 1955) 197–8

14 *The Poet Speaks*, 114

15 Day Lewis, C. *Transitional Poem* (London: Hogarth, 1929) 69

16 Day Lewis, C. *The Buried Day* (London: Chatto, 1960) 218

17 *The Buried Day*, 211

18 Day Lewis, C. "Foreword" to translation of *The Aeneid of Virgil* (London: Hogarth, 1961) viii

19 "Foreword" to *Aeneid*, viii

20 *The Buried Day*, 212–13

21 Roberts, M. (ed.) *New Country* (London: Hogarth, 1933) 32

22 Day Lewis, C. *The Buried Day*, 222

23 *The Poet Speaks*, 263

24 *John Cornford: A Memoir*, ed. P. Sloan (London: Cape, 1938) 125–33
25 Day Lewis, C. "Revolutionaries and Poetry", *Left Review*, I, 10 (July, 1935) 401

Chapter 7

1 Auden, W. H. "The Good Life" in *Christianity and the Social Revolution*, ed. J. Lewis, K. Polanyi and D. K. Kitchin (London: Gollancz, 1935)
2 "Psychology and Art Today" in *The Arts Today*, ed. G. Grigson (London: Lane, 1935) 20
3 "Jehovah Housman and Satan Housman" in *New Verse*, 28 (Jan., 1938) 16
4 "Yeats as Example", *Kenyon Review*, X, 2 (Spring, 1948): reprinted in *The Permanence of Yeats* (New York: Collier Books, 1961) 308–14
5 Spender, S. "W. H. Auden and His Poetry", *The Atlantic Monthly*, CXCII (1953) 74–9
6 Grubb, F. *A Vision of Reality* (London: Chatto, 1965) 153

Chapter 8

1 MacNeice, L. *The Strings are False* (London: Faber, 1965) 146
2 MacNeice, L. *I Crossed the Minch* (London: Longmans, 1938) 125 and 127–8
3 MacNeice, L. *Modern Poetry* (London: Oxford, 1938) 174–5
4 *I Crossed the Minch*, 195
5 MacNeice, L. *The Poetry of W. B. Yeats* (London: Oxford, 1941) 166
6 *Modern Poetry*, 197–8
7 *Modern Poetry*, "Preface" (No page number)
8 MacNeice, L. "Experiences with Images", *Orpheus*, II (1949)
9 "Experiences with Images"
10 Symons, J. "Everyman's Poems", *Twentieth Century Verse*, 11 (July, 1938) 69–71
11 "Experiences with Images"
12 *Modern Poetry*, 128
13 "Experiences with Images"
14 Betjeman, J. "Love is Dead" in *First and Last Loves* (London: Grey Arrow, 1960) 11

15 MacNeice, L. *I Crossed the Minch,* 219
16 Quoted in Stanford, D. *John Betjeman* (London: Spearman, 1961) 27
17 Bergonzi, B. "Culture and Mr. Betjeman", *The Twentieth Century,* 165, 984 (Feb., 1959) 137
18 Betjeman, J. "Topographical Verse" in *Slick but not Streamlined* (New York: Doubleday, 1947)

Chapter 9

1 Yeats, W. B. "Modern Poetry" in *Essays and Introductions* (New York: Macmillan, 1961) 499
2 Roberts, M. "Aspects of English Poetry", *Poetry,* XLIX, 4 (Jan., 1937) 213
3 Graves, R. and Hodge, A. *The Long Week-end* (London: Four Square, 1961) 295
4 "A Conversation with James Reeves", *The Review,* 11–12, 70
5 *Scrutiny,* III, 1 (June, 1934) 78
6 *Scrutiny,* II, 1 (June 1933) 72–3
7 *Scrutiny,* III, 1 (June, 1934) 76
8 *Scrutiny,* VII, 1 (June, 1938) 97

Chapter 10

1 *New Verse: an anthology* (London: Faber, 1939) 15
2 *New Verse: an anthology,* 16
3 *New Verse: an anthology,* 19
4 *New Verse: an anthology,* 16
5 *New Verse: an anthology,* 23
6 *New Verse: an anthology,* 23
7 See *The Harp of Aeolus* (London: Routledge, 1948)
8 Scarfe, F. *Auden and After* (London: Routledge, 1942) 69–70
9 "Introduction" to *The Collected Poems of Norman Cameron* (London: Hogarth, 1957)
10 Allott, K. *The Penguin Book of Contemporary Verse* (London: Penguin, 1950) 193
11 Grigson, G. *The Crest on the Silver* (London: Cresset, 1950) 162–3
12 Treece, H. *How I See Apocalypse* (London: Drummond, 1946) 58

Chapter 11

1 Barker, G. "Coming to London", *London Magazine*, 3, 1 (Jan., 1956)
2 Gascoyne, D. *A Short Survey of Surrealism* (London: Cobden-Sanderson, 1933) ix
3 Collected in Waldberg, P. *Surrealism* (London: Thames and Hudson, 1965) 76–80 (76)
4 Waldberg, 66–72 (70)
5 Waldberg, 72
6 Waldberg, 79
7 Gascoyne, 92

Chapter 12

1 *New Verse*, 11 (Oct., 1934) 12
2 Gascoyne, D. *A Short Survey of Surrealism* (London: Cobden-Sanderson, 1933) 90
3 Raine, K. *Defending Ancient Springs* (London: Oxford, 1967) 58
4 *Hölderlin's Madness* (London: Dent, 1937) 11
5 *Hölderlin's Madness*, 10
6 *New Verse*, 6 (Dec., 1933) 20
7 Barker, G. *Janus* (London: Faber, 1934) 143
8 Barker, G. *Alanna Autumnal* (London: Parton, 1933) 36–7
9 Barker, G. *The Dead Seagull* (London: Panther, 1968) 99
10 *Letters to Vernon Watkins* (London: Dent, 1957) 51
11 Barker, G. "The Miracle of Images", *Orpheus*, II (1949)
12 "The Miracle of Images"
13 *New Verse*, 11 (Oct., 1934) 22
14 O'Connor, P. *Memoirs of a Public Baby* (London: Faber, 1958) 123–4
15 *Memoirs of a Public Baby*, 139
16 *Memoirs of a Public Baby*, 170–1
17 *Memoirs of a Public Baby*, 199–200

Chapter 13

1 Thomas, D. "I am going to read aloud", *London Magazine* 3, 9 (Sept., 1956) 14

o

2 Grigson, G. "Recollections of Dylan Thomas" in *A Casebook on Dylan Thomas*, ed. J. M. Brinnin (New York: Crowell, 1960)

3 *Selected Letters of Dylan Thomas*, ed. C. Fitzgibbon (London: Dent, 1966) 195

4 "That sanity be kept", *Sunday Referee*, 3rd Sept., 1933

5 *Selected Letters*, 97

6 Blake, W. "The Marriage of Heaven and Hell"

7 "The Marriage of Heaven and Hell"

8 *Selected Letters*, 83

9 *Selected Letters*, 40

10 *Selected Letters*, 87

11 Maud, R. *Entrances to Dylan Thomas' Poetry* (Pittsburgh: 1963) 19

12 Scarfe, F. *Auden and After* (London: Routledge, 1942) 109–10

13 Olson, E. *The Poetry of Dylan Thomas* (Chicago: 1954) 84

14 Empson, W. "Collected Poems and Under Milk Wood" in *Dylan Thomas: A Collection of Critical Essays*, ed. C. B. Cox (Englewood Cliffs: Prentice Hall, 1966) 84–5

15 *Selected Letters*, 122

16 *Selected Letters*, 185–6

17 "Introduction" to *Adventures in the Skin Trade* by D. Thomas (London: Dent, 1955)

18 *Selected Letters*, 11

19 *Letters to Vernon Watkins* (London: Dent, 1957) 57

20 Tedlock, E. W. (ed.) *Dylan Thomas: The Legend and the Poet* (London: Mercury, 1963)

21 *Selected Letters*, 130

22 *Selected Letters*, 161

23 Thomas, D. "Notes on the Art of Poetry" in *Modern Poetics*, ed. J. Scully (New York: McGraw Hill, 1965) 185–7

24 *Letters to Vernon Watkins*, 13

25 *Letters to Vernon Watkins*, 16

26 *Selected Letters*, 115

27 *Selected Letters*, 198–9

28 *Selected Letters*, 232

29 *Letters to Vernon Watkins*, 17

30 Empson in Cox, 87

31 *Selected Letters*, 197

32 Fitzgibbon, C. *The Life of Dylan Thomas* (London: Dent, 1965) 200

33 *Selected Letters*, 109

34 *Selected Letters*, 191

35 *New Verse* 11 (Oct., 1934) 8

36 *New Verse* 11 (Oct., 1934) 9

37 *Selected Letters*, 151

Chapter 14

1 Swingler, R. "William Blake", *Left Review*, III, 1 (Feb., 1937) 23
2 Bronowski, J. "Recollections of Humphrey Jennings", *Twentieth Century*, CLXV, 983 (Jan., 1959) 48
3 Bronowski, J. *William Blake* (London: Penguin, 1954) 189
4 Marx, K. and Engels, F. *Manifesto of the Communist Party* (London: Lawrence and Wishart, 1934) 12
5 Bronowski, J. *The Poet's Defence* (Cambridge, 1959) 11
6 Jennings, H. *Poems* (New York: Weekend Press, 1951) No page numbers.
7 Raine, K. *Defending Ancient Springs* (London: Oxford, 1957) 47
8 *Left Review*, III, 1 (Feb., 1937) 34
9 *New Verse*, 25 (May, 1937) 16–19
10 *Defending Ancient Springs*, 105–6
11 *Defending Ancient Springs*, 28
12 *Letters to Vernon Watkins* (London: Dent, 1957) 17
13 Norris, L. (ed.) *Vernon Watkins* (London: Faber, 1970) 53
14 *Letters to Vernon Watkins*, 13
15 *Defending Ancient Springs*, 17

Chapter 15

1 Spender, S. *The Destructive Element* (London: Cape, 1935) 236
2 Isherwood, C. *Exhumations* (London: Methuen, 1966) 13 and 24
3 MacNeice, L. *The Strings are False* (London: Faber, 1965) 169
4 *Left Review*, II, 7 (April, 1936) 339
5 Symons, J. *The Thirties* (London: Cresset, 1960) 80
6 Auden, W. H. "Introduction" to *The Poet's Tongue*, ed. W. H. Auden and J. Garret (London: Bell, 1935) vii–viii
7 Auden. W. H. "Introduction" to *The Oxford Book of Light Verse* (London: Oxford, 1938)
8 Pudney, J. *Home and Away* (London: Joseph, 1960) 97
9 Auden, W. H. "Byron" in *Fifteen Poets* (Oxford, 1941) [1951] 295
10 *Oxford Book of Light Verse*, xvii
11 Plomer, W. *At Home* (London: Cape, 1958) 197
12 *Poetry*, 49 (Jan., 1937) 223–4
13 *At Home*, 198–200
14 *At Home*, 61
15 Auden, W. H. "Psychology and Criticism", *New Verse*, 20 (April–May 1936), 22

Chapter 16

1 Lehmann, J. *The Whispering Gallery* (London: Longmans, 1955) 219
2 Quoted in Wood, N. *Communism and British Intellectuals* (New York: Cornell, 1959) 59
3 *The Review*, 11–12, 19
4 Caudwell, C. *Studies in a Dying Culture* (London: Lane, 1938) xx–xxi
5 *New Verse* 25 (May, 1937) 22

Chapter 17

1 Graves, R. and Hodge, A. *The Long Week-end* (London: Four Square, 1961) 333
2 Cockburn, A. "To and from the Frontier", *The Review*, 16 (Oct., 1938) 10–16
3 Spender, S. Introduction to *Poems for Spain*, ed. S. Spender and J. Lehmann (London: Hogarth, 1939) 12
4 Letter of 29th Nov., 1962, quoted in Ford, H. D. *A Poet's War* (Philadelphia: U. of Pennsylvania, 1965) 288
5 Quoted in "A Note on the Text Used" in *Poetry of the Thirties*, ed. R. Skelton (London: Penguin, 1964) 41
6 Orwell, G. "Inside the Whale" in *Collected Essays* (London: Mercury Books, 1961) 145–6
7 Eliot, T. S. *Anabasis: A Poem by St. J. Perse* (London: Faber, 1930)
8 Spender, S. "Spain Invites the World's Writers", *New Writing*, IV (Autumn, 1937)
9 Lehmann, J. *The Whispering Gallery* (London: Longmans, 1955) 278

Chapter 18

1 *The Review*, 11–12, 24
2 *The White Horseman*, ed. J. F. Hendry and H. Treece (London: Routledge, 1941) 162
3 *The White Horseman*, 165
4 Symons, J. *The Thirties* (London: Cresset, 1960) 148

Chapter *19*

1 Isherwood, C. *Exhumations* (London: Methuen, 1966) 11–12
2 Spender, S. *World Within World* (London: Hamish Hamilton, 1951) 261
3 "Foreword" to *Poems, 1925–1940* (New York: Random House, 1941) xiii

Chapter *20*

1 MacNeice, L. "Subject in Modern Poetry" in *Essays and Studies*, XXII (Oxford: Clarendon, 1937)
2 Alvarez, A. "Introduction" to *The New Poetry* (London: Penguin, 1962)

INDEX

NOTE

There are separate entries for authors and other literary figures and organisations, and for periodicals and anthologies. Books by specific authors, prose pieces that are not whole books and poems are listed under authors, in that order. Only books or pieces of prose *mentioned* in the text are indexed, but all poems quoted from or mentioned are indexed. The Index covers only the text from Chapters 1 to 20, and not prefatory or appended material. There are no entries for politicians, political parties, historical events, etc. Names of any kind that appear in quoted material are not indexed.

Chapters or numbered sections of chapters devoted to a specific topic are indicated by putting their page numbers in bold type. Unpublished works appear with their titles in square brackets.

INDEX